SOCIOLOGY OF CRIME,
LAW, AND DEVIANCE

Volume 1 • 1998

SOCIOLOGY OF CRIME,
LAW, AND DEVIANCE

Volume 1 • 1998

SOCIOLOGY OF CRIME, LAW, AND DEVIANCE

Editor: JEFFERY T. ULMER
Department of Sociology and Anthropology
Purdue University

VOLUME 1 • 1998

Emerald

United Kingdom – North America – Japan –
India – Malaysia – China

Emerald Group Publishing Limited
Howard House, Wagon Lane, Bingley BD16 1WA, UK

First edition 1998.

British Library Cataloguing in Publication Data
A catalogue record for this book is available from the British Library

ISBN: 978-0-762-30282-6

Printed and bound in Great Britain by
CPI Antony Rowe, Chippenham and Eastbourne

CONTENTS

LIST OF CONTRIBUTORS

Celesta A. Albonetti	Department of Sociology University of Iowa
Tammy L. Anderson	Prevention Research Center University of Illinois, Chicago
Liqun Cao	Department of Sociology, Anthropology and Criminology Eastern Michigan University
Xiaogang Deng	Department of Sociology University of Massachusetts in Boston
John Dombrink	Department of Criminology, Law and Society University of California, Irvine
Gerald Globetti	Department of Sociology University of Alabama
Daniel Hillyard	Department of Criminology, Law and Society University of California, Irvine
Matthew R. Lee	Department of Sociology Louisiana State University
Celia C. Lo	Department of Sociology University of Akron
Karol Lucken	Department of Criminal Justice University of Central Florida

Gale Miller Department of Social and Cultural Sciences
Marquette University

Mark R. Pogrebin Graduate School of Public Affairs
University of Colorado, Denver

Eric D. Poole Graduate School of Public Affairs
University of Colorado, Denver

Edward S. Shihadeh Department of Sociology
Louisiana State University

A. Javier Treviño Department of Sociology
Wheaton College

PREFACE

Many scholars can think back to their days as undergraduates and recall a class that shaped their later research agendas, teaching interests, and careers. For me, it was a course at Susquehanna University called "Social Control," taught by a former student of Herbert Blumer named Frank Chase. "If you understand the processes and conflicts of social control in a society," Professor Chase would intone, "you will understand a great deal about that society." He also constantly gave us writing assignments on topics like the then-newly discovered AIDS epidemic, the apartheid regime in South Africa and the work of Nelson Mandela and Bishop Tutu, ABSCAM and other instances of governmental and corporate scandal, or even the aborted presidential candidacy of Senator Gary Hart. Topics like these, on the surface, seemed to have little to do with what we ignorant college sophomores thought of as social control. As the class went along, however, we learned that each and every one of these issues, and many other important ones facing contemporary society, all in some way involved efforts to impose or resist social control.

Later, a well-meaning professor in graduate school asked me, "Jeff, I thought you wanted to be a sociologist—why are you wasting your time on all this criminology stuff?" I stammered something inarticulate in reply, but what I wanted to tell him was that criminology involved social control. And social control, as Frank Chase taught me, was interrelated in complex ways with social inequalities of resources and power, political economy, organizational phenomena, cultural meanings, race and ethnic relations, gender issues, and other things sociologists are interested in.

Criminology, the sociology of law, and the sociology of deviance all revolve around the more generic sociological issue of social control. While I would not agree that social control is sociology's central notion (cf. Gibbs 1989), I would say that studying the processes by which rules of all kinds are made, enforced, broken, subverted, or resisted is also the opportunity to learn a great deal about stratification, power, organizations, gender, social psychology, demography, social movements, and more. I would add that those who study these latter topics would do well to read the work of their colleagues who study crime, law, and deviance (a point implied by Merton 1997).

This marks the inaugural volume of *Sociology of Crime, Law, and Deviance*. This new biennial series will publish theoretical and empirical contributions to—as the title suggests—sociological discourse on crime, law, or deviance. The series is similar in type and format to the many other series in sociology published by JAI, such as *Studies in Symbolic Interaction, Research on Democracy and Society, International Social Movement Research*, and *Current Perspectives on Social Theory*. Manuscripts submitted for the series typically were—and will continue to be—reviewed by two to three anonymous ad hoc referees with appropriate expertise in the topic, as well as myself, in a manner similar to a refereed journal.

Crime, law, and deviance are extremely broad topics, and I envision the series reflecting this breadth. The content of the series will include theoretical contributions, critical reviews of literature, empirical research, and methodological innovations. The series especially welcomes pieces that engage, review, or reconceptualize what is known and what remains to be understood about broad directions of research and theorizing. The following constitutes a "wish list" for contributions to future volumes:

- *The Sociology of Crime.* I would welcome studies of topics such as the social structural causes and correlates of crime, communities and crime, crime and socialization, criminal career trajectories, societal reaction to crime (e.g., studies of criminal labeling processes and stigma, police, courts, criminal sentencing, corrections, etc.), the politics of crime, fear of crime, domestic violence, white-collar crime, organized crime, gangs, race, gender, age and crime, critical theories of crime, historical and cross-national comparative research on crime, and other topics of general interest to social scientists who study criminology.
- *Sociology of Law.* Future contributions could address the criminal and civil law, legal cultures, the organization of legal work, the state and law making processes, law and social conflict, law and social change, the organization and activities of courts, formal and informal alternatives to law, historical and cross-national comparative analyses, and other related topics.
- *The Sociology of Deviance.* This category is the broadest of all, and in a sense it encompasses the other two categories. I would like to include studies of the social processes of defining and constructing deviance, as well as formal and informal social control. The series could therefore include examinations of topics such as the construction and treatment of mental illness, medicine as social control, social movements aimed at changing definitions of deviance or mobilizing social control, sexuality and social control, gender and social control, and other examples.

I also believe that the diversity of theoretical perspectives in sociology is a strength rather than a weakness (see Maines 1990). The series will therefore welcome studies that use a wide variety of theoretical approaches to crime, law, and deviance, so long as the studies represent a high quality of scholarship and make a significant contribution to the advancement of our understanding of the topic examined. Studies that develop new theoretical perspectives—such as the pieces by Treviño and Anderson in this volume—would be especially welcome.

Likewise, I believe that sociology's diversity of methodological approaches is also a strength. The series will therefore strive for a balanced mixture of works that draw on quantitative, qualitative, historical/comparative, experimental, and textual data and methods. The criteria for evaluating manuscripts in terms of data and method are the quality of the data, the competence with which research methods are used, and the appropriateness of the data and method for the topic under study.

I would also like the series to be visible to social scientists from other disciplines besides sociology, since many people in psychology, political science, history, anthropology, women's studies, and African American studies (to name just a few fields) are involved in research, theorizing, and policy analysis related to foci of this series. Therefore, the series welcomes submissions from non-sociologists whose work would overlap with sociological concerns.

This volume includes 10 pieces that certainly reflect some of the diversity of subjects, theoretical perspectives, and methodologies that characterize the study of crime, law, and deviance. In the section called "Crime and Criminal Justice," Celesta Albonetti uses data from cases under the U.S. Sentencing Guidelines to examine complex interactions between gender and guideline departures in terms of their effect on the sentencing of white-collar offenders. Her piece not only contributes to the empirical literature on criminal sentencing processes and policies but also makes important methodological contributions to techniques for statistically modeling sentencing outcomes. In addition, Albonetti's study addresses key conceptual issues in the social organization of formal social control, such as decision-making discretion and attempts to control it through policies like sentencing guidelines. In doing so, she expands on her previously articulated theory of judicial discretion and the role of status-based attributions in sentencing.

Matthew Lee and Edward Shihadeh analyze Interpol crime data from 26 countries to examine the direct and indirect relationships between unemployment, the availability of low skill jobs, and homicide and theft. In doing so, they put key ideas from social disorganization, economic deprivation, and social control theories to the test in a longitudinal, cross-national context. Their piece is an important contribution to the literature on macro-level criminology research, which often focuses only on the United States. Liqun Cao and Xiaogang Deng study a sample of first-time shoplifting offenders to test an integrated predictive model that incorporates Jack Katz's seductions theory of "sneaky thrill" crime as well as strain theory and differential association theory. Their piece also contributes to a larger debate in theory development among criminologists—a debate between the utility of the more traditional, Popperian model of theory competition and falsification versus the more recent trend toward theoretical integration and synthesis.

The next two pieces deal with problems and reforms in penology. Karol Lucken provides a critique of the theoretical and policy-oriented discourse surrounding penal reform over the past several decades. She argues that this discourse has been fragmented in focus, goals, and driving metaphors. She proposes an analytic approach that views in a more integrated way the theoretical goals of assessing the origins and consequences of formal social control and the more policy-oriented goals of evaluating the practical outcomes of penal reforms. Mark Pogrebin and Eric Poole draw from the sociology of work and occupations—in particular, conceptualizations of sexism in the work world—to examine sexism and sexual harassment among corrections officers. Their analysis of their qualitative interview data describes the work experiences of women corrections officers as they deal with sexism in the form of paternalism, exclusion, stress, and discrimination from their male colleagues.

The next section, which presents three pieces in the sociology of law, begins with John Dombrink's and Daniel Hillyard's examination of the processes by which Oregon voted to repeal a ban on assisted suicide. They examine the mobilization and countermobilization strategies of social movement organizations and interest groups on both sides of the debate. Their analysis illustrates that fundamental definitions, meanings, and moralities are potential sites of struggle and are created, maintained, and changed through individuals and groups exercising agency within historical and structural constraints. A. Javier Treviño attempts nothing less than a metatheoretical reorganization of the sociology of law through a rediscovery and exposition of four Eastern European pioneers of the field. Treviño uses five themes from these pioneers to articulate a formal theoretical and methodological framework for the sociology of law. Then, Gale Miller extends his and Jim Holstein's theory of dispute domains and dispute resolution by examining administrative hearings in a work incentive program. He contrasts program staff dispute resolution orientations and strategies with those of program clients, and details how the staff's dispute resolution process favored the program's legal and bureaucratic interests. He concludes with a discussion of his study's implications for reforming dispute resolution in public bureaucracies.

The final two pieces deal with deviant identities, activities, and consequences. Tammy Anderson develops a provocative new theory of drug *abuse* as opposed to drug *use*. Her theory admirably attempts to integrate micro-, meso-, and macro-level explanations for drug abuse. The central emphases of Anderson's theory are identity transactions and change, subcultural and cultural symbols and meanings, and structural contexts of opportunity, and she develops 12 propositions about their interrelationships. Celia Lo and Gerald Globetti then address the criticism that most theory and research in deviance either neglects or stereotypes female experience and behavior. They contribute to redressing this shortcoming by presenting an exploratory study of gender differences in the consequences of teenage alcohol use. They find that while boys and girls report similar experiences from drinking, they differ in their interpretations and accounts of those experiences.

Finally, I would like to thank Sue Oppenheim, Executive Editor at JAI Press. It was her idea to develop this series, and I am very grateful to her for inviting me to serve as its editor. I am also grateful to the reviewers listed in the following pages, who gave of their scarce time to help the authors improve their papers, and help me get this series off the ground. May the following 10 pieces be the first of many exciting and useful contributions to scholarship in crime, law, and deviance showcased by this series.

Jeffery T. Ulmer
Editor

REFERENCES

Gibbs, J. 1989. *Control: Sociology's Central Notion*. Urbana, IL: University of Illinois Press.

Merton, R.K. 1997. "On the Evolving Synthesis of Differential Association and Anomie Theory: A Perspective From the Sociology of Science." *Criminology* 35(3): 517-525.

Maines, D.R. 1990. "Pursuing the Simplifications in Smelser's Vision." *The American Sociologist* 21: 294-297.

REVIEWERS
for
Volume 1

The editor wishes to thank the following scholars for reviewing and assessing manuscripts submitted for consideration in Volume 1:

Peter Adler
University of Denver

Robert Agnew
Emory University

Ronald Akers
University of Florida

Emilie Allan
St. Francis College

David Altheide
Arizona State University

Tammy Anderson
University of Illinois at Chicago

Lonnie Athens
Seton Hall University

Michael Benson
University of Tennessee

Alan Booth
Penn State University

Todd Clear
Rutgers University

Francis Cullen
University of Cincinnati

William Gamson
Boston College

Valerie Jenness
Washington State University

Michael Katovich
Texas Christian University

Randy LaGrange
University of North Carolina at Wilmington

Donileen Loseke
University of South Florida

Kathleen Lowney
Valdosta State University

Jennifer McKinney
Purdue University

Albert J. Meehan
Oakland University

Dragan Milovanovic
Northeastern Illinois University

D. Wayne Osgood
Penn State University

Carolyn Perrucci
Purdue University

Joan Petersilia
University of California at Irvine

Robert Regoli
University of Colorado

Joachim Savelsberg
University of Minnesota

J. William Spencer
Purdue University

Robert Stebbins
University of Calgary

Darrell Steffensmeier
Penn State University

Jim Thomas
Northern Illinois University

Michael Tonry
Castine Research Corporation

Jerry Van Hoy
Purdue University

Samuel Walker
University of Nebraska at Omaha

PART I

FIVE STUDIES IN CRIME AND CRIMINAL JUSTICE

THE ROLE OF GENDER AND DEPARTURES IN THE SENTENCING OF DEFENDANTS CONVICTED OF A WHITE-COLLAR OFFENSE UNDER THE FEDERAL SENTENCING GUIDELINES

CELESTA A. ALBONETTI

ABSTRACT

This research examines the relationship between defendant's gender and sentence severity for defendants convicted of a white-collar crime and sentenced under the Federal Sentencing Guidelines in 1991-1992. With the enactment of the Federal Sentencing Guidelines in November 1987, judicial discretion was substantially limited by requiring judges to impose sentences within a narrow range as specified by the sentencing grid. However, provisions for guidelines departures and guilty pleas offer a mechanism through with sentence disparity linked to defendant characteristics may enter judicial decision making. This study examines the influence of defendant's gender on sentence severity by pursuing two stages of analysis. The first stage estimates

Sociology of Crime, Law, and Deviance, Volume 1, pages 3-48.

ISBN: 0-7623-0282-8

the direct effect of defendant's gender on sentence severity, controlling for guidelines-defined legally relevant variables. The second stage explores whether defendant's gender conditions the effect of guidelines departures and guilty pleas on sentence severity. Findings from the pooled tobit regression equation indicate that females receive more lenient sentences than males. In addition, the analysis indicates that pleading guilty and receiving a guidelines departure significantly reduce sentence severity. Findings from the gender-specific equations reveal that the effect of departures on sentence severity is conditioned by defendant's gender, to the advantage of female defendants. In addition, findings indicate that prosecutors and judges use guilty pleas similarly for males and females. Of the two sources of discretion under the Federal Sentencing Guidelines, my findings indicate that guidelines departures exert the stronger effect on the probability of imprisonment and on length of imprisonment.

INTRODUCTION

Whether sentence disparity is linked to defendant characteristics or to offense-related variables has been the focus of a substantial body of research during the past two decades. While much of this research estimated the effect of defendant characteristics on sentence severity under indeterminate sentencing practices (Smith and Damphousse 1996; Albonetti 1991, 1994; Rhodes 1991; Weisburd et al. 1991; Benson and Walker 1988; Eisenstein, Flemming, and Nardulli 1988; Peterson and Hagan 1984; Wheeler, Weisburd, and Bode 1982; Nagel and Hagan 1982, 1983; Hagan, Nagel, and Albonetti 1980; Hagan and Parker 1985; Lizotte 1978; Spohn, Gruhl, and Welch 1981-1982; Unnever 1982), another body of empirical studies explored this relationship in state jurisdictions governed by determinate or presumptive sentencing policies (Ulmer 1997; Ulmer and Kramer 1996; Dixon 1995; Knapp 1984; Kramer and Lubitz 1985; Clarke 1984; Zatz 1984; Miethe 1987; Moore and Miethe 1986; Martin 1984; Parent 1988; Boerner 1985, 1995; Quinn 1990; Washington State Sentencing Commission 1992). Taken together, this research has produced inconsistent findings of the effect of defendant characteristics on sentence outcomes.

In addition to these studies, a growing theoretical and empirical literature has developed that explicitly relates defendant's gender to sentence severity (Kruttschnitt 1980-1981; Kruttschnitt and Green 1984; Moulds 1980; Temin 1973; Nagel and Hagan 1982; Steffensmeier 1980; Rafter 1985; Daly 1987a, 1987b, 1994; Simpson 1989, to name a few). These studies, too, have produced mixed findings of the relationship between defendant's gender and sentence severity. After presenting a brief description of the federal sentencing guidelines, I review the findings from these studies and suggest a theoretical perspective from which to understand how defendant's gender affects sentence severity in the context of federal sentencing reform.

With the passage of the Sentencing Reform Act of 1984,[1] Congress established the United States Sentencing Commission for the purpose of developing a sentencing structure that would avoid "unwarranted sentencing disparity for defendants with similar records who had been found guilty of similar criminal conduct."[2] With the Sentencing Reform Act, Congress sought to reform federal sentencing practices by defining an overall sentencing policy of honesty, uniformity, and proportionality[3] Reflecting a shift from rehabilitation to deterrence and just deserts as the primary goal of sentencing, the federal sentencing guidelines are to systematically relate the type of illegal behavior, circumstances of the offense, and the defendant's criminal history to sentence outcomes. Offender characteristics are declared to be irrelevant to the sentencing process. According to Section 5H1.10 of the Federal Sentencing Guidelines, defendant's gender, race, socioeconomic status, creed, religion, and national origin are not to be considered at sentencing. Under the guidelines, determination of sentence severity at the federal level is to be based on offense characteristics, the defendant's role in the offense, and the defendant's criminal history. By so doing, the goals of uniformity and proportionality in sentencing outcomes would be realized.

With the enactment of the federal sentencing guidelines in November 1987, the wide latitude of judicial discretion that historically characterized federal sentencing was substantially limited by requiring federal judges to impose sentences within specified guidelines. Put simply, the federal sentencing guidelines were to reform sentencing by making the sentencing process more rational and certain. Judicial discretion was to be severely limited by a decision-making structure that explicitly defined the path to be followed when imposing sentence. However, the guidelines provide for judicial and prosecutorial discretion through sentence departures[4] and guilty plea agreements.[5] Recent legal and policy analyses (Gelacak, Nagel, and Johnson 1996; Gyurci 1994; Lee 1994; Standen 1993; Nagel and Schulhofer 1992; Nagel 1990; Purdy and Lawrence 1990; Breyer 1988) suggest that sentence departures, plea agreements, and provisions for "acceptance of responsibility"[6] are potential mechanisms by which the central goals of uniformity and proportionality in sentencing may be undermined. Consistent with the Sentencing Reform Act of 1984, the United States Sentencing Commission provided for departures from the guidelines range in cases that are characterized by "an aggravating or mitigating circumstance of a kind, or to a degree, not adequately taken into consideration by the Sentencing Commission . . . (18 U.S.C. 3553(b) and as cited in the U.S. Sentencing Commission Guidelines Manual, 1989, par. 1.6)." Framers of the Sentencing Reform Act intended such departures to be relatively rare (Gelacak et al. 1996).

Moreover, the federal sentencing guidelines specify situations for which the court may depart, either upward or downward, from the prescribed sentence range. For example, a judge may impose a sentence less than that specified by the guidelines when he/she is convinced that the defendant has accepted responsibility for his/her criminal actions[7] or that he/she has provided substantial assistance in investigating and prosecuting another defendant.[8] Examples of case characteristics that warrant consideration of an upward departure from the proscribed sentencing range include crimes in which the victim died,[9] the victim was abducted,[10] or the defendant's criminal activity was particularly heinous, brutal, or degrading to the victim.[11]

In summary, although the federal sentencing guidelines specify the "path" to sentencing that the judge is to follow, the guidelines permit departures and plea agreements that provide the opportunity for sentencing disparity. Since the federal guidelines leave the decision to judges on whether to depart, and by how much, judges continue to exercise some discretion at sentencing. Moreover, legal scholars and social scientists (Nagel and Schulhofer 1992; Berlin 1993; Lee 1994; Lowe 1987; Tonry 1996; Standen 1993; Steury 1989) argue that the federal sentencing guidelines enhanced prosecutorial discretion at both the charging stage of case processing and during guilty plea negotiations. The sociolegal significance of these mechanisms of discretion is in providing a nontrivial means of circumventing the central goal of the guidelines, namely, that of eliminating sentence disparity that is tied to defendant characteristics. Of particular interest to my research is whether the effect of sentence departures on sentence outcomes is conditioned by defendant's gender.

In a recent study of sentence outcomes for drug offenders sentenced under the federal sentencing guidelines in 1991-1992, Albonetti (1997) suggests that guilty pleas and sentence departures are two structural avenues of discretion within the federal guidelines through which sentence disparity may be tied to defendant's ethnicity. Her findings indicated ethnic-specific effects of departures on sentence severity. Specifically, white defendants receive significantly greater advantage from sentence departures than that received by either black or Hispanic defendants. However, she found that the effect of pleading guilty on sentence severity was similar for all three groups of defendants. These findings suggest the need to determine whether other defendant characteristics, such as gender, condition the effect of departures and guilty pleas on sentence outcomes under the federal sentencing guidelines.

Although a number of legal and policy analyses focuses on the role of gender in sentencing under the federal sentencing guidelines (Nagel and Johnson 1994; Wald 1995; Resnik 1995; Coughenour 1995; Cook 1995; Newton, Glazer, and Blackwell 1995; Daly 1995; McBride 1995; Raeder 1995; Sungaila 1995), research has yet to use multivariate analyses to estimate the *direct* and *conditioning* effects of defendant's gender on sentence severity under the federal guidelines. Nagel and Johnson's (1994) policy analysis of the federal sentencing guidelines emphasizes the need to empirically examine gender differences in sentencing under the new federal reform policies. In this chapter, I use a tobit, multivariate analysis to examine three questions. First, does defendant's gender significantly influence sentence severity for defendants convicted of a white-collar crime under the federal sentencing guidelines in 1991-1992? Second, do guidelines departures and guilty plea agreements affect sentence severity? Third, does the defendant's gender condition the effect of sentence departures and guilty pleas on sentence severity? If the effect of these process variables on sentence severity varies depending on the defendant's gender, this would strongly suggest that federal sentencing reform goals were being undermined by the sentencing structure created to eliminate sentence disparity.

PRIOR RESEARCH

Since the 1960s, the relationship between defendant's gender and punishment has received substantial and explicit attention (Green 1961; Reckless and Kay 1967; S. Nagel 1969; S. Nagel and Weitzman 1971; Kruttschnitt 1980-1981, 1982, 1984; Kruttschnitt and Green 1984; Moulds 1980; Temin 1973; Nagel and Hagan 1982; Steffensmeier 1980; Rafter 1985; Simpson 1989; Daly 1987a, 1987b, 1994). Other studies of the determinants of sentence severity have estimated the effects of defendant's gender as an important defendant characteristic in the legal and extralegal debate over the relative influence of ascribed characteristics and offense-related characteristics on sentence outcomes (Hagan et al. 1980; Wheeler et al. 1982; Benson and Walker 1988; Weisburd et al. 1991; Peterson and Hagan 1984; Albonetti 1991, 1994; Miethe and Moore 1985; Moore and Miethe 1986; Zatz 1984, to name a few). The central concern of this body of research was to examine whether female defendants are treated differently than male defendants. This literature reports that: gender is irrelevant to sentence outcomes (Miethe and Moore 1985; Moore and Miethe 1986; Zatz 1984; Albonetti 1991; Benson and Walker 1988); females are less likely to be imprisoned than males (Steffensmeier, Kramer, and Streifel 1993; Weisburd et al. 1991; Wheeler et al. 1982); females receive shorter periods of imprisonment (Hagan et al. 1980); there is a contextual effect of gender on length of imprisonment that is tied to government priorities in prosecution (Peterson and Hagan 1984); and females are more likely than male defendants to receive a suspended sentence (Albonetti 1994).

Much of the research on gender differences in sentencing is framed within a chivalry-paternalism, economic dependency/social status, or sex-role defined deviance perspective. For the purposes of my research, I review these perspectives with a focus on empirical studies of sentencing at the federal level and state court level, the latter including studies conducted in jurisdictions governed by either determinant or indeterminate sentencing. To date, research has not studied sentence disparity in white-collar crime cases under the federal sentencing guidelines. In this chapter, I draw from earlier research on sentence disparity linked to gender at both the federal and state levels of adjudication and suggest that an understanding of the effect of gender on sentence severity in white-collar offenses requires consideration of the net direct effect of gender on sentence outcomes and the conditioning effect, if any, of gender in the relationship between guilty pleas, guideline departures, and sentence severity. Before addressing these concerns, it is useful to review previous research that has analyzed the influence of defendant's gender on sentence outcomes.

The Gender-Sentence Relationship in the Context of Indeterminate Sentencing Practices

Beginning with the work of Green (1961), Reckless and Kay (1967), and S. Nagel (1969), early studies of the relationship of defendant's gender and sentence outcomes concluded that females received more lenient punishment then males. Green (1961) concluded that the gender differences in sentencing in Philadelphia could not be explained away by differences in prior record of convictions or severity of the convicted offense. In a reanalysis and extension[12] of Nagel's study, Moulds (1980) found that females were incarcerated at a lower rate than males. She concluded, "It is clear from the data that the criminal justice system treats women substantially differently from the way in which it treats men. This handling is pervasive regardless of race, type of crime, and prior record" (p. 293). She furthered noted, "It can be reasonably concluded from these findings that the term "chivalry factor", or perhaps more accurately, 'paternalism factor' is an appropriate one to describe the use of discretion by officials of the criminal justice system" (p. 293). Moulds' emphasis on paternalism and the accompanying emphasis on the power differentials between the genders spawned a substantial body of research to further explore, with more analytically sophisticated models, the relationship between defendant's gender and sentence outcomes. Moulds argued that the long-term consequences of preferential treatment of female defendants, especially the reluctance to impose a prison outcome, essentially reified the helpless, in-need-of-protection stereotype of women in society. She cautions:

> It is true that women do enjoy certain benefits of a chivalry factor. They are arrested, prosecuted, and sent to institutions less often than are men—the benefit to them is their freedom. A major cost to them, however, is the continuation of a state of public consciousness which holds that women are less able than men and are thus in need of special protective treatment. This results in extensive personal, psychological, social, economic, and political damage to the democratic notions of self-determination and equality (1980, p. 294).

The double-edged sword of "chivalry" was made explicit when Moulds (1980) introduced the paternalistic dimension of chivalry. The paternalistic aspect of sentencing was pointed out in Temin's (1973) legal analysis of Pennsylvania's Muncy Act[13] of 1964 and the court decision in *New Jersey State v. Costello.*[14] She provided evidence of the link between notions that females were more susceptible to rehabilitation and the longer prison stays received by women than men. Her analysis (1973) indicated that Pennsylvania was not unique in its practice of sentencing women to longer incarceration periods than men due to an image of women being more prone to rehabilitation. Temin (1973) documents how the female stereotype of being more responsive to rehabilitation became the justification for sentencing women to indeterminate sentences that resulted frequently in women serving more time in custody than males who were convicted of similar offenses. She notes (1973, p. 260) that in New Jersey, Connecticut, Iowa, Maine, and Maryland, women could be sentenced to indeterminate incarceration where men convicted of the same offense could be sentenced to a statutory maximum.

Among the earlier sentencing studies, research provides inconsistent findings of the relationship between defendant's gender and sentence severity. Baab and Furgeson (1967), S. Nagel and Weitzman (1971), Farrell and Swigert (1977), and Bernstein, Kelly, and Doyle (1977) found that females received more lenient treatment than males. However, Temin (1973) and Bernstein et al. (1977) found that males were given less severe dispositions. Hagan (1974) found that defendant's gender was unrelated to sentence outcomes when legally relevant variables were considered in the analysis.

Kruttschnitt's (1980-1981) study of California sentencing practices for females found offense-specific effects of the defendant's economic rank, respectability, and social integration on sentence severity. Specifically, being a housewife decreased sentence severity for assault cases but this measure of social integration did not significantly affect sentence outcomes for offenses of disturbing the peace, petty theft, forgery, or drug violations. Being a student decreased sentence severity for females convicted of disturbing the peace, assault, and drug violations. However, being on welfare significantly increased sentence severity for females convicted of petty theft, forgery, and drug violations. Regardless of offense type, having a criminal record, a negative measure of respectability, significantly increased sentence severity. Kruttschnitt (1980-1981) concluded that female defendants' social status influenced sentence outcomes, namely, that females who were more socially integrated, through various types of employment status, received sentence leniency and, thereby, were subjected to less governmental control as hypothesized by Black (1976). Essentially, Kruttschnitt's (1980-1981) findings suggest that differences among females were the basis of judicial discretion at sentencing. In a second study of California sentencing, Kruttschnitt (1982) hypothesized that to the extent that a female's dependency status involves high levels of social control, the defendant will receive less severe punishment. This hypothesis reflects Black's hypothesis that the "quantity of law varies inversely with the amount of other social controls" (1976, p. 107). Kruttschnitt concluded that her findings suggest that "the legal system prefers to exert little control over women whose lives presently contain an indicator of daily social control such as that entailed by economic dependency" (1982, p. 510).

Pursuing further an economic dependency explanation of gender differences in sentencing, Kruttschnitt and Green (1984) examined pre-trial release outcomes and the decision to incarcerate. Using data on males and females processed in Minneapolis during 1965-1980, they hypothesized that gender-based differences in formal and informal mechanisms of social controls account for gender differences in sentence severity. They found that, controlling for indicators of dependency (i.e., motherhood and source of support), female defendants are more likely to experience leniency at the pre-trial release stage of criminal adjudication and this directly influenced the likelihood of being incarcerated. In addition, they found that in only two of the 16 years was defendant's gender related significantly to the probability of imprisonment. This finding challenged Nagel and Hagan's (1982) hypothesis that gender differences in sentence outcomes would diminish over time as females became involved in more serious criminal behavior.

Kruttschnitt (1984) generated and tested hypotheses of gender-based status effects on sentence severity derived from Turk (1969) and Black (1976). She found that legally relevant variables (i.e., severity of the offense, and the presence of pending cases) affected sentence outcomes for female and for male defendants, but the effect was significantly different across the two groups. Examining Table 3 in Kruttschnitt (1984, p. 225) reveals important differences in the magnitude of the effect of two legally relevant variables. Having pending cases increases sentence severity for both genders, but the magnitude of the effects is significantly stronger for males than females. However, the opposite is observed for the effect of offense severity. Again for both groups of defendants. the effect of offense severity is to increase sentence severity, but this legally relevant variable produces a significantly stronger effect for females.

In addition, Kruttschnitt (1984) found that gender conditions the effect of pleading guilty on sentence severity. Pleading guilty did not produce a significant effect on sentence severity for females. However, for males, pleading guilty resulted in substantial and significant decreases in sentence severity. This finding and the finding of gender-related differences in the effect of two legally relevant variables on sentence severity supports the contention that females are more harshly punished than males when they commit more severe offenses, that females are less able to negotiate advantageous plea settlements, and that females benefit more than males from avoiding a history of court contacts. These findings will be returned to later in my analysis of sentencing under the federal sentencing guidelines.

Of particular interest to Kruttschnitt (1984) and Kruttschnitt and Green (1984) is the finding that females benefit at sentencing from their status as housewife or student, a benefit that is absent for males. They concluded that gender-based status affects sentencing to the advantage of females, with the caveat that their failure to find such effects for males could be due to the fact that in their study, only female defendants had single-parent responsibilities.

Another study that was influential in developing formulations of the relationship between gender and sentence outcomes is Daly's (1987a) analysis of lower New York criminal court sentencing patterns for four months during 1974-1975. Daly (1987a) suggested a revision of Kruttschnutt's (1982) social control formulation of the gender and sentencing relationship. Daly (1987a , p. 155) argues that previous findings of leniency in sentencing for females, compared to males, is the result not only of informal social controls that are exerted differentially on women but also of court officials' attempts to reduce the economic costs of replacing the care-taking responsibilities that women perform within the family and the social cost of victimizing children who are forced to live without a parent. She found support for her hypothesis of an inverse relationship between the levels of family dependency and sentence severity. Daly (1987a , p. 163-164) concluded that her findings indicate that the "sex-effect" on sentence outcomes is actually the by-product of the family dependency role that women are more likely to shoulder than men. In other words, the sentence leniency enjoyed by female defendants can be accounted for by gender differences in family responsibility. Daly's conclusion is founded on the following three findings: (1) men and women who are single and without child care responsibilities are sentenced similarly; (2) men ad women who are "familied" are treated more leniently than those who are "non-familied;" and (3) women who are "familied" are given more lenient sentences than similarly situated men. In a second study, Daly (1994) concluded that in similar cases sentenced in New Haven, females received a lower probability of incarceration than men. Daly (1994) argues that her findings point to the salience of family dependency and sentence outcomes.

Finally, Albonetti's (1991) study of sentencing in the District of Columbia found that, controlling for legally relevant variables and process variables, female defendants did not receive significantly more lenient sentences than male defendants. She found that legally relevant variables (e.g. type of offense, statutory severity, use of a weapon, and the defendant's record of prior convictions) and process-related variables (i.e., bail status and guilty pleas) exerted the strongest influence on sentence outcomes.

The Gender-Sentence Relationship in the Context of State Determinant/Presumptive Sentencing Guidelines

Since the early 1980s, the sentencing reform efforts at the state level have been a catalyst for numerous studies (Miethe and Moore 1985; Moore and Miethe 1986; Zatz 1984; Ulmer 1997; Ulmer and Kramer 1996; Kramer and Ulmer 1996; Dixon 1995; Steffensmeier et al. 1993) of the effects of defendant characteristics on sentence severity under determinant and presumptive sentencing guidelines. This research is particularly important to the research herein since studies of judicial discretion at the federal court level under federal sentencing guidelines are just beginning to be conducted. Although the federal sentencing guidelines scheme is different from the guidelines enacted in various state jurisdictions, research findings from these studies are suggestive of potentially important relationships between defendant characteristics and sentencing outcomes. Except for Steffensmeier et al. (1993), these studies have not explicitly focused on the effects of defendant's gender. However, they have included defendant's gender in their analysis. With this in mind, a number of multivariate studies of the determinants of sentence severity under state-level guidelines are reviewed, especially as they inform the gender-sentencing relationship.

Controlling for legally relevant variables, Miethe and Moore (1985) found that under the Minnesota sentencing guidelines, females were more likely than male defendants to receive a stayed sentence, that is, a sentence that was not executed. In their race-specific analysis of sentencing, Miethe and Moore (1985) found that the gender effect was present regardless of the defendant's race. They found that females were more likely than males to receive a stayed sentence, regardless of defendant's race. However, they also found that gender did not significantly affect the length of imprisonment imposed. Their race-specific analysis revealed that the effects of gender on length of imprisonment varied by defendant's race. For blacks, being female significantly shortened length of imprisonment, but for whites, being female was unrelated to sentence severity.

In a second study of Minnesota sentencing, Moore and Miethe (1986) found that defendant's gender did not significantly affect sentence outcomes for cases sentenced within the guidelines range. However, their findings indicate that females were less likely than males to be sentenced to jail. In addition, Moore and Miethe (1986) report that gender was unrelated to the decision to stay a sentence or the duration of the stayed sentence for those defendants sentenced outside the guidelines range.

Turning to research on sentencing outcomes under Pennsylvania sentencing guidelines, Steffensmeier et al. (1993) found that females were less likely than males to be sentenced to jail or prison. Further, they found that the effect of gender on sentence outcomes was reduced for cases that were sentenced within the guidelines. They reasoned that the observed 3% reduction in the probability of imprisonment due to the gender effect was due to females benefiting more than males from sentence departures. Examining the judges' reasons for imposing a sentence that departs from the guidelines, Steffensmeier et al. (1993) found that "judges viewed female defendants as less 'dangerous' or less culpable than their male codefendants, and as having more responsibilities and ties to the community (e.g., caregiving responsibilities)" (p. 433). They concluded that judges in Pennsylvania were influenced by the defendant's blameworthiness, practical concerns of childrearing, personal problems, and jail space. These concerns explained the gender-specific differences in the probability of incarceration. Finally, Steffensmeier et al. (1993) found that defendant's gender produces no significant effect on the length of imprisonment.

Kramer and Steffensmeier (1993) also found that females are sentenced more leniently than males but they are quick to note that the gender difference is small. Their region-specific analysis indicates that including defendant's gender in the length of sentence equation produces only a small contribution to R^2, the amount of explained variance in sentence severity. In a recent study, Ulmer and Kramer (1996) examined state-wide sentencing and county-specific sentencing patterns in Pennsylvania. They found that females received shorter periods of incarceration than males. However, it is important to note that the authors report that the gender effect again contributed little to the amount of explained variance in sentence severity.

Finally, Zatz's (1984) study of sentencing under California determinant sentencing policy found that defendant's gender was unrelated to sentence outcomes. Estimating the sentence equation separately for white, black, and Chicano defendants further revealed that gender did not produce a significant effect on length imprisonment. According to Zatz (1984), the effect of type of offense, defendant's record of prior prison commitments, and guilty pleas on sentence outcomes was conditioned by the defendant's ethnicity. Her analysis did not pursue whether defendant's gender conditioned the effect of these variables on sentence outcomes.

Gender and Sentencing in the Federal Courts

As noted earlier, sentencing under the Federal sentencing guidelines is just recently being studied with multivariate models. Albonetti's (1997) analysis of sentencing of drug offenders under the federal sentencing guidelines in 1991-1992 found that females received significantly shorter periods of imprisonment than males. This finding was obtained having controlled for guideline-defined legally relevant variables, guilty pleas, defendant's ethnicity, education level, citizenship status, and federal circuit. Her ethnic-specific analyses revealed that gender effect was significantly strong for white defendants than for black or for Hispanic defendants. She concluded that white defendants were more advantaged at sentencing than either black or Hispanic females.

A study by the United States Sentencing Commission (1991) and a subsequent analysis of the same data by the United States General Accounting Office (1992) indicated that preliminary findings that gender and race are related to sentence outcomes. Because of an inadequate sample size, these studies were unable to test hypotheses about sentencing under the federal sentencing guidelines (Tonry 1996). Nagel and Schulhofer's (1992) study of prosecutorial discretion under the federal sentencing guidelines offers insights into sentencing of defendant's convicted of a drug offense. Contrary to expectations, they found that the shift of discretion from judges to prosecuting attorneys did not result in greater disparity in sentence outcomes.

Using bivariate analyses of defendants convicted of embezzlement or larceny, Nagel and Johnson (1994) report gender differences in the percentage of defendants who received a sentence departure for other than offering substantial assistance. They also report differences in the percentage of defendants who were sentenced at the lowest level within the applicable guidelines cell. In the same study, Nagel and Johnson (1994) provide a legal analysis of the implications of the gender-neutral[15] structure of the federal sentencing guidelines. They conclude that gender-related issues, such as pregnancy, family ties, and parental responsibility are legally irrelevant to the decision to depart from the prescribed guideline sentence range (1994, p. 200).[16] They suggest that the emphasis on the offense, the defendant's role in the offense, and the defendant's criminal history, as mandated by the Sentencing Reform Act of 1984, essentially defined gender-specific biological conditions and social circumstances to be irrelevant to the decision to impose a sentence of imprisonment. However, Nagel and Johnson point out that an emphasis on the defendant's culpability does permit consideration of gender-specific aspects of the defendant's role in the offense such as coercion, duress, and abuse.[17] Sentence departures for these mitigating circumstances would be permitted and, as such, could account for females receiving more lenient sentences than males. In addition, the importance the guidelines place on the defendant's role in the offense opens the door for consideration of whether the defendant's actions were the result of either manipulations by a co-defendant or his/her dominant status over the female defendant. As Nagel and Johnson note, "To the extant that guidelines sentencing fails to permit judges to take this subordination adequately into account, it has a disparate impact on female offenders" (1994, pp. 211-212). The issues that Nagel and Johnson (1994) outline are central to the broader gender focus of earlier studies (Kruttschnitt 1980-1981; Kruttschnitt and Green 1984; Daly 1987a, 1987b, 1994).

Turning now to multivariate analyses of sentencing of defendants convicted of a white-collar crime prior to the federal sentencing guidelines, several studies are salient to the present gender-specific analysis of sentencing. A number of studies report that females receive more lenient sentences than males (Hagan et al. 1980, 1982; Hagan and Palloni 1986). In these studies, leniency was defined as shorter lengths of imprisonment. Other studies found that females were more likely than males to receive a non-imprisonment decision but gender did not produce a significant effect on length of imprisonment for the group of defendants receiving an imprisonment sentence (Wheeler et al. 1982; Weisburd et al. 1991). In an analysis of the sentencing of white-collar defendants, Albonetti (1994) found that being female was related to an increased probability of receiving a suspended sentence. Further, she found that case complexity conditioned the gender effect on sentencing. Specifically, females were more likely than males to receive a suspended sentence in cases that were medium low in complexity (false claims/statements, fraud, lending and institutional fraud, income tax evasion, and income tax felon) and in low complexity cases (embezzlement, forgery, larceny, and theft).

In a more recent study of sentencing of defendants convicted of a political crime, Smith and Damphousse (1996) found that gender failed to exert a significant direct effect of sentence length. They report that the effect of gender on sentence severity is indirect via an effect of crime severity. Their findings are contrary to Albonetti's (1996) that gender affected sentence length directly and indirectly via guilty pleas, case complexity, and statutory severity. The differences in findings may well be accounted for by differences in the type of federal offenses analyzed in the two studies. Smith and Damphousse (1996) examined sentences for political offenses while Albonetti's (1996) study focused on white-collar crimes.

Clearly, additional research is necessary to discover the subtle ways that gender influences sentencing decisions.

The research herein addresses direct effects of gender and mediating effects of gender in the relationship between guidelines departures and guilty pleas. The latter effect is particularly important since guideline departures and guilty pleas are mechanisms of discretion through which sentence disparity linked to defendant characteristics may significantly influence sentence severity under the federal sentencing guidelines (Standen 1993; Nagel and Johnson 1994; Albonetti 1997). This study seeks to determine how defendant's gender, if at all, contributes to understanding sentencing decisions under the federal sentencing guidelines.

Before presenting the results of the analysis of whether defendant's gender affects sentence outcomes for persons convicted of a white-collar offense and sentenced under the federal sentencing guidelines, it is important to describe the decision-making structure of the guidelines. Having done this, I generate hypotheses of gender differences in sentencing derived from a merger of uncertainty avoidance (March and Simon 1958; Simon 1957; Thompson 1967) and causal attribution (Hawkins 1981; Fontaine and Emily 1978; Carroll and Payne 1976) that was suggested in an earlier paper (Albonetti 1991).

FEDERAL SENTENCING GUIDELINES

With the Sentencing Reform Act of 1984, Congress established the United States Sentencing Commission and charged it with the responsibility of reforming federal sentencing. Senators Edward Kennedy and Orrin Hatch, the two sponsors of the Sentencing Reform Act, argued that: (1) sentencing at the federal level was largely determined by extra-legal defendant characteristics; (2) sentence outcomes were too lenient, especially for white-collar crimes and drug offenses; and (3) there should be "truth in sentencing"—that is, that defendants are to serve all the imposed sentence, minus a small reduction due to "good time." According to the authors of the Sentencing Reform Act, individualized sentencing based on a rehabilitation model of punishment was history. The new guidelines structure would substantially limit the amount, and change the form, of discretion previously enjoyed by federal judges prior to the sentencing guidelines.

Framers of the Sentencing Reform Act maintained that the wide latitude of judicial discretion, argued to be necessary under a rehabilitative, individualized sentencing policy, was no longer appropriate under a deterrent and retributive model of punishment. Furthermore, it was argued that judicial discretion was in large part responsible for the observed sentence disparities that were tied to extra-legal defendant characteristics. Sentencing reform would be accomplished by developing and enacting a presumptive sentencing scheme that would determine, within a narrow range, the length of imprisonment to be imposed upon a conviction. The guidelines were to insure that similarly situated offenders would be sentenced to similar levels of punishment. Differences in guidelines-defined legally relevant variables were to be the fundamental basis for sentence disparity (Wilkins and Steer 1990; Yellen 1993). Defendant characteristics such as gender, ethnicity, income, age, educational attainment, and citizenship status were to be structured out of the decision-making process at sentencing. The central goals of uniformity and proportionality in sentencing outcomes, expressed in the Sentencing Reform Act of 1984, pivot around the elimination of unwarranted disparity in punishment that results from systematic consideration of defendant characteristics in determining sentence outcomes. As noted earlier, Part H of the Federal Sentencing Guidelines Manual (U.S. Sentencing Commission 1989) specifies that defendant's race, sex, national origin, creed, religion, and socioeconomic status,[18] age,[19] education and vocation status,[20] mental and emotional conditions,[21] physical condition, including drug dependence and alcohol abuse,[22] previous employment record,[23] and family ties[24] as legally irrelevant to sentencing. This study focuses on the role gender plays, if any, in sentence outcomes under the federal sentencing guidelines.

Following Congressional directives to eliminate sentence disparity linked to defendant characteristics, the United States Sentencing Commission designed a sentencing process that theoretically limits judicial discretion by requiring judges to follow a path to sentencing outcomes that begins by identifying the approximate guideline, based on the convicted offense from the statutory index. This determines the base offense level. The judge is then to consider any increases to the base offense level due to the defendant's relevant conduct or any specific offense characteristics (e.g. the amount of dollar loss in embezzlement cases). The judge is to consider any applicable adjustments for acceptance of responsibility (3E1.2) and/or for offering substantial assistance to the government in the successful prosecution and conviction of another defendant (5K1.1).[25] The judge is also to consider special provisions for defendant's career criminal status. Following this series of steps to sentencing, the judge methodologically determines any additions/subtractions to the guideline base offense level, the vertical axis of the sentencing grid. The judge is then to determine the criminal history category (from 1 to 6), the horizontal axis of the grid. Having determined the scores on these two axes, the judge is to locate the intersecting cell and sentence within the prescribed range. By following this sentencing process, the Commission reasoned that judicial discretion would be limited and that sentence outcomes would be a function of systematic consideration of offense-related variables and the defendant's criminal history. As noted earlier, the judge may depart from a guidelines-prescribed sentence range in the presence of aggravating or mitigating circumstance that were not adequately considered by the U.S. Sentencing Commission. Such departures must be justified in writing and are subject to appeal.

It is important to keep in mind that the guidelines permit downward departures due to acceptance of responsibility (3E1.2) and for substantial assistance in prosecuting and convicting another defendant (5K1.1). I suggest that, although the sentencing guidelines represent a more formally structured decision-making system for imposing punishment than in the past, sentence departures and guilty plea negotiations are avenues through which proseuctorial and judicial discretion may enter the sentencing process. This study estimates the direct effect of guilty pleas and departures[26] on sentence severity and tests the conditioning effect of defendant's gender in the relationship among guilty pleas, departures, and sentence outcomes. The latter focus permits an examination of whether the influence of these two sources of discretion on sentence severity varies by defendant's gender.

THEORETICAL PERSPECTIVE

In an attempt to understand judicial discretion in a theoretical context that goes beyond the legal, extra-legal debate of previous research, Albonetti (1991) offered a reconceptualization of the social process of sentencing that integrates the structural perspective of rational decision making (March and Simon 1958; Simon 1957; Thompson 1967) with the social psychological perspective of causal attribution in punishment (Shaver 1975; Hawkins 1981; Carroll and Payne 1976; Heider 1958; Fontaine and Emily 1978; Lippman 1922). From the merger of the two perspectives, Albonetti (1991, p. 250) argues that judges "attempt to manage uncertainty in the sentencing decision by developing 'patterned responses' (March and Simon 1958; Simon 1957) that are themselves the product of an attribution process influenced by causal judgments." Essentially, the argument is that over time, judges construct defendant stereotypes that tie race and gender to predictions of future criminal activity. It is suggested that simplifying causal assumptions that attribute stable, enduring patterns of criminal activity (Shaver 1975; Fontaine and Emily 1978; Caroll and Payne 1976) increases the severity of the punishment. From the merger of uncertainty avoidance and causal attribution, I hypothesize that, controlling for guidelines-defined legally relevant case information (i.e., final offense level determined by the sentencing guidelines, the maximum sentence permitted under the guidelines, the defendant's total criminal history points), males will receive significantly longer prison sentences than females. Other defendant characteristics that are linked to negative stereotypes are expected to increase sentence severity (Albonetti 1997).

Turning to the effect of guilty pleas on sentence severity, previous studies (Albonetti forthcoming; Rhodes 1991; Miethe 1987; Hagan et al. 1980) found that pleading guilty significantly reduce the length of imprisonment. Albonetti (1997) found that pleading guilty resulted in a significant decrease in length of imprisonment for defendants convicted of a drug offense under the federal sentencing guidelines in 1991-1992. Furthermore, she found that this reduction was similar for black, Hispanic, and white defendants. Consistent with these findings and those of some legal scholars and social scientists (Standen 1993; Schulhofer and

Nagel 1989; Rhodes 1992; Purdy and Lawrence 1990; Gyurci 1994; Nagel and Schulhofer 1992; Steury 1989), I hypothesize that white-collar defendants who plead guilty will experience a significant decrease in length of imprisonment.

A number of legal scholars have focused on sentence departures under the federal sentencing guidelines (Gelacak et al. 1996; Lee 1994; Schulhofer 1980, 1992; Nagel 1990). Similar to guilty plea negotiations, guidelines departures may act to circumvent the central goals of uniformity and proportionality of the federal reform efforts. Under the federal sentencing guidelines, judicial and prosecutorial discretion, expressed in departures and guilty plea settlements, offer avenues through which defendant characteristics, such as gender, may circumvent the formal rational goals of sentencing as designed by the federal guidelines. With this in mind, my analysis examines the direct effects of gender, departures, and guilty pleas on sentence severity, controlling for guidelines-defined legally relevant variables, circuit effects, and defendant characteristics that offer rival explanations. Estimation of the direct effect of gender on sentence length is followed by a gender-specific analysis of the variables influencing length of imprisonment. Of particular interest at this stage of the analysis is whether a defendant's gender conditions the effect of sentence departures and guilty pleas, two sources of discretion, on sentence severity under the federal guidelines.

DATA AND ANALYTICAL PROCEDURES

To test the hypotheses specified above, I use the Monitoring of Federal Criminal Sentences, 1991-1992 data[27] for 7,079 defendants convicted of either money laundering, embezzlement, bribery, or fraud/larceny. This research consists of several stages of analysis. The preliminary stage involves an examination of univariate and bivariate statistics for variables thought to be related to sentence outcomes. With my interest in exploring whether defendant's gender conditions the effect of these variables on sentence severity, univariate statistics are provided separately for males and for females. Table 1 provides the coding and descriptive statistics for each variable in the analysis of the pooled group of white-collar defendants. In addition, Table 1 reports gender-specific descriptive statistics for each independent variable and the dependent. Appendix Table A.1 reports descriptive statistics for each of the federal circuits.[28]

The preliminary analysis also includes calculation of z-tests of differences in percentages (for nominal variables) and z-tests of differences in means (for interval and ratio variables) across gender. The null hypothesis of each test is that the percentages or means are equal for females and males. Rejection of the null hypothesis leads to further analyses that involve multivariate estimation procedures. Table 2 reports the obtained z-values.

The multivariate stage of my analysis involves estimating tobit regression equations of length of imprisonment. Maximum likelihood tobit equations are estimated instead of ordinary least squares regression for the purpose of generating unbiased and efficient estimates in the presence of left censored data (Long 1997; Breen 1996; Roncek 1992; Rhodes 1991; Moffitt 1982; McDonald and Moffitt 1980; Tobin 1958). Fifty-one percent of the 7,079 defendants received nonimprisonment sentences, that is, zero length of imprisonment. These observations are considered left-censored on the length of imprisonment dependent variable. According to McDonald and Moffitt (1980, p. 318), the tobit model is:

$$\begin{aligned} Y_t &= X_t\beta + u_t \quad \text{if } X_t\beta + u_t > 0 \\ Y_t &= 0 \quad \text{if } X_t\beta + u_t \leq 0, \text{ and} \\ & \quad t = 1,2,\ldots N, \end{aligned}$$

where N is the number of observations, Y_t is the dependent variable, length of imprisonment, X_t is a vector of independent variables, β is a vector of tobit coefficients, and u_t is an error term that is assumed to be normally distributed with zero mean and constant variance. As Tobin (1958) indicates, the tobit equation assumes an underlying stochastic unobserved latent variable with an expected value of $EY = X\beta F(z) + \sigma f(z)$, where $z = X\beta/\sigma$, $f(z)$ is the unit normal density, and $F(z)$ is the cumulative normal distribution function.

In addition to the ability to handle left-censored observations (zero length of imprisonment), tobit estimates can be decomposed into two components that are particularly meaningful to sentencing research. One component is an estimate of the effect of the independent variable on the *length of imprisonment for those defendants receiving a prison sentence*. The second component is an estimate of the effect of the same variable on the *probability of imprisonment for defendants receiving a nonimprisonment sentence*. In my analysis, decomposing the effects of defendant's gender, guilty pleas, and departures reveals how sentencing disparity, if found, is related to each of the two sentencing decisions. Such a decomposition is particularly informative given earlier findings (U.S. General Accounting Office 1992; Rhodes 1991; U.S. Sentencing Commission 1991) of the differential effect of these variables on the probability of imprisonment and length of imprisonment.

In addition to defendant's gender, the first tobit regression equation of length of imprisonment includes other defendant characteristics (e.g., ethnicity, age, number of dependents, education, log of annual income, non-U.S. citizenship), legally relevant variables (e.g., final guideline offense level—the vertical axis of the sentencing grid; total criminal points—the horizontal axis of the grid; guideline-defined maximum sentence applicable cell in the sentencing grid; type of white-collar offense; and number of counts), type of disposition (guilty plea or trial), whether or not there was a sentence departure, and dummy variables controlling for circuit effects. This equation will be estimated for the *pooled* group of white-collar defendants sentenced in 1991-1992 under the federal sentencing guidelines. The dependent variable, length of imprisonment, is transformed by $\log_e$ to reduce

Table 1. Descriptive Statistic and Coding for Variables Included in the Length of Imprisonment Model for Federal White Collar Crime Offenses, 1991-1992

Variables	*Coding*	*Pooled Group* N = 7079 %	*Female* N = 2295 %	*Male* N = 4784 %
Independent				
Hispanic[a] (X_1)	1=Hispanic	5	3	5
	0=Other	95	97	95
Black[a] (X_2)	1=Black	33	38	28
	0=Other	67	62	72
Gender (X_3)	1=Female	31		
	0=Male	69		
Education (X_4)	1= at least some college	17	10	19
	0=No college	83	90	81
Age (X_5)		$\bar{X}$ = 37.28	$\bar{X}$ = 35.34	$\bar{X}$ = 38.16
		s.d. = 11.52	s.d. = 11.06	s.d. = 11.61
Number of Dependents (X_6)		$\bar{X}$ = 1.91	$\bar{X}$ = 1.91	$\bar{X}$ = 1.91
		s.d. = 6.96	s.d. = 7.59	s.d. = 6.65
Non-Citizen (X_7)	1=Not U.S. Citizen	8	4	9
	0 = U.S. Citizen	92	96	91
Log Income (X_8)		$\bar{X}$ = 7.92	$\bar{X}$ = 8.17	$\bar{X}$ = 7.81
		s.d. = 3.57	s.d. = 3.20	s.d. = 3.73
Plea (X_9)	1 = Guilty	94	96	92
	0=Not Guilty	6	4	8
Guideline Offense Level (X_{10})	Final Offense Level	$\bar{X}$ = 9.57	$\bar{X}$ = 8.38	$\bar{X}$ = 10.10
		s.d. = 5.15	s.d. = 4.37	s.d. = 5.38

Criminal History Points (X_{11})		$\bar{X} = 1.83$ s.d. = 4.02	$\bar{X} = .96$ s.d. = 2.61	$\bar{X} = 2.23$ s.d. = 4.46
Guideline Maximum Sentence (X_{12})		$\bar{X} = 16.18$ s.d. = 17.88	$\bar{X} = 12.33$ s.d. = 11.34	$\bar{X} = 17.93$ s.d. = 19.91
Fraud (X_{13})	1 = Fraud	49	44	51
	0 = Other	51	56	49
Money Laundrying (X_{14})[c]	1 = Money Laundrying	5	4	6
	0 = Other	95	96	94
Embezzlement/Larceny (X_{15})[c]	1 = Embezzlement/Larceny	39	41	38
	0 = Other	61	59	62
Number of Counts (X_{16})	Convicted Counts	$\bar{X} = 1.88$ s.d. = 4.15	$\bar{X} = 1.56$ s.d. = 3.13	$\bar{X} = 2.02$ s.d. = 4.53
Departure (X_{17})	1=Sentence departs from guidelines	16	14	16
	0 = Sentence does not depart	84	86	84
Circuits				
Circuit 0[b]	District of Columbia	2	2	1
Circuit 1(X_{18})	ME, MA, NH, RI, PR	3	1	3
Circuit 2[b] (X_{19})	CT, NY, VT	7	6	8
Circuit 3 (X_{20})	DE, NJ, PA, VI	10	10	11
Circuit 4 (X_{21})	MD, NC, SC, VA, WV	10	10	11
Circuit 5 (X_{22})	LA, MS, TX	10	10	11
Circuit 6 (X_{23})	KY, MI, OH, TN	14	16	13
Circuit 7 (X_{24})	IL, IN, WI	7	7	7

(continued)

Table 1 (Continued)

Variables	Coding	Pooled Group N = 7079 %	Female N = 2295 %	Male N = 4784 %
Circuit 8 (X_{25})	AR, IA, MN, MO, NB, ND, SD	6	6	6
Circuit 9 (X_{26})	AZ, CA, HI, ID, MT, NV, OR, AK, WA, Guam, N. Mariana Islands	10	10	10
Circuit 10 (X_{27})	CO, KS, NM, OK, UT, WY	6	6	18
Circuit 11 (X_{28})	AL, FL, GA	15	14	14
Dependent				
Sentence Severity (Y)	Length of Imprisonment	$\bar{X} = 17.91$[d] s.d. = 20.30	$\bar{X} = 13.14$ s.d. = 14.63	$\bar{X} = 19.23$ s.d. = 21.42

Notes: [a] Reference category is white.
[b] Reference category is District of Columbia.
[c] Reference category is bribery.
[d] Mean and standard deviations reported as actual value for uncensored sentences. If censored cases (0 length of imprisonment) are included, the mean value for pooled defendants = 8.57, *s.d.* = 16.65; for female defendants, the mean = 4.37, *s.d.* = 10.46; the mean for males = 10.47, s.d. = 18.48.

positive skewness. Such transformations are typical in sentencing research (Wheeler et al. 1982; Weisburd et al. 1991).

Hypotheses of the *conditioning* effect of defendant's gender are tested by estimating the above tobit equation separately for females and for males. Using a *z*-test (Clogg, Petkova, and Haritou 1995) comparison of the coefficient estimates for guilty pleas and sentence departures across these two groups will indicate whether the effect of pleading guilty and sentence departures is dependent on the defendant's gender. By controlling for guidelines-defined legally relevant case information, the findings from the multivariate analyses of the conditioning effect of gender address the central goals of the federal sentencing reform, that is, whether similar defendants are sentenced similarly.

Taken together, the results from these empirical analyses will indicate the extent to which differences in sentence outcomes are the product of differences in guidelines-defined legally relevant offense characteristics, defendant characteristics, guidelines departures, and guilty pleas. Moreover, findings from the analyses test the extent to which sentencing disparity, if found, is the outcome of a more complex sentencing process that involves a conditioning effect of defendant's gender on the relationship between sentence departures, guilty pleas, and length of imprisonment.

FINDINGS

Table 1 indicates that the mean length of imprisonment for the pooled white-collar defendants, excluding left-censored cases, is 17.91 months (*s.d.* = 20.30). Of particular interest is the significant difference in mean length of imprisonment for females and males. Table 1 (columns 4 and 5) reveal that the mean length of imprisonment for female defendants is 13.14 months (*s.d.* = 14.63), compared to a mean length of imprisonment of 19.23 (*s.d.* = 21.42) for males. Table 2 reports a significant *z*-value of 14.00 ($p < .001$), indicating a rejection of the null hypothesis of equality of means across gender. This finding indicates that females were sentenced to significantly shorter periods of imprisonment than males. The tobit multivariate analyses will permit an assessment of whether this apparent gender-based disparity in sentencing is accounted for by gender differences in guidelines-defined legally relevant variables, departures, guilty pleas, other defendant characteristics, or federal circuit differences in sentencing practices.

Returning to the univariate statistics for the guidelines-defined legally relevant variables, Table 1 reports that for the pooled group of defendants, the mean guidelines offense level—the horizontal axis of the sentencing grid—is 9.57 (*s.d.* = 5.15). Findings in Table 1 and Table 2 ($z = 14.57$; $p \leq .001$) indicate that males, compared to females, are convicted of white-collar offense that carry a significantly higher guidelines offense level of the sentencing grid. Table 1 indicates that the mean number of criminal history points for the pooled defendants is 1.83 (*s.d.*

Table 2. Mean and Proportion Difference for Variables Across Defendants' Gender

	Test Statistic Value (z)
Independent Variables	
Hispanic (X_1)	4.17[a]
Black (X_2)	10.00[a]
Education (X_4)	10.00[a]
Age (X_5)	9.89[a]
Number of Dependents (X_6)	0
Non-Citizen (X_7)	8.33[a]
Log Income (X_8)	6.04[a]
Plea (X_9)	6.67[a]
Guideline Offense Level (X_{10})	14.57[a]
Criminal History Points (X_{10})	15.90[a]
Guideline Maximum Sentence (X_{12})	9.93[a]
Fraud (X_{13})	5.83[a]
Money Laundrying (X_{14})	4.00[a]
Embezzlement/Larceny (X_{15})	2.52[b]
Number of Counts (X_{16})	5.11[b]
Departure (X_{17})	2.99[a]
Circuit 0	5.00[a]
Circuit 1	6.67[a]
Circuit 2	3.08[a]
Circuit 3	1.25
Circuit 4	1.25
Circuit 5	1.25
Circuit 6	3.75[a]
Circuit 7	0
Circuit 8	0
Circuit 9	0
Circuit 10	14.12[a]
C ircuit 11	0
Dependent Variable	
Sentence Severity	14.00[a]

Notes: [a] $p < .001$
[b] $.01 < p \leq .05$.

= 4.02). Males have a significantly more serious history of criminal activity and exposure to criminal adjudication (Table 2, z = 15.90; $p < .001$) than females. Table 1 reports that the mean guidelines maximum sentence for the pooled group is 16.18 months ($s.d.$ = 17.88). For females, the mean length guideline maximum sentence is 12.33 months (*s.d.* = 11.34), and for males, the mean is 17.93 months (*s.d.* = 19.91). Table 2 reveals that this observed gender difference in guidelines maximum sentence is statistically higher for males ($z = 9.93$, $p < .001$). From these guidelines-defined legally relevant variables, it is clear that male defendants convicted of a white-collar crime and sentenced in 1991-1992 under the federal sentencing guidelines were convicted of more serious offenses, as defined by the structure of the guidelines grid, and that males represented a significantly more criminally active group than females. In addition, the findings in Table 1 and Table 2 indicate significant gender differences in the types of white-collar cases and in the mean number of convicted counts. The largest proportion of defendants were convicted of fraud (49%) with a significantly larger proportion of males being convicted of fraud than females (Table 2, $z = 5.83$, $p < .001$). Table 1 indicates that only 5% of the defendants were convicted of money laundering. Males represented a significantly larger percentage of money laundering convictions (Table 2, $z = 4.00$, $p < .001$). Thirty-nine percent of the defendants were convicted of embezzlement/larceny. In only this offense category is the percentage of females significantly greater than that for males (Table 2, $z = 2.52$, $.01 < p < .05$). This finding is consistent with Nagel and Johnson's (1994) findings. Finally, for the pooled group, the mean number of convicted counts is 1.88 (*s.d.* = 4.15). Table 2 reports that males are convicted of significantly higher number of counts than females ($z = 5.11$, $p < .001$).

In summary, the univariate statistics and *z*-tests of differences in parameter estimates across gender indicate significant gender differences in each of these guidelines-defined legally relevant offense and offense related variables. Except for the proportion of defendants convicted of embezzlement/larceny, the mean or proportion for males on each of these variables is higher than for females. Hypothetically, these gender differences in guidelines-defined variables could account for the observed significantly higher sentence length for males. The multivariate analysis, the basis for determining the net effect of defendant's gender on length of imprisonment, is estimated controlling for the effects of these guidelines-defined legally relevant variables.

Turning to the process-related variables in the analysis, Table 1 reports that 94% of the pooled defendants pled guilty and 16% received a sentence that departed from the federal guidelines. The *z*-values reported in Table 2 indicate significant gender differences in percentages for these two variables. Specifically, female defendants are more likely to plead guilty (96% compared to 92%) than males, but females receive a significantly lower percentage of sentence departures (14% compared to 16%). Again, this consistent with the descriptive statistics reported by Nagel and Johnson (1994). These gender-related percentage differences in guilty pleas and sentence departures are particularly interesting since, as I noted earlier, these are the two mechanisms through which discretion can structurally enter into sentencing. The multivariate analysis will estimate whether these differences significantly contribute sentence outcomes.

Table 3. Correlation Matrix for Variables in the Sentence Severity Equation of Federal White Collar Offense, 1991-1992

	X_1	X_2	X_3	X_4	X_5	X_6	X_7	X_8	X_9	X_{10}	X_{11}	X_{12}	X_{13}	X_{14}	X_{15}	X_{16}	X_{17}	X_{18}	X_{19}	X_{20}	X_{21}	X_{22}	X_{23}	X_{24}	X_{25}	X_{26}	X_{27}	X_{28}
X_2	−.16																											
X_3	−.04	.08																										
X_4	−.05	−.05	−.10																									
X_5	−.04	−.21	−.10	.14																								
X_6	.02	−.01	−.08	−.00	.02																							
X_7	.42	.03	.05	.02	−.07	.01																						
X_8	−.02	−.07	.01	.03	.07	.03	−.05																					
X_9	−.03	.02	−.14	−.06	−.11	−.02	−.01	.02																				
X_{10}	.06	−.13	−.14	.13	.19	.00	.06	−.06	−.23																			
X_{11}	.01	.10	−.17	−.10	−.06	.01	−.04	−.18	.01	−.02																		
X_{12}	.09	−.07	−.05	.06	.12	.00	.06	−.09	−.20	.83	.20																	
X_{13}	−.02	.02	−.02	.03	.04	−.01	.06	−.05	.01	.08	.11	.00																
X_{14}	.14	−.02	.06	.02	.04	−.01	.12	−.01	−.13	.46	−.02	.51	−.22															
X_{15}	−.05	.02	−.06	−.07	−.14	−.01	−.11	.05	.08	−.30	−.07	−.23	−.81	−.19														
X_{16}	−.01	−.02	−.04	.07	.06	−.01	−.02	−.00	−.27	.25	.01	.25	.08	.07	−.11													
X_{17}	.01	−.08	.12	.04	.07	−.02	.01	−.01	.02	.00	−.00	.23	.05	.14	−.12	.02												
X_{18}	.02	−.08	−.04	.07	.04	−.01	.00	.00	−.05	.06	−.02	.03	.03	−.02	−.03	.11	.02											
X_{19}	.04	.00	−.04	.01	−.01	−.02	.09	−.03	.01	.04	−.06	.02	−.03	.00	.01	.02	.09	−.04										
X_{20}	−.00	.02	−.02	−.02	.02	−.01	.01	−.05	.02	.05	−.00	.02	.06	−.04	−.06	.00	.12	−.05	−.08									
X_{21}	−.06	.03	−.02	−.00	−.02	−.03	−.03	−.01	−.01	−.03	.04	−.02	−.01	.00	.00	−.01	−.01	−.05	−.09	−.11								
X_{22}	.14	−.00	−.02	−.01	.01	−.01	.08	−.00	−.05	.10	.04	.12	.02	.09	−.06	−.03	−.01	−.06	−.09	−.11	−.12							
X_{23}	−.07	.04	.03	−.03	−.02	.01	−.06	−.01	.03	−.11	.02	−.07	−.02	−.04	.05	−.03	−.07	−.07	−.11	−.13	−.14	−.14						
X_{24}	−.04	.05	.00	−.01	.02	.01	−.06	.01	.01	.00	−.03	−.03	−.03	−.01	.03	−.01	−.03	−.04	−.07	−.09	−.10	−.10	−.12					
X_{25}	−.05	−.08	.00	.03	.05	−.01	−.05	.02	.02	.01	−.01	−.01	−.01	.01	.01	−.01	−.01	−.04	−.07	−.08	−.09	−.09	−.11	−.07				
X_{26}	.05	−.10	−.01	.00	−.00	.05	−.05	−.01	−.01	.01	.01	.01	−.01	.02	−.01	.00	.04	−.05	−.08	−.10	−.11	−.11	−.13	−.09	−.08			
X_{27}	−.02	−.08	.01	−.00	.02	.05	−.03	.03	−.01	−.05	−.01	−.04	.01	−.04	.01	−.02	−.03	−.04	−.07	−.08	−.09	−.09	−.11	−.07	−.06	−.08		
X_{28}	.00	.07	.05	−.00	−.04	−.02	.00	.03	−.01	−.02	−.00	.02	−.01	.01	.03	.04	−.06	−.07	−.12	−.14	−.15	−.15	−.18	−.12	−.11	−.14	−.11	
Y	.06	−.03	−.23	.07	.09	−.00	.09	−.18	−.22	.68	.38	.63	.11	−.26	−.22	.21	.01	.03	−.04	−.03	−.01	.12	−.06	−.02	.01	.00	−.03	.02

Table 1 reports that the pooled defendants are largely white males having less than a college education and a mean log income of 7.92. They are largely U.S. citizens with a mean age of approximately 37 years (*s.d.* = 11.52). *Z*-values provided in Table 2 indicate significant gender differences in the all but one of the defendant characteristics. The mean number of dependents is similar across defendant's gender. Compared to males, females are younger, have less education, and are more likely to be U.S. citizens and to report a higher log annual income. Thirty-eight percent of the female defendants are black, compared to 28% for males. A higher percentage of males than females are Hispanic. Again, the multivariate analysis that follows includes statistical controls for these variables.

Finally, Table 1 indicates that the two federal circuits contributing the largest percentage of defendants were Circuit 11 and Circuit 6. Circuit 3, Circuit 4, Circuit 5, and Circuit 9 each contributed 10% of the total cases. Table 2 reports significant gender differences in proportions of cases from the following circuits: Circuit 0, Circuit 1, Circuit 2, Circuit 6, and Circuit 10. With these observed gender differences in the percent of white-collar cases, the multivariate analysis will include 10 circuit dummy variables as control variables.

Turning now to the bivariate correlation matrix (Table 3) for the variables included in the tobit equations, several observations are noteworthy. Not surprisingly, guidelines offense level and guidelines maximum sentence exhibit the highest correlations with length of imprisonment. In general, the correlations reported in Table 3 are consistent with expectations. An examination of the correlation matrix reveals a strong correlation between guideline offense level and guideline maximum sentence. This is consistent with the structure of the federal sentencing guidelines. Consideration was given to excluding guideline maximum sentence from the regression analysis if the correlation indicated collinearity. The STATA program used to estimate the tobit equations automatically drops collinear variables. The program did not drop guideline maximum sentence from any of the estimated models. In addition, including guideline maximum sentence in the equation produced a significantly better fit, indicated by the change in the model chi-square and degrees of freedom. In the absence of evidence of collinearity between guideline offense level and guideline maximum sentence, and the substantive importance of both variables to sentencing under the federal guidelines, the decision was made to include both variables in the regression analysis.

Direct Effects

Table 4 provides the tobit coefficients, their standard errors, and the decomposition of the tobit estimates. As noted earlier, the tobit coefficient summarizes: (1) the effect of an independent variable on the length of imprisonment for defendants who received a prison sentence, and (2) the change in probability of a imprisonment for defendants who did not receive a prison decision (Long 1997; Roncek 1992; McDonald and Moffitt 1980). Focusing first on the net effect of defendant's

Table 4. Unstandardized Coefficient Estimates, Standard Errors, and Decomposition of Effects* for Variables Included in the Tobit Model** of Sentencing for White-Collar Crime Under the Federal Sentencing Guidelines, 1991-1992 (N = 7079)[a]

		Decomposition	
Variables	*Estimates*	c^1	c^2
Hispanic (X_1)	.17 (.09)	—	—
Black (X_2)	.15[d] (.04)	.05	04
Gender (X_3)	−.41[d] (.04)	−.15	−.12
Education (X_4)	.05 (.05)	.02	.01
Age (X_5)	−.01[d] (.00)	−.004	−.003
Number of Dependents (X_6)	−.01 (.01)	—	—
Non-Citizen (X_7)	.50[d] (.08)	.18	.14
Log Income (X_8)	−.04[d] (.00)	−.01	−.01
Plea (X_9)	−.28[d] (.07)	−.10	−.08
Guideline Offense Level (X_{10})	.43[d] (.00)	.15	.12
Criminal History Points (X_{11})	.21[d] (.00)	.08	.06
Guideline Maximum Sentence (X_{12})	−.04[d] (.00)	−.01	−.01
Fraud (X_{13})***	.26[d] (.08)	.09	
Money Laundrying (X_{14})***	−.49[d] (.12)	−.18	−.14
Embezzlement/Larceny (X_{15})***	.28[c] (.08)	.10	.08
Number of Counts (X_{16})	.01 (.01)	—	—

(continued)

Table 4 (Continued)

Variables	*Estimates*	*Decomposition* c^1	c^2
Departure (X_{17})	−1.33[d] (.05)	−.48	−.38
Intercept	−2.59[d] (.21)		

– *Log Likelihood* = 7633.00
Model Chi-square = 6396.11, *df* = 25, *p* = .000
Pseudo R^2 = .30

Notes: * Reported for significant estimates only.
** The model includes 11 circuit dummy variables with the District of Columbia as the reference category. Only the contrast of Circuit 3 compared to Circuit 0 is significant, therefore, for ease of presentation, the estimates for the circuit demography variables are reported in table A-4 in the Appendix.
*** Reference category is bribery.
[a] Number of uncensored values = 3,450; number of left-censored values = 3,629.
[b] Estimate significant at $.01 < p \leq .05$.
[c] Coefficient estimate significant $.001 < p \leq .01$.
[d] Coefficient estimate significant at $p \leq .001$.

gender on sentence severity, Table 4 indicates that females receive significantly less severe ($b = -.41, p \leq .001$) sentences than males. How this leniency is play out is expressed in the decomposition of the gender effect (Table 4, columns c^1 and c^2). For defendants convicted of a white-collar offense in 1991-1992 and sentenced under the federal sentencing guidelines, being female, compared to male, produces a 15% decrease in the log length of imprisonment for those receiving a prison sentence and a 12% decrease in the probability of incarceration. Contrary to the intent of the federal sentencing guidelines, not only does defendant's gender substantially affect the probability of receiving an imprisonment sentence but gender also affects the imposed length of imprisonment.

The strong inverse effect of gender on the probability of imprisonment is consistent with findings from studies of federal sentencing of white-collar offense prior to the enactment of the federal guidelines (Wheeler et al. 1982; Weisburd et al. 1991) and the effect is consistent with studies conducted in state-level courts under state sentencing guideline policies (Ulmer and Kramer 1996; Steffensmeier et al. 1993; Moore and Miethe 1986).

Turning next to the net effects of guidelines-defined legally relevant variables on sentence severity, Table 4 indicates that all but one of the legally relevant variables exert a significant influence on sentence outcomes. Only the number of convicted counts fails to research statistical significance. Guidelines offense level, the vertical axis on the sentencing grid, produces a significant ($b = .43, p \leq .001$) effect on sentence severity. Decomposing the tobit coefficient reveals that guidelines offense level exerts a .15 increase in the log length of imprisonment for offenders who received a prison sentence and a 12% increase in the probability of imprisonment for offenders who were not incarcerated. Criminal history points, the horizontal axis of the sentencing grid, produces a significant increase in sentence severity ($b = .21, p \leq .001$). Decomposing this effect indicates that increases in criminal history points produces a .08 increase in the log length of imprisonment for offenders who received a prison sentence and a 6% increase in the probability of imprisonment for offenders who were not incarcerated. Table 4 indicates that the effect of guideline maximum sentence is negative and small in magnitude ($b = -.04, p \leq .001$). Decomposing this effect reveals that the guidelines maximum sentence, a measure of statutory severity, decreases by −.01 the log length of imprisonment for offenders who were sentenced to some prison time and a 1% decrease in the probability of imprisonment for offenders who did not receive a prison sentence. This finding is particularly noteworthy since research on federal sentencing prior to implementation of the federal sentencing guidelines has consistently reported strong *increases* in sentence severity due to statute severity, conventionally measured as the highest sentence that can be statutorily imposed for the given offense. Under the federal sentencing guidelines structure, the comparable measure of statutory severity is the upper bound of the applicable guidelines cell which is defined by the intersection of the final offense level and the defendant's number of criminal history points. Albonetti (1997) also reports a significant negative effect for guidelines maximum sentence on length of imprisonment for defendants convicted of drug offenses in 1991-1992 under the federal sentencing guidelines. The negative effect of this variable may indicate judicial resistance to the increased harshness of sentences prescribed by the federal guidelines for white-collar offenses (see Tonry 1996).

Table 4 further indicates that the type of white-collar offense influences sentence severity. Controlling for the guidelines-defined legally relevant variables, convictions for fraud or embezzlement/larceny, compared to bribery, significantly increase sentence severity ($b = .26, p \leq .001$; $b = .28, p \leq .001$, respectively) while convictions for money laundering produce a substantial and significant decrease ($b = -.49, p \leq .001$). Decomposing the tobit coefficients for the effects of fraud and for embezzlement/larceny indicates that these two types of offenses produce similar effects on sentence outcomes. Being convicted of fraud, compared to bribery, increases by .09 the log length of imprisonment for offenders who received a prison sentence. Furthermore, a conviction for fraud increases by 7% the probability of being imprisoned for offenders receiving a sentence other than prison. Convictions for embezzlement/larceny, compared to bribery, result in a .10 increase in the log length of imprisonment for those offenders receiving an imprisonment decision and an 8% increase in the probability of imprisonment for offenders receiving a non-incarceration outcome. Table 4 indicates that convictions for money laundering, compared to bribery, produce a substantial decrease (−.18) in the log length of imprisonment for offenders receiving a prison sentence and a nontrivial 14% decrease in the probability of imprisonment for offenders receiving a non-incarceration outcome. Taken together, these results indicate that judges are systematically considering guidelines-defined legally relevant variables and type of white-collar offense when deciding the sentence severity.

Attention now turns to the effect of guidelines departures and guilty pleas, two sources for discretion to enter into the sentencing process. Table 4 indicates that both process-related variables exert significant decreases in sentence severity under the federal guidelines. Of the two variables, guideline departures produce the strongest effect ($b = -1.33$, $p \leq .001$) on sentencing. Decomposing this effect reveals that judicial departures from the guidelines in white-collar crime cases exerts a −.48 decrease on the log length of imprisonment for offenders receiving a prison sentence and a 38% decrease in the probability of incarceration for offenders receiving a non-incarceration sentence. These findings clearly indicate that one source of discretion under the federal guidelines produces nontrivial results on sentence severity.

The second process-related variable, guilty pleas, produces a significant decrease ($b = -.28$, $p \leq .001$) on sentence severity. Decomposing the tobit coefficient indicates that a guilty plea disposition, compared to a trial conviction, exerts a −.10 effect on the log length of imprisonment for offenders receiving a prison outcome and an 8% decrease in the probability of imprisonment for offenders receiving a nonincarceration sentence. These findings indicate that the type of disposition continues to exert significant and substantial influence on sentencing practices as observed in sentencing studies prior to the enactment of federal guidelines.

Finally, Table 4 reports that gender is not the only defendant characteristic that exerts a significant influence on sentence severity. According to the regression estimates in Table 4, black defendants receive more severe sentence outcomes ($b = .15$, $p \leq .001$) than white defendants. Being black, compared to white, produces a .05 increase in log length of imprisonment for defendants sentenced to prison and a 4% increase in the probability of being imprisoned for defendant who were not imprisoned. Compared to defendants who are U.S. citizens, defendants with non-U.S. citizenship receive significantly more severe sentences ($b = .50$, $p < .001$). This tobit estimate decomposes into an increase of .18 on the log length of imprisonment and a 14% increase in the probability of being imprisoned for those defendants not imprisoned. The significant effect of being a non-U.S. citizen is contrary to federal sentencing guidelines stipulations.

Two defendant characteristics produce significant, yet trivial, effects on sentence severity. Increases in defendant's age and income produce a small ($b = -.01$, $p \leq .001$ and $b = -.04$, $p \leq .001$) decrease in sentence outcomes. Finally, contrary to earlier studies of sentencing of white-collar defendants prior to the federal sentencing guidelines (Hagan et al. 1980; Nagel and Hagan 1982), defendant's educational attainment is unrelated to sentence outcomes.

Table 5. Unstandardized Coefficient and Standard Errors and Decomposition of Effects[a] for Variables Included in the Tobit Model of Sentencing for White-Collar Crime Under the Federal Sentencing Guidelines, 1991-1992, Estimated Separately by Gender*

	Female[a]			*Male*[a]		
		Decomposition			*Decomposition*	
Variable	*Est. (S.E.)*[e]	c^1	c^2	*Est. (S.E.)*[e]	c^1	c^2
Hispanic (X_1)	.16 (.22)	—	—	.16 (.10)	—	—
Black (X_2)	.08 (.08)	—	—	.18[d] (.05)	.07	.06
Education (X_4)	.22 (.13)	—	—	.03 (.06)	—	—
Age (X_5)	−.01[b] (.00)	−.003	−.003	−.01[b] (.00)	−.002	−.002
Number of Dependents (X_6)	−.01 (.01)	—	—	−.00 (.00)	—	—
Non-Citizen (X_7)	.36 (.21)	—	—	.51[c] (.14)	.20	.16
Log Income (X_8)	−.04[d] (.01)	−.01	−.01	−.04[d] (.01)	−.02	−.01
Guilty Plea (X_9)	−.35 (.18)	−.09	−.09	−.28[d] (.08)	−.11	−.09
Guideline Offense Level (X_{10})	.59[d] (.02)	.16	.15	.39[d] (.01)	.15	.12
Criminal History Points (X_{11})	.31[d] (.02)	.08	.08	.19[d] (.00)	.08	.06
Guideline Maximum Sentence (X_{12})	−.06[d] (.01)	−.02	−.02	−.03[d] (.00)	−.01	−.01
Fraud (X_{13})**	.23 (.23)	—	—	.26[c] (.09)	.10	.08
Money Laundrying (X_{14})**	−.82[c] (.30)	−.22	−.22	−.35[c] (.13)	−.14	−.11
Embezzlement/Larceny (X_{15})**	.20 (.23)	—	—	.30[c] (.09)	.12	.10
Number of Count (X_{16})	.01 (.01)	—	—	.01[b] (.00)	—	—
Departure (X_{17})	−1.92[d] (.13)	−.51	−.51	−1.17[d] (.06)	−.46	−.37
Intercept	−3.93[d] (.47)	—	—	−2.40[d] (.24)	—	—
−Log Likelihood	1933.61			5622.39		
Model $\chi 2$	1701.44, *df* = 27 (*p* = .000)			4448.24, *df* = 27 (*p* = .000)		
Pseudo R2	.31			.28		

Notes: *Reported for significant estimates only. Estimates for circuit dummy contrasts are reported in Table 5-A.

**Reference category is bribery.

[a]For the female defendants, the number of left-censored observations = 1508, the number of uncensored observations = 787; for male defendants, the number of left- censored observations = 2121, the number of uncensored observations = 2663.

[b]Estimates significant at $.01 < p \leq .05$.

[c]Estimates significant at $.001 < p \leq .01$.

[d]Estimates significant at $p < .001$.

[e]Standard errors reported in parentheses.

Conditioning Effects of Gender

With the findings from the tobit analysis that defendant's gender, sentence departures and guilty pleas *directly* affect sentence severity, interest turns to answering the third questions posed in this research: does defendant's gender condition the effect of sentence departures and guilty pleas on sentence severity? As noted above, legal scholars and social scientists (Gelacak et al. 1996; Gyurci 1994; Lee 1994; Nagel and Schulhofer 1992; Purdy and Lawrence 1990; Schulhofer 1980; Seymour 1992; Standen 1993; Steury 1989) suggest that the federal guidelines provisions for sentence departures and guilty pleas offer judges and prosecutors a mechanism through which to circumvent the goal of eliminating unwarranted sentence disparity linked to defendant characteristics. In a recent analysis of sentencing of drug offenders under the federal sentencing guidelines in 1991-1992, Albonetti (1997) found that defendant's ethnicity did not mediate the relationship between pleading guilty and sentence severity. However, she found that ethnicity significantly mediated the effect of sentence departures on sentence severity. With this in mind, this study estimates the tobit equation in Table 4 separately for females and males convicted of a white-collar offense under the federal sentencing guidelines in 1991-1992. Table 5 provides the tobit coefficients, their standard errors, and the decomposition of significant tobit coefficients for females and for males. Table 6 reports the z-values for tests of the null hypothesis that the coefficient estimates are *invariant* across defendant's gender.

Focusing first on the effect of guilty pleas, Table 5 reveals that pleading guilty produces a significant decrease ($b = -.28$, $p \leq .001$) on sentence outcomes for males. However, for females, the effect of pleading guilty is nonsignifcant. Among males who were sentenced to prison, pleading guilty, rather than going to trial, results in a $-.11$ decrease in log length of imprisonment. Furthermore, among males who were not sentenced to prison, there is a 9% reduction in the probability of being incarcerated. Consistent with Albonetti's (1997) findings, Table 6 reveals that the difference in the effect of pleading guilty on sentence outcomes is not statistically significantly across gender.

Turning now to the effect of sentence departures, Table 5 indicates that departures from the sentencing guidelines produce a substantial decrease in sentence severity for females ($b = -1.92$, $p \leq .001$) and for males ($b = -1.17$, $p \leq .001$). The z-value of 5.24 ($p \leq .01$) reported in Table 6 warrants a rejection of the null hypothesis that the effect of sentence departures is similar across gender. These findings reveal that sentence departures, a source of discretion, differentially advantage females compared to males. This advantage is expressed in greater decreases in the log length of imprisonment and in greater reductions in the probability of being imprisoned. Earlier research on the sentencing of white-collar defendants prior to the federal sentencing guidelines (Wheeler et al. 1982; Weisburd et al. 1991) found that judges were more reluctant to imprison females than males. The findings from the present study indicate that this reluctance continues under the federal sentencing guidelines.

Table 6. Z-Test* for Differences in Regression Estimates Across Defendant's Gender

Variables	*Females Compared to Males*
Hispanic (X_1)	—
Black (X_2)	—
Education (X_4)	1.36
Age (X_5)	0
Number of Dependents (X_6)	—
Non-Citizen (X_7)	.67
Log Income (X_8)	0
Plea (X_9)	.36
Guideline Offense Level (X_{10})	9.09[a]
Criminal History Points (X_{11})	6.00[a]
Guideline Maximum Sentence (X_{12})	3.00[a]
Fraud (X_{13})	.24
Money Laundrying (X_{14})	1.44[a]
Embezzlement/Larceny (X_{15})	.40
Number of Counts (X_{16})	—
Departure (X_{17})	5.24[a]

Notes: * z-values reported as absolute values.
[a] z-values significant at $p \leq .01$ (two-tailed test.

Furthermore, this study reveals that the sentence departures are a key discretionary mechanism through which sentence leniency, linked to gender, is facilitated.

The "evil woman" thesis (Chesney-Lind 1977; Singer 1973; Smart 1977; Velimesis 1975; Nagel and Hagan 1983) argues that more severe punishments are imposed on females when their illegal behavior contradicts gender-based stereotypes. According to this thesis and consistent with the uncertainty avoidance/causal attribution perspective, females who are convicted of offenses that are associated with relatively severe punishment are predicted to receive more severe sentences than their similarly situated males. These theoretical perspectives can be examined by testing whether the effects of guidelines-defined legally relevant variables on sentence severity is invariant for females and males. Support for these perspectives would be found if the effect of guidelines-defined variables on sentence outcome resulted in significantly more punitive sentences for females than males.

The findings reported in Tables 5 and 6 indicate that increases in the final guidelines offense level produce significant increases in sentence severity for both females (.59, $p \leq .001$) and males (.39, $p \leq .001$). Consistent with the two theoretical perspectives, the increase in sentence severity is greater for females than for males ($z = 9.09$, $p \leq .01$, Table 6). The latter finding is particularly revealing. Although the *direct* effect of being female is to produce a more lenient sentence than that received by males (Table 4), the *conditioning* role of gender is that female defendants are punished more severely than males in terms of the vertical axis of the sentencing grid, the final guidelines offense level. Comparing the results of the decomposition of effects across gender (Table 6) is informative. The difference in the effect of final guideline offense level on the log length of imprisonment is similar (.16 and .15 for females and males, respectively) but the effect of this variable on the probability of receiving an imprisonment outcome is different and to the disadvantage of female defendants. Contrary to earlier findings based on sentencing practices prior to federal sentencing reform (Weisburd et al. 1991; Wheeler et al. 1982; Hagan et al. 1980), among defendants who are given a prison sentence, females experience a higher increase in the probability of being imprisoned than males (Table 5, .15 and .12 for females and males, respectively). Pre-guideline resistance to sentencing females to prison (Weisburd et al. 1991; Wheeler et al. 1982) is reversed under the federal sentencing guidelines.

Turning now to the comparison of the effect of criminal history points, the horizontal axis on the sentencing grid, on sentence severity across the males and females, the findings reported in Tables 5 and 6 reveal significantly different (z = 6.00, $p \leq .01$) effects across gender. For both groups, increases in the number of criminal history points increase sentence severity ($b = .31$, $p \leq .001$ for females and $b = .19$, $p \leq .001$ for males). But females receive significantly more punitive effects than males. This finding is consistent with the uncertainty avoidance/causal attribution perspective and the evil women theory. Decomposing the tobit estimates reveals the gender differences in punishment. Table 6 indicates that increases in the number of criminal history points produces the same increase in the log length of imprisonment ($b = .08$) for both genders. However, the gender difference is played out in the probability of imprisonment for each gender. Females experience a higher increase in the probability of being imprisoned (.08) than males (.06). Taken together, the findings of gender differences in the effect of two central features of the guidelines structure, final guidelines offense level and number of criminal history points, suggests that females are more severely punished for counter-gender stereotypes centering around offense-related information and prior criminal involvement.

The effect of guidelines maximum sentence, the upper bound within the sentencing grid cell, significantly decreases sentence severity for males and for females. Table 5 indicates that the effect is small in magnitude, with female defendants receiving the larger reduction. The z-value (3.00, $p \leq .01$) reported in Table 6 reveals that the difference in tobit coefficients is statistically significant. Comparing the decomposition estimates across gender reveals that female defendants experience only a slightly lower reduction in length of imprisonment for those receiving a prison sentence and a slightly lower reduction in the probability of being incarcerated for those not receiving an incarceration sentence. Although the effects of guideline maximum sentence are small, the negative effect of this variable is particularly noteworthy. As noted earlier, research on sentence severity has consistently found a positive effect of statutory severity on sentence severity.

This negative effect suggests judicial resistance to the increased harshness of sentences imposed under the federal sentencing guidelines for convictions for white-collar offenses. Nagel and Johnson (1994) and Tonry (1996) point out that Congress instructed the Sentencing Commission to create a sentencing structure that, among other goals, increased substantially the penalties assigned for white-collar and drug offenses. By substantially reducing judicial discretion, the sentencing guidelines encroached on judicial autonomy. Resistance to such encroachment may well be expressed by judges imposing sentences closer to the lower bound of the cell when the upper bound of the guideline grid cell is viewed as more severe than the sentences imposed prior to implementation of the federal sentencing guidelines. Findings from this analysis are consistent with this interpretation.

Table 6 indicates that the effects of the three white-collar crime dummy variables on sentencing is invariant across gender. Findings in Table 5 and Table 6 indicate that the influence of offense-related variables on sentence outcomes are captured by guidelines-defined offenses measures (e.g., final guidelines offense level, guidelines maximum sentence) rather than the particular type of offense.

Turning now to the effects of extra-legal variables on sentence outcomes, Table 5 and Table 6 indicate that defendant's gender does not condition the effect of ethnicity, education, age, citizenship status, income, or the number of dependents. Of particular interest is the finding that the number of dependents is unrelated to sentence outcomes, regardless of gender. Earlier research from an informal social control emphasis suggested that sentence leniency for females was tied to being "familied" (Daly 1987a, 1994) and to the general dependence-caretaking status (Kruttschnitt and Green 1984; Steffensmeier et al. 1993) that females disproportionately experience. My analysis reveals that, under the federal sentencing guidelines, sentence leniency for females is not tied to such considerations. Taken together, these findings of an absence of gender-specific effects of defendant characteristics is consistent with the intent of the federal sentencing reform, namely, to eliminate sentence disparately linked to family responsibility, education, age, and ethnicity.

Finally, Table 5 indicates that being a non-U.S. citizen significantly increases sentence severity ($b = .51$, $.001 < p \leq .01$) for only male defendants. This increase penalty is evidenced in the decomposition of the tobit estimate. Table 5 indicates that being a non-U.S. citizen increases by .20 the log length of imprisonment for male defendants receiving a prison sentence and a 16% increase in the probability of being imprisoned for those not imprisoned. This finding is contrary to the federal sentencing guidelines directive that citizenship is not ordinarily relevant to sentencing.

SUMMARY AND CONCLUSION

Under the federal sentencing guidelines, sentence disparity linked to defendant characteristics is to be eliminated by restricting judicial discretion at sentencing.

This overarching goal of sentencing reform may well be undermined by the very sentencing guidelines that were enacted to produce uniformity and proportionality in sentence outcomes. Provisions for sentence departures and for guilty plea negotiations offer a means through which prosecutorial and judicial discretion can circumvent the formal, rational decision-making structure prescribed by the guidelines (Standen 1993; Schulhofer and Nagel 1989; Rhodes 1992; Purdy and Lawrence 1990; Gyurci 1994; Lee 1994; Steury 1989). Albonetti's (1997) recent research on sentencing of drug offenders under the federal sentencing guidelines provides empirically evidence of ethnic-specific effects of departures on sentence severity. Steffensmeier et al.'s (1993) analysis of sentencing under Pennsylvania guidelines leads them to concluded that females benefited more from guidelines departures than males. These two multivariate studies of sentence outcomes under different sentencing guidelines structures, together with the legal and policy analyses, suggest the need to empirically examine the direct effect of guidelines departures on sentence severity under the federal sentencing guidelines.

In this study, I posed three questions that are pivotal to the federal sentencing reform efforts and to the larger value of equal protection under the law. First, does defendant's gender systematically influence sentence outcomes under the federal sentencing guidelines? Second, do guidelines departures and guilty pleas significantly affect sentencing? Third, does gender condition the effect of guidelines departures and guilty pleas on sentence outcomes? Using data on 7,079 defendants convicted of a white-collar crime and sentenced under the federal sentencing guidelines in 1991-1992, I used multivariate tobit equations to estimate the net effect of defendant characteristics, guidelines-defined legally relevant variables, offense information, departures, and guilty pleas on sentence severity. The analyses controlled for circuit-specific sentencing practices. Tobit estimates were decomposed to uncover the effect of each variables on: (1) the probability of imprisonment for defendants who were not imprisoned, and (2) the length of imprisonment for those who received a prison sentence.

Regarding the first question, the results from the pooled analysis indicate that females receive more lenient punishment than males, controlling for circuit-specific sentencing practices, guidelines-defined legally relevant variables, process variables, and other defendant characteristics. Sentence leniency for females is expressed in shorter periods of imprisonment and in a lower probability of being incarcerated. This finding is generally consistent with findings of sentencing practices for defendants convicted of a white-collar offense prior to the federal sentencing guidelines. As such, this strongly suggests the federal sentencing guidelines have not eliminated gender-based sentencing in white-collar cases.

Specifying the social process that accounts for gender-related sentence leniency is difficult. As noted in the literature, a number of theories are offered. Kruttschnitt (1980-1981) hypothesized that higher levels of social integration, typically experienced by females, account for the more lenient sentences imposed on females, compared to males. In a subsequent study, Kruttschnitt (1982) concluded that gender-based sentence leniency could be explained in terms of the greater economic dependency experienced by females. She reasoned that economic dependency is a source of social control over females and in the face of this higher level of control, judges decided to impose less severe punishment for females than for males. Kruttschnitt (1982) and Kruttschnitt and Green (1984) hypothesize an intervening effect of social control, measured by economic dependency, in the relationship between defendant's gender and sentence severity. Since the Monitoring of Federal Criminal Sentences, 1991-1992, data do not contain measures of economic dependency, I am unable to test Kruttschnitt's (1980-1981, 1982) and Kruttschnitt and Green's (1984) explanation of the effect of gender on sentence severity under the federal sentencing guidelines.

The observed nonsignificant effect of the defendant's number of dependents on sentence severity in the pooled analysis and in the gender-specific analysis contradicts Daly's (1987a) theory that family and caretaking responsibilities influence sentence outcomes. However, it is important to note that my analysis does not represent a thorough empirical test of Daly's (1987a) theory, again due to limitations in the available measures of being "familied," having other caretaking responsibilities, and the estimated cost to the government for child care if the defendant is sentenced to prison.

Drawing from the uncertainty avoidance/causal attribution merger suggested by Albonetti (1991), I hypothesized that females receive less severe sentence outcomes than males because judges are less likely to attribute stable and enduring patterns of illegal behavior to females. Steffensmeier notes, "These same attributional processes may also lead to the conception of the female offender as being more amenable to 'rehabilitation' and less likely to transgress in the future than male defendants. In this view, the perceived permanence of the behavior and the extent to which the offender is perceived as being susceptible to change may help account for differential responses to male and female defendants" (1980, pp. 351-352). I suggest that it is the link between gender-based attributions of enduring illegal behavior and judges' desires to reduce the uncertainty of surrounding sentencing decisions that contributes to the preferential sentencing outcomes observed in this study. However, in this study, it was considered important to determine how gender-specific sentencing outcomes are realized within the structure of the federal sentencing guidelines.

Turning to the second question, the findings indicate that pleading guilty and receiving a sentence departure significantly reduces sentence severity under the federal guidelines. In fact, sentence departures produce the largest effect on both sentencing outcomes. Receiving a departure from the prescribed guidelines range results in a substantial decrease in length of imprisonment and in the probability of being imprisoned. Pleading guilty, rather than going to trial, produces a nontrivial reduction in length of imprisonment and in the probability of imprisonment. These findings support theoretical arguments of legal scholars and social scientists that prosecutorial and judicial discretion, provided by guilty pleas and guidelines departures, continues to influence sentencing and may circumvent the formal goals of uniformity and proportionality in sentence outcomes. With the sentencing reform goal of directly linking offense-related variables and the defendant's record of prior criminal activity to sentence severity, the observed substantial negative effect of guidelines departures and guilty pleas on sentence outcomes points to the need to empirically test whether the sentence reductions, resulting from these two provisions of the federal sentencing guidelines, may contribute to gender-based sentence leniency suggested by the univariate analysis.

The third question I posed in this study focuses on gender-specific effect of guilty pleas and guidelines departures on sentence severity under the federal guidelines. My findings reveal that for both females and males, judges use guideline departures as a means for reducing the sentence severity that would otherwise be imposed by the applicable guidelines range. However, the effect of guidelines departures on sentence severity is greater for females than for males, thereby contributing to the observed gender-based sentence leniency for defendants sentenced for a white-collar offense under the federal sentencing guidelines. Moreover, the findings reveal that prosecutors and judges use guilty pleas similarly for males and for females. Of the two sources of discretion, my findings indicate that guidelines departures exert the stronger effect on sentence severity. This is consistent with Albonetti's (1997) findings of sentencing practices for defendants convicted for drug offenders under the federal sentencing guidelines. One might argue that such a finding indicates that the use of discretion is far more visible under the guidelines since judges are required to explain in writing their reason for giving a departure from the applicable guidelines range. There is merit to this suggestion. However, the findings from this study indicate a lack of uniformity in the use of sentence departures that results in sentence disparity that is tied to defendant's gender and to defendant's ethnicity Albonetti (1997).

Additional findings are noteworthy. From the pooled analysis, it is clear that guidelines-defined legally relevant variables affect sentence severity. Consistent with the federal sentencing guidelines, the final guidelines offense level—the vertical axis of the sentencing grid—substantially increases sentence severity. Moreover, the findings demonstrate that federal judges systematically consider the defendant's number of criminal history points, the horizontal axis of the grid. These effects are in the expected direction. However, contrary to earlier sentencing studies, the variable that measures the maximum legal penalty that can be imposed, guideline maximum sentence, is small in magnitude and acts to decreases sentence severity. I suggest that the negative direction of the coefficient may be understood in terms of the widespread judicial resistance to legislative targeting of white-collar crimes for substantially harsher punishment under the federal sentencing reform. The findings that the negative effect of guidelines maximum sentence is significantly stronger for females than males suggests that judges are even more resistant to imposing the harsher punishments on females convicted of a white-collar offense. Albonetti's (forthcoming) analysis of sentencing outcomes for drug offenders under the federal sentencing guidelines revealed similar findings to those obtained in this analysis of sentencing for offenders convicted of white-collar crimes. Future research should examine whether the observed negative effect of guideline maximum sentence on sentence severity is found for other federal offenses.

Finally, the finding that gender mediates the effects of final guidelines offense level and the defendant's number of criminal history points is noteworthy. My analysis demonstrates that these two axes of the sentencing grid are not uniformly applied across gender. The significantly stronger effect of these variables on sentence severity for females is consistent with an uncertainty avoidance/causal attribution and evil woman theories of sentencing. From these perspectives, females who are convicted of criminal behavior and accompanying specific offense characteristics that yield relatively high values for the final guidelines offense level, and who score relatively high on the criminal history scale, are females who represent counter-gender stereotypes and, as such, approach the "evil woman" attribution and are punished more severely than males with similar attributes. Considering the findings of preferential treatment of females and the gender-specific effect of final guideline offense level and the defendant's number of criminal history points strongly suggest that sentencing in white-collar crime cases under the federal sentencing guidelines reflects the corollary relationship between the chivalry/paternalism thesis and the evil woman thesis (Nagel and Hagan 1983). As Nagel and Hagan propose, "Thus it may be that women are preferentially treated, compared to men, until such time as the basis for that preferential treatment—chivalry or paternalism—is rendered inappropriate. Then, by virtue of the seriousness of the offense charged, the lessening of the presumption of innocence, and the evidence of deviation from traditional female patterns of behavior, the woman is moved into the evil women category, and preferential treatment ceases" (1983, pp. 136-137).

Returning to the pooled analysis, the findings reveal that defendant's gender is not the only defendant characteristics that produces a net effect on sentence severity under the federal guidelines. Results indicate that older defendants and those with higher incomes received leniency. Black defendants and non-U.S. citizens received harsher sentences than did whites and U.S. citizens. These findings also suggest that sentence disparity under the federal sentencing guidelines continues to be influenced by legally *irrelevant* defendant characteristics. Previous research (Hagan et al. 1980) indicated that defendant's educational attainment was related to sentence severity. Findings from this study of sentencing under the federal sentencing guidelines reveals that defendant's education was not a determinant to sentence severity for white-collar offenders sentenced in 1991-1992. Finally, my analysis reports that Hispanic defendants convicted of a white-collar offense did not receive significantly different sentences than whites.

In summary, the findings from this study reveal that defendant's gender is related to sentence outcomes under the federal sentencing guidelines. Females receive more lenient punishment than males. This study indicates that sentence departures is a mechanism through which this leniency is provided. Guilty pleas appear to be less important as an avenue of imposing gender-specific sentencing outcomes. Furthermore, findings indicate that, under the federal sentencing guidelines, females who represent counter-gender stereotypes are sentenced more severely than are similarly situated males. Future research should be conducted to explore these findings for other offense categories.

ACKNOWLEDGMENTS

The author wishes to thank the research staff of the United States Sentencing Commission, especially Cameron Counters, John Scalia, Jr., and Linda Drazga Maxfield, for their help in understanding the complex nature of the data (U.S. Sentencing Commission Monitoring of Federal Criminal Sentencing, 1991-1992) used for this research.

APPENDIX

Table A.1. Unstandardized Coefficient Estimates, Standard Errors, and Decomposition of Effects* for Variables Included in the Tobit Model of Sentencing for White-Collar Crime under the Federal Sentencing Guidelines, 1991-1992 (*N* = 7079)

		Decomposition	
*Variables***	*Estimates*	c^1	c^2
Circuit 1 (X_{18})	-.11 (.18)		
Circuit 2 (X_{19})	-.31 (.17)		
Circuit 3 (X_{20})	-.35[a] (.16)	.10	.09
Circuit 4 (X_{21})	.03 (.16)		
Circuit 5 (X_{22})	.30 (.16)		
Circuit 6 (X_{23})	.03 (.16)		
Circuit 7 (X_{24})	.00 (.16)		
Circuit 8 (X_{25})	.15 (.17)		
Circuit 9 (X_{26})	.00 (.16)		
Circuit 10 (X_{27})	.16 (.17)		
Circuit 11 (X_{28})	.13 (.16)		

Notes: *Reported for significant estimates.
**Reference category is District of Columbia.
[a]Estimate significant at .01 < p ≤ .05..

Table A.2. Unstandardized Coefficient, Standard Errors and Decomposition of Effects* for Variables Included in the Tobit Model of Sentencing for White-Collar Crime Under the Federal Sentencing Guidelines, 1991-1992, Estimated Separately by Gender

	Female			*Male*		
		Decomposition			*Decomposition*	
Variable	*Est. (S.E.)*	c^1	c^2	*Est. (S.E.)*	c^1	c^2
Circuit 1 (X_{18})	.30 (.41)	—	—	.06 (.22)	—	—
Circuit 2 (X_{19})	–.52 (.33)	—	—	–.17(.20)	—	—
Circuit 3 (X_{20})	.68[a] (.31)	–.18	–.18	–.17 (.19)	—	—
Circuit 4 (X_{21})	.15 (.30)	—	—	.09 (.19)	—	—
Circuit 5 (X_{22})	.03 (.30)	—	—	.44a (.19)	—	—
Circuit 6 (X_{23})	–.11 (.29)	—	—	.16 (.19)	.17	.14
Circuit 7 (X_{24})	–.13 (.31)	—	—	.11 (.20)	—	—
Circuit 8 (X_{25})	.19 (.31)	—	—	.19 (.19)	—	—
Circuit 9 (X_{26})	–.14 (.31)	—	—	.14 (.19)	—	—
Circuit 10 (X_{27})	.04 (.32)	—	—	.31 (.20)	—	—
Circuit 11 (X_{28})	–.08 (.29)	—	—	.28 (.19)	—	—

Notes: * Provided for significant estimates.
[a] Significant at $p \leq .05$.

NOTES

1. Pub. L. No. 98-473, 98 Stat. 1987 (1984) (codified as amended at 18 U.S.C. 3551-3586 (1988)).
2. 28 U.S.C. 991(b) (1) (B) (Supp. 1993).
3. U.S.S.G. Part A - Introduction.
4. U.S.S.G. Part K - Departures, 5K1.1 through 5K2.15.
5. U.S.S.G. Chapter 6, Part B - Plea Agreements, 6B1.1 through 6B1.4.
6. U.S.S.G 3E1.1.
7. U.S.S.G. 3E1.1.
8. U.S.S.G. 5K1.1.
9. U.S.S.G. 5K2.1.
10. U.S.S.G. 5K2.4
11. U.S.S.G. 5K2.8.
12. Whereas S. Nagel (1969) analyzed limited his analysis of federal and state data to two types of offenses, Moulds (1980) included all offenses in her reanalysis of Nagel's data.
13. P.L. 1311, see Pa. Stat. Ann.tit.61 566 (1964).
14. 59 N.J. 334, 282 A.2d 748 (1971).
15. See U.S.S.G 5H1.10.
16. See U.S.S.G. 5H1.6 states, "Family ties and responsibilities and community ties are not ordinarily relevant in determining whether a sentence should be outside the guidelines. Family ties that are complied with are relevant in determining whether to impose restitution and fines."
17. According to U.S.S.G. 5K2.12, "If the defendant committed the offense because of serious coercion, blackmail or duress, under circumstances not amounting to a complete defense, the court may decrease the sentence below the applicable guideline range."
18. See U.S.S.G. 5H1.10. age,[19]
19. See U.S.S.G. 5H1.1.
20. See U.S.S.G. 5H1.2. The guidelines indicate that education and vocational skills "are not ordinarily relevant in determining whether a sentence should be outside the guidelines, but the extent to which a defendant may have misused special training or education to facilitate criminal activity is an express guidelines factor" (par. 5.35).
21. See U.S.S.G. 5H1.3.
22. See U.S.S.G. 5H1.4.
23. See U.S.S.G 5H1.5.
24. See U.S.S.G 5H1.6.
25. According to the federal sentencing guidelines, prosecuting attorneys must file a motion for a 5K1.1 departure before the court can consider such a departure; see Part K - Departures, Guidelines Manual (1989).
26. Research on sentencing under the Pennsylvania sentencing guidelines (Ulmer 1977; Kramer and Ulmer 1996) analyzed departures as a sentence outcome. While this is a meaningful approach, my research focuses on how avenues of discretion may influence sentence severity. Judicial departures are one such avenue. As such, I treat departures as a process-related variable. Under the federal sentencing guidelines, a departure is not considered a sentence outcome.
27. The data for this research are U.S. Sentencing Commission Monitoring of Federal Criminal Sentencing, 1991-1992, ICPSR version. Washingon, DC: U.S. Sentencing Commission [producer], 1992. Ann Arbor, MI: Inter-university Consortium for Political and Social Research [distributor], 1992.
28. Throughout this chapter, I report federal circuit estimates in separate tables. This is done for ease of reporting and seems reasonable since only one circuit contrast achieved statistical significance in the tobit regression equation provided in Table 4 and Table A.1.

REFERENCES

Albonetti, C.A. 1991. "An Integration of Theories to Explain Judicial Discretion," *Social Problems* 38: 247-266.

Albonetti, C.A. 1994. "The Symbolic Punishment of White-Collar Offenders." Pp. 269-282 in *Inequality, Crime and Social Control*, edited by G.S. Bridges and M.A. Myers, Boulder, CO: Westview.

Albonetti, C.A. 1996. "The Process of Federal Sentencing: A Legal-bureaucratic Model of the Variables Affecting Length of Imprisonment for White-Collar Offenders Prior to the Federal Sentencing Guidelines." Paper presented at the American Sociological Association Meetings, New York.

Albonetti, C.A. 1997. "Sentencing under the Federal Sentencing Guidelines: An Analysis of the Effects of Defendant Characteristics, Guilty Pleas, and Departures on Sentence Outcomes for Drug Offenses, 1991-1992." *Law and Society Review* 31: 601-634.

Baab, G.W., and W.R. Furgeson 1967. "Texas Sentencing Practices: A Statistical Study." *Texas Law Review* 45: 471-403.

Benson, M.L., and E. Walker 1988. "Sentencing the White-Collar Offender." *American Sociological Review* 53: 294-202.

Berlin, E.P. 1993. "Comment: The Federal Sentencing Guidelines' Failure to Eliminate Sentencing Disparity: Governmental Manipulation Before Arrest." *Wisconsin Law Review* 1993: 187-30.

Bernstein, I., W. Kelly, and P. Doyle. 1977. "Societal Reaction to Deviants: The Case of Criminal Defendants." *American Sociological Review* 42: 743-795.

Black, D. 1976. *The Behavior of Law*. New York: Academic Press.

Boerner, D. 1985. *Sentencing in Washington: A Legal Analysis of the Sentencing Reform Act of 1981*. Seattle, WA: Butterworth.

Boerner, D. 1995 "Sentencing Guidelines and Prosecutorial Discretion." *Judicature* 78: 196-200.

Breen, R. 1996. *Regression Models: Censored, Sample Selected, or Truncated Data*. Thousand Oaks, CA: Sage.

Breyer, S. 1988. "The Federal Sentencing Guidelines and the Key Compromises Upon Which They Rest." *Hofstra Law Review* 17: 1-50.

Carroll, J.S., and J.W. Payne 1976. "The Psychology of the Parole Decision Process: A Joint Application of Attribution Theory and Information Processing Psychology." Pp. 109-123 in *Cognition and Social Behavior*, edited by J.S. Carroll and J.W. Payne, Hillsdale, NJ: Erlbaum.

Chesney-Lind, M. 1977. "Judicial Paternalism and the Female Status Offender: Training Women to Know Their Place." *Issues in Criminology* 8: 51-59.

Clarke, S.H. 1984. "North Carolina's Determinate Sentencing Legislation." *Judicature* 68: 140-152.

Clogg, C.C., E. Petkova, and A. Haritou 1995. "Symposium on Applied Regression Statistical Methods for Comparing Regression Coefficients between Models." *American Journal of Sociology* 100: 161-193.

Cook, J.A., Jr., 1995. "Gender and Sentencing: Family Responsibility and Dependent Relationship Factors." *Federal Sentencing Reporter* 8: 145-147.

Coughenour, J.C. 1995. "Separate and Unequal: Women in the Federal Criminal Justice System." *Federal Sentencing Reporter* 8: 142-144.

Daly, K. 1987a. "Discrimination in the Criminal Courts: Family, Gender, and the Problem of Equal Treatment." *Social Forces* 66: 152-175.

Daly, K. 1987b. "Structure and Practice of Familial-Based Justice in a Criminal Court." *Law and Society Review* 21: 267-290.

Daly, K. 1994. *Gender, Crime, and Punishment*. New Haven, CT: Yale University Press.

Daly, K. 1995. "Gender and Sentencing: What We Know and Don't Know from Empirical Research." *Federal Sentencing Reporter* 8: 163-167.

Dixon, J. 1995. "The Organizational Context of Criminal Sentencing." *American Journal of Sociology* 100: 1157-1198.

Eisenstein, J., R. Flemming, and P. Nardulli 1988. *The Contours of Justice: Communities and Their Courts.* Boston, MA: Little Brown.

Farrell, R.A., and V.L. Swigert 1978. "Prior Offense Record as a Self-fulfilling Prophecy." *Law and Society Review* 12: 437-453.

Fontaine, G., and C. Emily 1978. "Causal Attribution and Judicial Discretion: A Look at the Verbal Behavior of Municipal Court Judges." *Law and Human Behavior* 2: 323-337.

Gelacak, M.S., I.H. Nagel, and B.L. Johnson 1996. "Departures under the Federal Guidelines: An Empirical and Jurisprudential Analysis." *Minnesota Law Review* 81: 299-266.

Green, E. 1961. *Judicial Attitudes in Sentencing.* London: Macmillan.

Gyurci, J. 1994. "Note: Prosecutorial Discretion to Bring a Substantial Assistance Motion Pursuant to a Plea Agreement: Enforcing a Good Faith Standard." *Minnesota Law Review* 78: 1253-1283.

Hagan, J. 1974. "Extra-Legal Attributes and Criminal Sentencing: An Assessment of a Sociological Viewpoint." *Law and Society Review* 8: 857-884.

Hagan, J., I.H. Nagel, and C.A. Albonetti. 1980. "The Differential Sentencing of White-Collar Offenders in Ten Federal District Courts." *American Sociological Review* 45: 802-820.

Hagan, J., I.H. Nagel, and C.A. Albonetti. 1982. "The Social Organization of White-Collar Sanctions: A Study of Prosecution and Punishment in the Federal Courts." Pp. 259-275 in *White-Collar and Economic Crime*, edited by P. Wickman and T. Dailey, Lexington, MA: D.C. Heath and Company.

Hagan, J., and A. Palloni 1986. "'Club Fed' and the Sentencing of White-Collar Offenders Before and After Watergate." *Criminology* 24: 603-622.

Hagan, J., and P. Parker 1985. "White-collar Crime and Punishment: The Class Structure and Legal Sanctioning of Securities Violations." *American Sociological Review* 50: 302-316.

Hawkins, D.F. 1981. "Causal Attribution and Punishment for Crime." *Deviant Behavior: An Interdisciplinary Journal* 2: 207-230.

Heider, F. 1958. *The Psychology of Interpersonal Relations.* New York: Wiley.

Knapp, K.A. 1984. *The Impact of the Minnesota Sentencing Guidelines: Three Year Evaluations.* St. Paul, MN: Minnesota Sentencing Guidelines Commission.

Kramer, J.H., and R.L. Lubitz 1985. "Pennsylvania's Sentencing Reform: The Impact of Commission-Established Guidelines." *Crime and Delinquency* 31: 481-500.

Kramer, J.H., and D. Steffensmeier. 1993. "Race and Imprisonment Decisions." *The Sociological Quarterly* 34: 357-376.

Kramer, J.H., and J. Ulmer 1996. "Sentencing Disparity and Guideline Departures." *Justice Quarterly* 13: 81-106.

Kruttschnitt, C. 1980-1981. "Social Status and Sentences of Female Offenders." *Law and Society Review* 15: 247-265.

Kruttschnitt, C. 1982. "Women, Crime, and Dependency." *Criminology* 19: 495-413.

Kruttschnitt, C. 1984. "Sex and Criminal Court Dispositions: The Unresolved Controversy." *Research in Crime and Delinquency* 21: 213-232.

Kruttschnitt, C., and D.E. Green 1984. "The Sex-Sanctioning Issue: Is It History?" *American Sociological Review* 49: 541-551.

Lee, C.K.Y. 1994. "Prosecutorial Discretion, Substantial Assistance, and the Federal Sentencing Guidelines." *UCLA Law Review* 42: 105-180.

Lippman, W. 1922. *Public Opinion.* New York: Harcourt Brace.

Lizotte, A.J. 1978. "The Extra-Legal Factors in Chicago's Criminal Courts: Testing the Conflict Model of Criminal Justice." *Social Problems* 25: 564-580.

Long, J.S. 1997. *Regression Models for Categorical and Limited Dependent Variables.* Thousand Oaks, CA: Sage.

Lowe, C.J. 1987. "Modern Sentencing Reform: A Preliminary Analysis of the Proposed Federal Sentencing Guidelines." *American Criminal Law Review* 25: 1-57.

March, J.G. and H.A. Simon 1958. *Organizations*. New York: Wiley.

Martin, S.E. 1984. "Interests and Politics in Sentencing Reform: The Development of Sentencing Guidelines in Pennsylvania and Minnesota." *Villanova Law Review* 29: 21-13.

McBride, M.R. 1995. "Gender Issues in Federal Sentencing: A View from Probation." *Federal Sentencing Reporter* 8: 154-156.

McDonald, J.F., and R. A. Moffitt 1980. "The Uses of Tobit Analysis." *The Review of Economics and Statistics* LXII: 318-213.

Miethe, T.D. 1987. "Charging and Plea Bargaining Practices under Determinate Sentencing: An Investigation of the Hydraulic Displacement of Discretion." *Journal of Criminal Law and Criminology* 78: 155-176.

Miethe, T.D., and C.A. Moore 1985. "Socioeconomic Disparities under Determinate Sentencing Systems: A Comparison of Preguideline and Postguideline Practices in Minnesota." *Criminology* 23: 337-363.

Moffitt, R. 1982. "The Tobit Model, Hours of Work and Institutional Constrains." *The Review of Economics and Statistics* 64: 510-515.

Moore, C.A., and T.D. Miethe 1986. "Regulated and Unregulated Sentencing Decisions: An Analysis of First-Year Practices Under Minnesota's Felony Sentencing Guidelines." *Law and Society Review* 20: 253-277.

Moulds, E.F. 1980. "Chivalry and Paternalism: Disparities of Treatment in the Criminal Justice System." Pp. 277-299 in *Women, Crime and Justice*, edited by S. Datesman and F. Scarpitti. New York: Oxford Press.

Nagel, I.H. 1990. "Structuring Sentencing Discretion: The New Federal Sentencing Guidelines." *Journal of Criminal Law and Criminology* 80: 883-843.

Nagel, I.H., and J. Hagan. 1982. "The Sentencing of White-Collar Criminals in Federal Courts: A Socio-Legal Exploration of Disparity." *Michigan Law Review* 80: 1427-1465.

Nagel, I.H., and J. Hagan. 1983. "Gender and Crime: Offense Patterns and Criminal Court Sanctions." Pp. 91-144 in *Crime and Justice: An Annual Review of Research*, Vol. 4, edited by M. Tonry and N. Morris. Chicago, IL: The University of Chicago Press.

Nagel, I.H., and B.L. Johnson. 1994. "The Role of Gender in a Structured Sentencing System: Equal Treatment, Policy Choices, and the Sentencing of Female Offenders under the United States Sentencing Guidelines." *The Journal of Criminal Law and Criminology* 85: 181-121.

Nagel, I.H., and S.J. Schulhofer. 1992. "A Tale of Three Cities: An Empirical Study of Charging and Bargaining Practices under the Federal Sentencing Guidelines." *Southern California Law Review* 66: 501-566.

Nagel, S. 1969. *The Legal Process from a Behavioral Perspective*. Homewood, IL: Dorsey Press.

Nagel, S., and L. Weitzman. 1971. "Women as Litigants." *Hastings Law Journal* 23: 171-198.

Newton, P.J., J. Glazer, and K. Blackwell. 1995. "Gender, Individuality and the Federal Sentencing Guidelines." *Federal Sentencing Reporter* 8: 148-153.

Parent, D.G. 1988. *Structuring Criminal Sentences: The Evolution of Minnesota's Sentencing Guidelines*. Stoneham, MA: Butterworth.

Peterson, R.D., and J. Hagan 1984. "Changing Conceptions of Race: Towards An Account of Anomalous Findings of Sentencing Research." *American Sociological Review* 49: 56-70.

Purdy, D.A., Jr., and J. Lawrence. 1990. "Plea Agreements under the Federal Sentencing Guidelines." *Criminal Law Bulletin* 26: 483-408.

Quinn, T.J. 1990. "Delaware Sentencing Guidelines Achieving Their Goals." *Overcrowded Times* 1: 1-2.

Raeder, M.S. 1995. "The Forgotten Offender: The Effect of the Sentencing Guidelines and Mandatory Minimums on Women and Their Children." *Federal Sentencing Reporter* 8: 157-162.

Rafter, N.H. 1985. *Partial Justice: Women in State Prisons, 1800-1935*. Boston, MA: Northeastern University Press.

Reckless, W.C., and B.A. Kay. 1967. *The Female Offender.* Consultant's Report presented to the President's Commission on Law Enforcement and Administration of Justice.

Resnik, J. 1995. "Sentencing Women." *Federal Sentencing Reporter* 8: 134-136.

Rhodes, W. 1991. "Federal Criminal Sentencing: Some Measurement Issues with Application to Pre-Guideline Sentencing Disparity." *The Journal of Criminal Law and Criminology* 81: 1002-1033.

Rhodes, W. 1992. "Sentence Disparity, Use of Incarceration, and Plea Bargaining: The Post-Guideline View from the Commission." *Federal Sentencing Reporter* 5: 153-155.

Roncek, D.W. 1992. ""Learning More From Tobit Coefficients: Extending a Comparative Analysis of Political Protest."*American Sociological Review* 57: 508-523.

Schulhofer, S.J. 1980. "Sentencing Reform and Prosecutorial Power." *University of Pennsylvania Law Review* 126: 550-577.

Schulhofer, S.J. 1992. "Assessing the Federal Sentencing Process: The Problem is Uniformity, Not Disparity."*American Criminal Law Review* 29: 833-873.

Schulhofer, S.J., and I.H. Nagel 1989. "Negotiated Pleas Under the Federal Sentencing Guidelines: The First Fifteen Months." *American Criminal Law Review* 27: 231-288.

Seymour, J.G. 1992. "Downward Departures From The Federal Sentencing Guidelines Based on the Defendant's Drug Rehabilitative Efforts." *The University of Chicago Law Review* 59: 837-864.

Shaver, K.G. 1975. *An Introduction to Attribution Process.* Cambridge, MA: Winthrop.

Simon, H. 1957. *Administrative Behavior: A Study of Decision Making Processes in Administrative Organizations.* New York: Macmillian.

Simpson, S.S. 1989. "Feminist Theory, Crime, and Justice." *Criminology* 27: 605-631.

Singer, L.R. 1973. "Women and the Correctional Process." *American Criminal Law Review* 11: 295-208.

Smart, C. 1977. *Women, Crime and Criminology: Feminist Critique.* London: Routlede & Kegan Paul.

Smith, B.L., and K.R. Damphousse. 1996. "Punishing Political Offenders: The Effect of Political Motive on Federal Sentencing Decisions." *Criminology* 34: 289-221.

Spohn, C., J. Gruhl, and S. Welch. 1981-1982. "The Effect of Race on Sentencing: A Re- Examination of an Unsettled Question." *Law and Society Review* 16: 72-88.

Standen, J. 1993 "Plea Bargaining in the Shadow of the Guidelines." *California Law Review* 81: 1471-1438.

Steffensmeier, D. 1980. "Assessing the Impact of the Women's Movement on Sex-Based Differences in the Handling of Adult Criminal Defendants." *Crime and Delinquency* 23: 344-357.

Steffensmeier, D., J. Kramer, and C. Streifel. 1993. "Gender and Imprisonment Decisions." *Criminology* 31: 411-446.

Steury, E.H. 1989. "Prosecutorial and Judicial Discretion." Pp. 93-109 in *The U.S. Sentencing Guidelines: Implication for Criminal Justice*, edited by D.J. Champion. New York: Praeger.

Sungaila, M-C. 1995. "Taking the Gendered Realities of Female Offenders into Account: Downward Departures for Coercion and Duress." *Federal Sentencing Reporter* 8: 169-172.

Temin, C.E. 1973. "Discriminatory Sentencing of Women Offenders: The Argument of ERA in a Nutshell." *American Criminal Law Review* 11: 355-372.

Thompson, J.D. 1967. *Organizations in Action.* New York: McGraw-Hill.

Tobin, J. 1958. "Estimation of Relationships for Limited Dependent Variables." *Econmetrica* 26: 24-36.

Tonry, M.H. 1996. *Sentencing Matters.* New York: Oxford University Press.

Turk, A. 1969. *Criminality and the Legal Order.* Chicago, IL: Rand NcNally.

Ulmer, J.T. 1997. *The Social Worlds of Sentencing: Court Communities Under Sentencing Guidelines.* Albany, NY: State University of New York Press.

Ulmer, J.T., and J.H. Kramer 1996. "Court Communities Under Dilemmas of Formal Rationality and Sentencing Disparity" *Criminology* 34: 383-308.

Unnever, J.D. 1982. "Direct and Organizational Discrimination in the Sentencing of Drug Offenders." *Social Problems* 30: 212-225.

U.S. General Accounting Office. 1992. *Sentencing Guidelines: Central Questions Remain Unanswered: A Report to Congressional Committees.* Washington, DC: U.S. General Accounting Office.

U.S. Sentencing Commission, 1989. *Guidelines Manual.* Washington, DC: The United States Sentencing Commission.

U.S. Sentencing Commission. 1991. *The Federal Sentencing Guidelines: A Report on the Operation of the Guidelines System and Short-Term Impact on Disparity in Sentencing, Use of Incarceration, and Prosecutorial Discretion and Plea Bargaining.* Washington, DC: U.S. Sentencing Commission.

Velimesis, M. 1975. "The Female Offender." *Crime and Delinquency Literature* 7: 94-112.

Wald, P.M. 1995. "\'What About the Kids?': Parenting Issues in Sentencing." *Federal Sentencing Reporter* 8: 137-141.

Washington State Sentencing Guidelines Commission. 1992. *A Decade of Sentencing Reform: Washington and Its Guidelines, 1981-1991.* Olympia, wa: Washington State Sentencing Guidelines Commission.

Weisburd, D., S. Wheeler, E. Waring, and N. Bode. 1991. *Crimes of the Middle Classes: White-Collar Offenders in the Federal Courts.* New Haven, CT: Yale University Press.

Wheeler, S., D. Weisburd, and N. Bode. 1982. "Sentencing the White-Collar Offender: Rhetoric and Reality." *American Sociological Review* 47: 641-659.

Wilkins, W.W., Jr. and J.R. Steer 1990. "Relevant Conduct: The Cornerstone of the Federal Sentencing Guidelines," *South Carolina Law Review* 41: 495-431.

Yellen, D. 1993. "Illusion, Illogic and Injustice: Real-Offense Sentencing and the Federal Sentencing Guidelines." *Minnesota Law Review* 78: 403-465.

Zatz, M.S. 1984. "Race, Ethnicity, and Determinate Sentencing: A New Dimension to an Old Controversy," *Criminology* 22: 147-171.

LABOR MARKET STRUCTURE, UNEMPLOYMENT, AND CRIME:
THE INDIRECT EFFECT OF LOW-SKILL JOBS ON HOMICIDE AND THEFT IN 26 COUNTRIES

Matthew R. Lee and Edward S. Shihadeh

ABSTRACT

Although low-skill, entry-level jobs have historically facilitated social mobility, evidence from the late 1970s and early 1980s confirms that many countries have witnessed a decline in the availability of such jobs. This shift in the structure of the labor force has resulted in high rates of unemployment among low-skill workers and may be linked to high rates of crime. Using Interpol crime data for the years 1965-1984, we examine the direct and indirect relationship between the availability of low-skill jobs and the rates of homicide and theft. The findings reveal that a decline in the availability of low-skill work increases crime rates indirectly by first raising rates of unemployment. We model these relationships for 26 countries and find that the analysis supports a macro-social link between serious crime and cross-national variations in labor market structure.

Sociology of Crime, Law, and Deviance, Volume 1, pages 49-64.

ISBN: 0-7623-0282-8

INTRODUCTION

Urban research from the early Chicago school documented the process by which foreign immigrants and rural migrants settled in cities where low-skill jobs were widely available (Park, Burgess, and McKenzie 1925; Wirth 1928). Although poor and densely populated, these areas were active industrial centers, with an emphasis on entry-level employment. This labor market structure provided residents the opportunity for social mobility and the potential for relocation to peripheral areas of the city. Upwardly mobile residents were then replaced by a successive wave of immigrants who replicated this process of assimilation and mobility. But a reorganization of urban labor markets has taken place in which low-skill jobs have been replaced by high-skill jobs, thus economically isolating low-skill residents in center cities (Berry and Kasarda 1977; Kasarda 1989).

A similar process occurred in the international labor market during the 1970s and early 1980s. In the postwar period, there was substantial economic growth throughout the industrial countries and around the world (Peet 1987). Labor shortages, especially in Western Europe, led to mass migrations of foreign low-skill populations to the booming industrial complexes (Fielding 1995). Unfortunately, the decline and relocation of centers of industrial production in the 1970s and early 1980s exacerbated the economic problems of low-income and poorly educated urban residents by depriving them of access to jobs commensurate with their skill levels (Castles and Kosack 1973, 1985).

A second research tradition descended from the Chicago school analyzes the structural correlates of crime across macro-social units. Such studies examine not the individual-level determinants of crime, but the macro-level structures that are associated with high rates of offending. A substantial body of research in this area places economic hardship as a key predictor of high rates of crime. Indeed, evidence suggests that economic deprivation in a variety of forms, including unemployment, is associated with high rates of crime (Chiricos 1987; Sampson 1987; Shihadeh and Ousey forthcoming).

Our objective is to intersect these two ideas to examine the indirect effect of low-skill jobs on serious crime via its relationship with unemployment. Specifically, we suggest that blocked access to low-skill jobs increases the rates of unemployment, which in turn, raises the rates of serious crime. The impact of deindustrialization and the flight of entry-level jobs is a major concern to sociologists (e.g., Kasarda 1993; Shihadeh and Ousey forthcoming; Wilson 1987). For instance, Shihadeh and Ousey (forthcoming) recently found that the availability of low-skill jobs in major U.S. cities is indirectly related to the rates of homicide via its effect on employment prospects. While this relationship holds true for the United States, there are no studies examining this potentially important issue at the international level. And so, using a cross-national sample, we examine whether U.S. and foreign labor markets dominated by low-skill employment also have low rates of joblessness and, indirectly, low rates of crime. We test this indirect effect for 26 countries over a 20-year period.

BACKGROUND

In the early part of the twentieth century, the United States had an abundance of low-skill employment in industrial centers, and this drew large numbers of both foreign immigrants and rural migrants to major urban areas (Park, Burgess, and McKenzie 1925). Settling into low-income and densely populated ethnic enclaves in inner cities, expansion of the low-skill job sector gave these newly arrived groups access to the mainstream economy and social institutions and, by implication, the opportunity for social mobility. As center-city residents adjusted to urban life, they moved to the outlying areas, away from ethnic ghettos in the urban core. Thus, while the inner cities were characterized by poverty, overcrowding, and poor living conditions, the local economy provided a mechanism by which poorly skilled residents could gradually improve their life chances. As groups gradually improved their socioeconomic standing and relocated to the peripheral areas, they were then replaced by successive waves of residents that replicated this process of assimilation and mobility.

The underlying force driving this process was the availability of low-skill employment in expanding metropolitan areas (Kasarda 1993). Although such jobs were low paid and offered few benefits, they provided low-skill first-generation migrants an entry point into the labor force. Such opportunities were then further bolstered by the extensive economic growth in the postwar period, when both unemployment and income inequality declined and health care and educational services increased (Margolin and Schor 1990).

Rapid growth in manufacturing and other low-skill industrial work after World War II occurred not only in the United States but in other countries as well. In Western Europe, for instance, the postwar boom was accompanied by large-scale migration flows first from the peripheral areas of Europe and then from the Third World (Hollifield 1992; King 1995). Between 1945 and the early 1970s, an estimated 30 million workers and their dependents moved to Western Europe (Castles 1984). Like the early migrant streams to the United States, these foreign workers generally had few educational credentials and were hired to work in low-skill and low-income jobs.

But in the 1970s and early 1980s, there was a worldwide decline in the manufacturing base of low-skill work which displaced thousands of low-skill migrant workers (King 1995). This structural change closely paralleled that which occurred in the United States. For instance, Peet (1987, p. 37) documents massive declines throughout Europe between 1975 and 1982 in the mainstay of low-skill employment, manufacturing. A number of countries experienced precipitous declines in their manufacturing base, including Belgium (–23.3%), The Netherlands (–15.3%), the United Kingdom (–23.2%), Italy (–12%), France (–10.5%), and Germany (–7.5%). Overall, Western Europe experienced a loss of 6 million jobs in manufacturing between 1974 and 1983 (Peet 1987, p. 30).

The contraction of low-skill industrial sectors in the United States and Europe was accompanied by an expansion of high-skill employment sectors, those dominated by government jobs and information, business, and professional services. This industrial transformation may have been prompted by changes in technology (Berry and Kasarda 1977) or by a structural reorganization of urban areas (Kasarda 1993). But on a wider, international level, the decline of low-skill employment in more industrialized countries may have been part of a sorting process in which wealthier countries transferred low-skill jobs to peripheral countries in their local regions or beyond, to Third World countries (Fielding 1995). This is consistent with the view that industrialized countries have exported low-skill jobs and have instead fostered the growth of high-skill employment in order to compete more effectively in the global economy (Kegley and Wittkopf 1996, 1988). Indeed, global cities such as Toronto, New York, London, and Paris serve as headquarters for administering a worldwide production system with few national boundaries.

ECONOMIC DEPRIVATION AND CRIME

A classic idea in criminology is that economic deprivation is related to the rates of crime. Indeed, a wide range of theories posit such factors as poverty and unemployment as key explanatory factors in explaining variation in the rates of crime. Of particular note, evidence reveals that unemployment rates are positively related to crime rates. While there are some results to the contrary, Chiricos' (1987) review of 63 studies tempers any doubt that joblessness has a weak or nonexistent relationship to crime. His review indicates that the vast majority of cross-sectional aggregate studies reveal a positive and significant relationship between unemployment and crime (see also Box 1987).

Few studies have examined the unemployment-crime relationship at the cross-national level. Krohn (1976), using Interpol data for a sample of countries, finds little or no relationship between unemployment and property or total crime rates, and a moderate positive relationship between unemployment and homicide rates. In contrast, McDonald (1976) finds no relationship between unemployment and homicide rates. Similarly, in a pooled cross-sectional time-series analysis of homicide rates in 18 countries, Pampel and Gartner (1995) find no relationship between unemployment and homicide.

From the point of view of theory, unemployment is traditionally viewed as creating economically motivated offenders (Bonger 1916; Cantor and Land 1985).[1] Although it is likely that economic deprivation plays a nontrivial role in motivating individuals to commit crime, as a stand-alone perspective, it is seriously limited. As Sampson and Wilson (1995) note, such explanations rely on a "materialist fallacy," that material need necessarily produces criminal behavior. The idea that violent crimes such as murder, robbery, aggravated assault, and even some serious property crimes are prompted by materialist needs misses the full complexity of the unemployment-crime relationship. These motivationally based explanations have not fared well empirically, and the modern welfare state buffers against the full force of poverty and unemployment, which militates against the motivating effects these conditions may produce (Allan and Steffensmeier 1989).

A second problem with motivationally based theories is the assumption that macro-level relationships are an additive function of individual-level processes. For instance, Blau and Blau (1982) maintain that highly stratified environments generate frustration and aggression among those at the bottom end of inequality. These feelings are especially pronounced when inequalities are based on ascriptive characteristics such as race, and can ultimately find expression in various forms of violence. Although structural elements are an important part of the Blau's framework, individual-level social psychological processes are also integral to their framework. But our view is that since macro-social theory is meant to articulate the emergent properties of collectives, such reductionism is unnecessary.

In light of these shortcomings, we argue that widespread economic hardship as experienced through unemployment has serious negative consequences for all elements within communities, consequences that go far beyond the mere creation of motivated offenders. As Shihadeh and Ousey (forthcoming, pp. 8-9) note, "widespread deprivation is an embedded structural condition that can delegitimize conventional norms and weaken the capacity of communities to cultivate allegiance to mainstream institutions" such as the labor force. So, the availability of work opportunities is a vital resource not only to specific individuals but to the community as a whole. Regular employment is more than a way for individuals to make a living, it constitutes a community-wide framework for daily behavior. It is one of the many conduits by which communities channel members into mainstream, middle-class adulthood. Opportunities for stable work help foster a work ethic and make it easier for communities to confer mainstream values and normative patterns of interaction.

But when unemployment and economic deprivation are widespread and deeply embedded, communities lack the capacity to regulate their members according to acceptable lines of action, including those which restrain the use of violence (Anderson 1994). Thus, the above discussion suggests that cross-national variations in labor market structure may be related to variations in the rates of serious crime. Although these links are theoretically important, prior research has neither proposed nor measured this at the cross-national level. In what follows, we examine whether countries with a short supply of low-skill jobs have high rates of unemployment and, in turn, high rates of crime.

RESEARCH DESIGN

To test our model, we use the Correlates of Crime data set (Bennett 1989), a collection of crime statistics from Interpol and relevant social, economic, and political variables for 52 countries for the years 1960-1984. The sample includes nations representing the seven major regions of the world, although no non-market nations are included. Given the finite nature of the population, this precludes the possibility of a random sample. Therefore, by necessity, we employ a purposive sampling technique. Due to missing data for one or more of the structural variables, the final sample consists of 26 nations and covers the years 1965-1984.[2] Despite some limitations, these data are nonetheless regarded as one of the most comprehensive sources available for cross-national comparisons of the structural predictors of crime.

Dependent Variables

Each of the crime variables are taken from Interpol data. The homicide rate is officially categorized as murders or acts performed with the purpose of taking a human life, excluding manslaughter or abortion. The second crime indicator, theft, includes the total number of both major and minor thefts.[3] These variables are standardized as rates per 100,000 using United Nations population data.

In the past, researchers have expressed concern over the use of cross-national crime data (Vigderhous 1978; Wilkins 1980). Specifically, definitions of certain crimes and the measurement and classification of these crimes may be systematically biased across countries. Krohn (1978) reports that if these disparities do exist, their effects are minimal because serious crimes (particularly homicide) are narrowly defined and are well reported. Further, Bennett and Lynch (1990), in assessing the error structure and reliability of the four major cross-national crime data sets available, acknowledge that it is impossible to assess which data set is superior in terms of validity. They conclude that for analytic cross-sectional designs, no statistical differences in measurement between available data sets exists. As with U.S. data, we expect a greater degree of validity for homicide rates than for theft rates.

Independent Variables

Our two key substantive predictors are low-skill jobs and unemployment. Low-skill jobs is derived as the percentage of the entire workforce that is employed in the industries of mining, quarrying, manufacturing, construction, and public utilities (electricity, gas, water, and sanitation).This is consistent with usage in U.S. studies (see Kasarda 1993; Shihadeh and Ousey forthcoming). Unemployment reflects the percentage of all people in the labor force that are unemployed.

Although this information is a part of the Correlates of Crime data set, the original source is the International Labor Organization.

We also include a number of control variables in our models. To control for differences in police efficiency, we also include another measure from Interpol data, the clearance rate, which is the ratio of crimes cleared to the total number of offenses. A crime is cleared when the offender has been identified by the police and/or when the offender is convicted. According to prior research (Bennett 1991a, 1991b; Pampel and Gartner 1995), increases in female labor force participation weakens the capacity of communities to exert social control, particularly over individuals of crime-prone age. This may be the case, although we recognize that this indicator has multiple interpretations, and so we include it as one of many potential controls for the social context of crime. Female labor force participation is the percentage of all females that are in the labor force.

We also include a control for the economic context of crime, economic development, measured as the total GDP per capita. This is an important control since highly developed countries are more apt to make the transition away from low-skill jobs to higher-order, technologically oriented jobs. Thus, the degree of economic development is intrinsically tied to labor market structure and, by consequence, the availability of low-skill jobs.

Our models contain three standard demographic measures as well. Population size is the mid-year estimate of the national population. Population density is the national population divided by the total land area in square kilometers. These variables are transformed to their natural logs in the regression models in order to induce normality in their highly skewed distributions. Percent urban is the percentage of the total population who reside in non-rural areas of the country. Each of these measures are also contained in the Correlates of Crime archive and are drawn from data published by the United Nations.[4]

Analytical Techniques

We estimate our models using a pooled cross-sectional research design. Since the number of cross-section units is greater than the number of time periods, it is appropriate to use an ordinary least-squares estimator as our chief analytical tool (Sayrs 1989; Stimson 1985). An advantage of this model is that pooling the data increases the number of cases and the number of degrees of freedom, avoiding the problems typically associated with small sample sizes. Of course, such pooled designs introduce the possibility of autocorrelation. Fortunately, the Durban-Watson statistics reported in the tables are centered around a value of 2.0, suggesting neither positive nor negative autocorrelation in our sample of countries.[5]

Our models first predict unemployment. We then follow with models that predict crime rates. The indirect effects of independent variable i on j, ij, is derived using the well-known structural equation formula (for an example, see Shihadeh and Ousey forthcoming)

$$\lambda_{ij} = \beta_{ij} 1 * \beta_{jk} 2$$

where β_{ij} 1 is the parameter estimate from model 1 of the exogenous variable i (low-skill jobs) predicting the mediating variable j (unemployment), and β_{jk} 2 is the parameter estimate from the second model where mediating variable j (unemployment) is predicting variable k (homicide or theft). Testing the significance of indirect effects is derived from developments by Clogg, Petkova, and Shihadeh (1992). The formula takes the form:

$$S^2 (d_k) = S^2 (b_k) - S^2 (b^*_k) \delta^2_v / \delta^2_\varepsilon$$

where $S^2(d_k)$ is the estimated variance of variable (d), $S^2 b_k$ is the sampling variance of variable (k) in the full model, and $S^2 b^*_k$ is the sampling variance of variable (k) in the reduced model multiplied by the ratio of mean square errors (see also Clogg, Petkova, and Haritou 1995, p. 1274). The t-statistic for this formula is:

$$t = d_k / S(d_k)$$

Diagnostics indicate that parameter instability due to high correlations among the independent variables (multicollinearity) is not a problem with these analyses. None of the models contain independent variables with first-order correlations greater than $r = .75$ and most are far below that. Additionally, the variance inflation factors associated with each of the parameter estimates are all below 3.4.

RESULTS

Table 1 presents the descriptive measures for the variables used in the analysis. Several features stand out. As expected, the mean cross-national homicide rate is

Table 1. Descriptive Statistics of National-Level Variables, 1965-1984

	Mean	*Std. Dev.*	*Range*
Homicide Rate	3.87	2.95	.13-16.66
Total Theft Rate	1,607.12	1,574.46	46.00-6,641.00
Low-Skill Jobs	29.41	10.39	8.00-48.10
Unemployment	3.45	3.42	.00-19.64
Female Labor Force Participation	24.10	10.10	2.50-42.30
Economic Development	3,965.08	3,870.14	34.69-15,334.64
Urban Population	60.16	23.79	14.70-99.90
Population Size	33,154,819	50,183,247	333,000-240,000,000
Population Density	23,324	70,686	112.90-421,800
Clearance Rate	.50	.20	.09-.94

relatively low, only 3.87 per 100,000 population, while the theft rate is higher, at 1,607 per 100,000. Nonetheless, both of these rates are far lower than the corresponding UCR rates for the United States. In addition, an average of one-third of all jobs in this sample of countries are classified as low-skill (29.41), while only 3.45% of the population is unemployed. Roughly one-quarter of the labor force is comprised of female workers (24.10), and the majority of the population lives in urban areas (60.16%). The standard deviations of the means, however, indicate considerable variability across countries in our sample. Indeed, in several instances, the standard deviations are roughly equal to or greater than the mean itself, suggesting that our sample is far from monolithic on these social and economic indicators.

Results from the pooled OLS regression analyses predicting unemployment are shown in Table 2. Model one shows the results for models predicting unemployment. In conformity with our expectations, the results reveal an exceedingly strong association between the national-level structure of labor markets and national unemployment rates. As the results suggest, the percentage of the labor force in low-skill jobs is nearly the best predictor of unemployment ($B = -.662$), topped only by the effect of urban population ($B = .697$). Thus, a one standard deviation rise in the availability of low-skill jobs is associated with a two-thirds decline in unemployment. In plain terms, this implies that when low-skill jobs are widely available, unemployment rates tend to be low.

The second model in Table 2 predicts homicide rates for our sample of countries. The results lend support to the idea of an indirect effect of low-skill jobs on crime rates, via the rates of unemployment. Note that unemployment in this second model is the best predictor of homicide rates ($B = .387$). That is, as unemployment rates rise, so do national-level homicide rates. Combining these two direct effects, low-skill jobs on unemployment, and unemployment on homicide, yields a substantial indirect effect of low-skill jobs on homicide. The indirect effect, listed at the top of the last column, is $B = -.256$. We interpret this to mean that a one standard deviation rise in the availability of low-skill jobs is indirectly associated with a one-quarter standard deviation decline in the rates of homicide. Indeed, the indirect effect is not only significant, it is as large or larger than the bulk of the direct effects in either model. This offers strong support to the idea that access to entry-level jobs has potentially major implications for the homicide rate at the international level.

Interestingly, low-skill jobs also have a negative direct effect on homicide rates, an effect that appears to augment the indirect effect via unemployment. From the results in the second model, it appears that a rise in the availability of low-skill jobs is associated directly with declines in the homicide rate ($B = -.147$). Thus, it appears that labor market structure has an effect on homicide rates independent of unemployment.

There are several other noteworthy features of Table 2. For instance, it appears that unemployment rates tend to be higher in countries with higher levels of

Table 2. Pooled Cross-Sectional OLS Regression Models Predicting Unemployment and Homicide 1965-1984, Direct and Indirect Effects

	Unemployment		*Homicide*		
	b	*Beta*	*b*	*Beta*	*Indirect*
Low-Skill Jobs	−.218	−.662**	−.042	−.147*	−.256*
Female Labor Force Participation	.008	.024	.020	.067	.091
Economic Development	.000	.208**	.000	−.002	.080*
Urban Population	.100	.697**	−.101	−.084	.270*
Population Size (ln)	.238	.116**	−.335	−.190**	.045*
Population Density (ln)	.110	.056	−.215	−.127**	.022
Clearance Rate	1.737	.104*	−.783	−.054	.040
Unemployment		—	.333	.387*	
R-squared		.30		.20	
N		520		520	
Durbin-Watson		2.02		2.19	

Notes: *$p <= .05$.
**$p <= .01$.

economic development ($B = .208$, model 1). From the point of view of our heuristic framework, this is not surprising. There are substantive similarities between this and the low-skill job variable, and this is supported by a first-order correlation of .50 (not reported). Indeed, as our earlier discussion suggests, markets of more developed nations tend to be dominated by high-skill employment sectors. Such countries, having made the transition away from entry-level jobs, are likely to have a significant population of under-educated individuals who are economically isolated by this market transition and, therefore, more vulnerable to unemployment. In the empirical terms of our models, this means that economic development shares variance with low-skill jobs. So it is not surprising that economic development also has a significant indirect effect on homicide ($B = .080$).

To strengthen our inferences, we apply the same specification to examine indirect effects of low-skill jobs on theft rates. These results are presented in Table 3. According to the indirect effects in the third column, low-skill jobs have a negative indirect effect on the rates of theft, via unemployment ($B = -.049$). As entry-level jobs become more widely available, the rates of theft decline. Although the indirect effect of low-skill jobs is not as large as in the prior set of models, it is nevertheless significant, lending further support to the view that countries with labor markets that have strong opportunities for low-level employment tend to have low rates of crime.

Further reinforcing these findings is the observed effect of economic development. As in the prior model, the level of economic development has a small but

Table 3. Pooled Cross-Sectional OLS Regression Models Predicting Unemployment and Theft 1965-1984, Direct and Indirect Effects

	Unemployment		*Theft*		
	b	*Beta*	*b*	*Beta*	*Indirect*
Low-Skill Jobs	−.218	−.662**	3.880	.026	−.049*
Female Labor Force Participation	.008	.024	40.773	.262**	.002
Economic Development	.000	.208*	.122	.301**	.015*
Urban Population	.100	.697**	19.130	.289**	.052*
Population Size (ln)	.238	.116**	−30.590	−.033	.009*
Population Density (ln)	.110	.056	−142.853	−.158**	.004
Clearance Rate	1.737	.104*	−1411.403	−.183**	.008*
Unemployment		—	33.905	.074*	
R-squared		.30		.67	
N		520		520	
Durbin-Watson		2.02		2.49	

Notes: *$p <= .05$.
**$p <= .01$.

significant indirect effect on the rates of theft (.015). Given the conceptual overlap between these two variables, this finding adds further fuel to our contention that market transitions away from entry-level employment have potentially harmful consequences in the form of unemployment and crime.

There are some points of departure between the results in Tables 2 and 3. First, while the results in Table 2 revealed a direct effect of low-skill jobs on homicide, no corresponding direct effect on theft rates is observed here in Table 3. In contrast, while economic development had no direct effect on homicide in Table 2, it has a substantial one in the second model of Table 3.

On a subsidiary note, we observe that the clearance rate is significant in the model predicting theft in Table 3 ($B = -.183$). We speculate that the negative relationship between clearance rates and theft rates is due to a swamping effect on police departments. Theft is a high frequency crime. Consequently, the efficiency of law enforcement agencies may be compromised in the context of particularly high rates of theft. This is further supported by the lack of association between clearance rates and homicide rates back in Table 2. Homicide warrants not only greater priority and less discretionary authority for police, it also is a comparatively rare event. Unlike the situation for theft, it is less likely that clearance rates would be statistically related to homicide rates. Nonetheless, since the results of Table 3 reveal significant cross-jurisdictional variations in the efficiency of law enforcement, clearance rates are an important control in cross-national studies, particularly for those analyzing property crimes.

DISCUSSION AND CONCLUSION

This study links two distinct theoretical streams within sociology, one based on how entry-level jobs provided an impetus for the social mobility of low-income residents, and the other based on a long tradition of identifying the structural predictors of crime in macro-social units. Applying this combined heuristic framework to a sample of countries, we find that nations whose labor markets contain greater proportions of low-skill jobs tend to have lower rates of both homicide and theft. The causal link between low-skill jobs and crime is indirect, via the rates of unemployment. Specifically, as the proportion of low-skill jobs increases, unemployment rates decline. In turn, as unemployment rates decline, so do the rates of homicide and theft. Thus, countries with labor markets dominated by low-skill jobs tend to have low rates of violence and theft.

There are several implications of these findings. First, although the cross-national resorting of entry-level jobs is presumed to enhance global competitiveness, such a strategy is not without its disadvantages. One serious consequence of a flight of low-skill jobs is that substantial numbers of undereducated and poorly skilled individuals are structurally isolated from participation in the labor force. Significant segments of the population are denied the primary means by which individuals secure a successful and middle-class adulthood. In plain terms, a loss of low-skill jobs severely restricts the economic prospects of low-skill individuals because the bottom rung of the job ladder is removed.

Second, the long tradition of macro-social research on crime has focused mainly on processes that are internal to communities (Bursik and Grasmick 1993; Sampson 1987; Shihadeh and Flynn 1996; Shihadeh and Steffensmeier 1994; Smith and Jarjoura 1988; Warner and Pierce 1993). But this study suggests that crime rates may also be related to the larger political, social, and economic structures of nations (see also Neuman and Berger 1988). As our results show, a cross-national reorganization of labor market structures has implications for both the economic well-being of residents and national rates of violent and property crime.

Finally, our analysis demonstrates the utility of examining both direct and indirect effects. Removing direct-effect constraints has two important advantages. First, it encourages the cross-fertilization of two or more distinct theoretical areas, thus illuminating new causal paths to crime. Second, because of the conceptually wider reach of this approach, criminological research can go beyond the incessant reshuffling of well-used variables and examine a broader range of potential predictors of crime.

APPENDIX

Variable Definitions

Homicide: Any act performed with the purpose of taking a human life, in whatever circumstances. This definition excluded abortion but includes infanticide.

Theft: Theft with dangerous aggravating circumstances (e.g., robbery, violent theft, burglary, house breaking) as well as all other thefts not listed above.

Crime Cleared: A case is "cleared" when any of the following four conditions are met: (1) The offender has been convicted; (2) The offender was caught red-handed, even if he/she subsequently denies guilt; (3) The offender has been identified: provided the police are certain, it makes no difference whether he/she is arrested, under provisional release, at large, or dead; or (4) Inquiries have revealed that no criminal offense occured.

Population: Mid-year estimate of the nation's population.

Population Density: The nation's population divided by the toal land area in square kilometers.

Urban Population: Urban population is defined as the percentage of the total population who reside in cities and towns. The definition of cities and towns are the purview of the reporting nation.

Unemployment: All persons above a particular age who, on a specified day or for a specified week, were in the following categories: (1) Workers available for employment whose contract of employment had been terminated or temporarily suspended and who were without a job and seeking work for pay or profit; (2) Persons who were available for work during a specified period and were seeking work for pay or profit who were never previously employed or whose most recent status was other than that of employee; (3) Persons without a job and currently available for work who had made arrangements to start a new job at a date subsequent to the specified period; and (4) Persons on temporary or indefinite layoff without pay.

Female Labor Force Participation: The proportion of the female population that participates in the labor force.

Industrial Labor Force Participation: The proportion of the labor firce which is involved in industrial activities such as mining, quarrying, manufacturing, construction, and public utilities (electricity, gas, water, and sanitary services).

Gross Domestic Product: A measure of the total final output of a nation's economy—all goods produced and services rendered within its territory by residents and nonresidents without regard to its allocation among domestic and foreign claims, in U.S. dollar equivalents. Its value is calculated before deductions are made for depreciation and other capital consumption allowances.

Note: All Definitions are from Bennett (1989).

NOTES

1. Although Cantor and Land (1985) fail to find evidence of the motivational effect of unemployment on crime, they provide a well-articulated, high-quality test of both the motivational and opportunity components of the unemployment and crime relationship.

2. The sample contains the following countries: United States, Canada, England/Wales, Australia, Luxembourg, West Germany, France, Austria, Finland, Sweden, Norway, Denmark, Japan, Korea, Singapore, Indonesia, Fiji, Cyprus, Morocco, Libya, Sri Lanka, Syria, Israel, Nigeria, Zambia, and Chile.

3. We use total thefts rather than just major thefts because the definition of the latter is likely to vary substantially across countries. In contrast, the more inclusive measure of total thefts is likely to include all thefts of any kind and will likely give a more accurate picture of the total level of property crime in a given country.

4. While macro-level resesarch on homicide often includes a control for the age structure of the population, we exclude it from this analysis. The age variable contained in this archive measures only the male juvenile population under 14 years of age. The actual crime-prone age group is roughly 15-24 (see Steffensmeier et al. 1989) and so this variable completely misses the target population. In fact, it measures the age structure of only one segment of the population that is not at risk for crime (ages 0-14 and 25 and over). The age variable in this archive has its origins from developmental research of the United Nations, where the size of the youth population is of substantive interest. Unfortunately, it has little value in controlling for crime-prone age groups and its inclusions in such models is nonsequiter.

5. We also analyzed a series of fixed effects models. With just dummy variables for each year (with 1965 excluded as the reference year), most of the indicators do not reach statistical significance, suggesting that unmeasured temporal effects do not influence rates of crime in this sample. Models with dummy variables for each nation (with the United States excluded as the reference country) introduced severe multicollinearity (see Stimson 1985), making interpretation impossible.

REFERENCES

Allan, E.A., and D.J. Steffensmeier. 1989. "Youth, Underemployment, and Property Crime: Differential Effects of Job Availability and Job Quality on Juvenile and Young Adult Arrest Rates." *American Sociological Review* 54: 107-123.

Anderson, E. 1994. "The Code of the Streets." *Atlantic Monthly* (May): 81-94.

Bennett, R.R. 1989. "Correlates of Crime Data Set Documentation." Unpublished paper, Department of Justice, Law, and Society, The American University, June.

Bennett, R.R. 1991a. "Development and Crime: A Cross-National, Time-Series Analysis of Competing Models." *The Sociological Quarterly* 32(3): 343-363.

Bennett, R.R. 1991b. "Routine Activities: A Cross-National Assessment of a Criminological Perspective." *Social Forces* 70(1): 147-163.

Bennett, R.R., and J.P. Lynch. 1990. "Does a Difference Make a Difference? Comparing Cross-National Crime Indicators." *Criminology* 28(1): 153-182.

Berry, B.J.L., and J.D. Kasarda. 1977. *Contemporary Urban Ecology*. New York: Macmillan.

Blau, J.R., and P.M. Blau. 1982. "The Cost of Inequality: Metropolitan Structure and Violent Crime." *American Sociological Review* 47: 114-129.

Bonger, W.A. 1916. *Criminality and Economic Conditions.* Boston, MA: Little, Brown, and Co.
Box, S. 1987. *Recession, Crime and Punishment.* Totowa, NJ: Barnes and Noble Books.
Bursik, R.J., and H.G. Grasmick. 1993. *Communities and Crime: The Dimensions of Effective Community Control.* New York: Lexington Books.
Cantor, D., and K.C. Land. 1985. "Unemployment and Crime Rates in the Post-World War II United States: A Theoretical and Empirical Analysis." *American Sociological Review* 50: 317-332.
Castles, S. 1984. *Here for Good: Western Europe's New Ethnic Minorities.* London: Pluto Press.
Castles, S., and G. Kosack. 1973. *Immigrant Workers and Class Structure in Western Europe.* Oxford, UK: Oxford University Press.
Castles, S., and G. Kosack. 1985. *Immigrant Workers and Class Structure in Western Europe*, 2nd edition. Oxford, UK: Oxford University Press.
Chiricos, T.G. 1987. "Rates of Crime and Unemployment: An Analysis of Aggregate Research Evidence." *Social Problems* 34(2, April): 187-212.
Clogg, C.C., E. Petkova, and A. Haritou. 1995. "Statistical Methods for Comparing Regression Coefficients Between Models." *American Journal of Sociology* 100(5, March): 1261-1293.
Clogg, C.C., E. Petkova, and E.S. Shihadeh. 1992. "Statistical Methods for Analyzing Collapsibility in Regression Models." *Journal of Educational Statistics* 17: 51-74.
Fielding, A. 1995. "Mass Migration and Economic Restructuring." Pp. 7-18 in *Mass Migration in Europe: The Legacy and the Future*, edited by R. King. Chichester, UK: John Wiley and Sons.
Hollifield, J.F. 1992. *Immigrants, Markets, and States: The Political Economy of Postwar Europe.* Cambridge, MA: Harvard University Press.
Kasarda, J.D. 1989. "Urban Industrial Transition and the Underclass." *Annals of the American Academy of Political and Social Sciences* 501: 26-47.
Kasarda, J.D. 1993. "Urban Industrial Transition and the Underclass." Pp. 43-64 in *The Ghetto Underclass*, edited by W.J. Wilson. Newbury Park, CA: Sage.
Kegley, C.W., Jr., and E.R. Wittkopt. 1988. *The Global Agenda: Issues and Perspectives.* Boston, MA: McGraw-Hill.
Kegley, C.W., Jr., and E.R.Wittkopt. 1996. *American Foreign Policy: Pattern and Process.* New York: St. Martins Press.
King, R. 1995. "European International Migration 1945-1990: A Statistical and Geographical Overview." Pp. 19-39 in *Mass Migration in Europe: The Legacy and the Future*, edited by R. King. Chichester, UK: John Wiley and Sons.
Krohn, M.D. 1976. "Inequality, Unemployment and Crime: A Cross-National Analysis." *The Sociological Quarterly* 17: 303-313.
Krohn, M.D. 1978. "A Durkheimian Analysis of International Crime Rates." *Social Forces* 57(2): 654-670.
Margolin, S., and J. Schor 1990. *The End of the Golden Age.* Oxford, UK: Clarendon Press.
McDonald, L. 1976. *The Sociology of Law and Order.* London: Faber and Faber.
Neuman, W.L., and R.J. Berger. 1988. "Competeing Perspectives on Cross-National Crime: An Evaluation of Theory and Evidence." *The Sociological Quarterly* 29(2): 281-313.
Pampel, F.C., and R. Gartner. 1995. "Age Structure, Socio-Political Institutions, and National Homicide Rates." *European Sociological Review* 11(3, December): 243-260.
Park, R.E., E.W. Burgess, and R.D. McKenzie. 1925. *The City.* Chicago, IL: University of Chicago Press.
Peet, R. 1987. *International Capitalism and Industrial Restructuring.* Boston, MA: Allen and Unwin.
Sampson, R.J. 1987. "Urban Black Violence: The Effect of Male Joblesness and Family Disruption". *American Journal of Sociology* 93: 348-382
Sampson, R.J., and W.J. Wilson. 1995. "Toward a Theory of Race, Crime, and Urban Inequality." Pp. 37-54 in *Crime and Inequality*, edited by J. Hagan and R.D. Peterson. Stanford, CA: Stanford University Press.

Sayrs, L.W. 1989. *Pooled Time Series Analysis*. Quantitative Applications in the Social Sciences, Series no. 07-070. Newbury Park, CA: Sage.

Shihadeh, E.S., and N. Flynn. 1996. "Segregation and Crime: The Effect of Black Social Isolation on Rates of Black Urban Violence". *Social Forces* 74(4, June): 1325-1352.

Shihadeh, E.S., and G. Ousey. Forthcoming. "Industrial Restructuring and Crime: The Link Between Entry Level Jobs, Black Employment and Black Violence in Central Cities." *Social Forces*.

Shihadeh, E.S., and D.J. Steffensmeier. 1994. "Economic Inequality, Family Disruption, and Urban Black Violence: Cities as Units of Stratification and Social Control." *Social Forces* 73: 729-751.

Smith, D.A., and G.R. Jarjoura. 1988. "Social Structure and Criminal Victimization." *Journal of Research in Crime and Delinquency* 25(1): 27-52.

Steffensmeier, D.J., E.A. Allan, M.D. Harer, and C. Streifel. 1989. "Age and The Distribution of Crime." *American Journal of Sociology* 94: 803-831.

Stimson, J.A. 1985. "Regression in Space and Time: A Statisical Essay." *American Journal of Political Science* 29: 914-947.

Vigderhous, G. 1978. "Methodological Problems Confronting Cross-Cultural Criminological Research Using Official Data." *Human Relations* 31(3): 229-247.

Warner, B.D., and G.L. Pierce. 1993. "Reexamining Social Disorganization Theory Using Calls to the Police as a Measure of Crime." *Criminology* 31(4): 493-517.

Wilkins, L.T. 1980. "World Crime: To Measure or Not to Measure." Pp. 17-41 in *Crime and Deviance: A Comparative Perspective*, edited by G. Newman. Beverly Hills, CA: Sage.

Wilson, W.J. 1987. *The Truly Disadvantaged: The Inner City, The Underclass, and Public Policy*. Chicago, IL: University of Chicago Press.

Wirth, L. 1928. *The Ghetto*. Chicago, IL: University of Chicago Press.

SHOPLIFTING:
A TEST OF AN INTEGRATED MODEL OF STRAIN, DIFFERENTIAL ASSOCIATION, AND SEDUCTION THEORIES

Liqun Cao and Xiaogang Deng

ABSTRACT

Although shoplifting has plagued retail stores across the nation for years, understanding of this widespread social problem is limited. Previous literature has identified a number of factors that lead to such behavior, but thus far, few studies have tested multifactors simultaneously in one model. In this study, we propose that seduction theory, strain theory, and differential association theory are largely compatible and can be integrated into one model to gain a better understanding of the behavior of shoplifting. Based on a sample of convicted first-time shoplifters, our analysis indicates that the three theories are indeed complementary, and our combined model significantly improves the predictive power of any of the theories taken separately. The idea that shoplifting is encouraged by thrill-seeking, economic motivation, and differential association is supported by our data.

Sociology of Crime, Law, and Deviance, Volume 1, pages 65-83.

ISBN: 0-7623-0282-8

INTRODUCTION

Consistent with renewed efforts to integrate various theories of crime (Bernard 1989; Bernard and Snipes 1996; Cullen 1983; Elliott, Ageton, and Cantor 1979; Elliott 1985; Groves and Lynch 1990; Thornberry 1989; Tittle 1989), the current study uses an integrated criminological model to study a sample of first-time convicted shoplifters. Heeding the call to reconcile structuralist and subjective theories of crime (Groves and Lynch 1990), this integrated model includes not only classic sociological theories of strain and differential association but also the new phenomenological theory of seductions.[1]

The current study contributes to shoplifting literature and to theory construction in several ways. First, shoplifting is important for study because it is one of the most widespread forms of contemporary theft (Klemke 1992; Baumer and Rosenbaum 1984; Ray 1987). Second, although both Merton (1938) and Sutherland (1947) used theft to illustrate their theories, few empirical studies since then have actually tested their theories with theft or shoplifting as the dependent variable. Thus, the roles of strain and differential association in explaining shoplifting are only assumed, rather than specified empirically.

Third, while many scholars (see Hirschi 1979; Stinchcombe 1968) argue that various criminological theories are competing against one another, others (Akers 1989; Cao and Maume 1993; Elliott 1985; Groves and Lynch 1990; Tittle 1989) contend that some of these theories complement one another. We agree with the argument that many of the sociological theories of crime, such as differential association theory and strain theory, actually complement each other. The differences between these theories merely reflect differences in focus or emphasis rather than fundamentally opposed views of the world. In many ways, combining the theories into one model not only allows each theory to capture its unique areas of criminality in the dependent variable but also increases the explanatory power of the new model.

Fourth, Agnew (1995) has urged criminologists to reexamine the central component of the leading theories of crime causation focusing on the motivation for crime. Since the motivation in crime and deviance may vary widely from person to person, this task suggests the relevance of phenomenological theories of crime. Traditional criminological theories, such as strain, tend to focus on the offender's background, which is seen as predisposing people to criminal behavior. Katz (1988) argues that a more complete picture of crime needs to take both background and foreground factors into consideration. He contends that shoplifting has a certain seductive power that cannot be readily explained by either strain or differential association theory. Groves and Lynch (1990) called for possible merging of structuralist theories with subjective theories of crime.

This study incorporates Katz's theory into our integrated model and examines empirically his "thrill" or seduction perspective that has rarely been assessed previously. Shoplifting, appearing as an example of both structural and sensational crimes, becomes a good candidate to test this integrated model.

Fifth, in the past, theory testing has been conducted mainly among adolescents, and the applicability of these findings to adults is questionable. In contrast, we have a sample of first-time convicted adult shoplifters.

In brief, this study takes a crime-specific and theory-integrated approach to the study of shoplifting behavior. It examines such motivations for shoplifting as those contained in strain theory, differential association theory, and seduction theory and tests the empirical validity of our integrated criminological model. In the following section, we first discuss the major findings in shoplifting research and then examine three major theories and their empirical findings.

RESEARCH ON SHOPLIFTING

Shoplifting is a widespread social phenomenon. Baumer and Rosenbaum (1984) suggested that shoplifting is so pervasive that approximately 40% of all persons in the United States have shoplifted at some point in their lives. In a large-scale study of high school students, 63% of the subjects admitted to having shoplifted at some time in their lives (Klemke 1982). Another general population sample has indicated that shoplifting is so common that one out of every 12 shoppers admitted that he or she had shoplifted recently (Ray 1987). It is quite possible that many otherwise law-abiding citizens are involved in shoplifting, and thus it is not surprising that some studies have found that shoplifters do not conform to the stereotype of typical property offenders. Won and Yamamoto (1968), for example, found that shoplifting tends to be committed more by middle-class persons and that shoplifters tend to be relatively well-educated. While clearly a criminal activity, Turner and Cashdan (1988) contended that shoplifting borders on what one might consider a "folkcrime."

In considering the motives for shoplifting, Kraut (1976) argued that unlike drug addiction, insanity, or violent crime, shoplifting is not fueled by complex motives. The motive underlying most shoplifting is essentially the same as for normal shopping: the acquisition of goods at a minimum cost. Kraut (1976) listed four categories of motives for his college-student sample: economics, revenge, excitement, and social pressure. Moore's study (1984) of 300 shoplifters partially supported Kraut's view: the primary motive for shoplifting is financial gain or personal benefit, and the secondary motive is impulse. Klemke (1982) described two major clusters of motivations among his high school student sample: economic motivations (poverty and self-indulgence) and sporting motivations (fun, excitement, and getting away with something). Yates (1986) classified her shoplifters' motives into three categories: shoplifting for profit or gain and two levels of "nonsensical" shoplifting (i.e., shoplifting not motivated by need or desire). The leading reason for shoplifting in Ray's (1987) general population sample was economic stress. Turner and Cashdan (1988) reported that of the various motives offered by college students for shoplifting, "poverty," "self-indulgence," and "fun" or "thrill" were the top reasons. Recently, Wood et al. (1997) found a significant correlation between shoplifting and sensation.

This literature review indicates that shoplifting is a crime that involves a large proportion of people and that the major motivations of shoplifting may be grouped into two main categories: structural strain and a sense of thrill. Few of these studies, however, attempted to apply criminological theories to explain participation in shoplifting. Accordingly, this present analysis fills a gap in shoplifting literature. Although all criminological theories, in one way or another, are able to explain some variation in shoplifting, it seems that three perspectives are particularly relevant in our integration effort:[2] differential association theory, strain theory, and seduction theory. Limited by our data, we focus only on these three perspectives.

THEORETICAL EXPLANATIONS APPLIED TO SHOPLIFTING

Sutherland's (1947) differential association theory[3] suggests that criminal behavior is learned through differential association or social relationships oriented toward people who approve of crime or hold values conducive to crime. Learning criminal behavior occurs within intimate personal groups—family, friends, and peers. Accordingly, individuals become law violators when there is an excess of definitions favorable to violation of law over definitions unfavorable to violation of law. In our case, individuals are more likely to shoplift if they have definitions favoring thieving and if they have many associates who approve of shoplifting.

Many empirical studies support the claims of differential association theory. Tittle, Burke, and Jackson (1986) found that exposure to criminal definitions does seem to generate crime. Differential association theory has also been supported in studies of alcohol use (Akers et al. 1989), marijuana use (Orcutt 1987), and drug consumption (Johnson, Marcos, and Bahr 1987).

In the area of shoplifting, Klemke (1982) found that various significant others, such as parents, siblings, and close friends, can affect a person's shoplifting behavior. Bales' research (1982) suggested that peer support was the most important predictor of shoplifting in his random sample. Gold's study (1970) indicated that young offenders are more likely to shoplift with their friends. These studies, however, were not designed to test differential association theory on shoplifting. The core concept of Sutherland's theory—favorable definition to crime—was not measured.

Merton's (1938) anomie/strain theory views crime as an outcome of incongruence in the social system. Strain may arise from an imbalance between socially approved goals and the availability of socially approved means of achieving them. Merton's original theory has seldom been tested (Messner 1988) and has often been reduced from its macro to micro level of individual experiences with frustration (Burton and Cullen 1992).

Empirical tests of strain theory at the individual level[4] have yielded mixed results (for a detailed review of the literature, see Burton and Cullen 1992). The critical problem with testing efforts lies in how to operationalize key constructs (Burton and Cullen 1992). Most previous measures of strain theory suffer from having a single explanatory variable (Elliott et al. 1979). The contribution to strain theory from Cloward and Ohlin has not been fully understood (Cullen 1988) or utilized (Menard 1995). In addition, as in the case of differential association theory, shoplifting has seldom been used as the primary dependent variable in testing strain theory; instead, it often appears in the delinquent scale as one of several dozen delinquent acts.

Criticism of differential association theory has concentrated on three major issues: (1) it ignores the importance of social structure (Agnew 1992); (2) it cannot be applicable to different crimes (Cameron 1964; Lemert 1953); and (3) it overlooks the non-economic factors of crime (Cameron 1964; Katz 1988). In contrast, criticism of strain theory can be summarized as follows: (1) it does not acknowledge such factors as that lower-class boys may not share common goals with middle-class boys (Hirschi 1969; Tittle, Villemez, and Smith 1978) and that people from other social classes also commit crime (Hirschi 1969); (2) the theory overlooks individual decision-making (Clarke 1980) and emotional reactions (Katz 1988) and overemphasizes the importance of material success (Agnew 1992; Katz 1988); and (3) the theory ignores problems in measurement and operationalization of the key variables (Burton and Cullen 1992; Cullen 1988).

Cohen (1955), Cloward and Ohlin (1960), and Elliott and Voss (1974) have all attempted to integrate Merton's strain theory and Sutherland's differential association.[5] In their works, delinquency is regarded as a result of goal-blockage and as the outcome of an affiliation with delinquent friends, who provide the strained adolescent with social support for and opportunities to engage in delinquency. However, from both the literature review on shoplifting and latest empirical studies (McCarthy 1995; Wood et al. 1997), it seems necessary to include a measure of thrill and excitement in the study of shoplifting.

In this regard, Katz (1988) presents a phenomenological theory of shoplifting. Based on a college student sample, he observed that shoplifters had sufficient money to pay for what they stole and that even when the object was economically beyond their reach, their aim was not necessarily to use the booty. Furthermore, "even in desperately poor areas adolescent thieves turn to theft for emotionally compelling rather than materially necessary reasons" (p. 79). Initial experiences in sneak thefts by poor, working-class, and middle-class youths, alike, appear to be more projects in constructing "sneaky thrills" than efforts to satisfy previously defined material needs. Therefore, Katz concluded that shoplifting has a fascinating seductive power that stimulates potential offenders to shoplift in certain situations, even without much compelling financial need or influence from significant others.

Although at first glance Katz's theory of crime seems to contradict sociological theories about shoplifting, a closer examination reveals that many elements of his theory are consistent with previous sociological theories. As McCarthy (1995) pointed out, Katz was not the first to highlight the role of situational variables.

Sutherland (1947) and Gibbons (1971) both recognized proximate effects in the etiology of crime. Cohen (1955) made the argument that delinquent behavior is *unnecessarily* utilitarian in nature, and Bordua (1961) admonished theorists to recognize the enjoyment that accompanies many offenses. Excitement or sensation-seeking was also recognized as an important element in crime commission by Zuckerman (1979), Wood et al. (1995, 1997), and Matza and Sykes (1961). It is Katz, however, who systematically wove these themes into a theory of seduction. As discussed earlier, a repeated theme in the shoplifting literature is that many people engage in it for thrills. Thus, it is appropriate to include Katz's theory in a study of shoplifting.

An Integrated Model

Each of the theories we have discussed offers a unique view of crime, but none of them alone adequately addresses the multicausal nature of crime (for a discussion of multiple causes of crime, see Alexander 1987; Elliott 1985; Groves and Lynch 1990; Knorr-Cetina and Cicourel 1981). Strain and differential association are sociological theories and tend to be indeterminate (Cullen 1988), but they cannot sufficiently explain what makes offenders decide when to commit crime and what type of crime to commit (Clarke 1980). Katz's theory represents a phenomenological approach that focuses on emotional experiences not addressed by sociological theories, but it is criticized for overlooking structural factors. Therefore, combining these theories into one model may capture the complex nature of shoplifting because these theories seem to complement one another. Indeed, Groves and Lynch (1990) argue that structural-oriented theories should attempt to integrate subjective approaches so that an integrated view of crime can enhance our knowledge of crime.

Based on the above discussion, we construct an integrated model that includes strain theory, differential association theory, and seduction theory. In this model, strain theory accounts for the significant impact of social structure on behavior that is not properly addressed by the other two theories. Also, deprived opportunities and frustration may provide motivations for association with delinquent peers and acceptance of criminal culture. Differential association theory focuses on how the nature of association influences subsequent behavior. Katz's theory helps us understand why some people shoplift for non-economic motivations.

Our method of theoretical integration is what Hirschi (1979) called "side-by-side" integration. Although it is simple, it does help answer two of the crucial questions in integration: whether the theories are compatible (that is, whether by adding variables of one theory the explanatory power of the other theory is washed out), and whether the combined model increases the explained variation in shoplifting. We propose that the integrated model does both: each theory can retain its unique area of explained variation in shoplifting and the combined model can increase the total explained variation in shoplifting.

Specifically, we shall test the following hypotheses derived from each of the theories. First, from strain theory, three hypotheses are deduced:

Hypothesis 1. The frequency of shoplifting is higher for those who are obsessed by their immediate material goals, such as obtaining the latest clothes and electronics.

Hypothesis 2. Those who feel that their opportunity to achieve financial success has been blocked tend to shoplift more.

Hypothesis 3. Those who perceive shoplifting as a solution to achieve their goals engage in more shoplifting acts.

It is important to note that the last hypothesis has not been tested in empirical studies. The variable perceived solution is developed to address the concern raised by Cloward and Ohlin (1960) and Cullen (1983) that criminal adaptation is indeterminate in nature. Frustration of goals will not by itself explain individuals' involvement in a specific type of crime. It is necessary to consider whether or not people perceive criminal involvement, such as shoplifting, as an adaptive solution to their strain. Previous tests of strain theory have not yet measured this indeterminate aspect of criminal adaptation.

Second, from differential association theory, two hypotheses are deduced:

Hypothesis 4. The higher one scores in the measure of definitions favorable to crime, the more frequently one shoplifts.

Hypothesis 5. The more deeply one is involved with deviant association, the more frequently one shoplifts.

Third, from Katz's seduction theory, the following hypothesis is deduced:

Hypothesis 6. Gaining a sense of sneaky thrill at crime scenes increases the frequency of shoplifting.

METHOD

Sample

The subjects for this study were recruited from a Stop Shoplifting School Program in a large northeastern city. The program is designed to reduce first-time shoplifters' risk of recidivism. First-time arrested shoplifters are referred by the court to the program. The second author of this study went to the school every month for nine months to conduct the in-class survey with the help of two research assistants (see Deng 1997 for a detailed discussion of the issue). Five hundred and seventy-six questionnaires were distributed among all those who attended the school. Special efforts were made to assure the respondents that the study was completely anonymous and that their responses would not have any detrimental effects on their future. Except for nine refusals and another 19 blank questionnaires, 548 respondents completed their questionnaires, representing a return rate of 95%.

Although all program attendants pleaded guilty for alleged shoplifting in courts, 127 (or 21%) in the survey denied ever engaging in shoplifting.[6] We treat those who denied their shoplifting as missing even though they were officially identified as shoplifters. The final sample size is 433. Table 1 reports the means and standard deviations of demographic characteristics and dependent variables of the sample.

Since only convicted first-time shoplifters were surveyed, our sample is not representative of the general population of shoplifters. Further, unlike other street crimes such as robbery or burglary, shoplifters usually have to go through two justice systems: the private and public justice systems (Hindelang 1974). Normally shoplifters are caught red-handed in a store, which has its own security personnel. The store security guard has discretionary power and may or may not notify the police, who, once informed, also can decide whether or not to process the case officially. Shoplifting apprehension is a filtering process, and at each stage of the process some shoplifters vanish (May 1978).

Measurement

Dependent Variable

The dependent variable in this study is shoplifting frequency. It is worth noting that we are not analyzing why some people shoplift and others do not. Instead, we are analyzing why, among convicted shoplifters, some people shoplift more than others. To arrive at the number of past shoplifting acts, respondents were asked to report how many times they had shoplifted before their arrest. The response category in the frequency scale is open-ended. To curb the problem of extreme skewness, however, we recoded extreme cases into several ordinal categories that are above the fourth quartile. On average, the respondents admitted shoplifting 27 times with a standard deviation of 38 (see Table 1).

Independent Variables

Building on the previous research, we used multiple-item measures of the variables. For each item, a Likert scale was used to rate the respondents' answers from 1 = strongly agree to 6 = strongly disagree. When necessary, the responses were

Table 1. Sociodemographic Characteristics of the Sample and Dependent Variables ($N = 433$)

Variables	*Mean*	*Percentage*	*Standard Deviation*
Sociodemographic Variables			
Age	27.46		12.83
Education	12.08		2.79
Gender (female = 1)	.47		.49
Income	3.24		2.59
$0-$16,000		34	
$16,001-$32,000		24	
$32,001-$56,000		26	
$56,001 or more		16	
Race			
Whites		68	
African Americans		20	
Hispanics		7	
Others		5	
Dependent Variable			
Shoplifting	27.21		37.84

recoded so that a higher score on an item indicated the presence of strain, subculture, attitudes favorable to criminal definition, or thrills.

Strain Measures

There are three measures derived from strain theory: immediate material goals, blocked opportunities, and perceived solutions. For the measure of immediate material goals, respondents were asked to rate the extent to which they wanted to possess the latest clothes and the latest electronics goods. These materials are socially valued goals, since they represent an individual's success through conspicuous consumption (Veblen 1912)—an eagerness to display wealth by the elaborate consumption of goods. Strain results when a person's desire for materials is strong and the ability to pay is weak. This measure improves the previous measures of strain by focusing on immediate material goals rather than on more global and remote discrepancy between educational, occupational, or middle-class aspirations. The reliability of this measure is .71.

For blocked opportunities, a scale consisting of three items was developed: "I am satisfied with my opportunities to reach my goals"; "I am satisfied with my present financial situation"; and "I am satisfied when comparing myself with other American families." This scale taps both a sense of blocked opportunities

(Item 1) as well as a sense of relative deprivation (Item 3). The reliability of this measure is .75.

The third measure—perceived solutions—is a one-item scale: after respondents recalled their first shoplifting experience, they were asked why they continued to do it. One of the statements was that "shoplifting could offer an easy and quick solution to my needs." This variable assesses the respondents' intended adaptation for their strain. Cloward and Ohlin (1960) argued, building on Merton, that it is necessary to consider whether adaptation or opportunities for engaging in delinquency are available for individuals who experience strain. Accordingly, the coincidence of structural strain and available criminal solution is the final push for an individual to commit a criminal offense (in our case, shoplifting). This measure captures this coincidence.

Differential Association Measures

There are two measures of central constructs derived from differential association theory—definitions favorable to criminality[7] and deviant association. Definitions favorable to crime include four items: (1) it is O.K. to shoplift when people are unemployed; (2) it is O.K. to shoplift if people are poor; (3) to get ahead, you may have to do something which is not legal; and (4) it is all right to do things that are not legal if you can get away with it. These items tap a person's degree of tolerance for shoplifting and the moral validity of violating the law. The reliability coefficient of the scale is .81.

The index of deviant association is consisted of three items: (1) whether one has shoplifting friends; (2) how much one's friends would approve of the shoplifting activity; and (3) how likely it is that one's best friends would be picked up by the police. The reliability coefficient of the scale is .68. Deviant association captures not only whether the respondent has shoplifting friends but also whether shoplifting is socially approved among those friends and the extent of the friends' involvement in shoplifting.

Measure of Thrills

According to Katz (1988, p. 4), "something causally essential happens" just prior to the commission of a crime. Offenders' emotions subdue their rational selves, and they experience an overpowering sense of being determined by the environment. To tap this "magical" and "transformative" experience, we included the following three items to form the seduction of a sneaky thrill scale: (1) it is exciting to shoplift; (2) sometimes I find it exciting to do things for which I might get in trouble; and (3) sometimes I feel it is exciting to get around the law. This multiple scale attempts to capture the various components of a sneaky thrill: seduction by theft, thieving, and euphoric thrills. The reliability coefficient of the scale is .76.

Control Variables

Five demographic variables were controlled for in the study: age, education, gender, income, and race. Table 1 reports their means and standard deviation. Age is coded as the respondent's natural age in years at the time of the survey. The mean age of the sample is 27.5 with a standard deviation of 12.8. Education is measured by the respondents' self-claimed formal schooling in years with a sample mean of 12. Respondents' gender is coded as a dummy variable where male = 1 and female = 0. Fifty-three percent (292) of the respondents are males and the rest are females. Income is an ordinal variable with eight categories, starting from $0-8,000 with intervals of $8,000—except the next-to-last category, which is $56,001-63,000, and the last category, $63,001 or above. To control for racial and ethnic differences in shoplifting, two binary variables—African American and Hispanics—are constructed with whites as the omitted or benchmark category. Sixty-eight percent (366) of our sample are whites, 20% (107) are African Americans, 7% (36) are Hispanics, and 5% various other ethnic minorities.

RESULTS

Three equations were developed to explain the frequency of shoplifting. The first equation reports the results of regression analysis with strain theory's measures and demographic control variables; the second equation adds into Equation 1 the measures of differential association theory; and the third equation, our complete model, includes all 12 variables. Table 2 presents these results. Only standardized coefficients are shown.

As expected by strain theory, our analyses indicate that immediate material goals and perceived solutions are positively related to the frequency of shoplifting. Blocked opportunities do not affect shoplifting. In addition, the control variables of age and being African American are significantly related to the frequency of shoplifting. The older one is, the less likely one will shoplift, and being African American significantly decreases the likelihood of shoplifting. Other control variables—education, gender, income, and being Hispanic—are not statistically significant. The model as a whole explains 13% of the variance in shoplifting.[8]

In Equation 2, when the measures of differential association theory are introduced, the significant effect of immediate goals from strain theory becomes insignificant. Definitions favorable to deviance do not affect shoplifting significantly. Deviant association, however, is significantly related to the frequency of shoplifting acts. Among the control variables, the age effect is also reduced to insignificance, while being African American continues to reduce the likelihood of shoplifting. The model significantly increases the explained variance in shoplifting by 4 percent.

Moving from Equation 2 to Equation 3, it is found that our measure of seduction theory is significantly related to the frequency of shoplifting. Furthermore, adding

Table 2. Regression of Self-Reported Shoplifting Acts on the Integrated Model (B values)[a]

Explanatory Variables	Equation 1	Equation 2	Equation 3
Strain Theory			
Immediate goals	.11*	.02	.01
Blocked opportunity	–.02	–.03	–.02
Perceived solution	.27***	.21***	.18***
Differential Association Theory			
Definition of law	—	.11	.07
Deviant association	—	.18***	.16**
Seductions Theory			
A sense of sneaky thrill	—	—	.14*
Control Variables			
Age	–.10*	–.03	–.03
Education	–.03	–.01	–.01
Gender	–.05	–.01	–.00
Income	.01	.02	.00
African-Americans	–.11**	–.12**	–.10*
Hispanics	–.02	–.04	–.03
Constant	29.75	6.49	3.15
R-square	.13	.17	.19

Notes: [a]N = 433.
*$p < .05$.
**$p < .01$.
***$p < .001$.

that measure does not affect the significance of the other theoretical constructs in the equation, indicating that it captures a unique area of variance in shoplifting. Inclusion of this variable significantly improves the model's overall fit: the complete model explains 19% of the variance in shoplifting. Although one may expect the model to be stronger, it is important to remember the limitations of our sample: we do not have a comparison of non-shoplifters, and only those who committed at least one shoplifting act appear in our sample.

Our analyses indicate that the constructs derived from the three theories are more powerful explanatory variables than the socioeconomic background characteristics, such as age and race. In the final model, only race remains to be a significant predictor of the shoplifting. Whites are found to be more likely than African Americans to participate in shoplifting. Interestingly, the strain theory measure—perceived solutions—accounts for 18% of the total explained variance in shoplifting. It leads the list of the significant predictors, followed by deviant association, and thrills. Being African American is the weakest predictor.

DISCUSSION

Facing the multidimensional nature of crime, some researchers have called for blending the different theories concerning crime (though some others are critical; see Einstadter and Henry 1995 for a critical assessment of integration in criminology). An integrated model of sociological and phenomenological theories of crime has been tested and largely supported with the frequency of shoplifting as the dependent variable. While rivalry between theories exists,[9] these theories are largely complementary. In our final model, variables from different theories are able to retain their unique area of explained criminality and contribute to the model's increased explained variance.

Our analyses, however, need to be interpreted with caution. Our sample is limited to convicted shoplifters. The detection rate for shoplifting is low (Klemke 1992), and most shoplifters go through two justice systems. The convicted shoplifters thus may represent a selective group of offenders. Minority members may be overrepresented in our sample. In addition, our method of integration is simple and exploratory. Even so, the current study does contribute to our effort to better understand shoplifting and to theoretical integration in the sense that the combined model with variables of both sociological and phenomenological theories has significantly improved the predictive power of any of the models taken separately. At minimum, the idea that shoplifting is encouraged by thrill-seeking, and not necessarily just by economic motivation and differential association, has survived our empirical scrutiny.

Several other findings of our study are also important. First, like the previous literature on shoplifting, our study confirms, at the theoretical level, that both structural strain and differential association are critical to understanding the widespread nature of shoplifting. Shoplifting remains an important area of the sociological study both because of the social harm and of the sheer quantity of cases involved.

Second, shoplifting as a multidimensional phenomenon requires multiple approaches to understand it. Criminologists should take offenders' subjective orientations seriously (Groves and Lynch 1990) and examine motivational process thoughtfully (Agnew 1995). As the data of Katz (1988), McCarthy (1995), and Wood et al. (1997) all demonstrate, the thrills provided by shoplifting and some crimes are seductive. Our analyses confirm that the attraction of crime is an inseparable part of criminality although other factors are also important. If our goal is to understand the etiology of crime, it is necessary to reconcile various theories.

It should be noted that Katz's theory is not the only theory that uses sneaky thrill to explain crime. Gottfredson and Hirschi's (1990) self-control also employs the notion of thrills. The two theories have different assumptions about human nature and the causes of crime. Self-control theory proposes that the pleasure-seeking nature of human beings determines individual propensity to crime, and risk-taking is one of six indicators of low self-control. In contrast, Katz maintains that the sensual dynamics of crime can invoke an emotional reaction from offenders. In other words, regardless of everything else, crime has an intrinsic value to the offenders. Since sneaky thrill is central in Katz's theory, we employ his theory in our integrated model. We recognize that we did not fully test Katz's original theory, which is more rich and complex, and our measure of sneaky thrill needs further refinement. Our intention here is to show the empirical utility of an integrated model and to stimulate more research using integrated approaches to theory.

Third, our measure of perceived solution in strain theory raises some interesting issues. Previous tests of strain theory have ignored the indeterminate nature of adaptation in strain theory. We establish the link between strain and criminal adaptation. As a result, unlike previous studies testing strain theory with learning theory (Akers and Cochran 1985) or differential association theory (Burton et al. 1994), the significant effect of strain theory did not wash out in our analyses; in fact, perceived solution is the most powerful explanatory variable of all. This finding lends support to the argument of McCarthy's study (1995) that we should pay more attention to the situational aspects of perceived material needs/solutions, as well as to any "sneaky thrills" that come from such crimes. The other two measures of strain theory—immediate goals and blocked opportunities—are not significant in the full model; this is consistent with previous tests of strain theory (see Burton and Cullen 1992, but also Agnew et al. 1996).

Fourth, our measure of deviant association shows a significant effect on shoplifting. This finding is consistent with previous studies using the similar measure (Akers et al. 1989; Johnson et al. 1987; Matsueda 1988; Orcutt 1987; Tittle et al. 1986). Probably because our measure captures not only whether people have criminal friends but also whether theft is socially approved, inclusion of this index measure seems to make our other measure of differential association theory—definition favorable to criminality—less important.

Finally, the finding that whites shoplift more frequently than blacks merits discussion. Since people in our sample went through the filters of both private and public justice systems, it is possible that the result that whites admitted more shoplifting is a true reflection of their behavior pattern: only the most hardened and most frequent white shoplifters are caught and processed. Past research indicates that African Americans are more likely than whites to be hassled (Browning et al. 1994), to be stopped and frisked (Massachusetts Attorney General 1990), and to be arrested (Smith, Visher, and Davidson 1984). Other studies suggest that African Americans are more likely to be arrested on less stringent evidentiary criteria than whites (Hepburn 1978; Petersilia 1983). Since blacks are more closely watched, they have less opportunity to steal, and any petty theft behaviors are more likely to be caught and to be brought to the attention of the courts. As a result, infrequent African American shoplifters were included in our sample.

In summary, this study provides another piece of evidence that the theoretical integrated model is the preferred choice of methodology in understanding shoplifting. This finding contributes to the larger debate in theory development: whether criminologists should stick to the past pattern of theory falsification through theory competition or should embrace the new trend of theory integration. Our analysis seems to tilt toward the new trend. Our analyses support the argument that not only is it possible to reconcile different theories of crime but also that such reconciliation should be encouraged in the future within sociology/criminology and across academic disciplines. Moreover, future research should extend this integrative approach to other forms of crime, such as murder and rape.

ACKNOWLEDGMENT

This study was made possible through financial assistance from the Mike Dimond Fund and Baldy Center for Law and Social Policy at the SUNY at Buffalo. The authors thank Simon Singer for his advice in designing the survey, and Judith Peters of the Western New York Better Business Bureau for her cooperation at the Stop Shoplifting School. We also thank Francis T. Cullen, Stuart Henry, and Alethea Helbig for their helpful comments on the earlier versions of this paper.

NOTES

1. In *A Primer in the Psychology of Crime*, Shoham and Seis (1993, p. 127) argue that Katz's theory is "an excellent combination of both existential and phenomenological approaches to the study of crime."

2. Hirschi's social control theory (1969) is also relevant to explanations of shoplifting. Our data, however, do not contain direct measures of social control theory, such as attachment and involvement. In an extension of social control theory to adult criminality, Sampson and Laub (1993) found that adult criminal behavior is influenced by social ties to the adult institutions of informal social control (such as family and work).

3. Social learning theory (Akers 1985; Burgess and Akers 1966) is not discussed here because our data do not contain measures of *"imitation" and "differential reinforcement."* Both are crucial ingredients of the theory.

4. We omit a discussion of Agnew's (1985, 1992) revision of strain theory. Although very valuable, Agnew's approach broadens the concept of strain to include several sources of stress or strain that are not structurally-generated, as he has admitted (Agnew 1995). Neither do we discuss testing Merton's strain theory at the macro-structural level, since this is, according to Messner (1988), a road not taken.

5. Liska, Krohn, and Messner (1989, p. 17) called these attempts a "classic example of middle range or small integration."

6. No matter what assurances we gave, some respondents refused to admit to shoplifting. A comparison of those who refused and those who admitted to shoplifting indicated that there were no significant differences in gender, race, income, and education and that older people were found to be significantly less likely to admit to the behavior.

7. Although this variable measures respondents' attitude toward law, as one reviewer accurately pointed out, one it could also be argued that it could be labeled as "neutralizing definition." Sykes and Matza's (1957) theory could be seen as a further development of differential association. Since our focus is to test differential association theory rather than neutralization theory, it seems more relevant to label it definitions of law.

8. A product term of immediate goals and blocked opportunity was included to test the possible interaction effect. This product term is not significant, and the inclusion of the variable did not increase the explained variation either. As a result, we decided not to present these results in our table.

9. By introducing variables of differential association theory, the significant effect of immediate goals of strain theory becomes insignificant.

REFERENCES

Agnew, R. 1985. "A Revised Strain Theory of Delinquency." *Social Forces* 64: 151-164.

Agnew, R. 1992. "Foundation for a General Strain Theory of Crime and Delinquency." *Criminology* 30:47-87.

Agnew, R. 1995. "Testing the Leading Crime Theories: An Alternative Strategy Focusing on Motivational Processes." *Journal of Research in Crime and Delinquency* 32: 363-398.

Agnew, R., F.T. Cullen, V.S. Burton, Jr., T.D. Evans, and R.G. Dunaway. 1996. "A New Test of Classic Strain Theory." *Justice Quarterly* 13: 681-704.

Akers, R.L. 1985. *Deviant Behavior: A Social Learning Approach*, 3rd edition. Belmont, CA: Wadsworth.

Akers, R.L. 1989. "A Social Behaviorist's Perspective on Integration of Theories of Crime and Deviance." Pp. 23-36 in *Theoretical Integration in the Study of Deviance and Crime*, edited by S.F. Messner, M.D. Krohn, and A.E. Liska. Albany, NY: SUNY Press.

Akers, R.L., and J.K. Cochran. 1985. "Adolescent Marijuana Use: A Test of Three Theories of Deviant Behavior." *Deviant Behavior* 6: 323-346.

Akers, R.L., A. La Greca, J. Cochran, and C. Seller. 1989. "Social Learning and Alcohol Behavior among the Elderly." *Sociological Quarterly* 30: 625-638.

Alexander, J.C. 1987. *Twenty Lectures*. New York: Columbia University Press.

Bales, K. 1982. "Contrast and Complementary in Three Theories of Criminal Behavior." *Deviant Behavior* 3: 155-174.

Baumer, T., and D.P. Rosenbaum. 1984. *Combating Retail: Theft: Programs and Strategies*. Boston, MA: Butterworth.

Bernard, T.J. 1989. "A Theoretical Approach to Integration." Pp. 137-59 in *Theoretical Integration in the Study of Deviance and Crime*, edited by S.F. Messner, M.D. Krohn, and A.E. Liska. Albany, NY: SUNY Press.

Bernard, T.J., and J.N. Snipes. 1996. "Theoretical Integration in Criminology." Pp. 301-348 in *Crime and Justice: A Review of Research*, Vol. 20, edited by M. Tonry. Chicago, IL: The University of Chicago Press.

Bordua, D.J. 1961. "Delinquent Subcultures: Sociological Interpretations of Gang Delinquency." *The Annals of the American Academy of Political Science* 338: 119-136

Browning, S.L., F.T. Cullen, L. Cao, R. Kopache, and T.J. Stevenson. 1994. "Race and Getting Hassled by the Police." *Police Studies* 17: 1-12.

Burgess, R.L., and R.L. Akers. 1966. "A Differential Association-Reinforcement Theory of Criminal Behavior." *Social Problems* 14(Fall): 128-147.

Burton, V.S., and F.T. Cullen. 1992. "The Empirical Status of Strain Theory." *Journal of Crime and Justice* XV: 1-30.

Burton, V.S., F.T. Cullen, D. Evans, and R.G. Dunaway. 1994. "Reconsidering Strain Theory: Operationalization, Rival Theories, and Adult Criminality." *Journal of Quantitative Criminology* 10: 213-239.

Cameron, M.O. 1964. *The Booster and the Snitch: Department Store Shoplifting*. New York: Free Press of Glencoe.

Cao, L., and D.J. Maume, Jr. 1993. "Urbanization, Inequality, Lifestyles and Robbery: A Comprehensive Model." *Sociological Focus* 26: 11-26.

Clarke, R.V. 1980. "Situational Crime Prevention: Theory and Practice." *British Journal of Criminology* 20: 136-147.

Cloward, R., and L. Ohlin. 1960. *Delinquency and Opportunity: A Theory of Delinquent Gangs*. New York: Free Press.

Cohen, A. 1955. *Delinquency Boys: The Culture of the Gang*. New York: Free Press.

Cullen, F.T. 1983. *Rethinking Crime and Deviance Theory*. Totowa, NJ: Rowman and Allenheld.

Cullen, F.T. 1988. "Were Cloward and Ohlin Strain Theorists? Delinquency and Opportunity Revisited." *Journal of Research in Crime and Delinquency* 25: 214-241.

Deng, X. 1997. "Deterrent Effects of Initial Sanction on First-time Apprehended Shoplifters." *International Journal of Offender Therapy and Comparative Criminology* 34: 284-297.

Einstadter, W., and S. Henry. 1995. *Criminological Theory: An Analysis of Its Underlying Assumptions*. Philadelphia, PA: Harcourt Brace College Publishers.

Elliott, D.S. 1985. "The Assumption that Theories can be Combined with Increased Explanatory Power: Theoretical Integrations." Pp. 123-149 in *Theoretical Methods in Criminology*, edited by R. Meier. Beverly Hills, CA: Sage.

Elliott, D.S., S.S. Ageton, and R.J. Canter. 1979. "An Integrated Theoretical Perspective on Delinquent Behavior." *Journal of Crime and Delinquency* 16: 3-27.

Elliott, D.S., and H.L. Voss. 1974. *Delinquency and Dropout*. Lexington, MA: D.C. Heath.

Gibbons, D.C. 1971. "Observations on the Study of Crime Causation." *American Journal of Sociology* 77: 262-278.

Gold, M. 1970. *Delinquent Behavior in an American City*. Belmont, CA: Brooks/Cole.

Gottfredson, M., and T. Hirschi. 1990. *A General Theory of Crime*. Stanford, CA: Stanford University Press.

Groves, W.B., and M.J. Lynch. 1990. "Reconciling Structural and Subjective Approaches to the Study of Crime." *Journal of Research in Crime and Delinquency* 27: 348-375.

Hepburn, J.R. 1978. "Race and the Decision to Arrest: An Analysis of Warrants Issued." *Journal of Research in Crime and Delinquency* 15: 54-73.

Hindelang, M.J. 1974. "Decisions of Shoplifting Victims to Invoke the Criminal Justice Process." *Social Problems* 21: 580-593.

Hirschi, T. 1969. *Causes of Delinquency*. Berkeley, CA: University of California Press.

Hirschi, T. 1979. "Separate and Unequal is Better." *Journal of Research in Crime and Delinquency* 16: 34-37.

Johnson, R.E., A.C. Marcos, and S.J. Bahr. 1987. "The Role of Peers in the Complex Etiology of Adolescent Drug Use." *Criminology* 25: 323-340.

Katz, J. 1988. *Seductions of Crime: Moral and Sensual Attractions in Doing Evil*. New York: Basic Books.

Klemke, L.W. 1982. "Exploring Juvenile Shoplifting." *Sociology and Social Research* 67: 59-75.

Klemke, L.W. 1992. *The Sociology of Shoplifting*. Westport, CT: Prager.

Knorr-Cetina, K.D., and A. Cicourel. 1981. *Advances in Social Theory and Methodology: Towards an Integration of Micro and Macro Sociology*. London: Routledge & Kegan Paul.

Kraut, R.E. 1976. "Deterrent and Definitional Influences on Shoplifting." *Social Problems* 23: 358-368.

Lemert, E.M. 1953. "Isolation and Closure Theory of Naive Check Forgery." *Journal of Criminal Law, Criminology and Police Science* 44(September-October): 293-307.

Liska, A.E., M.D. Krohn, and S.F. Messner. 1989. "Strategies and Requisites for Theoretical Integration in the Study of Crime and Deviance." Pp. 1-19 in *Theoretical Integration in the Study of Deviance and Crime*, edited by S.F. Messner, M.D. Krohn, and A.E. Liska. Albany, NY: SUNY Press.

Massachusetts Attorney General. 1990. *Report of the Attorney General's Civil Rights Division on Boston Police Department Practices*. Boston, MA: Massachusetts Attorney General.

Matsueda, R.L. 1988. "The Current State of Differential Association Theory." *Crime and Delinquency* 34(3): 277-306.

Matza, D., and G.M. Sykes. 1961. "Juvenile Delinquency and Subterranean Values." *American Sociological Review* 26: 712-719.

May, D. 1978. "Juvenile Shoplifters and the Organization Store Security: A Case Study in the Social Construction of Delinquency." *International Journal of Criminology and Penology* 6: 137-160.

McCarthy, B. 1995. "Not just 'for the Thrill of It': An Instrumentalist Elaboration of Katz's Explanation of Sneaky Thrill Property Crime." *Criminology* 33: 519-538.

Menard, S. 1995. "A Developmental Test of Mertonian Anomie Theory." *Journal of Research in Crime and Delinquency* 32: 136-174.

Merton, R. 1938. "Social Structure and Anomie." *American Sociological Review* 3: 672-682.

Messner, S.F. 1988. "Merton's 'Social Structure and Anomie': The Road Not Taken." *Deviant Behavior* 9: 33-53.

Moore, R.H. 1984. "Shoplifting in Middle America: Patterns and Motivational Correlates." *International Journal of Offender Therapy and Comparative Criminology* 28: 53-64.

Orcutt, J.D. 1987. "Differences Association and Marijuana Use: A Closer Look at Sutherland (with a Little Help from Becker)." *Criminology* 25: 341-358.

Petersilia, J. 1983. *Racial Disparities in the Criminal Justice System*. Santa Monica, CA: Rand.

Ray, J. 1987. "Every Twelfth Shopper: Who Shoplifts and Why?" *Social Casework: The Journal of Contemporary Social Work* 68(4): 234-239.

Sampson, R.J., and J.H. Laub. 1993. *Crime in the Making: Pathways and Turning Points Through Life*. Cambridge, MA: Harvard University Press.

Shoham, S.G., and M. Seis. 1993. *A Primer in the Psychology of Crime*. New York: Harrow and Heston.

Smith, D.A., Christy Visher, and Laura A. Davidson. 1984. "Equity and Discretionary Justice: The Influence of Race on Police Arrest Decisions." *Journal of Criminal Law and Criminology* 75: 234-249.

Stinchcombe, A. 1968. *Constructing Social Theories*. New York: Harcourt, Brace and World.

Sutherland, E.H. 1947. *Principles of Criminology*, 4th edition. Philadelphia, PA: J.B. Lippincott.

Sykes, G.M., and D. Matza. 1957. "Techniques of Neutralization: A Theory of Delinquency." *American Sociological Review* 22: 664-670.

Thornberry, T.P. 1989. "Reflections on the Advantages and Disadvantages of Theoretical Integration." Pp. 51-60 in *Theoretical Integration in the Study of Deviance and Crime*, edited by S.F. Messner, M.D. Krohn, and A.E. Liska. Albany, NY: SUNY Press

Tittle, C.R. 1989. "Prospects for Synthetic Theory: A Consideration of Macro-Level Criminological Activity." Pp. 161-178 in *Theoretical Integration in the Study of Deviance and Crime*, edited by S.F. Messner, M.D. Krohn, and A.E. Liska. Albany, NY: SUNY Press.

Tittle, C.R., M.J. Burke, and E.F. Jackson. 1986. "Modeling Sutherland's Theory of Differential Association: Toward an Empirical Clarification." *Social Forces* 65: 405-432.

Tittle, C.R., W.J. Villemez, and D.A. Smith. 1978. "The Myth of Social Class and Criminality: An Empirical Assessment of the Empirical Evidence. *American Sociological Review* 43: 643-656.

Turner, C.B., and S. Cashdan. 1988. "Perception of College Student's Motives for Shoplifting." *Psychological Reports* 62: 855-862.

Veblen, T. 1912. *The Theory of the Leisure Class*. New York: Macmillan.

Won, G., and G. Yamamoto. 1968. "Social Structure and Deviant Behavior: A Study of Shoplifting." *Sociology and Social Research* 53: 44-55.

Wood, P.B., J.K. Cochran, B. Pfefferbaum, and B.J. Arneklev. 1995. "Sensation Seeking and Delinquent Substance Use: An Extension of Learning Theory." *Journal of Drug Issues* 25: 173-193.

Wood, P.B, W.R. Gove, J.A. Wilson, and J.K. Cochran. 1997. "Nonsocial Reinforcement and Habitual Criminal Conduct: An Extension of Learning Theory. *Criminology* 35: 335-366.

Yates, E. 1986. "The Influence of Psycho-social Factors on Non-Sensical Shoplifting." *International Journal of Offender, Therapy and Comparative Criminology* 30: 203-211.

Zuckerman, M. 1979. *Sensation Seeking: Beyond the Optimal Level of Arousal.* Hillsdale, NJ: Erlbaum.

ANALYZING PENAL REFORM: CAN THEORY AND POLICY EVER MEET?

Karol Lucken

ABSTRACT

For the past two decades, penal reform has become the focus of much criminological research. Emerging from this research, however, are decidely different analytical styles and priorities. One body of research has been theoretical and has centered on interpreting the origins and social control outcomes of national penal reform movements. The other body of research has been policy oriented and has centered on the effectiveness of individual program efforts. As a result, penal reform research has been dominated by metaphors that reflect punishment's necessarily suspect functions or by statistics that provide empirical data without understanding. The need for penal reform research that adheres to neither extreme is apparent. This paper reviews this fragmented penal reform research in order to formulate an analytical approach that advances theoretical and policy developments simultaneously.

Sociology of Crime, Law, and Deviance, Volume 1, pages 85-103.

ISBN: 0-7623-0282-8

INTRODUCTION

Garland (1990) has observed that punishment, like the crime it is intended to deal with, has become just as chronic a social problem. Cohen (1985) has similarly remarked that the quest for the causes of crime has been superceded by the quest for finding "what works." Indeed, over the past two decades, criminological research has increasingly focused on punishment practices and institutions. Of particular interest to many scholars are the penal reform movements of the nineteenth and twentieth centuries. For example, beginning in the 1970s, numerous studies examined the origins and social control outcomes associated with the prison (Ignatieff 1978; Foucault 1977; Melossi and Pavarini 1981; Rothman 1971; Takagi 1975), juvenile court (Platt 1969; Schlossman 1977), probation/parole (Rothman 1980), and diversion/decarceration (Austin and Krisberg 1981; Blomberg 1977; Cohen 1985; Scull 1977). Inspired by the revisionism of the "new criminology" (Taylor, Walton, and Young 1973), these studies cited accelerated social control as a patterned consequence of penal reform efforts. Accordingly, metaphors such as "net-widening," "stronger and different nets," and "carceral archipelago" came to dominate the penal reform literature vocabulary (Blomberg 1995).

By the late 1980s, the intermediate punishment movement became the focus of penal reform research (Baird and Wagner 1990; Blomberg, Bales, and Reed 1993; Byrne and Pattavina 1992; Erwin 1990; Latessa 1987; Lilly, Ball, and Wright 1987; MacKenzie and Parent 1992; Pearson and Harper 1990; Petersilia 1987; Petersilia and Turner 1990, 1993; Petersilia, Turner, and Deschenes 1992). Guided by more pragmatic objectives, this body of research evaluated the outcomes of individual reform programs. Studies examined the capacity of various intermediate punishment programs (e.g., home confinement, intensive supervision probation) to reduce prison overcrowding and recidivism and provide more punitive sanctions. To date, conflicting findings have been reported regarding intermediate punishment's degree of effectiveness.

Emerging from this penal reform research overall are decidely different analytical styles and priorities. In fact, it can be argued that in the penal reform research, theory and policy have been compartmentalized. The earlier penal reform research, which is sociological-historical in content, was dominated by theoretical abstractions. The more recent (intermediate punishment) penal reform research, which is more practical-empirical in content, has been dominated by statistical particulars. For example, McMahon (1990) asserts that the diversion research has been based as much on ideological metaphors as on statistical evidence. Matthews (1987) claims that adequate understanding of decarceration has been hindered by theoretical overgeneralizations and weak methodologies. And Lemert (1993) has argued that the day-to-day reality of punishment has been lost in a monopoly of "surreal" penal reform narratives.

Conversely, intermediate punishment research has been empirically more rigorous, but also atheoretical and narrow in scope. With few exceptions (i.e., Blomberg and Lucken 1994; Petersilia 1987), little attention has been devoted to clarifying the conditions and processes that contribute to program outcomes. Thus, program outcomes have been quantitatively measured but not qualitatively understood. At best, it can be concluded that the success or failure of various intermediate punishment programs is contingent upon several factors. Those factors have not been systematically explored, leaving unanswered the essential question, "why do some programs work, while others do not?"

While appeals for concrete accounts, better explanation, and policy relevancy abound in the penal literature of the nineties (Blomberg 1995; Duff and Garland 1994; Garland 1990; Lemert 1993; Pisciotta 1994), a strategy that facilitates their blending has not been clearly articulated. Thus, there is an apparent need to translate the fragmented penal reform literature into recommendations for more integrated penal reform studies. In response to this need, this paper reviews the penal reform literature with a view to formulating an approach that advances theoretical and policy developments simultaneously.

The literature review that follows falls short of exhausting the research on the subject of penal reform. Rather, the review illustrates the polar approaches in the study of penal reform and the implications of that polarity. The opening section of the review addresses the theoretical research, as represented by sociological-historical studies of the prison, juvenile court, probation/parole, and diversion/decarceration. The subsequent section addresses the policy research, as represented by practical-empirical studies of the latest penal reform movement of intermediate punishment. These sections are succeeded by a discussion of an alternative approach to analyzing penal reform.

BUILDING THEORY: EARLY PENAL REFORM RESEARCH

Penal reform as an object of critical study has its roots in the social and academic turbulence that gave rise to labeling theory and the various strands and derivatives of Marxist theory in the analysis of crime, law, and deviance. Consequently, early penal reform research became entangled in the dialectics of functionalism in seeking to expose the true meaning and impact of historical and contemporary reform efforts. Conventional interpretations of penal reform as mere acts of benevolence were dismissed as illusory, as penal reform efforts came to be viewed as utilitarian enterprises that expanded control over the masses. A number of perspectives have been responsible for the "demystification" of penal reform and they are classified quite simply here as organizational, radical, and social context (for additional typologies, see Garland 1990; Howe 1994).

Organizational Perspective

Evolving from the ideas of Weber, an organizational perspective highlights the "good intentions, bad consequences" (Cohen 1985) paradox in penal reform. Most notably, these frameworks call attention to the undermining forces of bureaucratic imperatives. It is argued that in the interest of organizational survival, maintenance, and expansion, the originating ideas and goals of penal reform are predictably displaced. This argument is featured most prominently in the work of Blomberg (1977), Rothman (1980), and Austin and Krisberg (1981).

Employing a functional systems framework to the study of a reform movement, Blomberg (1977) finds a disjunction between the goals and practices of a California diversion program. He argues that populations previously not considered appropriate for control are drawn into this reform's various intervention strategies. Thus, he concludes that diversion extended, rather than reduced, the formal control exercised by the juvenile court, citing conflicting objectives, ambiguous treatment technology, resource scarcity, and operational uncertainty as the organizational culprits.

In Rothman's *Conscience and Convenience*, the organizational perspective is given perhaps its fullest elaboration. In his analysis of the Progressive Era reforms, Rothman contends that well-meaning reforms are systematically subverted by bureaucratic considerations. He argues that reform ambitions, no matter how conscientiously they are conceived, must find an organizational constituency if they are to win enactment. For example, Rothman claims that the reforms of probation and parole were widely received because of their numerous practical advantages to the operators of criminal justice and mental health; wardens supported parole because it facilitated institutional control, and state attorneys supported probation because it facilitated plea bargaining and, therefore, higher conviction rates. Though the Progressive reforms *failed* in the eyes of their designers, the reforms *succeeded* in meeting the managerial and administrative objectives of their users.

Austin and Krisberg (1981) argue as well that organizational dynamics have functioned to resist, distort, and frustrate the original purposes of a number of reform movements (diversion, deterrence, due process). Though the authors concede that penal reforms are inevitably affected by the contradictions inherent in the broader political-economic structure, they also propose that crime control ideologies, agency values, and power and authority act as sources of conflict among the organizations associated with the reform's administration (police, corrections, law enforcement). Such organizations engage in competition with one another, reacting to a given reform based on its perceived value to organizational survival. Much like Blomberg and Rothman, Austin and Krisberg contend that the primary effect of reform activity is the creation of wider, stronger, and different nets of control.

Radical Perspective

For the purposes of this review, a radical perspective refers to both the power position of Foucault (1977) and the range of positions that directly or indirectly owe their allegiance to the writings of Marx. As a whole, these positions have concentrated on the relationship between social organization and penal reform and the associated questions of what punishments are "like" and what they are "for" (Hudson 1996). Consequently, penal reform has become synonymous with notions of political economy, class control, and fiscal crisis and disassociated from notions of civility, benevolence, and "disinterested" reformers.

Takagi's (1975, p. 279) opening statement in his analysis of the Walnut Street Jail illustrates this point explicitly: "Most of us have been led to believe that the 'gentle and humane' Quakers founded the prison as an alternative to the sanguinary English laws then in effect, and that the idea of a prison was based upon the prevailing theory of humane reason." Takagi argues instead that the prison enabled the development of a strong centralized government. Penal powers came to be monopolized by the state (via the prison) as problems of law and order arose from the ascendancy of the new bourgeoisie establishment.

Platt (1969, p. xiv) makes a similar argument when he states that the juvenile court and other "child saving" reforms "were intertwined with profound developments that were taking place in the political economy at the end of the 19th century." He argues that the child saving reforms, though not removed entirely from concerns for "salvation" and "protection," were part of a corporate class movement aimed at devising new forms of control to protect the power and privilege of the economic elite. Thus, compulsory education and youth reformatories alike prepared children for a future of industrial labor. According to Platt, the diversified control spawned by the child-savers' "paternalistic" impulses was, in effect, a civil defense against the threatening and unseemly behaviors of the lower-class.

Following in the footsteps of Rusche and Kirchheimer (1939), Melossi and Pavarini establish the connection between the rise of the capitalist mode of production and the origins of the modern prison. In *The Prison and the Factory*, they propose that the initial function of the prison was to transform a recalcitrant peasant class into a socially manageable proletariat workforce. Workhouses, houses of correction, and prisons, in particular, served as a training ground for instilling the values needed for submission to the new bourgeois way of life.[1]

In his vivid account of the transition of penal power from visible brutal attacks on the body to invisible manipulations of the soul, Foucault (1977) links penal reform to the requisites of political power. However, unlike his Marxist contemporaries, Foucault is less concerned with tracking who or what is responsible for penal reform (Garland 1990) and more concerned with constructing the anatomy of the power relations that lie within. By dissecting the prison and displaying the associated invention of discipline, the operational dimensions of this penal reform come into full view. It is discovered that the penal project of modernist society relies on such subtle technologies of power as knowledge, observation, regimentation, and routine to render deviant subjects "docile," normal, and self-controlled.

In *Decarceration,* Scull argues that deinstitutionalization was a response to a fiscal crisis engendered by the contradictions of capitalism. As budgetary pressures on the state intensified during the 1960s and 1970s, noninstitutional methods of dealing with problem populations became increasingly attractive. Scull contends that the rise of the welfare state, and its associated "social investments" (O'Connor 1970) made segregative forms of control too expensive and too difficult to justify, particularly for the insane. Thus, deinsitutionalization was motivated by the need for cheap control rather than a belief in the humanity and effectiveness of community-based alternatives for the "bad" and the "mad."

Social Context Perspective

The social context perspective is so designated because of its meta-view of history and its search for penal reform meaning in a more generalized set of factors. The primary assumption of this perspective is that penal reforms represent functional solutions to problems brought about by impending social change. According to this perspective, social change embodies demographic, political, economic, and cultural shifts. This "complicated intentions" (Cohen 1985) interpretation of penal reform originated with the work of Rothman (1971) and has been replicated in the work of Schlossman (1977).

In *The Discovery of the Asylum,* Rothman argues that the prison emerged as the dominant form of punishment as public perceptions of social chaos escalated in postrevolutionary America. "The idea of the asylum took form in the perception, in fact the fear, that once-stable social relationships were now in the process of unraveling threatening to subvert social order and social cohesion" (1971, p. xxiv). Jacksonian angst over the lost order of the Colonial Era led to the development of the prison, which was to be a microcosm of a perfectly organized community. Ultimately, the prison was to serve as a model to a morally disintegrating society and as a reform vehicle for subsequently morally weakened offenders.

In *Love and the American Delinquent,* Schlossman (1977) argues that the juvenile court was a product of the turn-of-the-twentieth-century times. He bases this conclusion on the fact that legal precedence for establishing a juvenile court had been in place long before its implementation. Schlossman contends that the juvenile court was implemented only when the prevailing social thought and social conditions coincided with the allowances of the law. These social prerequisites included anti-institutional sentiments sparked by an enlightened penal philosophy, and the emergence of class-based neighborhoods sparked by urbanization, immigration, and industrialization.

Collectively, this research has provided enlightening and countering views of the various forces that shape penal reform and social control. Richly descriptive historical inquiries reveal that penal reforms are mobilized, structured, and implemented in accordance with organizational preservation, repression, fiscal crisis, or various social transformations. However, the explanatory powers of these perspectives are not without certain limitations. For example, in remarking on the social context perspective, Forst (1978) notes that it is not sufficient to merely study the national mood or general social conditions of a given time; one must also attend to the individuals and groups which have the power to formulate penal policy. Nor is it sufficient to rely on perspectives that necessarily implicate these individuals and groups in the conscious or unconscious reproduction of class relations or penal organizations (Cohen 1985; Garland 1990). The recognition of these and other limitations has led a number of penal scholars to advocate theoretical synthesis (Blomberg 1995; Cohen 1985; Garland 1990; Pisciotta 1994) and one other scholar (Lemert 1993) to doubt whether these "elegant" and "provocative" theories can advance the understanding of penal reform beyond their earlier usage.

DEVELOPING POLICY: RECENT PENAL REFORM RESEARCH

The absence of theory from the more recent penal reform research might suggest that Lemert is not alone in his skepticism. Noticeably missing from the intermediate punishment research are substantive probes of this reform's origins and operations. Queries of "intentions" and "meaning" are instead reduced to three pragmatic questions relating to outcomes. Specifically: can intermediate punishment reduce prison overcrowding and recidivism and can it provide more punitive sanctions?

Reducing Institutional Overcrowding

It has been suggested that in the absence of prison overcrowding and scarcity of fiscal resources, the incentive to develop intermediate punishments would disappear (Lurigio and Petersilia 1992). The foremost objective of intermediate punishment has been to provide relief to overburdened correctional systems by diverting offenders into less costly community-based alternatives. The research thus far has produced mixed findings regarding this reform's effectiveness as a diversion strategy.

Erwin (1986) found that Georgia's Intensive Supervision Program (ISP) acted as a true diversion, citing a 10% decrease in the proportion of convicted felons imprisoned. Using discriminant analysis, Erwin reported that those placed in the program more closely resembled the prison population than those sentenced to regular probation. Using criminal justice and jail documents, Lilly, Ball, and Wright (1987) also found that a Kentucky home incarceration program served as an alternative to jail. The authors base this conclusion on the facts that 80% of the offenders participating in the program had previously served jail time and 96% of the program participants had prior convictions.

In contrast, Blomberg et al. (1993) found that prison populations in Florida increased following the implementation of the state's home confinement program. Using felony conviction, home confinement, and prison population data in a pre/post program evaluation design, the authors found that Florida increasingly relied on prison for drug and non-drug convictions during home confinement's operation. The study showed that during the program's operation, the probability of a prison sanction increased while the probability of a non-prison sanction—namely, probation and/or home confinement—decreased.

Baird and Wagner's (1990) assessment of Florida's home confinement program produced both negative and positive results. The authors examined pre/post program incarceration rates and compared offenders receiving probation, jail, home confinement, and prison. A multivariate analysis was also conducted to determine what sanction home confinement participants would have received in the program's absence. Baird and Wagner concluded that the program did not initially reduce the proportion of offenders going to prison. However, they noted that after a period of time, a true diversion rate of 50% was achieved.

The findings of Blomberg and Lucken (1994) and Petersilia and Turner (1993) cast further doubt on the capacity of intermediate punishment to reduce reliance on incarceration. Using statistical reports and participant observation, Blomberg and Lucken found that a Florida county intermediate punishment program increased the likelihood of technical violations. Between 1985 and 1989, average monthly probation violation rates increased by 238%, while average monthly probation caseload sizes increased by only 2%. During that same period, the county's jail population increased by 245%, despite the expanded use of community-based alternatives and county arrest increases of only 87%. Petersilia and Turner's (1993) study of 14 ISP programs in nine states also found that ISP increased the occurrence of technical violations and, therefore, prison populations. In a majority of the sites, intensive supervision produced approximately twice the number of technical violations as routine supervision.

Reducing Recidivism

Through increased control and surveillance, it is expected that intermediate punishment can also reduce recidivism. It is assumed that offenders will be deterred from committing new offenses for fear that their behavior will be swiftly detected and responded to. Intermediate punishment's record on recidivism has, by comparison, been more consistent. Erwin (1986) found that less than 1% of Georgia's ISP participants were convicted of a violent offense while participating in the program. She also compared ISP participants with a cohort of high-risk regular probationers and prison releasees. An 18-month follow up revealed that while revocation rates were higher for ISP, it yielded the lowest rate of subsequent serious crime.

Employing an experimental design, Petersilia and Turner (1990) examined recidivism rates for ISP programs in three California counties. The authors reported that there were no significant differences in new arrests between intensive and regular probationers, even though the surveillance of intensive probationers was two to three times greater than that of regular probationers. The authors concluded that ISP has no apparent effect on recidivism, and may do no more than monitor the offender's success or failure in meeting the technical conditions of ISP (see also Petersilia and Turner 1993).

Petersilia et al. (1992) examined drug intensive supervision programs and reached a similar conclusion. The study involved 500 offenders in seven jurisdictions in five states that were randomly assigned to ISP or a routine supervision program. They found the ISP programs were no more effective than the routine supervision programs in curbing offender recidivism. Specifically, there were no differences in recidivism outcomes between ISP and routine supervision; however, there were vast differences in recidivism rates across programs.

Latessa (1987) also reports that overall recidivism rates for intensive probationers were not significantly different from the control group, even though the intensive probationers were a much higher risk group of offenders (i.e., less educated, less employable, with more serious prior criminal records). Intensive probationers had slightly more misdemeanor and felony arrests, felony convictions, and technical violations than the comparison group, though the differences were not significant. During the follow-up period, the two groups were similar with regard to the proportion remaining on probation, absconding, being revoked, and being reincarcerated.

Using survival analysis, Pearson and Harper (1990) found a New Jersey's ISP program held recidivism rates (i.e., new offenses only) to a reasonable level. Ninety percent of all ISP admissions remained in the community for up to 1,020 days without being convicted of a new offense. Of those who completed the program successfully, only 3% were rearrested after they had been granted unconditional discharges from ISP. Of those committing new offenses, property crimes, followed by drug crimes, were the most prevalent. Less than 10% of the new crimes involved violence.

Punitive Sanctions

In contrast to traditional probation and parole, intermediate punishment is primarily retributive and incapacitative in its philosophical objectives. The findings regarding intermediate punishment's capacity to effectively control offenders remain equivocal. Pearson and Harper (1990) found that New Jersey's intensive supervision probation (ISP) program provided substantially higher levels of punishment and supervision than regular probation or parole. Offenders were required to pay fines, perform community service, adhere to curfews, and participate in rehabilitative programs such as Alcoholics Anonymous and Narcotics Anonymous. Monthly reports of ISP officer contacts revealed that the frequency of contacts (i.e., phone, personal, urinalysis tests) met and/or exceeded program objectives.

Blomberg and Lucken (1994) also found that intermediate punishment was more punitive than routine supervision. Much like the New Jersey program, offenders were exposed to multiple conditions, including fines, treatment, Alcoholics/Narcotics Anonymous, urinalysis, community service, and restitution. The fact that offenders often preferred incarceration to the rigors of the program provided a further indication of the program's punitiveness.

The findings of Latessa (1987) and Lemert (1993) indicate otherwise. Comparing intensive probationers with a similar group of regular probationers, Latessa found intensive supervision probationers were receiving significantly more contacts than the comparison group. Yet, the number of face-to-face contacts was still below the program goal. Latessa concluded that the Ohio program did not provide the number of "high quality" contacts to warrant the label of "intensive supervision."

Lemert found that supervision styles under a punitive probation model were no different than supervision styles under the rehabilitative probation model. Using interview data from four California county probation departments, he found that under conditions of resource scarcity, officers gave greater attention to high-risk cases and scant attention to low-risk cases, an age-old practice he terms "bank-loading." Lemert concluded that the California experience belied any claims of a "new" (Feeley and Simon 1992) era in punishment.

The findings of the intermediate punishment research demonstrate the variegated nature of this reform's performance record. Similar programs have produced different results (e.g., Latessa, Pearson/Harper on punitiveness), different methodologies have produced like conclusions (e.g., Erwin, Baird/Wagner, Lily/Ball/Wright on diversion; Pearson/Harper, Petersilia, Latessa on recidivism), and like methodologies have produced different conclusions (e.g., Latessa, Lemert, Blomberg/Lucken on punitiveness). In the absence of a theoretical perspective and/or an investigation into a program's origins or operations, it is difficult to determine what accounts for the mix of intermediate punishment program outcomes. In particular, the findings presented in each study do not make clear why some programs have been successful or unsuccessful or, more specifically, why a single program has met certain goals and not others.

What is clear is that the intermediate punishment research has proceeded with scarce reference to questions of "true" function. In fact, Tonry (1990) is alone in his speculations on intermediate punishment.[2] Tonry declares that this reform, despite its failures, is a success because it serves latent political, institutional, and professional interests. While this interpretation certainly gives cause for thought, it is without empirical foundation. Consequently, as presented, the finding is of dubious *practical* value.

The preceding literature review has attempted to illustrate the contrasting approaches in penal reform research and the theoretical and policy gaps created by these contrasting approaches. At one extreme are the sweeping interpretations about the intentions and consequences of national penal reform movements. These interpretations locate penal reform within the context of social, political, economic, or organizational exigencies that ultimately lead to accelerated social control. At the other extreme are statistical details about the diversionary, recidivism, and punishment outcomes of local or state reform programs. These details indicate what specific programs in different jurisdictions can and cannot do. Thus, with the former approach, the motivations and practices responsible for reform processes have been oversimplified, and, with the latter approach, the motivations and practices responsible for reform processes have been overlooked altogether.

However, the call to integration does not rest on the simple fact that because two different and incomplete bodies of punishment research exist, they must necessarily be merged to obtain a completed penal reform assessment. After all, it could be argued that the statistical findings from program evaluations could more or less confirm the theoretical contentions of the broader sociohistorical research. Rather, the case for integration rests in the fact that penal motives, and therefore function, can not be ascribed without corroborative operational and outcome data, and that outcome data is limited in its implications without knowledge of a reform's operations and originating context. More specifically, the two bodies of research are designed with entirely different hypotheses in mind and their respective findings can not be properly linked when the decisions, activities, and intentions that provide the glue are not part of either analysis or, most importantly, the same analysis.

AN INTEGRATED APPROACH

It is from this assortment of strengths and weaknesses that an alternative approach to penal reform analysis comes into focus. To better address the corresponding questions of penal reform function and effectiveness, it is proposed that a theoretical (sociohistorical) framework be applied to the study of local or state reform programs, which has typically been overseen by a policy (practical-empirical) framework exclusively. To illustrate the form and utility of this integrated approach, a summarized example of its application is provided. This is followed by an expanded discussion of what the approach entails.

An integrated approach has been expressly employed by the author in an article-length case study of a local penal reform (Lucken 1997). In this study, the reform's origins, operations, and outcomes are examined through many theoretical lenses to enable a broader description of reform activities and a broader interpretation of the meaning of these activities.

In employing this approach, the origins of the reform could be traced to a number of interacting events, individuals, and motives. It was discovered that the prosperity of the local industry depended on a clean, safe streets image. This lead to a long-standing informal policy of arresting and transporting to jail minor "visible" offenders, who were incarcerated in a distinctively "lock-em-up and throw away the key" environment. This policy ultimately contributed to jail overcrowding and inmate disruptions, which contributed to multiple lawsuits and, finally, the demand for reform. This reform demand culminated in the ongoing development of a number of rehabilitative and punitive community-based programs that were each oversold to local politicians as the cheap alternative. Thus, the economic interests of the business community and the political concerns and (penal) philosophical beliefs of the county commission and the sheriff's department each played a critical and distinct role in the reform's origins.

Analysis of the reform's operations revealed that these programs were primarily used as alternatives to jail, as intended. However, they were also used as supplements to each other. Through the frequent imposition of combination sentences (i.e., jail followed by probation), an offender could find him/herself on probation and home confinement at the same time, or probation, alternative community service, and work release at the same time. This operational tendency evolved from the organizational activities of independently operating sanctioning agents (e.g., judges, work release, and home confinement personnel) and the belief that overlapping controls were more beneficial and deserved than detrimental and counterproductive. Consequently, the increase in technical violations that resulted from the "piling up of sanctions" was not ill-perceived. Rather, it was viewed as a logical extension of the offenders' irresponsibility and lack of discipline. Thus, the reform's operations were a function not only of organizational factors but also of ideological factors that assumed the form of a "middle-class measuring rod" (Cohen 1955) when imposing offender expectations.

The study concluded that there was a positive side to the "piling up of sanctions." In many instances, treatment was administered, community service was performed, and restitution and child support were collected. However, the overriding goal of reducing jail populations and costs went unrealized. Increased technical violations and subsequent returns to jail negated the initial diversionary impact of the programs. The use of programs as supplements to each other further confounded potential diversionary effects because programs with relatively small capacities (i.e., relative to the jail population) were simultaneously supervising the same offender clientele.

Consistent with the aims of an integrated approach, the findings of the study have implications for both theory and policy. For example, the apparent incompatibility between the interests of capital and the interests of the state—the business community supported a pro-arrest, pro-incarceration policy, while local government supported the less costly policy of releasing offenders into the community—challenges the premises of political economy. The findings also demonstrate that while strategic organizational self-preservation is an inevitable feature of the reform process, the element of chaos (e.g., the independent and unwitting actions of diverse sanctioning agents) is an equally powerful determinant of operational practices. Policy-wise, this study indicates that more programs are not necessarily better, unless community-corrections guidelines can structure their use in a way that maximizes their potential.

Inasmuch as the aforementioned example only indicates what an integrated approach can yield, an accounting of research procedure is warranted. It should be noted, however, that this procedure is not intended to be a rigidly codified evaluation design; imposing such a scheme would reinvent the wheel that lead to the problem that is the subject of this paper. To discuss the assumptions of the approach and what the approach is and is not, and to outline the principal research questions associated with the approach, is perhaps a more useful and appropriate means of articulating the procedure.

An integrated approach is grounded in two assumptions. The first assumption is that a penal reform's origins, operations, and outcomes constitute a cumulative and interrelated process and, therefore, should be studied as an integrated whole. The second assumption is that penal reform exhibits a complexity of purpose that cannot be captured through singular theoretical perspectives (see Blomberg 1995; Cohen 1985; Garland 1990). Cohen's "deposits" metaphor aptly describes these two assumptions.

Cohen (1985) employs the concept of "deposits" to demonstrate how several theoretical perspectives can be combined for better explanation of penal reform. He notes that varying perspectives (i.e., progress, organizational, ideological, professional, and political economy) are more interdependent than antithetical in the sense that the interests represented by each perspective leave behind "deposits" that are drawn upon by the interests represented by the next perspective. The concept of "deposits" (interdependence) refers not only to the need for a multiple theoretical perspective in examining penal reform origins, operations, and outcomes but also to the relationship between a reform's origins, operations, and outcomes. The forces that underly a reform's origins leave behind "deposits" that shape the operations of penal reform. The reform's operations, in turn, generate "deposits" that ultimately shape the reform's outcomes.

With these assumptions in mind, the approach begins with an examination of a reform's origins. This examination explores the political, economic, and organizational context of the jurisdiction of interest as it pertains to the development of the reform idea and the motives of the reformers. Thus, it seeks to address the theoretical questions of who are the reformers and why has the reform occurred and, ultimately, the broader theoretical question of penal reform function. In this portion of the analysis, then, an integrative approach is essentially a sociological-historical micro-study that provides an added insight into why the reform was implemented in the manner observed.

In examining the reform's operations, an integrative approach evolves into a modified process evaluation. It is modified in the sense that it does not reach the level of comprehensiveness found in a study devoted solely to process evaluation and, unlike a process evaluation, it probes the perceptions and/or ideology of the actors directly involved in the reform's operation. Thus, the internal dynamics of the reform program are explored to determine what the actual operations are and why they are organized and carried out as they are. This information, in turn, lays the proper foundation for an assessment of program outcomes (Patton 1978).

In the final stage of penal reform analysis, an integrated approach involves multi-goal evaluation (Blomberg 1984). In other words, the reform's impact is not measured in terms of officially selected outcomes exclusively. Both positive and negative unintended outcomes are considered, which enriches the broader theoretical discussion of whether there is consistency between penal reform words and deeds.

Overall, an integrated approach blends the abstract with the concrete for the purpose of identifying, explaining, and interpreting a particular program's origins, operations, and outcomes, the relationships therein, and, in effect, why some programs do or do not work. This approach is dependent upon varied and flexible methods of data collection, including documents, interviews, observation, surveys, and statistical reports. Thus, the approach is both qualitative and quantitative, with an emphasis on the former. In sum, the approach is a mosaic of integrative initiatives (e.g. integrated methodology, integrated theory, integrating theory and policy) that expands and redefines understanding of program effectiveness and punishment as a social institution more broadly.

The following set of research questions offer some final details on the procedure underlying an integrative approach. The questions provide a conceptual outline of sorts for those seeking to apply an integrated approach in the study of penal reform.

Origins

1. What has prompted the reform movement; what events have preceded and/or coincided with the development of the reform idea, and are they economic, political, social/cultural and/or organizational in nature?
2. Who are the reform actors (e.g., criminal justice, non-criminal justice individuals and agencies)?
3. What factors (e.g., economic, political, professional, philosophical, organizational) have motivated the reform actors; what are the perceptions and interests that govern their decision making?

Operations

1. What are the reform's major operational features (e.g., who are the intended client targets, who are the actual targets, what are the intended services and punishments, what services and punishments are actually being administered)?

2. What individuals/organizations (non-criminal justice, criminal justice) are directly involved in these practices?
3. What factors shape the perceptions and decisions of these individuals/organizations (e.g., ideological, professional, organizational)?
4. In what ways did the reform's origins impact the reform's implementation and operation?

Outcomes

1. What are the reform's positive intended and unintended outcomes?
2. What are the reform's negative unintended outcomes?
3. How did the various operational practices contribute to the various outcomes?

PROSPECTS FOR AN INTEGRATED APPROACH

This review has called attention to problems and voids that are hardly unique to penal reform scholarship. Calls for theoretical integration in research on crime and crime control have a long history (Elliot 1985; Jeffery 1977; Liska, Krohn, and Messner 1989), as do calls for policy relevancy (Belumstein 1992; Petersilia 1990) and calls for bridging theory and policy (Liska 1993; Sherman 1974).[3] For example, Elliot (1985) contends that explanatory powers in criminology have been embarrassingly low because of searches that look for single causes of deviancy. Petersilia (1990) has warned that criminological research has become increasingly statistically complex and, thus, increasingly removed from the needs of criminal justice policymakers. Blumstein has argued that, in light of the irrationality of the nation's drug policy, an important mission for criminologists is the "generation of knowledge that is useful in dealing with crime and the operation of the criminal justice system" (1993, p. 1). Finally, Sherman (1974) has asked whether [police] sociologists can and should answer the questions of [police] practitioners.

However, efforts to confront in one project the problems of parochial knowledge, single-factor explanations, and theory/policy disunity have been few and far between in criminological research and in penal reform research specifically.[4] The dearth of such comprehensive research efforts is not entirely surprising, as there are several interrelated barriers that may well prevent an integrated approach from becoming anything other than a scarcely used supplement to the prevailing narrower approaches.

For example, this type of analysis does not originate from a computer-based data set, or what Christie (1997) terms the "compelling archives." Thus, it promises to be a lengthy undertaking, the feasibility of which has been all but destroyed by the "McDonaldization" (Ritzer 1993) of academic publishing requirements;

"McDonaldization" refers to the process by which the principles of the fast-food industry are increasingly found in every facet of American society. Second, in the relentless pursuit of scientific rigor, research that emphasizes case study analysis and/or qualitative methods is often relegated to secondary status in the academic community (Athens 1997; Christie 1997). Those who engage in this line of research are often dismissed as "children of a lesser science" in certain criminological circles.

The partitioning of research skills serves as yet another impediment to an integrated approach. The loose coupling of theory and policy reflects, to a large degree, the division of labor that has evolved in the discipline and the divergent interests that have accompanied that division. For example, there are quantitative empiricists who are inclined towards highly technical program evaluations and social control theorists who are inclined towards highly conceptual evaluations of the bigger penal reform picture. It is recognized that these barriers are formidable, but they need not be impenetrable.

SUMMARY AND CONCLUSIONS

This paper has reviewed two decades of penal reform research in an attempt to resolve the unsettled paradigms that have resulted. Proposed is an integrated approach that merges the sociohistorical style of one body of penal reform research with the empirical-practical style of another body of penal reform research. The concept of "deposits" communicates the major assumptions of this approach, namely, that multiple factors shape penal reform and that penal reform is a process defined by the interconnectedness of origins, operations, and outcomes. The approach, however, does not aspire to impose or isolate specific cause-and-effect relationships in the penal reform process. Rather, it identifies relationships better characterized as somewhat linear, intermittent and varying in degrees of priority. The information gleaned from this approach can nevertheless be woven together to tell a program's story in a way that is meaningful to theory and policy. The application of an integrated approach accomplishes what Sherman (1974) proposed when he argued that "pure" research should develop more specific foci for its general theories and "applied" research should develop a broader view of the local problems it studies.

ACKNOWLEDGMENT

The author thanks Thomas Blomberg, anonymous reviewers, and Sharon Marosi for their most helpful comments.

NOTES

1. Melossi and Pavarini add that, in the postindustrial age, the prison accommodates labor market demands by absorbing surplus populations. In refining this argument, Melossi (1985) and others (Box and Hale 1982; Hale 1989) argue that the relationship between the economy and punishment is mediated by human "agency" (Greenberg 1977). Under this conception, penal actors are not viewed as collaborators in grand capitalist schemes, nor are they freed from the hegemonic influence of the economic structure. Instead, it is suggested that these relatively "autonomous" actors are moved by ideology. For example, harsher punishments are imposed in periods of economic downturn because they (i.e., judges) believe unemployment causes crime (Melossi 1985) or that the unemployed are weak and ammoral and therefore more likely to be criminal (Hale 1989). While these analyses do not speak directly to the issue of penal reform, the explication of ideology is an important link in furthering understanding of the motivations of actors involved in the reform process.

2. Feeley and Simon (1992) address the function of intermediate punishment indirectly in their "new penology" thesis. They argue that the managerial objectives of the "new penology" are due in part to a growing underclass. Thus, they contend that intermediate punishment, one of the many strategies of the "new penology," serves a purely custodial function.

3. Calls for bridging theory and policy are distinguished from calls for policy relevancy as theory can easily be disgarded in the effort to conduct policy relevant research.

4. Several book projects have addressed certain elements of an integrated approach (e.g., Simon 1993; Griset 1991). However, Bullington et al.'s (1986) article-length analysis of the success of Massachussetts' deinstitutionalization policy best approximates the application of a fully integrated approach. The authors examine the social context of juvenile policy at three points in time, namely, "before the era of reform," "during the era of reform," and "during the closing months of reform." This study yields the theoretically and policy relevant finding that political and organizational concensus may not be a precondition for the success of a reform when an dynamic reform leader is present. The findings also raise the questions of whether brash and risky tactics are necessary for the success of radical reform and what conditions must prevail for reforms to survive once revolutionary leaders have departed from the scene.

REFERENCES

Athens, L. 1997. *Violent Criminal Acts and Actors: Revisited.* University of Illinois Press.

Austin, J., and B. Krisberg. 1981. "Wider, Stronger, and Different Nets: The Dialectics of Criminal Justice Reform." *Journal of Research in Crime and Delinquency* 18: 165-196.

Baird, C., and D. Wagner. 1990. "Measuring Diversion: The Florida Community Control Program." *Crime and Delinquency* 36(1): 112-125.

Blomberg, T. 1977 "Diversion and Accelerated Social Control." *The Journal of Criminal Law and Criminology* 68(2): 274-282.

Blomberg, T. 1984. *Juvenile Court and Community Corrections.* Lanham, MD: University Press of America, Inc.

Blomberg, T. 1995. "Beyond Metaphors: Penal Reform as Net-Widening." Pp.45-61 in *Punishment and Social Control,* edited by T.G. Blomberg and S. Cohen. New York: Aldine De Gruyter.

Blomberg, T., W. Bales, and K. Reed. 1993. "Intermediate Punishment: Redistributing or Extending Social Control?" *Crime, Law, and Social Change* 19(2): 187-201.

Blomberg, T., and K. Lucken. 1994. "Stacking the Deck by Piling Up Sanctions: Is Intermediate Punishment Destined to Fail?" *Howard Journal* 33(1): 62-80.

Blumstein, A. 1992. "Making Rationality Relevant." *Criminology* 31(1): 1-16.

Box, S., and C. Hale. 1982. "Economic Crisis and the Rising Prison Population in England and Wales." *Crime and Social Justice* 17(1): 20-35.

Bullington, B., J. Sprowls, D. Katkin, and H. Lowell. 1986. "The Politics of Policy: Deinstitutionalization in Massachussetts 1970- 1985." *Law and Policy* 8(4): 507-524.

Byrne, J.M., and A. Pattavina. 1992. "The Effectiveness Issue: Assessing What Works in the Adult Community Corrections System." Pp. 281-303 in *Smart Sentencing*, edited by J.M. Byrne, A.J. Lurigio, and J. Petersilia. Newbury Park, CA: Sage.

Christie, N. 1997. "Four Blocks Against Insight: Notes on the Oversocialization of Criminologists." *Theoretical Criminology* 1(1): 13-23.

Cohen, A. 1955. *Delinquent Boys*. New York: Free Press.

Cohen, S. 1985. *Visions of Social Control*. Cambridge, UK: Polity Press.

Duff, A., and D. Garland. 1994. "Introduction: Thinking About Punishment." Pp. 1-43 in *A Reader on Punishment*, edited by A. Duff and D. Garland. Oxford, UK: Oxford University Press.

Elliot, D.S. 1985. "The Assumption that Theories Can Be Combined with Increased Explanatory Power: Theoretical Integrations." Pp. 123-149 in *Theoretical Methods in Criminology*, edited by R.F. Meir. Beverly Hills, CA: Sage.

Erwin, B.S. 1986. "Turning Up the Heat on Probation in Georgia." *Federal Probation* 2(1): 17-24.

Erwin, B.S. 1990. "Old anEd New Tools for the Modern Probation Officer." *Crime and Delinquency* 36(1): 61-74.

Feeley, M., and J. Simon. 1992. "The New Penology: Notes on the Emerging Strategy of Corrections and Its Implications." *Criminology* 30(4): 449-474.

Forst, M.L. 1978. *Civil Commitment and Social Control*. Lexington, MA: Lexington Books.

Foucault, M. 1977. *Discipline and Punish*. New York: Vintage Books.

Garland, D. 1990. *Punishment and Modern Society: A Study in Social Theory*. Oxford, UK: Clarendon Press.

Greenberg, D. 1977. "The Dynamics of Oscillatory Punishment Processes." *The Journal of Criminal Law and Criminology* 68(4): 643-651.

Griset, P. 1991. *Determinate Sentencing: The Promise and the Reality of Retributive Justice*. Albany, NY: State University of New York Press.

Hale, C. 1989. "Economy, Punishment and Imprisonment." *Contemporary Crises* 13(3): 327-350.

Howe, A. 1994. *Punish and Critique*. London, UK: Routledge Press.

Hudson, B.A. 1996. *Understanding Justice*. Buckingham, UK: Open University Press.

Ignatieff, M. 1978. *A Just Measure of Pain: The Penitentiary in the Industrial Revolution 1750- 1850*. London: MacMillan Press.

Jeffery, C.R. 1977. *Crime Prevention Through Environmental Design*. Beverly Hills, CA: Sage.

Latessa, E.J. 1987. The Effectiveness of Intensive Supervision with High Risk Probationers. Pp. 99- 12 in *Intermediate Punishments: Intensive Supervision, Home Confinement, and Electronic Surveillance*, edited by B.R. McCarthy. Monsey, NY: Criminal Justice Press.

Lemert, E. 1993. "Visions of Social Control: Probation Considered." *Crime and Delinquency* 39(4): 447-461.

Lilly, J.R., R.A. Ball, and J. Wright. 1987. "Home Incarceration with Electronic Monitoring in Kenton County, Kentucky: An Evaluation." Pp. 189-203 in *Intermediate Punishments: Intensive Supervision, Home Confinement, and Electronic Surveillance*, edited by B.R. McCarthy. Monsey, NY: Criminal Justice Press.

Liska, A. 1993. "A Review of Confronting Drunk Driving: Social Policy for Saving Lives by H. Lawrence Ross." *American Journal of Sociology* 99(4): 556-557.

Liska, A.E., M.D. Krohn, and S.F. Messner. 1989. "Strategies and Requisites for Theoretical Integration in the Study of Crime and Deviance." Pp. 1-19 in *Theoretical Integration in the Study of Deviance and Crime: Problems and Prospects*, edited by A.E. Liska, M.D. Krohn, and S.F. Messner. Albany, NY: State University of New York Press.

Lucken, K. 1997 "Dynamics of Penal Reform." *Crime, Law, and Social Change* 26(4): 367-384.

Lurigio, A.J., and J. Petersilia. 1992. "The Emergence of Intensive Probation Supervision Programs in the United States." Pp. 3-17 in *Smart Sentencing*, edited by J.M. Byrne, A.J. Lurigio, and J. Petersilia. Newbury Park, CA: Sage.

MacKenzie, D.L., and D.G. Parent. 1992. "Boot Camp Prisons for Young Offenders." Pp. 103-119 in *Smart Sentencing*, edited by J.M. Byrne, A.J. Lurigio, and J. Petersilia. Newbury Park, CA: Sage.

Matthews, R. 1987. "Decarceration and Social Control: Fantasies and Realities." *International Journal of the Sociology of Law* 15(1): 39-60.

McMahon, M. 1990. "Net-Widening: Vagaries in the Use of a Concept. *British Journal of Criminology* 30(2): 121-149.

Melossi, D. 1985. "Punishment and Social Action: Changing Vocabularies of Punitive Motive Within a Political Business Cycle." *Current Perspectives in Social Theory* 6(2): 169-197.

Melossi, D., and M. Pavarini. 1981. *The Prison and the Factory.* Totowa, NJ: Barnes & Noble Books.

O'Connor, J. 1970. "Some Contradictions of Advanced U.S. Capitalism." *Social Theory and Practice* 1(1): 1-11.

Patton, M.Q. 1978. *Utilization-Focused Evaluation.* Beverly Hills, CA: Sage.

Pearson, F.S., and A.G. Harper. 1990. "New Jersey's Intensive Supervision Program." *Crime and Delinquency* 36(1): 75-86.

Petersilia, J. 1987. "Georgia's Intensive Probation: Will the Model Work Elsewhere?" Pp. 15-30 in *Intermediate Punishments: Intensive Supervision, Home Confinement and Electronic Surveillance,* edited by B.R. McCarthy. Monsey, NY: Criminal Justice Press.

Petersilia, J. 1990. "Policy Relevance and the Future of Criminology." *Criminology* 29(1): 1-15.

Petersilia, J., and S. Turner. 1990 "Comparing Intensive and Regular Supervision for High-Risk Probationers: Early Results From an Experiment in California." *Crime and Delinquency* 36(1): 87-111.

Petersilia, J., and S. Turner. 1993. "Intensive Probation and Parole." in *Crime and Justice: A Review of Research,* Vol. 17., edited by M. Tonry. Chicago, IL: University of Chicago Press.

Petersilia, J., S. Turner, and E.P. Deschenes. 1992. "Intensive Supervision Probation for Drug Offenders." Pp. 18-37 in *Smart Sentencing*, edited by J.M. Byrne, A.J. Lurigio, and J. Petersilia. Newbury Park, CA: Sage.

Pisciotta, A.W. 1994. *Benevolent Repression.* New York: New York University Press.

Platt, A. 1969. *The Child Savers: The Invention of Delinquency.* Chicago, IL: The University of Chicago Press.

Ritzer, G. 1993. *The McDonaldization of Society.* Newbury Park, CA: Pine Forge Press.

Rothman, D. 1971. *The Discovery of the Asylum.* Boston, MA: Little, Brown.

Rothman, D. 1980. *Conscience and Convenience: The Asylum and its Alternatives in Progressive America.* Glenview, IL: Scott, Foresman.

Rusche, G., and O. Kirchheimer. 1939. *Punishment and Social Structure.* New York: Columbia University Press.

Schlossman, S.L. 1977. *Love and the American Delinquent: The Theory and Practice of "Progressive" Juvenile Justice, 1825-1920.* Chicago, IL: University of Chicago Press.

Scull, A. 1977. *Decarceration.* New Brunswick, NJ: Rutgers University Press.

Sherman, L. 1974. "The Sociology and the Social Reform of the American Police: 1950-1973." *Journal of Police Science and Administration* 2(3): 255-262.

Simon, J. 1993. *Poor Discipline: Parole and the Social Control of the Underclass, 1980-1990.* Chicago, IL: University of Chicago Press.

Takagi, P. 1975. "The Walnut Street Jail: A Penal Reform to Centralize the Powers of the State." *Federal Probation* 39(4): 18-26.

Taylor, I., P. Walton, and J. Young. 1973. *The New Criminology.* London: Routledge & Kegan Paul.

Tonry, M. 1990. "Stated and Latent Functions of Intensive Supervision Probation." *Crime and Delinquency* 36(1): 174-191.

SEX, GENDER, AND WORK:
THE CASE OF WOMEN JAIL OFFICERS

Mark R. Pogrebin and Eric D. Poole

ABSTRACT

This paper examines the nature of a sexualized work environment and adjustment strategies of female deputy sheriffs working in four county jails and three local adult detention centers. Semi-structured interviews were conducted with 108 women deputies. The findings suggest that women correctional officers experience various problems stemming from sexism and sexual harassment by their male co-workers. The impact of and response to these work problems are explored.

INTRODUCTION

During the past 20 years, there has been a dramatic increase in the number of women correctional officers working in the nation's jails. The employment gains that women have realized in local corrections are even more dramatic when compared with their employment in other areas of the criminal justice system. Women currently comprise a larger percentage of correctional officers working in jails

Sociology of Crime, Law, and Deviance, Volume 1, pages 105-124.

ISBN: 0-7623-0282-8

(24.2%) than in either state (18.0%) or federal (11.0%) adult correctional facilities (Maguire and Pastore 1995, pp. 91, 94). Among full-time sworn law enforcement personnel, women make up 15.4% of the deputies in sheriffs' departments (the law enforcement agencies that typically operate local jails), yet only 8.1% and 4.6% of officers in local police departments and state police agencies, respectively, are female (Maguire and Pastore 1994, pp. 51-52).

Despite women's increased nationwide presence in corrections work, the position of female jail officer is a unique form of nontraditional work for women; it is qualitatively different from other work in that violence is prevalent in the work environment and, also, the job is perceived to be a highly sex-typed male one requiring qualities of dominance, aggressiveness, and authoritativeness (Belknap 1991). Female qualities of nurturing, sensitivity, and understanding are thought by many male jail officers to be not merely unnecessary but potentially detrimental to job performance. Because female officers are expected to conform to masculine sex-typed work norms, it is likely that the integration problems faced by women entering this occupation are severe; however, little research attention has been focused on female officers working in local jails (see Kissel and Katsampes 1980; Belknap 1991).

Based on studies of women working as guards in male prisons, sexism and sexual harassment have emerged as persistent obstacles to work-force integration (Jurik 1985; Pollock 1986; Zimmer 1986; Farnworth 1992). Women correctional officers experience a hostile work environment where they endure resentment, harassment, and discrimination (Zupan 1992). The research suggests that male officers seek to maintain male dominance and subordination of female co-workers by sexualizing the prison work environment. What is lacking almost entirely from the research literature is a focus on the impact of the sexualized work environment on women jail officers. The present paper seeks to lay an initial qualitative research foundation upon which this area of concern may be addressed.

We frame our study by focusing on gender as a normative system, a pervasive network of interrelated norms and sanctions through which female and male behavior is evaluated and controlled (West and Zimmerman 1987). This conception of gender as a scheme of interpersonal evaluations is, of course, implicit in most critiques of the concepts of "femininity" and "masculinity." Guided by how workplace perceptions and practices bear a close relation to these sociocultural constructions of reality, we stress what Padavic (1991, p. 279) has described as the "re-creation of gender in the male workplace" and what Stockard and Johnson (1980, p. 10) has termed "the reproduction of male dominance in everyday interactions."

Diverse studies of the gender system have irrefutably shown how the subordination of women is sustained through their being socialized for, and restricted to, limited aspirations, options, roles, and rewards (Millett 1971; Hochschild 1973; Dworkin 1974; Laws 1979; Kosinar 1981; Jacobs 1989). The heavy significance of such factors, and of the basic learning processes and major societal institutions that produce and perpetrate them, is unquestionable. Equally important is the role of interpersonal evaluation in ordinary life situations. In particular, informal social control must be recognized as a key mechanism that backs up and enforces many of the restrictions and limitations placed on women. There are various ways, then, in which gender—as a sociocultural complex of meanings, behaviors, and assessments—is instilled and maintained. Hochschild (1973) identifies and compares four main perspectives adopted in studies of women and the gender system. One focuses on the nature of biological and psychological "sex differences"; a second emphasizes "sex roles and the norms which govern them"; a third treats "women as a minority group"; and the fourth—a "politics of caste" outlook—stresses power differentials and exploitation as a tool of control. As Hochschild notes, these alternative approaches reflect different disciplinary traditions, tend to favor different "conceptual vocabularies," and may carry different implications with respect to social change and public policy. In the present work, the first orientation ("sex differences") receives little attention. Each of the other three approaches, however, provides concepts and emphases that are useful for the analysis of women's work experiences. Our central concepts of "gender norms" has close ties to the study of "sex roles," even if our present focus on reinforcement in daily interaction departs somewhat from the more usual stress on socialization. In exploring the basic perceptions and responses through which women are devalued, the analogy to deviance labeling and stigmatization will prove valuable. Finally, power and control differentials are used as critical sensitizing concepts in examining the sexualization of the work setting in general, and sexual harassment in particular. In developing an overview of women working in jail, it is therefore unnecessary, and might even prove counter-productive, to attempt to adopt one of these orientations. The sociological penchant for identifying supposedly competing "schools" should not lead us to neglect points on which otherwise different approaches may converge or complement each other. Because the topic of women working in traditional male occupations is highly complex, to study it, we may well need a varied arsenal of sociological concepts and outlooks.

THE SEXUALIZED WORK ENVIRONMENT

Both early studies and the contemporary literature reveal that women who have entered a variety of traditionally male occupations have faced discriminatory hiring and assignment practices, resistance and opposition from male co-workers, and inadequate on-the-job training (Kanter 1977; Meyer and Lee 1978; Walshok 1981; Gruber and Bjorn 1982; O'Farrell and Harlan 1982; Gray 1984; Jacobs 1989; Swerdlow 1989). The experiences of women entering the corrections field are illustrative of these organizational obstacles and challenges to changing occupational norms in a work setting undergoing integration (Bowersox 1981; Crouch and Alpert 1982; Petersen 1982; Jurik and Halembra 1984; Jurik 1985; Zimmer

1986, 1987; Zupan 1986). To understand the persistence of an organizational climate of resentment, skepticism, and hostility toward women working in corrections, we must first examine the nature of the occupational norms that are at stake.

Occupational norms have traditionally been linked to work segregation by sex (Coser and Rokoff 1971; Laws 1979; Stockard and Johnson 1980; Jacobs 1989). For the most part, the sex typing of specific jobs is arbitrary and follows one basic rule: men and women are different and should be doing different things. Such stereotypical thinking has long sustained the stigmatization of those who violate such norms of occupational segregation, thus reinforcing sex-role typing in the workplace. Sex-role stereotypes function to keep women in ancillary and supportive roles rather than in positions of independence, authority, and leadership (Safilios-Rothschild 1979). A consequence for women who challenge these sex-role stereotypes is the negative evaluation of their skills, capabilities, and competence.

Negative reactions to or sanctioning of occupational "deviants" constitutes a powerful social control mechanism in maintaining a polarized male and female work force (Laws 1979; Schur 1984). Particularly when women enter what have traditionally been viewed as ultra-masculine occupations, intense reactions are expected to occur. Several common responses are likely to be found in such situations of female occupational deviance (Schur 1979). Consciousness of the deviant's femaleness will be heightened. Consciousness of the female's deviance also will be high, and she will be devalued, restricted, and otherwise punished for it. Finally, male workers may convince themselves that a woman who commits such occupational deviance deserves whatever she gets. Women come to be viewed as "fair game" for whatever abuses—verbal or physical, sexual or otherwise—male co-workers decide to dispense. In such a work situation, then, a specific imputation of deviance to the woman is used to rationalize diverse forms of male deviance directed toward her (Schur 1984). This rationalization suggests that harassment may sometimes implicitly constitute punishment for women's perceived violation of specific gender norms.

Zimmer (1986, p. 202) argues that for women corrections officers, the effect of tokenism (i.e., being in the numerical minority) is "overpowered by the effects of sexism." That is, the fact that male officers believe that women are unsuited to the job of prison guard is based upon the gender differences between men and women: "Being viewed as inferior is not the same as being viewed as different" (Zimmer 1986, p. 203). While women in nontraditional work settings may perform the job as well as men, they tend not to be seen as being men's equals. In many situations, then, systemic sexism is primarily responsible for women's problems on the job.

Some observers contend that a generalized perception of threat to male power and control on the part of male workers lies behind most harassment in the workplace (Erez and Tontodonato 1992). It is important, however, to keep in mind that something besides occupational power and control is involved in the harassment phenomenon. As MacKinnon (1979, p. 162) notes:

> The sense that emerges from incidents of sexual harassment is . . . [that men] want to know that they can go this far this way any time they wish and get away with it. . . . The practice seems an extension of their desire and belief that the woman is there for them, however they may choose to define that.

Harassment functions to sustain both male workplace power and male power to treat women as sexual objects. Workplace harassment, then, is not merely a result of women's vulnerability as tokens or as violators of occupational norms (Zimmer 1988). On the contrary, it also reflects the socialized and reinforced tendency of male co-workers to view women primarily as visual sexual objects (MacKinnon 1979). From this standpoint, harassment of women workers has as much to do with the daily harassment they experience in many other contexts as it has to do with the specific features of women's work situations.

The sexualized work environment embodies the treatment of women as objects and a denial of personal autonomy (Farley 1978). According to MacKinnon (1982, p. 541), "Sexual objectification is the primary process of the subjection of women." This process is thus central to perceptions of female violations of occupational norms and gender roles, as individual women are submitted to standardized and stereotype-laden categorizations and responses. In this respect, the sexualized work environment is the linchpin of occupational (and economic) inequality (Martin 1989). The research presented here seeks to explore the dimensions of the sexualized jail setting that women corrections officers face and to understand the significance of gender in their work experiences.

METHOD

Four county jails and three adult detention centers located in four counties in the Denver metropolitan area were selected for the present study. These facilities were managed and staffed by personnel from four sheriffs' departments. Utilizing personnel rosters of deputy sheriffs provided by the respective facilities, we drew a 50% systematic random sample ($n = 135$) of all female officers from each institution.[1] We contacted sampled officers individually in order to inform them of the purpose of the study, request their participation, and obtain informed consent. A total of 119 women agreed to participate, and interview times were then scheduled. Because of conflicts related to vacation, sick leave, work assignment, transfer, and so forth, interviews with 11 women could not be conducted. Thus, the present study was based on interview data from 108 women deputies. Their ages ranged from 24 to 51 (median = 37), and their length of experience at their present facility ranged from one to 15 years (median = 5).

Interviews were conducted at the respective facilities in private conference rooms, library carrels, or visitation rooms during off hours. Each interview lasted approximately 90 minutes and was tape recorded with the subject's consent. A semi-structured interview format was used, which relied on sequential probes to pursue leads provided by subjects. This allowed the deputies to identify and elaborate on important domains they perceived to characterize their experiences in jail work, rather than the researchers eliciting responses to structured questions.

The interview tapes were transcribed for qualitative data analysis, which involved a search for general relationships among categories of observations. Employing grounded theory techniques similar to those suggested by Glaser and Strauss (1967), we categorized the data into conceptual domains of jail work experiences as identified by the women deputies, as follows: paternalism, exclusion, work stress, and career prospects.

We should note that in all seven facilities, women officers were assigned to supervise both male and female inmates. The duties of jail deputies were the same for both male and female officers. This is an important occupational issue because many jails in this nation do not permit women officers to work in male inmate housing units, which results in unequal opportunities for women to advance within the organizations.

FINDINGS

Paternalism

According to Belknap (1991), the conflict between gender-role norms and occupational-role norms in jail work poses unique obstacles for female officers. The traditional male attitude about the inherent masculine nature of the job of jail guard makes the prospect of a female co-worker particularly offensive to some men officers. For example, corrections officers associate masculinity with physical ability and view the use of force as a defining feature of the job (Belknap 1991). Jurik (1985) reports that male officers believe that women are incapable of exercising sufficient physical force to perform the social control tasks required to control incorrigible inmates; moreover, women are often seen as less reliable in back-up or cover roles when handling violent encounters with inmates. Implicit trust and reliance that an officer will come to another's aid and use any means necessary to protect a peer's life are vital components of the work expectations among corrections officers. Male staff are fearful that the presumed physical limitations of women will place officers at greater risk and make the environment potentially more threatening and dangerous because of the inmates' perception of diminished staff ability to maintain control.

Zimmer (1986) reports that female officers are afforded few opportunities to build skills or gain confidence in controlling prisoners in threatening situations. Since women are perceived as weak, indecisive, emotional, and timid, male officers tend to take charge in physical encounters between women deputies and inmates. This action, although necessary when aiding a fellow officer as back-up, reinforces male feelings of physical superiority over women and diminishes the status of female officers. One woman officer describes her experience:

> I've been on many codes [officer back-up] when there is a physical altercation going on and male officers have run in with me and I'm shoved aside so the guys can get in on the fight. . . . I don't know if it's ego. Some of it's patronizing, some protective—"We've got to take care of the little women."

The attitude that female officers need protection from aggressive inmates is also shared by supervisory staff. Instead of developing policy which is inclusive of women in these dangerous encounters, supervisory personnel tend to reinforce the stereotype of women's heightened vulnerability. Two deputies illustrate this problem:

> We had a fight in the girls' pod day room, and there was all this concern all of a sudden that we can't have two female officers in the pod. . . . It's just not safe. The male supervisors think we can't handle it.

> [Male supervisors] don't think we can rough it up like the male officers do—that we can't take it like the men, that we are more likely to get injured or something. They don't even want to give us a chance to prove ourselves.

If women corrections officers are not afforded the opportunity to resolve inmate physical altercations, they will be restricted in their repertoire of social control techniques. To the extent that supervisory personnel reinforce this subordinate position, women officers will have limited opportunities to demonstrate their physical abilities and gain experience and confidence in the skilled use of force. Such paternalistic treatment thus serves to undermine the authority of women officers and calls in question their ability to perform their job:

> A male deputy . . . in front of some inmates . . . put his arm around me and said, "Dear, I'm going to go to lunch. Can you handle this?"

The paternalistic treatment of women is in itself a denial of their basic role identity as agents of security and control. The notion that women officers cannot take care of themselves subjugates them in their work relations with men, as well as imputing diminished capacities in their routine job performance. In her participant observer role as a coal handler in a power plant, Padavic (1991, p. 286) reports that paternalistic treatment made her "unsure of [her] abilities, afraid of undertaking something new, doing it wrong, and thereby confirming a stereotype." Millett (1971, p. 37) further notes that while paternalism is tauted as "a palliative to the injustice of women's social position, chivalry is also a technique for disguising it."

The irony of the self-fulfilling prophecy that operates in the jail setting is twofold. First, women officers who are subjected to paternalistic protection and control are not given the opportunity to develop or prove their physical skills, which in turn tautologically confirms the male co-workers' stereotypes. Second, when women officers are treated as marginal employees who are perceived in need of protection, they may experience heightened anxiety, exhibit less self-confidence, and even react in inappropriate or unsatisfactory ways. Thus, the circle is complete—paternalistic actions serve to foster the stereotypical behavior that in turn confirms the original expectations.

Exclusion

Pollock (1986) notes that the guard subculture is an important component of work socialization, especially in regard to handling inmates. Yet, male officers tend to adhere to a cult of masculinity that serves to isolate women co-workers as outsiders (Belknap 1991). Excluding women staff from the informal organizational network of male deputies often forces the women to learn much of the job on their own. As a result of this purposive exclusion, women are denied occupational socialization opportunities and the sense of belonging associated with collegial relations. Because much of the job training is done on an informal basis as situations arise, the isolation of female officers undermines their ability to learn the particulars and peculiarities of the job from experienced male colleagues.

Zimmer (1986) notes that female officers are viewed by many of their male peers as inferior and are therefore denied entree to the officer subculture. One deputy describes her experience of exclusion from informal work networks:

> The male officers go out for drinks after work. Nobody ever bothers to tell me until later on and I find out just in conversation.... I once asked a male deputy to let me know when the shift goes out and he said that he knows that some of the men bother me, so he didn't ask me along.

The social exclusion of women deputies makes them easy targets for jocular aggression and derogatory nicknames; moreover, male work group solidarity may be enhanced by directing humor at female officers. This "laughter of inclusion" (Dupreel 1928) affirms the gender distinctions and relative male superiority (Davies 1982). Innuendo, insinuation, and character assassination are effective strategies in maintaining social distance and social boundaries between the male in-group and the female out-group. As one deputy notes:

> You're always mindful of your position here. You're at work doing your job, but you always feel somehow you don't really belong here.

In short, women officers are often ostracized and belittled by their male co-workers. The male officers view women with a mixture of hostility and resentment, treating them with disdain or simply ignoring them (Jurik 1985; Zimmer 1986; Van Voorhis et al. 1991).

According to Millett (1971), men have a vested interest in sustaining conventional sexual distinctions in role relationships, which reflect a recognition and acceptance of gender-based status and power differentials. Here we can see a link between gender identity and work role dynamics. Gender norms and work relationships are concerned with maintaining boundaries—moral, social, and psychological. Imputed male work superiority and dominance require female devaluation and subordination. Thus, Dworkin (1974, p. 44) asserts: "The truth of it is that he is powerful . . . when contrasted with her."

Sustaining male workplace superiority dictates that women be isolated so that they cannot compete with males. In this way, the strength of women's efforts to compete determines the force required by men to limit or restrict these attempts. Change on one side of the equation invariably affects the other side as well. It is the perception of a threat, regardless of whether that perception is well founded, that constitutes a central basis for resistance to change and triggers the systematic devaluation of women workers (Kanter 1977).

When male workers' conceptions of their masculinity are closely linked to the nature and conditions of their work (particularly in what have traditionally been viewed as ultra-masculine occupations, such as coal mining, steel manufacturing, firefighting, corrections, etc.), they are especially likely to feel threatened by female job entrants and to resort to more overt subjugation (Meyer and Lee 1978; Walshok 1981; Gray 1984; Swerdlow 1989). Of course, if women are cowed into lowering their aspirations or limiting their efforts, it may not matter whether this happens because their workplace threats to men are real or imagined. Either way, and however indirectly, the overall subjugation of females would again be taking its toll in lost work contributions and occupational achievements.

Work Stress

Fox and Hesse-Biber (1984) suggest that certain forms of workplace harassment and abuse are so commonly tolerated that many women have come to regard such activity as inevitable and as virtually a condition of employment. These researchers report that women are reluctant to try to do anything about harassment out of fear of reprisals that may include being fired, demoted, passed over for promotion or a raise, transferred to an undesirable job, or given a poor performance evaluation. In hopes of protecting their job security, female officers often accept and endure the harassment as part of the work environment. Such stressful work conditions often produce feelings of anger, irritability, fear, anxiety, powerlessness, and depression (see Erez and Tontodonato 1992; Morash and Haar 1995). Two women deputies described the types of emotional problems they have had to face:

> I became something of a zombie. I was emotionally numb. I didn't care about anything or anyone and as a result I was very lonely and isolated. Even at parties or at other social occasions I just didn't feel comfortable. . . . People like to talk about work, tell stories, you know. But I couldn't bring myself to talk about what I did at work.

I had trouble sleeping and my home life suffered a lot. . . . I was hurting a lot and pulled back from my own husband. He didn't know what was wrong and I couldn't tell him about it or even explain it myself.

Research in law enforcement agencies has shown that women and minority officers are especially vulnerable to the psychological and physiological disorders associated with sustained exposure to job-related stress (Johnson 1991; Bartol et al. 1992). For example, Wexler and Logan's (1983, p. 53) study of the sources of stress among women officers in a large metropolitan police department indicated that their greatest obstacle was in demonstrating that they could be effective officers without compromising their femininity:

The most significant stressors seem to be ones in which others were denying them as officers, as women, or both. It is psychologically a very threatening and uncomfortable situation when one's self-perception is substantially different from the perception of others. This is particularly the case when such fundamental identities are at stake as one's gender and profession.

Individuals who feel or know they are deemed marginal employees experience anxiety and are more sensitive about their job performance, often assuming a defensive posture, attempting to overcompensate to prove others wrong in their attitudes, or otherwise reacting in ways that may be perceived as inappropriate or undesirable (Timmins and Hainsworth 1989; Wright and Saylor 1991). Two deputies relate their reactions:

I found that I would lose my temper over the littlest of things. . . . Stupid little things would happen and I would start crying.

I just stayed mad. I became defensive. I had a big chip on my shoulder. I hated the constant abuse and kept thinking that one day I would just kill someone.

The job stress experienced by women working in jails is further exacerbated by their lack of access to the peer-group support structure of fellow male deputies. The informal work subculture often functions to reduce stress, providing individual officers a forum within which they can vent safely. Women deputies' lack of acceptance in this traditional male fraternity denies them a critical organizational coping mechanism to mitigate the impact of work-related stress (Cullen et al. 1985; Van Voorhis et al. 1991).

Female officers sometimes attempt to deal with their male co-workers by adopting a "give-and-take" approach, a sort of verbal jousting. This tactic, however, is risky, as shown by two women deputies:

Bantering back and forth with the men takes a lot of stress out of the situation and kind of neutralizes the harassment we experience. But once it goes beyond or crosses the line, there seems to be no course of action for female officers.

I was kidding with a couple of guys out in the parking lot about my pathetic love life and we were talking about going out to get a drink . . . when out of the blue one of them grabbed my

> head, pulled me up to his face, and stuck his tongue in my mouth. I was shocked and disgusted—just humiliated by that.

Such inability on the part of female deputies to engage in verbal horseplay on an equal footing with male co-workers reflects their lack of acceptance in the work subculture. Pogrebin and Poole (1988, p. 184) observe, "Joking relations among peers generate feelings of implicit understanding and camaraderie, thus strengthening group norms and bonds." The rub is that women deputies are not accepted as "peers" in the jail work setting; thus, women may find that their attempts to act like "one of the boys" via joking relations are met with "punitive" responses from male co-workers (Seckman and Couch 1989).

Career Prospects

Women in corrections routinely experience derision, hostility, and exclusion from male supervisors and co-workers. Their attitudes toward job commitment and aspirations to advance in the profession are adversely affected by such treatment (Belknap 1991). Chapman et al. (1983) report that female corrections officers perceive unequal opportunities and unequal treatment in promotion. Poole and Pogrebin (1988) uncover a similar perception among women police officers; specifically, after only three years on the job, policewomen view their chances of ever being promoted as greatly diminished. A veteran officer with many years of working in the patrol side of the sheriff's department tells of her disappointment in not having an opportunity for advancement:

> I came off the street as a road deputy after 12 years on the front lines. I really did think I had the skills to come here and make some rank and do well, but that will never happen.

Jurik (1985) claims that supervisors who are biased against females working as corrections officers use performance evaluations to discourage them and keep them in subordinate positions. Since performance history is a critical criterion in advancement to supervisory ranks, women officers are viewed as less promotable. One deputy notes the nature of the inequality:

> There is one woman who really is an exceptional deputy and I like her a lot. She is really strong and stern and she knows her job very well. If she were a man, they would think she is the best deputy in the world, but because she is female they think she is a bitch. But if a male deputy would act like her, they would promote him real fast.

In those rare instances when a female officer receives a choice assignment or a promotion, she is perceived by male staff as not having earned it. For example, females are often teased about trading sexual favors for advancement:

> There are men on this job that think any time a woman gets ahead the first thing out of their mouth is: "Oh, I wonder who she's sleeping with?" . . . That's their way of dealing with women who're better than them.

Such sexist attributions of female career advancement serve to impede the acceptance of women into the work subculture, which robs them of important training, peer support, sponsorship, and access to inside information for job assignments and promotional opportunities (Zimmer 1986). If sexist attitudes and actions are allowed to prevail, women officers are unlikely to be seen as capable of becoming supervisors and joining the ranks of management.

Among those women in our sample who had attained supervisory positions ($n = 6$), there was a consensus that they now experience more hostility and resistance than they had encountered when they were line officers. These women perceive greater resentment on the part of not only the male line staff but their fellow male supervisors as well:

> I finally realized after years on the job that I've been playing gin rummy and the men have been playing poker. . . . We are socialized to be a team player and sacrifice for the good of the group. . . . Men are like sharks. Play on a team with sharks, they'll eat you alive.

> I'm under the microscope every day of the week, in everything I say and do. Many are just waiting and watching for me to slip up so they can say I can't handle it.

> [As a woman supervisor] you're out there on your own. There's no backup, no support, no "Nice job." Well, that's not entirely so. Some will say one thing to your face, then another behind your back.

Supervisory work in many respects is associated with male role characteristics such as independence, initiative, forcefulness, competitiveness, and tough-minded objectivity (Kosinar 1981). Ironically, although the image of the supervisor emphasizes masculine traits, the actual tasks that the supervisor performs are not exclusively those associated with maleness. Compassion, understanding, and interpersonal warmth, traits associated with the female role, have been shown to be just as important to supervisory success as the male qualities (Brown 1981; Pollock 1995). Moreover, women in supervisory positions in jail are a new phenomenon, representing a complete reversal of the historically all-male management staff and directly challenging the traditional conceptions of the relationship between sex and power.

Given the greater exclusiveness of supervisory positions, especially in the inner circles of upper management, the entry of women into positions of increased status and power may be seen as disruptive and detrimental to the intimacy, solidarity, and informality of the nearly all-male colleague group. And exclusion from this more powerful male management subculture again results in a lack of access to information, contacts, and informal participation, representing yet another barrier to career advancement.

Another source of resistance to women supervisors is the organizational perception that women simply do not make good managers. They are often viewed as overbearing, domineering, inflexible, and overly concerned with bureaucratic routines and details (Rosen and Jerdee 1973; Schein 1973). The women supervisors in our study did report sex differences in how they do their jobs. And these differences seem to originate in their performance as line officers. For example, Worden (1993) reports that women police officers emphasize rules and regulations more and exercise discretion less frequently than do their male counterparts. This is because the standard operating procedures define roles and evaluation criteria, establishing a level playing field with the men. Women jail officers similarly perceive "going by the book" as a safer method of operation, thus avoiding risky discretionary decision making which may lead to criticism.

> I've learned it's best to know the rules and stick to them in everything you do in here. Someone's always waiting for you to mess up . . . so it's better to have rules you can rely on to do your job. . . . Because if a female officer messes up because she wasn't following the rules, then it's made ten times worse.

And most women in our sample also believe that adhering to rules and regulations is a function of their gender socialization:

> Women pay more attention to detail, more strict abidance to the rules. I mean, the rules are the rules, that's the way we've been socialized. We follow the rules or we lose our turn. And we follow the rules well. Even if some rules don't make sense, if it's a rule, we still follow it.

Thus, it is likely that women officers who have successfully survived and advanced in the jail organization still embrace these work strategies, tending to rely on what has worked for them in the past. The consequences of employing such a work strategy in the role of manager, however, are deleterious, if not predictable, as three women supervisors observe:

> I'm firm but fair and run things by the book. For a man, that's OK. For a woman, it's just being a "bitch." . . . There's definitely a double standard here.

> I would say the male supervisors want to be liked and handle things much more loosely . . . [than I do]. They don't want to be seen as the "bad guy." So they'll delegate . . . to others so they don't get criticized. . . . I'm not here to be their buddy. I'm here to do the best job I can. So I can't "loosen up" or "take it easy" or "giv'em a break." That's not my style. Because I'll tell you right now, there's no "good ole gal" network going to back me up or cover for me if I can't do my job.

> On my last [performance evaluation] I received several negative comments about how I handle officers. . . . I was criticized for how I write them up. They think I'm too picky and that I demand too much.

Kanter (1977) argues that negative perceptions of women in supervisory positions reflect sex differences in power and influence within organizations. In particular, performance ratings by supervisors are affected by the supervisor's power and influence, and more powerful supervisors generate higher morale, tend to be less rigid and authoritarian, and are generally better liked. Powerless supervisors, on the other hand, are more likely to be controlling in their relationships with subordinates, show favoritism, and generate lower morale. Since men are more likely to be in formal positions of power and authority and to be part of the informal networks of organizational influence, differences in the perception and behavior of female supervisors are more a function of the unequal distribution of organizational power than a reflection of sex differences in managerial or personal style (South et al. 1982).

DISCUSSION

Women jail deputies find themselves in an occupational dilemma. Many male jail officers harbor negative attitudes toward competent women co-workers because they perceive women who can perform their job-related tasks satisfactorily as threatening. On the other hand, they view female officers who fail to perform the job adequately as confirming the stereotypical "unfitness" of female workers. Thus, the better officers women become, the greater their threat to the male establishment.

Several observers have noted that gender remains the defining or controlling (i.e., master) status in traditionally male occupations, with women treated first on the basis of their sex role and second on the basis of their work role (Williams 1989; Reskin and Roos 1990). Hunt (1990) argues that gender-based norms support discriminatory practices and sexual harassment in the work setting, which in turn reinforce and maintain power differentials. The sexualized work environment is intended to keep a woman subservient by making her feel unwelcome, insecure, and fearful. The strategy is to exert control through intimidation and humiliation.

The consequences of institutional sexism may be such as to discourage aspirations and restrict opportunities, or to instill fear of being maligned or punished for even trying. In short, sexism may reduce the efforts of females to demonstrate their full potential. Systematic devaluation of women's work roles easily becomes self-fulfilling and self-perpetrating. It can create and maintain conditions that minimize the need for males to confront evidence contradicting their stereotypes or to experience dissonance when they demean female coworkers (Schur 1984).

Sexual harassment represents a violation of Title VII of the U.S. Civil Rights Act, which bans sex-based discrimination (Deitch 1993). Any conduct which has the purpose or effect of substantially interfering with an individual's work performance or creating an intimidating, hostile, or offensive working environment is prohibited; moreover, employers have an affirmative duty to take "all steps necessary" to prevent such conduct and to take remedial actions when it does occur. Yet, we find a great deal of misunderstanding as to what constitutes sex-based discriminatory practices. For example, Gutek and Morasch (1982, p. 59) note that "men are more likely than women to project sexuality into ambiguous behavior between sexes at work, and to feel that such sexuality is appropriate in the work environment"; consequently, what female workers perceive as unwelcome sexual advances may be viewed by male employees as innocent flattery. Konrad and Gutek (1986) further report that males employed in male-dominated jobs are less inclined than men working in gender-integrated jobs to define their gender-based behavior toward women co-workers as sexual harassment. It appears that gender-integrated work settings foster a greater congruence of definitions of acceptable behavior between the sexes, which may serve to reduce the nature and extent of gender-based behavioral misunderstandings.

A complicating factor in effecting change in the jail setting is the social pathology of a male-dominated work culture. The occupational culture of jail work is based on the values and eccentricities of a cult of masculinity, largely exemplified in behaviors such as aggression, taunting, horseplay, and sexually related conversation and innuendo (Belknap 1991). Despite significant increases in the number of women in local corrections, the generally higher caliber (and more educated) people entering the field, better professional training, and implementation of policies to control sexual harassment and related misconduct, the long-established characteristics of the occupational culture largely remain (see Zupan 1992; Belknap 1996). Since survival in the informal organization requires adherence to the subcultural norms, women must develop appropriate adjustment or coping strategies not only in doing their jobs but also in managing their work relations with male officers. Men tend to misinterpret culturally related behaviors of women jail deputies—largely holding them to a double standard—and cannot understand why they are accused of harassment or conduct unbecoming an officer.

The sexualized work environment of the jail is thus grounded in and supported by a combination of structural factors (e.g., occupational segregation, tokenism, hierarchical power arrangements) and cultural themes and processes (e.g., occupational norms, gender-based stereotypes, status inequality) that become manifest in social interaction. The subordination of women in and at work unquestionably promotes sexual exploitation in the workplace (Millett 1971). Such exploitation, in turn, reinforces women's overall socioeconomic subordination (see MacKinnon 1979, 1982). Sex discrimination and job segregation regularly place working women under male supervision and control, heavily dependent on males for their economic security. Because of their subordinate economic and occupational situations, most women have neither autonomy nor authority in workplace relations (Kanter 1977). These consequences of the sexualized work environment thus have implications that go beyond the job itself.

The prevailing opinion of female officers in all seven facilities was that the elimination of harassment in local corrections organizations was dependent on top administrators enforcing policies against sexual harassment. Belknap (1991) asserts that the corrections work environment cannot improve until there are fundamental changes in male officers' attitudes toward their female peers. As long as sexist stereotypes are allowed to pervade the work setting, women officers will be viewed and treated as second-class workers. Lovrich and Stohr (1993) further argue that managers and supervisors in corrections need to transform the work environment into one where women officers are recognized and appreciated as valuable resources and are fully integrated into both formal and informal organizational cultures, both of which must be intolerant of sexual and gender harassment. Also, there must be a strong advocacy role adopted by jail administrators in order for female deputies to gain equal opportunities for career advancement.

In order to minimize harassing behavior in the jail setting, administrators need to invest in the career development of all employees, advance the ideals of professionalism, and establish closer linkages to line staff (Zimmer 1989; Belknap 1996). Such a work climate would help to lower the level of animosity and offensive behavior directed at women officers by male co-workers. The "affirmative duty" of jail management lies not simply in fostering a general atmosphere which will combat harassing behavior but also in implementing proactive mechanisms to monitor and prevent the conditions that give rise to such actions.

The organization of corrections work itself plays a role in producing and reinforcing workplace attitudes and behavior and, thus, the extent to which sexism and sexual harassment may be institutionally tolerated (Morton 1991). These discriminatory practices and subsequent difficulties faced by women officers can be affected significantly if the organization implements adequate administrative strategies to promote gender integration and institutionalize measures to provide equality of opportunity.

CONCLUSION

The presence of women in what has long been an exclusively male occupation creates a multitude of individual and organizational conflicts. The workplace functions as a complex occupational and organizational entity that shapes a workers' perception of self and others. The relationship between gender and organizational status reveals that those work roles assigned to women are seen as appropriate extensions of their more diffuse social role of nurturance. These arrangements can act to reflect, magnify, or distort gender differences, which then confirm prevailing stereotypes and organizational norms. This situation has culminated in male co-workers and supervisors' limited and often inaccurate appraisal of women officers' true potential and capabilities in the field.

To persist with this state of affairs is untenable because evaluating female officers on the basis of male sex-typed norms distracts from the organization's efforts to implement competency-based standards and reduces its ability to analyze work problems and formulate solutions. The jail must demonstrate a philosophical commitment to the thorough integration of women within the formal and informal organizational structure. The more barriers women face in accessing informal channels of information and conflict resolution, the more they are compelled to respond formally, with the associated implications of lesser control and power. Jail officers, whether male or female, are less likely to perform effectively if they are not perceived as exercising legitimate authority under conditions of equality.

The nature and scope of jail work continue to increase in complexity, presenting new job expectations and challenges for male and female officers alike. Given the need to adjust and respond to changing organizational demands, it becomes more critical that officers have the opportunity to hone their unique talents and utilize their special skills with greater latitude. Developing alternative or multiple work strategies would permit officers to maximize their effectiveness and accomplish tasks otherwise beyond their capacity. An important initiative in realizing such change in organizational culture is to flatten the hierarchical control mechanisms and eliminate the administrative pressures for worker uniformity that have served to reinforce and maintain traditional job stereotypes in the jail setting. Finally, Wexler and Quinn (1985) report that the number of women present in an organization is a critical mass variable in facilitating gender integrated work groups. This finding would seem to encourage more aggressive recruitment and retention of women officers, who by their sheer numbers may promote the development of an androgynous work culture where an individual officer's success is predicated on ability rather than sexual physiology.

NOTE

1. Inmate and officer distributions by sex for each facility are shown below, along with the respective sample sizes and number of study participants. Facilities labeled A-D are jails; facilities E-G are detention centers:

	Facility						
	A	*B*	*C*	*D*	*E*	*F*	*G*
Inmates							
Male	279	391	656	1739	218	475	541
Female	18	34	67	172	27	53	35
Officers							
Male	38	158	146	285	105	159	92
Female	21	26	29	81	45	27	36
50% Sample of Female Officers	11	13	15	41	23	14	18
Female Study Participants	10	10	13	30	18	12	15

REFERENCES

Bartol, C.R., G.T. Bergen, J.S. Volckens, and K. Knoras. 1992. "Women in Small-Town Policing: Job Performance and Stress." *Criminal Justice and Behavior* 19: 240-259.

Belknap, J. 1991. "Women in Conflict: An Analysis of Women Correctional Officers." *Women and Criminal Justice* 2: 89-115.

Belknap, J. 1996. *The Invisible Woman: Gender, Crime, and Justice*. Belmont, CA: Wadsworth.

Bowersox, M.S. (1981). "Women in Corrections: Competence, Competition, and the Social Responsibility Norm." *Criminal Justice and Behavior* 8: 491-499.

Brown, L.K. 1981. *The Woman Manager in the United States*. Washington, DC: Business and Professional Women's Foundation.

Chapman, J.R., E.K. Minor, P.P. Rieker, T.L. Mills, and M. Bottum. 1983. *Women Employed in Corrections*. Washington, DC: U.S. Government Printing Office.

Coser, R.L., and G. Rokoff. 1971. "Women in the Occupational World: Social Disruption and Conflict." *Social Problems* 18: 535-554.

Crouch, B.M., and G.P. Alpert. 1982. "Sex and Occupational Socialization Among Prison Guards: A Longitudinal Study."*Criminal Justice and Behavior* 9: 159-176.

Cullen, F.T., B.G. Link, N.T. Wolfe, and J. Frank. 1985. "The Social Dimensions of Correctional Officer Stress." *Criminal Justice and Behavior* 9: 159-176.

Davies, C. 1982. "Ethnic Jokes, Moral Values, and Social Boundaries." *British Journal of Sociology* 33: 383-403.

Deitch, C. 1993. "Gender, Race, and Class Politics and the Inclusion of Women in Title VII of the 1964 Civil Rights Act." *Gender and Society* 7: 183-203.

Dupreel, E. 1928. "Le Probleme Sociologique du Rise" [The Sociological Problem of Laughter]. *Revue Philosophique* 106: 213-260.

Dworkin, A. 1974. *Woman Hating*. New York: E.P. Dutton.

Erez, E., and P. Tontodonato. 1992. "Sexual Harassment in the Criminal Justice System." Pp. 227-252 in *The Changing Roles of Women in the Criminal Justice System*, edited by I.L. Moyer. Prospect Heights, IL: Waveland Press.

Farley, L. 1978. *Sexual Shakedown*. New York: McGraw Hill.

Farnworth, L. 1992. "Women Doing a Man's Job: Female Prison Officers Working in a Male Prison." *Australian and New Zealand Journal of Criminology* 25: 278-296.

Fox, M.F., and S. Hesse-Biber. (1984). *Women at Work*. Palo Alto, CA: Mayfield.

Glaser, B.G., and A.L. Strauss. 1967. *The Discovery of Grounded Theory: Strategies for Qualitative Research*. Chicago, IL: Aldine.

Gray, S. 1984. "Sharing the Shopfloor: Women and Men on the Assembly Line." *Radical America* 18: 69-88.

Gruber, J.E., and L. Bjorn. 1982. "Blue-Collar Blues: The Sexual Harassment of Women Autoworkers." *Work and Occupations* 4: 271-298.

Gutek, B.A., and B. Morasch. 1982. "Sex-Ratios, Sex-Role Spillover, and Sexual Harassment of Women at Work." *Journal of Social Issues* 38: 55-74.

Hochschild, A.R. 1973. "A Review of Sex Role Research." Pp. 249-267 in *Changing Women in a Changing Society*, edited by J. Huber. Chicago, IL: University of Chicago Press.

Hunt, J. 1990. "The Logic of Sexism Among Police." *Women and Criminal Justice* 1: 3-30.

Jacobs, J.A. 1989. *Revolving Doors: Sex Segregation and Women's Careers*. Stanford, CA: Stanford University Press.

Johnson, L. 1991. "Job Strain Among Police Officers: Gender Comparisons." *Police Studies* 14: 12-26.

Jurik, N.C. 1985. "An Officer and a Lady: Organizational Barriers to Women Working as Correctional Officers in Men's Prisons." *Social Problems* 32: 375-388.

Jurik, N.C., and G.J. Halembra. 1984. "Gender, Working Conditions, and the Job Satisfaction of Women in a Non-Traditional Occupation: Female Correctional Officers in Men's Prisons." *Sociological Quarterly* 25: 551-566.

Kanter, R.M. 1977. *Men and Women of the Corporation*. New York: Basic Books.

Kissel, P.J., and P.L. Katsampes. 1980. "The Impact of Women Corrections Officers on the Functioning of Institutions Housing Male Inmates." *Journal of Offender Counseling, Services and Rehabilitation* 4: 213-231.

Konrad, A.M., and B.A. Gutek. 1986. "Impact of Work Experiences on Attitudes Toward Sexual Harassment."*Administrative Science Quarterly* 31:422-438.

Kosinar, P. 1981. "Socialization and Self-Esteem: Women and Management." Pp. 31-41 in *Outsiders on the Inside: Women and Organizations*, edited by B.L. Forisha and B.H. Goldman. Englewood Cliffs, NJ: Prentice-Hall.

Laws, J.L. 1979. *The Second X: Sex Role and Social Role*. New York: Elsevier.

Lovrich, N.P., and M.K. Stohr. 1993. "Gender and Jail Work: Correctional Policy Implications of Perceptual Diversity in the Work Force." *Policy Studies Review* 12: 66-84.

MacKinnon, C.A. 1979. *Sexual Harassment of Working Women*. New Haven, CT: Yale University Press.

MacKinnon, C.A. 1982. "Feminism, Marxism, Method, and the State: An Agenda for Theory." *Signs* 7: 515-544.

Maguire, K., and A.L. Pastore. 1994. *Sourcebook of Criminal Justice Statistics 1993*. U.S. Department of Justice, Bureau of Justice Statistics. Washington, DC: U.S. Government Printing Office.

Maguire, K., and A.L. Pastore. 1995. *Sourcebook of Criminal Justice Statistics 1994*. U.S. Department of Justice, Bureau of Justice Statistics. Washington, DC: U.S. Government Printing Office.

Martin, S.E. 1989. "Sexual Harassment: The Link Joining Gender Stratification, Sexuality, and Women's Economic Status." Pp. 57-75 in *Women: A Feminist Perspective*, edited by J. Freeman. Mountain View, CA: Mayfield.

Meyer, H.H., and M.D. Lee. 1978. *Women in Traditionally Male Jobs: The Experiences of Ten Public Utility Companies*. U.S. Department of Labor, Employment and Training Administration. Washington, DC: U.S. Government Printing Office.

Millett, K. 1971. *Sexual Politics*. New York: Avon Books.

Morash, M., and R.N. Haar. 1995. "Gender, Workplace Problems, and Stress in Policing." *Justice Quarterly* 12: 113-140.

Morton, J.B. 1991. *Change, Challenge, and Choices: Women's Role in Modern Corrections*. Laurel, MD: American Correctional Association.

O'Farrell, B., and S. Harlan. 1982. "Craftworkers and Clerks: The Effect of Male Coworker Hostility on Women's Satisfaction with Nontraditional Jobs." *Social Problems* 29: 252-265.

Padavic, I. 1991. "The Re-Creation of Gender in a Male Workplace." *Symbolic Interaction* 14: 279-294.

Petersen, C.B. 1982. "Doing Time with the Boys: An Analysis of Women Correctional Officers in All-Male Facilities." Pp. 437-460 in *Criminal Justice and Women*, edited by B.R. Price and N. Sokoloff. New York: Clark Boardman.

Pogrebin, M.R., and E.D. Poole. 1988. "Humor in the Briefing Room: A Study of the Strategic Uses of Humor Among Police." *Journal of Contemporary Ethnography* 17: 183-210.

Pollock, J.M. 1986. *Sex and Supervision: Guarding Male and Female Inmates*. New York: Greenwood.

Pollock, J.M. 1995. "Women in Corrections: Custody and the 'Caring Ethic'." Pp. 97-116 in *Women, Law and Social Control*, edited by A.V. Merlo and J.M. Pollock. Boston, MA: Allyn and Bacon.

Poole, E.D., and M.R. Pogrebin. 1988. "Factors Affecting the Decision To Remain in Policing: A Study of Women Officers." *Journal of Police Science and Administration* 16: 49-55.

Reskin, B.F., and P.A. Roos. 1990. *Job Queues, Gender Queues: Explaining Women's Inroads Into Male Occupations*. Philadelphia, PA: Temple University Press.

Rosen, B., and T.H. Jerdee. 1973. "The Influence of Sex-Role Stereotypes on Evaluation of Male and Female Supervisory Behavior." *Journal of Applied Psychology* 57: 44-48.

Safilios-Rothschild, C. 1979. *Sex Role Stereotypes and Sex Discrimination: A Synthesis and Critique of the Literature*. U.S. Department of Health, Education, and Welfare, National Institute of Education. Washington, DC: U.S. Government Printing Office.

Schein, V.E. 1973. "The Relationship Between Sex Stereotypes and Requisite Management Characteristics." *Journal of Applied Psychology* 57: 95-100.

Schur, E.M. 1979. *Interpreting Deviance*. New York: Harper & Row.

Schur, E.M. 1984 *Labeling Women Deviant: Gender, Stigma, and Social Control*. Philadelphia, PA: Temple University Press.

Seckman, M.A., and C.J. Couch. 1989. "Jocularity, Sarcasm, and Relationships." *Journal of Contemporary Ethnography* 18: 327-344.

South, S.J., C.M. Bonjean, J. Corder, and W.T. Markham. 1982. "Sex and Power in the Federal Bureaucracy: A Comparative Analysis of Male and Female Supervisors." *Work and Occupations* 9: 233-254.

Stockard, J., and M.M. Johnson. 1980. *Sex Roles*. Englewood Cliffs, NJ: Prentice-Hall.

Swerdlow, M. 1989. "Men's Accommodations to Women Entering a Nontraditional Occupation: A Case of Rapid Transit Operatives." *Gender & Society* 3: 373-387.

Timmins, W.M., and B.E. Hainsworth. 1989. "Attracting and Retaining Females in Law Enforcement." *International Journal of Offender Therapy and Comparative Criminology* 33: 197-205.

Van Voorhis, P., F.T. Cullen, B.G. Link, and N.T. Wolfe. 1991. "The Impact of Race and Gender on Correctional Officers' Orientation to the Integrated Environment." *Journal of Research in Crime and Delinquency* 28: 472-500.

Walshok, M.L. 1981. *Blue-Collar Women: Pioneers on the Male Frontier*. New York: Anchor Books.

West, C., and D.H. Zimmerman. 1987. "Doing Gender." *Gender and Society* 1: 125-151.

Wexler, J.G., and D.D. Logan. 1983. "Sources of Stress Among Women Police Officers." *Journal of Police Science and Administration* 11: 46-53.

Wexler, J.G., and V. Quinn. 1985. "Considerations in the Training and Development of Women Sergeants." *Journal of Police Science and Administration* 13: 98-105.

Williams, C.L. 1989. *Gender Differences at Work: Women and Men in Nontraditional Occupations*. Berkeley, CA: University of California Press.

Worden, A.P. 1993. "The Attitudes of Women and Men in Policing: Testing Conventional and Contemporary Wisdom." *Criminology* 31: 203-237.

Wright, K.N., and W.G. Saylor. 1991. "Male and Female Employees' Perceptions of Prison Work: Is There a Difference?" *Justice Quarterly* 8: 505-524.

Zimmer, L.E. 1986. *Women Guarding Men*. Chicago, IL: University of Chicago Press.

Zimmer, L.E. 1987. "How Women Reshape the Prison Guard Role." *Gender and Society* 1: 415-431.

Zimmer, L.E. 1988. "Tokenism and Women in the Workplace: The Limits of Gender-Neutral Theory." *Social Problems* 35: 64-73.

Zimmer, L.E. 1989. "Solving Women's Employment Problems in Corrections: Shifting the Burden to Administrators." *Women and Criminal Justice* 1: 55-80.

Zupan, L.L. 1986. "Gender-Related Differences in Correctional Officers' Perceptions and Attitudes." *Journal of Criminal Justice* 14: 349-361.

Zupan, L.L. 1992. "The Progress of Women Correctional Officers in All-Male Prisons." Pp. 323-343 in *The Changing Roles of Women in the Criminal Justice System*, edited by I.L. Moyer. Prospect Heights, IL: Waveland Press.

PART II

THREE STUDIES IN THE SOCIOLOGY OF LAW

MANIFESTATIONS OF SOCIAL AGENCY IN THE 1994 REFORM OF OREGON'S ASSISTED SUICIDE LAW

John Dombrink and Daniel Hillyard

ABSTRACT

This paper examines how social reformers were successful in convincing a majority of voters in one American state (Oregon) to repeal their state's ban on assisted suicide in cases of competent, terminally ill adults who repeatedly ask physicians to prescribe a lethal dose of medication. This paper describes the political conduciveness of the Oregon electorate to assisted suicide reform, the mobilization of proponent and opponent campaigns, the framing of issues within the opposing campaigns, and their planning and execution of strategies and counter-strategies. The roles of public opinion, organized medicine, organized religion, and key activists and their organizational bases are described in great detail. Our analysis of the motives, intentions, deliberations, and choices of organizational and citizen activists adds to the sociolegal literature on the role of social agency in law and morality.

Sociology of Crime, Law, and Deviance, Volume 1, pages 127-154.

ISBN: 0-7623-0282-8

INTRODUCTION

In 1994, Oregon voters successfully used the ballot initiative to allow terminally ill patients to request and receive lethal medicine prescribed by their physicians so that they can end suffering by ending their lives. That achievement extended the collective definition of death with dignity well beyond what has been allowed anywhere in the world. The measure took effect in October 1997, as the Oregon Death with Dignity Act. In November 1997, a repeal effort—Measure 51—failed by a large margin. On March 25, 1998, the first legal assisted suicide in Oregon under this law was reported to have taken place. The United States Supreme Court has chosen not to review a Federal Appellate Court's upholding of the 1994 measure.

No other polity, not even The Netherlands, permits assisted suicide as a matter of law. Dutch law prohibits physician-assisted suicide, yet, through a series of legal decisions and prosecutorial and medical community guidelines, physicians who follow a number of requirements can provide voluntary euthanasia with no threat of prosecution (see Griffiths, Weyers, and Bood 1998 for a learned treatment of these developments.)

This paper traces how and why the proponents in Oregon were successful in getting voters to amend the state ban against assisted suicide, allowing physicians to prescribe a lethal dose of drugs to end the unbearable suffering of competent, terminal adults who request such medical services.

During the 1990s, social reform efforts to establish a general "right to die" contracted into efforts to legalize voluntary physician-assisted suicide for the competent, terminally ill. The ardent public interest in physician-assisted suicide began to grow in June 1990 when Janet Adkins, a Portland, Oregon woman, flew to Michigan and became the first person known to have requested a Michigan pathologist named Jack Kevorkian to help her commit suicide. The manner of Adkins's suicide—inhalation of carbon monoxide from a canister supplied by a virtual stranger in the back of a dilapidated old van parked in a remote campground, and later self-promoted by Kevorkian himself—became a worldwide story.

Despite the change from the 1970s onward in laws regulating the right to withdraw treatment and life-support (Glick 1992; Hoefler 1994), before the news of Jack Kevorkian and Janet Adkins, there was virtually no public interest in the specific issue of assisted suicide. A nationwide Gallup poll about opinions on death and dying conducted a month before Adkins's suicide is a good measure of the public's generally nonsupportive attitude toward assisted suicide: the survey did not even include questions about physician-assisted suicide. At that time, 49% of respondents agreed that terminally ill patients have a moral right to commit suicide (that number was up from 40% in 1975). Within a year, state and national polls showed that physician-assisted suicide and euthanasia were supported by 75% of adults under 35 and half of adults over 50. Many citizens' groups, professional associations, and religious organizations sought to influence the course of this fast-changing public opinion, facilitating movement of the physician-assisted suicide debate onto the political agenda.

Proponents of physician assistance in hastening death decided to bring the issue directly before voters. In Washington (1991) and California (1992), reform measures that would have legalized forms of physician-assisted suicide were ahead in early polls, but ended in defeat (Hillyard and Dombrink forthcoming). In 1994, however, reform activists in Oregon were successful in getting voters to pass the world's first law permitting physician-assisted suicide. The theme of this paper is understanding the role of human agency—in the patterns of mobilizing political action, framing issues, and planning and executing strategies and counter-strategies—in the reform of assisted suicide law in Oregon.

Some researchers studying how and why criminal law changes have focused on the social status of the deviant (Skolnick and Dombrink 1978; Lempert 1974). Others have studied opportunities for social activism, including "policy windows" in state and national politics and the activities of "moral entrepreneurs" (Kingdon 1984). Some have described specific behaviors causing moral dissonance among a populace that stimulate appeals to change a law, the indicators of this problem, and the definition of it as a social problem. Others have focused on the events that focus public attention and the policy alternatives available, as well as the ebbs and flows of the national mood, political leadership, concerns of interest groups, and public opinion (Calavita 1992; DiChiara and Galliher 1994; Gusfield 1997; Traynor and Glantz 1996). McCann (1994, 1996) adds that any adequate explanation of political action must examine the diverse deliberations, motives, choices, and intentions of reform activists.

This paper examines how the proponents and opponents of amending Oregon's assisted suicide law actually thought about their tactical efforts. It examines how they deliberated about moral dissonance, state and national politics, and public and media opinion, as well as how they reasoned in quite variable, complex, sophisticated ways. The paper relies on in-depth interviews and archival analyses of media reports, legal texts, and campaign literature, speeches, and debates. With these data, the proponent and opponent campaigns in Oregon are compared and contrasted to the prior campaigns in Washington and California. The analysis emphasizes contextual and situational factors that influenced the motivations, deliberations, choices, and actions of political subjects in each state. While others have emphasized other aspects of the process (Annas 1994; Campbell 1995), the conclusions of this paper explore how the dynamic, indeterminate, contingent, interactive processes of judgment, choice, and reasoned intentionality of people in action—that is, social agency—can matter and have influence in how and why law changes.

The paper is structured in six parts. In the first part, we review a literature on the dynamics of social agency and legal change, focusing on issues of law and morality. The second part reviews the national interest in and Oregon's conduciveness toward reform of assisted suicide law. The third part details why campaign participants were motivated to get involved in the assisted suicide debate and how their roles developed. The fourth part looks inside the deliberations of campaign proponents and opponents and reveals the dialectical nature of their tactical efforts. The fifth part narrates the campaign battle and emergence of counter-strategies. Finally, the sixth part analyzes how the interactive processes of judgment and reasoned intentionality culminated in choices that, when compared and contrasted to the prior initiative campaigns in Washington and California, appear to have influenced how and why only reformers in Oregon were successful in changing assisted suicide law.

METHODS

Between 1993 and 1994, local, regional, and national archives of major newspapers discussing the Oregon initiative were examined. Previously, the unsuccessful physician-assisted suicide initiatives in Washington in 1991 and California in 1992 were examined (Hillyard and Dombrink forthcoming). Campaign offices in Oregon were visited, and campaign and educaitonal materials, articles, newsletters, solicitations, and other movement texts were collected. Data was collected from the parties' own media collections. These media data were supplemented with scholarly commentary on the campaign participants, strategies, and tactics. Finally, 15 key campaign participants and supporters from both sides of the campaign debate in the three campaign states were interviewed face-to-face, using a semi-structered instrument. Informants were asked why reform was sought and how they became involved in the reform debate. They were asked about their roles in the campaigns and their assessments of the efficacy of various framing strategies.

LEGAL REFORM ISSUES PRESENT IN THE ASSISTED SUICIDE EXAMPLE

This paper traces how and why the proponents in Oregon were successful in getting voters to amend the state ban against assisted suicide, allowing physicians to prescribe a lethal dose of drugs to end the unbearable suffering of competent, terminal adults who request such medical services.

These human phenomena can be characterized in terms of the dynamics of social agency and legal change. One can categorize the dynamics involved in how and why laws change as: (1) identification of a social problem and appeals to solve it by changing the law; (2) attention to national mood, political leadership, interests groups, and public opinion; (3) opportunities for social activism through political pressure; (4) policy and strategic alternatives; (5) the social status of the deviant; and (6) the diverse contingent and indeterminate deliberations, choices, and intentions of reform activists.

Analyses of how and why the law changes have tended to focus on a number of concepts: conduciveness or specific behaviors causing moral dissonance among a populace that stimulates appeals to change a law (DiChiara and Galliher 1994; Bonnie and Whitebread 1974; Kaplan 1971; Musto 1973; Reagan 1997; Skolnick 1978); the relative power of constituent groups seeking legal reform (Chambliss and Seidman 1982; Chambliss and Zatz 1993); the role of social stigma (Bonnie and Whitebread 1974; Kaplan 1971; Himmelstein 1983; Schur 1980); opportunities for social activism, including "policy windows" in state and national politics (Kingdon 1984); mobilization—the events that focus public attention and the activities of "moral entrepreneurs (DiChiara and Galliher 1994)); issue framing and the social status of the deviant (Lempert 1974; Skolnick and Dombrink 1978); the reasons why groups seek legal reform—for example, increased power for the state, revenue enhancement (Skolnick 1978); concern for those harmed by criminalization (Himmelstein 1983; Kaplan 1971); disillusionment with wasted resources and unwise legal policy, as in the "war on drugs" (Bayer and Oppenheimer 1993; Currie 1993; Kleiman 1992) or the right to privacy or liberty (Herman 1994; Jenness 1993; Luker 1978; Reagan 1997; Tribe 1992; Vaid 1995); policy alternatives available (DiChiara and Galliher 1994); and strategies and counter-strategies.

Many versions of the role of interest groups on the development of criminal law—whether criminalization, decriminalization, legalization, or recriminalization—have concentrated on different variables. This includes Becker's (1963) concept of the moral entrepreneur, Duster's (1970) study of class-based moral definitions of an activity, Timberlake's (1963) explanation of the role of the rising middle class and the nascent progressive movement in temperance politics, Reinarman and Levine's (1989, 1997) examination of the production of a moral panic surrounding crack cocaine, and Bonnie and Whitebread's (1974) concentration on the racial impetus behind marijuana legislation.

Many of these studies have concentrated on the area of vice and the use of law in the area of morality. DiChiara and Galliher (1994) analyzed the people and events that led to changes in several states' marijuana laws during the 1970s (see also Galliher and Basilick 1979; Galliher and Cross 1982; Galliher, McCartney, and Baum 1974). In a study of the growth of legal gambling in Nevada, Skolnick (1978) described the destigmatization of an industry associated with illegal gambling, organized crime, and other vices. Dombrink and Thompson (1990) described the ways in which those stigmas prevented the success of campaigns for the introduction of legal gambling in other states. In areas like prostitution, analysts have explained that there has been no significant shift in legal approaches due to the limited power of prostitutes themselves (Weitzer 1991).

Steinhoff and Diamond (1977) focused on the role of the medical profession in the liberalization of abortion laws in Hawaii. Other analyses have described the role of legal reform groups, while Luker (1984) described the world views of opponent and proponent activists, and Craig and O'Brien (1993), Garrow (1994), Reagan (1997), Staggenborg (1991), Tribe (1992), and Condit (1990) described how the terminology and popular framing of abortion language accompanied legal reform and societal reevaluation of the law surrounding abortion.

Steinhoff and Diamond (1977) found, in a study of abortion law repeal in Hawaii, that it was not the efforts of pro-choice groups campaiging for change that prompted repeal of that state's abortion laws. Instead, they maintain, repeal efforts succeeded because they were proposed as a conservative issue, one which appealed to traditional values already suported by the middle class, and were promoted by high-status actors—physicians.

DiChiara and Galliher (1994) examined similar phenomena in their analysis of marijuana decriminalization, noting that demographic changes in the typical marijuana user during the 1960s and 1970s provided the key social context for the reform of marijuana laws (DiChiara and Galliher 1994, p. 44; Himmelstein 1983).

Two factors served to focus attention for a time on the legal controls rather than the drug itself: bureaucratic, law enforcement problems and moral dissonance. The arrest of affluent users and fears of parents of youthful marijuana users seemed unjust in a system of nominal sentences for large-scale dealers and selective enforcement of marijuana laws. These concerns were reinforced by a 1972 report by the National Commission on Marijuana & Drug Abuse, which disclosed evidence of difficulties in marijuana law enforcement across the United States.

DiChiara and Galliher analyzed this phenomenon in terms of Chambliss' observation that in any historical period, law is created to help resolve the existing "contradictions, conflicts, and dilemmas. . . . The most important of these dilemmas and conflicts are those that derive from the economic and political structures of the times," but that "often, resolutions of particular conflicts and dilemmas not only create further conflicts, but also spotlight other contradictions which may have been dormant," leading to further resolutions (DiChiara and Galliher 1994, p. 43). In the case of marijuana decriminalization, this dialectical process of legal and social change led away from *de jure* decriminalization toward *de facto* decriminalization, the latter being an effective means of reducing the moral dissonance inherent in the arrest of high-status individuals while still retaining the presence of criminal penalties, an ideal resolution of the additional conflict that developed as a consequence of the decriminalization laws themselves (DiChiara and Galliher 1994, p. 73).

In a study of the reform of New York state prostitution laws, Roby (1969) identified three bases for reformers' power: their expertise, their ability to muster support, and their political and financial backing. The conditions for groups' power varied from stage to stage in the reform process. Roby identified several bases for these groups obtaining power:

> 1) their awareness of the various actions taken and to be taken in the formulation or enforcement of the law; 2) their recognition of the importance of these actions to their interests; 3) their professional (especially legal) knowledge or expertise; 4) their public (scattered and unorganized) support gained through their expertise and conscious appeals to the community; 5) their political and financial support by organized groups; 6) their personal charisma; and 7) their means to informally withhold needed support or cooperation from that significant actor (Roby 1969, p. 109).

The sociolegal factors that run throughout this literature also run throughout the physician-assisted suicide reform movement: identification of a social problem and appeals to solve it by changing the law; opportunities for social activism through political pressure; policy and strategic alternatives; the social status of the deviant; and attention to national mood, political leadership, interest groups, and public opinion. The remaining sections of this paper trace manifestations of social agency in the reform of Oregon's assisted suicide law.

National and State Conduciveness

National Conduciveness

Increasingly over the past decade, legal scholars, medical professionals, public policy experts, ethicists, clergy, and the general public have grappled with the weighty and complicated issues of the ending of life in medical settings (Anspach 1993; Battin 1994; Callahan 1987, 1990, 1992, 1993; Glick 1992; Hoefler 1994; Jonsen 1990; Meisel 1992; Nuland 1994; Rothman 1991; Zussman 1992). These issues have arisen in the wake of a dramatic increase in the use of advanced diagnostic and therapeutic techniques and medical technology to prolong life in its final days (Belkin 1993; Callahan 1990). The proliferation of public interest in advance directives, following the widely anticipated decision of the Supreme Court in *Cruzan* (*Cruzan v. Director, Missouri Department of Health* (497 U.S. 261 (1990))—in which advanced directives were supported—has been one outcome of the rights consciousness of persons considering end-of-life issues (Cantor 1993).

In testimony before Congress, Dr. Kathleen Foley, Director of the Project on Death in America, summarized the factors contributing to public and professional interest in physician-assisted suicide:

> The re-emergence of advocacy groups for both physician-assisted suicide and euthanasia in the 1980's and 1990's has come from numerous factions and multiple factors. These groups include both physician advocates and public advocacy groups, including the Hemlock Society and Compassion in Dying, to name only a few. The multiple medical, social and economic factors framing this discussion include: advancements in high technological medical support systems for patients with respiratory and cardiac failure; changes in the trajectory of dying, with large numbers of patients with cancer and AIDS alive for months and years following the diagnosis of an incurable illness; the increasing age of the population; the greater emphasis on patient autonomy; a concerted policy shift from societal to individual rights; and the highly debated limitations in health care resources, particularly for patients with chronic, incurable illness (Foley 1996, p. 13).

The perception that modern medicine does little to reduce this suffering has also been a major impetus for the right-to-die movement. As Schneiderman and Jecker explained, "medical treatment has come to be viewed by many as an unleashed menace rather than as a beneficent healing process" (Schneiderman and Jecker 1995, p. 40). In addition, many physicians and legal reform advocates have contended that *de facto* legalization of assisted suicide exists now, through the procedures of "terminal sedation" and use of the morphine drip (Quill 1996; Preston 1994).

This identification of a problem with how people die has translated into opportunities for social activism through political pressure. But since suicide has traditionally been viewed as a deviant act, and assisted suicide a crime, much of the debate has centered on the rights of terminally ill persons vis-à-vis society in general.

Because it is bad politics and constitutionally suspect to distinguish a person's right to life by his/her health condition, efforts to change law and social policy governing the rights of the person who seeks physician-assisted suicide have focused on the concept of individual autonomy (Battin 1994; Dombrink forthcoming; Dworkin 1993). While individual autonomy has swayed many as an important principle; nevertheless, others fear that certain populations—such as the aged (Logue 1993), the poor, the disabled, and the uninsured—may be too vulnerable to the economic and social pressures that abound in the process of life-and-death decision making. Some analysts, for example, are skeptical of reform efforts because of the conflict of interest between profit seeking by insurance companies, hospitals, and other interests, and a desire to promote various changes in end-of-life policies, especially changes that may not recognize or honor the rights of patients. Additionally, there is suspicion that physician paternalism and power may actually dominate individual autonomy, which has led some skeptics to cast the issue of physician-assisted suicide as a fight for power in a competition between physicians and patients. Rothman (1991), for example, has characterized the expansion of rights as flowing from a series of changes in the relationships between patients and physicians over the last several decades. In this framework, the notion of "patients' rights," which have expanded in many areas (Macklin 1993), characterizes the rights consciousness that has developed around medical decision making, as end-of-life decisions have become more complex and imposing in the wake of technological developments.

In terms of identifying the policy alternatives available, the deep divisions within the physician community, health industry, and national and local medical associations have been important. In the various campaigns and court cases, doctors and medical associations have lined up almost evenly on opposite sides of the issue. Some medical groups and individual physicians have tried to draw interest away from assisted suicide, calling for better training in pain management and increased concentration on caring, not curing. All this interest and debate transpires in an area in which key legal-social-medical terms are vague and still changing, mostly because terminal prognoses are highly uncertain. Several studies from medicine and social science (Capron 1994; Zussman 1992) have observed that certainty is elusive in the context of resuscitation and other decisions to treat or not to treat, a factor which necessarily prevents easy application of any legal rules in this area.

State Conduciveness

Magleby describes Oregon (as well as California and Washington) as an "initiative prone" state (Magleby 1994, p. 232). Not only was Oregon the first state to adopt an initiative process, but citizen law-making has often been used in grand social movements. For example, Oregon is one of four states that adopted women's suffrage by initiative, Oregon was one of the early states to decriminalize marijuana possession and use (though it later recriminalized them), and it has passed a umber of municipal laws protecting gays and lesbians (and defeated two anti-gay statewide measures).

As indicated by this representative history, many Oregon citizens view themselves as social progressives. Yet, they do not feel that freedom is derived from government; in fact, many view centralized government as the bane of individual liberty. However, there is a solid sense of state sovereignty when "Oregonians" feel themselves pressured by "outside" political pressures.

Oregonians also disdain religious pressure. Says Mary Jo Tully, a religious educator who serves as chancellor for the Archdiocese of Portland in Oregon, "This diocese does not have the resources of the larger and more Catholic archdioceses." In fact Catholics, although the largest religious group, are only about 12% of the population. Overall, Oregon is 62% unchurched.

Hence, Oregon is a unique state, both in terms of the long history of Oregon citizens using the initiative power as a tool of legal and social change and in terms of Oregon citizens' defiance toward both religious activism within the state and political pressure from outside the state. These factors make the state seem generally conducive to political change. Moreover, its recent history, with progressive changes in the rights of the dying and the funding of health care, made the state seem specially conducive to changing the laws governing hastening the deaths of terminally ill patients.

Starting with Oregon's early codification of "living will" legislation, Oregon law increasingly reflected a right of consumers to give voice to their end-of-life values through effective legal planning. The state already had a detailed legal framework for using advance directives and making decisions on behalf of incapable patients who lacked advance directives. In addition, the issue of rationing the state's money for Medicare patients, which had raised ethical concerns similar to those in the assisted suicide debate, become a topic of public discussion in the late 1980s and early 1990s (Weiner 1992). In Oregon, data were gathered from the general population by an organization examining health decisions, to measure the relative importance of health outcomes. Individual values were assessed using a quality-of-well-being scale in a telephone survey of 1,000 Oregon residents. Additionally, views oncommunity values were solicited from 1,048 citizens who participated in small group discussions at 47 community meetings held in all but two counties throughout the state. Participants were asked to prioritize nine categories of health services, to identify and discuss the values underlying their priorities, and to identify key shared values about health care. The assessment of community values on controversial health care issues was also a key factor in mobilizing public interest in the physician-assisted suicide debate in Oregon.

By 1994, thanks in part to continued interest in Jack Kevorkian, people's understanding of the issues surrounding death and dying went beyond the level of public knowledge during the earlier campaigns in Washington and California. Three things happened: (1) communities around the state were joined by satellite for a public debate on the merits of physician-assisted suicide; (2) a small group of prominent citizens (including the parents of Janet Adkins) started an organization called Oregon Death with Dignity; and (3) a campaign to get the issue of physician-assisted suicide on the Oregon ballot was mobilized.

Mobilizing a Voter Initiative Campaign

Our informants—all key political participants—described instrumental activities, structural pressures, and expressive activities in roughly three stages of the initiative process: defining a need, framing the discourse for debate, and explaining the outcome.

Building a Coalition and Achieving Consensus

The chief petitioners for Measure 16 were Barbara Coombs Lee, a nurse and attorney, and Dr. Peter Goodwin, a physician and university professor. Each had excellent community and professional standing with many years of experience and service in health care. Together, they sought to build a coalition of people with professional and community integrity and reputations. Their goal was to secure voter confidence that the coalition truly aimed to achieve what was best for patients and physicians in terms of what could actually be accomplished by changing the law (Duncan 1996; Goodwin 1996; Stutsman 1996).

Barbara Coombs Lee and Dr. Goodwin both became involved in euthanasia reform on account of their personal experiences in caring for dying patients. Each felt that many physicians have no penchant for, and that some are even intransigent about, becoming intimate with their patients, especially with regard to helping them die. Yet, according to Dr. Goodwin, this is not the fault of physicians, for nothing in their training teaches them how to help dying patients die.

> Traditionally, patients were generally given very high doses of morphine and left to die by the inch. The family was left waiting somewhere and in most cases was not even informed that the patient was officially dying. Physicians were trained that it is harmful to give family the bad news until it is over. These medical practices are deplorable (Goodwin 1996).

Dr. Goodwin's own life was profoundly affected the first time a patient asked him for assistance with dying. "It felt as if my blood froze," he said. "I realized that with all my technical knowledge about diagnosing and treating, I knew nothing about helping people die. And there was nowhere to turn—not to my colleagues, my association, the literature. There was literally no guidance anywhere" (Goodwin 1996). So he joined the Hemlock Society and served as a board director, waiting for an opportunity like Measure 16 to come along.

When interest in a ballot initiative finally did come along in 1993, reformers started without a law in mind, believing instead that they should first learn what people actually wanted. To gain that knowledge, leaders of the newly formed organization "Oregon Right to Die" organized a forum of physicians, nurses, hospice workers, and pharmacists, as well as terminal patients, their families, and people who had watched loved ones suffer protracted deaths or botched suicides. The goal was to get a bare view of the problems surrounding the care of the dying and to develop possible options that could realistically work. The consensus was achieved without regard to the opposition. For example, Dr. Goodwin stresses that while omitting injections from the consensus and subsequent legislation had a very favorable political impact, that is not why they were omitted. "They were omitted because doctors overwhelmingly felt like they could not and would not provide them, and patients expressed very little interest in having them available" (Goodwin 1996).

Crafting a Law

Barbara Coombs Lee and Dr. Goodwin teamed up with Eli Stutsman, a highly skilled attorney and campaign strategist, for help with crafting a law and running the campaign. The law would allow a patient with six months to live to ask a doctor to prescribe a lethal dose of drugs to end unbearable suffering. At least two doctors would have to first agree that the patient's condition was terminal. The patient would have to request the drugs at least three times, and the third request must be in writing. Most important, the law would leave it to the patient to take the final step and self-administer the drugs.

The Oregon ballot measure contained a strategic element that was aimed at correcting the concerns of opponents during the Washington and California initiatives. That strategy was to include numerous strict assurances of voluntariness. For example, in order to receive a prescription for medication to end his or her life, a patient must make two oral and one written request. At least 15 days must pass between the oral requests, and at least 48 hours must pass between the written request and writing the prescription. Furthermore, no prescription can be issued until the patient is determined to be free of psychological or psychiatric disorder, or depression causing impaired judgment. Additionally, only physicians who treat patients for terminal illnesses are qualified to write prescriptions for life-ending medication. Moreover, all interactions between a physician and patient with regard to obtaining lethal drugs are required to be documented in the patient's medical records, and there is a provision for random review of those records by the Oregon State Health Division. Most importantly, the law allows physicians to prescribe life-ending medication only; in the end, the medicine must be self-administered (i.e., lethal injections, mercy killing, and active euthanasia remain illegal).

Opponents set out to convince voters that assuring voluntariness is not possible. They said physicians are often accused of abandoning patients on the threshold of death because: (1) they do not like to concede when death is imminent, and (2) they typically dodge communications with patients and loved ones concerning issues of death. Supporters counterclaimed, "The Oregon Death with Dignity Act is designed to foster communication between dying patients and their attending physician. The Act respects, and we believe will strengthen, the physician-patient relationship, by allowing unrestricted communication between the dying patient and his or her physician."

Campaign Strategies

Framing the Debate

Barbara Coombs Lee articulated the proponent position:

> You shouldn't have to suffer through a prolonged and agonizing death against your will. Measure 16 says decisions at the end of life are yours to make—free from unwanted unconstitutional government interference—with your family and physician at your side.

Pat McCormick, spokesman for the Coalition for Compassionate Care countered:

> It's open to abuse because it fails to require mental health evaluations and family notification. It leaves those without access to good health care vulnerable to facing suicide as the least costly treatment option ("State Demos Urge Party" 1994, p. B6).

A spokesman for the Oregon Pharmacists Association explained that organization's opposition to Measure 16: "Pharmacists are educated in the healing arts to prolong life in the treatment and healing of illnesses and injuries. Our organization views Measure 16 as a direct contradiction to that" (O'Keefe 1994b, p. 19). The Oregon Hospice Association opposed Measure 16, urging people to consider alternatives such as aggressive pain management and hospice care. Thomas Reardon, an Oregon physician and AMA board member, agreed, estimating that 90% of end-of-life pain could be treated (O'Keefe 1994b).

Eli Stutsman, legal counsel for Oregon Right to Die, countered that the proposed law would merely "codify existing medical practice for the terminally ill." Dr. Goodwin concurred: "The physicians who are presently involved and have kept it secret, and who are in the closet, so to speak, will now be able to speak to their colleagues and say, 'I will do this in the future because I think it's appropriate care.'"

As these statements illustrate, the debate presented numerous complex issues: compassion for suffering and the dying; fear that any exception to a total ban against assisted suicide would be abused; claims that the law was being skirted already, hence change would allow inter-professional and patient-physician candor; counterclaims that direct physician assistance in death would actually harm the image of the profession; claims that there would be even broader moral and social harms; and appeals to seek less controversial alternatives.

Distancing the Reformers from Their Radical Colleagues

Derek Humphry is acknowledged as the initiator of the assisted suicide reform movement in the United States. However, Measure 16 strategists saw him as a political liability, fearing his views might scare away voters worried that the measure was just the beginning of radical societal experiments to help people kill themselves (O'Keefe 1994c). Indeed, Humphry advocates lawful assisted suicide not only in cases of terminal illness but also for sufferers of advanced rheumatoid arthritis and others who are "hopelessly ill." Moreover, he strongly argues that injections must be lawful because in some cases swallowing pills actually worsens a patient's condition. He characterized Measure 16 as but a step in the right direction and said it would be used as a lever to get lethal injections legalized (Humphry 1996).

Campaign strategists regarded Humphry's exclusion from the day-to-day politics as "necessary to get the Leigh Dolins of the world to the table" (Stutsman 1996). Dolin, incoming president of the Oregon Medical Association, is widely regarded as having been a key figure in the OMA's executive decision to take no official position on Measure 16. Professionally, Dolin was neither for or against the measure; his view was that the issue of whether to legalize some cases of assisted suicide should be decided by Oregon voters. That deference to voters made Dolin's acquiescence[1] in Measure 16 crucial, in the minds of the proponents' campaign engineers. Hence, they carefully maneuvered to alleviate his worries about being linked with Humphry.

The maneuvers to mobilize moderated state leaders like Dolin illustrate the role of social agency in legal change. Eli Stutsman and Barbara Coombs Lee tensely balanced between extolling Humphry's enormous role in the assisted suicide reform movement and isolating their campaign from his "fringe" agenda. On the one hand, Stutsman and Coombs Lee met with Humphry to debate whether to include lethal injections in the measure. The meetings were long and laden with emotion (Humphry 1996; Stutsman 1996). Humphry lost the debates, he said, to the campaign strategists who thought "this halfway measure will bring the medical professionals to their side" (O'Keefe 1994c). On the other hand, Coombs Lee publicly rebutted Humphry's suggestion that the proponents were playing to physicians. Nine days before the election, for example, Barbara Coombs Lee distanced the Oregon Right to Die campaign from Humphry, stating, "Measure 16 was designed to find the common ground with a moderate, rational and safe solution to a problem facing Oregonians. It was not designed to satisfy the fringe element on either side of this issue, not Derek Humphry and not the archbishop" (O'Keefe 1994c).

With all of Humphry's prestige and the history of his efforts, could he have just sought his own goals instead of conceding to the narrower goals of the Measure 16 proponents? For a while, Humphry felt as if he had lost his long battle to legalize lethal injections (Humphry 1996). Yet, he said, "In fact, Measure 16 will prove me right." He cited a Dutch study that confirmed that in one of four cases, swallowing pills actually worsens a patient's condition. Patients become comatose or suffer even greater pain, taking two to four days to die, which is precisely the kind of lingering death they seek to avoid. At that point, their only deliverance from suffering is a lethal injection, he believes. In fact, he said, that is why Dutch law allows a doctor to administer a lethal injection if a patient does not die within 48 hours (Humphry 1996). "If the true purpose of assisted suicide is to relieve suffering, patients and physicians will see for themselves that a law like Measure 16 that does not include injections is inadequate. So while at first I thought this [Measure 16] was the end of my book [*Final Exit*], in fact my book will be even more significant as people realize that obtaining drugs is not enough" (Humphry 1996, cf. 1991). In conclusion, Humphry views his compromise with Measure 16 campaign strategists not as a concession but as a maneuver toward vindicating his convictions about the need for lethal injections.

Was Derek Humphry's exclusion from the coalition of Measure 16 proponents a facade or a verifiable political strategy? Humphry's bootstrap characterization of Measure 16 is flatly contradicted by Eli Stutsman, the central campaign strategist for the proponents of Measure 16. According to Stutsman and others,[2] it was Humphry's persistence about injections that alienated people like Dr. Leigh Dolin, who was the incoming president of the Oregon Medical Association (OMA) when the campaign for Measure 16 was launched. To secure nonresistance from moderate state leaders such as Dolin, Humphry was asked not to attend the deliberations between campaign strategists and wary community leaders. He was assured that the meeting participants knew his views already, and cautioned that his militancy might destroy the chance to cultivate key political support. He reluctantly conceded that any level of lawful assisted suicide was better than the status quo and agreed not to enter the meetings without invitation. He also made it clear in media interviews that he did not speak for the Measure 16 campaign. (By contrast, he was publicly perceived as a campaign spokesperson for both Washington's Initiative 119 and California's Proposition 161.) Instead, he proclaimed himself to be "more of the conscience of our movement. . . . I take a longer, historic view and a more honest view. But I'm not involved in day-to-day politics, so I can afford that" (O'Keefe 1994c).

As this account illustrates, pro-campaign strategists had to achieve a fragile balance between satisfying Humphry's desire to be included in the overall assisted suicide movement and diplomatically distancing their campaign from his more aggressive agenda. Certainly, therefore, Humphry's exclusion from the coalition was much less a facade than a verifiable political strategy. Then again, hardly anyone realized or paid attention to the fact that Humphry quietly helped raise about 20% of the $1 million dollars spent on the proponents' campaign. "It is a fact that I've written at least three fund-raising letters for them," Humphry said (O'Keefe 1994c). Thus, although it was misleading to imply that the Hemlock Society funded the entire campaign—an insinuation that some opponents made in an apparent attempt to disparage Oregon Death with Dignity—"it is quite unlikely that the campaign could have succeeded without it" (Stutsman 1996). In conclusion, only a carefully planned, tightly executed, and exhaustively guarded strategy enabled pro-Measure 16 tacticians to obtain everything they wanted: the assent of moderate state leaders, Humphry's alliances with financial backers, and a majority of the votes.

Physician Neutrality

Polls and surveys at regional and national levels indicate that the physician profession is deeply split over the issue of active euthanasia (Cohen 1994). In two rigorous surveys, 60% of 2,700 physicians who treat terminal patients supported legalizing physician-assisted suicide, and 56% of physicians and 66% of adults supported legalization (Dworkin 1996).

However, the American Medical Association (AMA) strongly condemns physicians providing lethalities, regardless of voluntariness. The AMA was also active in opposing both the Quill and Glucksberg lawsuits heard by the United States Supreme Court in 1997 and the variety of state legislative proposals to decriminalize physician-assisted suicide.

In Washington and California, the state medical associations stood along with the Catholic Church as primary opponents of aid-in-dying initiatives. The position of the AMA and the actions of state associations in Washington and California contributed to expectations that the OMA House of delegates would vote to oppose Measure 16.

In Oregon, Dr. Goodwin's longtime public interest in death with dignity, his professional status as a teaching physician at Oregon Health Sciences University, and his personal relationships with roughly six in 10 family physicians in the state gave him insights that made him uniquely capable of accurately assessing the level of physician tolerance or support for various levels of physician-aided death. When the campaign for Measure 16 commenced, Dr. Goodwin informally surveyed 20 Oregon family physicians. Half of the respondents said they would be comfortable prescribing medication for a patient's use in suicide, but none wanted to give lethal injections. Based on this survey, Goodwin advised the Oregon Medical Association (OMA) to neither support nor oppose Measure 16.

When the OMA House of Delegates convened to consider Measure 16, the common wisdom was that the delegates would vote to oppose the measure. But that sentiment changed during 90 minutes of intense, emotional debate. Dr. Goodwin reported his informal survey results to the group, suggesting an even split between physicians on the matter of prescribing lethalities. Other delegates spoke about their experiences with patients and with their own parents, siblings, and other relatives. An equal number of physicians shared personal experiences in which assisted suicide would have been a good option.

Dr. Lee Dolin, then President-elect of the OMA, remembers the debate as the longest, most solemn that he can remember. When Dolin spoke, he reasoned that the wide differences of opinion among physician leaders suggested the organization ought neither support nor oppose the measure. Instead, he advocated the position that patients and the general public should decide what they want from physicians. His sentiment might be accurately summarized as follows: if physicians agree on what to do about the profoundly personal experience of dying, can we rightfully tell everyone else what they ought to do? Thus, the decision not to take an official position occurred probably not because physicians abdicated their moral judgment toward patients, as Campbell contends (Campbell 1994, p. 147) but because the participants were evenly split over providing lethal prescriptions, just as were the physicians in Dr. Goodwin's informal survey.

Physician neutrality accomplished a lot: it informed voters that at least half of physicians supported and would even implement physician-assisted suicide; it removed physicians from their previous opposition partnership with organized religion; and, most importantly, it is considered by proponents and opponents alike as a key to amending assisted suicide law in Oregon.

The Campaign Battle and Emergence of Counter-Strategies

Opposition Strategies

Opponents of the proposed law included Oregon Right to Life, the Oregon Health Care Coalition, the Oregon State Council of Senior Citizens, and the Oregon Hospice Association.

Religious organizations—particularly the Catholic Church—played prominent roles in defeating earlier aid-in-dying initiative campaigns in Washington and California, and they were the primary opponent in Oregon. The Church provided funds for the opponent campaign. Pat McCormick, an opposition leader, said that more than 75% of the $1.5 million in contributions sent to his campaign to defeat Measure 16 came from Catholic sources, including $300,000 from donations in churches (O'Keefe 1994a, p. A1). Parish priests, moreover, used their pulpits as a forum for sermons against the initiatives. An article in *The Oregonian* described one aspect of the effort: "Archbishop William J. Levada of the Diocese of Portland and Bishop Thomas J. Connolly of the Diocese of Baker have instructed their priests to preach against the measure on Sunday Sept 18, and to collect money a week later to defeat it" (O'Keefe 1994a). Priests were also encouraged to remind parishioners about the sanctity of life, especially in old age. Additionally, church membership rolls were used for distributing materials opposing the measures. For example, 200,000 copies of an eight-page voter's guide produced by the Oregon Family Council were distributed in 1,600 churches (O'Keefe 1994a). Said Jeff Sugerman, Executive Director of Oregon Right to Die, "This politicking from the pulpit clearly shows our opponent's intention to promote Catholic religious doctrine by influencing Oregon voters" (O'Keefe 1994b).

Church leaders and other opponent organizations executed a second, more secular strategy, as well. *The Oregonian* summarized the arguments as: (1) doctors would become killers, contrary to their oath to the role of healer; (2) current methods for predicting the imminence of death are unreliable ("Misjudgment of a patient's condition could end life prematurely"); (3) family rights would be violated; (4) a slippery slope would be created, leading to court judgments allowing lethal injections when patients cannot swallow medication; (5) people may kill themselves to avoid financial costs ("The right to die may well become the duty to die."); and (6) depressed patients may be at most risk ("Depressed patients will likely go untreated"). Citing these problems, opponents claimed the proposed law lacked safeguards, a claim that became the key message of their ads and appeals.

The group Physicians and Nurses Against Measure 16, for example, placed a full-page advertisement in *The Oregonian*, which read: "Need a second opinion?" The ad listed many names of those opposing Measure 16 and continued: "How about hundreds of them? Physicians and nurses from all parts of Oregon are speaking out in clear opposition to Ballot Measure 16. Former United States Surgeon General C. Everett Koop, M.D. says that 'Measure 16 is ripe for abuse.' The American Medical Association hopes 'the voters of Oregon will honor the healing role of physicians and vote against Ballot Measure 16.' Medical professionals are letting their voices be heard. On November 8, we need to hear yours."

The AMA Intercedes

In October, the governing board of the American Medical Association announced its opposition to Measure 16 and sent delegates to Oregon to join the opposition (O'Keefe 1994b). Thomas Reardon, a Portland physician and AMA national board member, explained the AMA's decision: "It's fundamentally inconsistent with the physician's professional role in taking care of patients. Our basic tenet is to do no harm. . . . There was a concern that this was a major issue not only for Oregon, but the country."

Leigh Dolin, then President-elect of the Oregon Medical Association, rebutted: "We'll see how Oregonians feel about outsiders trying to tell them how to vote" (O'Keefe 1994b, p. 19). Dr. Goodwin termed the AMA's action "inappropriate and paternalistic" (O'Keefe 1994b, p. 19). A spokesman for Oregon Right to Die agreed: "The fact is, this is just another out-of-state group coming in and saying this is wrong. What do Oregonians care what the AMA in Chicago says about this?" (O'Keefe 1994b, p. 19).

Final Weeks

In Washington and California, the proponents ran out of money before the crucial last 10 days of the campaign—a time when T.V., radio, and print messages and images were essential (Hillyard and Dombrink 1997; Stutsman 1996). The opponents blasted the media with frightening images and slogans. Yet, the proponents had no money to counterattack. Not so in Oregon, where Measure 16 strategists had saved money to wage a strong media campaign during the final days before the vote. Nevertheless, as in Washington and California, as the election came closer there was a narrowing of support for the initiative and predictions of defeat (McLaughlin 1994; Rubenstein 1994, p. A1). In early September, a viewer poll conducted by television station KPTY indicated that the measure was ahead 63% to 31% (Mapes 1994). Support was highest among young voters and lowest among older voters, and there was equally strong support among Democrats, Republicans, and independents. After the opponents' advertising blitz, however, a poll for *The Oregonian* and television station KATU showed the expected vote narrowing. The poll reported that the strongest opposition came from women, those over 55, and those who considered themselves very religious.

Just days before the election, *The Oregonian*, the state's highest circulation daily newspaper, editorialized against the measure:

> Four realities are at the core of why the state should not become a co-conspirator in assisted suicide: (1) almost all pain experienced by the dying can be successfully managed; (2) virtually all clinical depression among the dying can be successfully treated; (3) such treatment is available to all Oregonians, rich and poor; and (4) when doctors control pain and relieve depression, suicide requests among the dying virtually vanish.

The editorial concluded: "Measure 16 places the most vulnerable at the greatest risk."

The editorial quoted from the report of the New York State Task Force on Law and Life (1994):

> No matter how well the guidelines are framed, this treatment would be delivered in the context of social inequality and bias that exists in society, including medical services. Those who are poor, elderly, lack access to good medical care or are members of minority groups will be at greatest risk" ("Offer Dignity" 1994, p. C6).

Election Results

Measure 16 passed narrowly, with only 51 percent of the vote. A breakdown of the results by county showed that the vote was 55% for and 45% against in the population-rich Portland-metro counties of Multnomah, Washington, and Clackamas. It passed in 13 other counties throughout the state and lost in the remaining, most rural 20 counties, which have smaller populations ("How Many Voted" 1994).

EXPLAINING SUCCESS

Problem Identification

The Oregon initiative debate took place at the end of a two-year period in which the Clinton Administration failed to convince Congress to enact a wide-ranging reform of the nation's health care system. Several polls from the 1992 election described the anxiety of the nation's electorate related to their own health care. The issue had been seen as pivotal in one U.S. Senate race and was used as an example of middle-class economic anxiety in the Clinton-Bush race. Opponents of the Measure 16 initiative sought to tie their concerns to this anxiety, stating:

> Under managed care plans, physicians' earnings can be directly related to how well they control costs. The poor, the elderly and the disabled are the most likely to feel pressured to choose lethal drugs to end their lives rather than more expensive treatment (Oregon Secretary of State 1994, p. 131).

At the same time, proponents of physician-assisted suicide pointed to cultural and historical concerns about changes in the care of the dying. They noted that during the period from 1920 until 1960, advanced surgical techniques, antibiotics, techniques for the administration of intravenous fluids and drugs, the development of respiratory support systems, and improved therapeutic and diagnostic techniques greatly increased life expectancy as well as changing the locus of death from homes to hospitals and nursing home institutions. The institutionalization of death, moreover, has given physicians even greater control over the process of dying. Yet, there is a strong consensus that physicians remain inadequately trained to care for the dying. Moreover, physicians are deterred economically from providing palliative care. Patients typically do not understand their right to refuse treatment or to demand withdrawal of unwanted treatment, and advance care planning has barely been implemented. Still, data from death certificates reveal that approximately 62% of the 2.3 million annual deaths occur in hospitals, 16% occur in nursing homes, and only 17% occur in homes (Foley 1996).

These cultural and historical changes have given rise to a long list of cultural and personal fears such as: "How will I die?" "Where will I die?" "Who will care for me?" "Will I be alone, or accompanied by loved ones?" "Will my pain be controlled?" "Will my cultural, religious, and spiritual beliefs by respected?" "Will my advance directives be heeded?" "How will my care be paid for?" Proponents of physician-assisted suicide raise these concerns as clear indications of a social problem that can be solved by amending assisted suicide law.

Conduciveness

Proponents of change could rest their hopes for success on Oregon. A national survey conducted by Our Sunday Visitor indicated that only 43% of registered voters supported Measure 16 nationally, but in Oregon the Measure was supported by 60% early in the campaign (Bates and O'Keefe 1994, p. A16). Additionally, Oregon is a unique state both in terms of its long history of citizens using the initiative power as a tool of legal and social change, and in terms of citizens' defiance toward both organized religion and outside political pressure. Chet Orloff, the director of the Oregon Historical Society, claimed: "This measure is in keeping with Oregon. Throughout history Oregon seems to be out there ahead of other states in testing things" (Bates and O'Keefe 1994). John Pridonoff, the Executive Director of Hemlock Society USA, based in Eugene, said: "Oregonians tend to be more open-minded to a wide variety of opinions. That climate was very important" (Bates and O'Keefe 1994). Referring to the status of Oregon as a relatively secular place, Historian E. Kimbark MacColl added, "Oregon has never been a strong church state" (Bates and O'Keefe 1994). Orloff supported this sentiment: "The fact that there has been no dominant religion has allowed a moral flexibility that a lot of states don't have" (Bates and O'Keefe 1994).

Deliberation and Choice Making

Analysis of the Measure 16 campaign reveals a lot about social agency in terms of policy and strategic alternatives. Reform strategists carefully assessed the Oregon electorate and honed in on key political attitudes. Accordingly, voluntariness and individual choice became the centerpiece of their campaign. They further argued that the provisions in the law requiring multiple requests for a prescription and physician assessment a patient's capacity to make voluntary health care decisions would strengthen the physician-patient relationship. This was an important strategic choice in the wake of the Washington and California initiative failures, where opponents argued that physicians tend to abandon terminal patients, rendering most of the alleged safeguards ineffective.

The Catholic Church's strategies are equally indicative of deliberation and choice. On the one hand, they sought to educate believers about the immorality of taking human life in any instance, since life is sacred and human are mere stewards of life given by God. On the other hand, they ran a tenacious secular campaign geared toward educating the secular public about the potential dangers of allowing doctors to help kill their patients, especially when so many Americans cannot afford good health care.

The deliberations of the Oregon Medical Association are especially interesting. The common wisdom was that the OMA would officially oppose Measure 16. Dr. Leigh Dolin and Dr. Peter Goodwin both emphasized the gravity of the long, emotional debate that finally resulted in the decision to let voters decide the issue without political pressure from physicians. That decision had two immediate impacts. It allowed for the impression that Measure 16 might not have been as poorly written as opponents claimed—at least in the official opinion of the physicians' organization. And it left the Church alone as the primary group against the proposed law (unlike in Washington and California, where the Church and physicians worked side by side). Given the anti-religion sentiment of Oregonians, the appearance of religious groups standing alone helped the proponents' campaign. Ironically, perhaps, OMA neutrality also created another benefit for proponents because it led to intercession by the American Medical Association, which played into Oregonian's opposition to "outside" pressure. This series of strategic choices and their repercussions illustrate the contingency and indeterminacy of social agency

The Social Status of the Deviant

Lempert (1974) observed that pressure for decriminalization occurs to the extent that high-status individuals are identified as violators of the law. His reasoning is that deviant, law-violating behavior creates a "moral dissonance" whereby an actor is simultaneously seen as having high social status and low moral status (Lempert 1974, p. 5). DiChiara and Galliher demonstrated that the pressures leading to marijuana decriminalization had precisely the origins Lempert predicted. Moral dissonance was also a precursor of change in the assisted suicide law.

Barbara Coombs Lee argues that the term "suicide" is pejorative as it tends to raise in people's minds an image of a desperate, lonely, violent act that leaves colleagues, friends, and family confused. The kind of "aid-in-dying" that she and Dr. Goodwin sponsored with Measure 16, on the other hand, is compassionate, peaceful, dignified, and it includes loved ones and helps them understand (Coombs Lee 1997). In fact the measure provided that, "Actions taken in accordance with this Act shall not, for any purpose, constitute suicide, assisted suicide, mercy killing, or homicide, under the law."

Moral dissonance in its broader complexity is pointedly reflected in the amicus brief of a group of bioethicists in support of the reformers:

> The word "suicide" does not differentiate among the death of a teenager coping with the struggles of adolescence, a middle-aged family man facing financial ruin, and an eighty-year old cancer patient who seeks to avoid further protracted pain and suffering when her death is near. Unlike the first two tragic illustrations, there can be a sense of meaningfulness, emotional resolution, and communicative culmination, including gratitude for a life now complete, in the "suicide" of the dying patient who seeks both to avoid bad death and to bring life to an inevitable but appropriate close (amicus brief submitted in both *Vacco v. Quill* and *Washington v. Glucksberg*).

These observations illustrate considerable moral dissonance between social paternalism and compassion, depending largely on the health condition of the individual. In appeals to solve this "problem" by changing the law, the debate revolves around American society's general interest in preserving life and our equally significant values of liberty and individual choice.

The jurisprudence that has evolved around the withholding and withdrawal of treatment suggests that assurances of voluntariness provide the key to opportunities for death-and-dying reform through social activism. Similarly, after the

Measure 16 election, an analysis in *The Oregonian* (Bates and O'Keefe 1994) concluded that by removing doctors one step from the actual suicide, proponents were able to frame the debate as a matter of autonomy and personal choice.

Three years later, Professor Albert Jonsen, Chair of the Department of Medical History and Ethics at the University of Washington School of Medicine, agreed (Jonsen 1997). In our present cultural and historical context, a law allowing mercy killing is politically too volatile. The Holocaust, says Jonsen, linked mercy killing (voluntary euthanasia on the grounds of autonomy, and sometimes non-voluntary euthanasia on the grounds of compassion) with involuntary euthanasia. The threat of genocide, however, is mitigated by Oregon's requirements of mental competence, terminality, multiple requests, and, most important, self-administration. And since suicide is not illegal and the mere writing of a prescription is not homicide, Oregon's requirements of voluntariness serve jurisprudential purposes, as well (Jonsen 1997).

Yet, determining which assisted suicides are moral and/or legal on the basis of health status—or more precisely, on longevity—still raises many worries about what might happen to socially/politically/economically marginalized sick people.

For example, the New York State Task Force Report on Law and Life advised against legalizing any form of assisted suicide because:

> No matter how well the guidelines are framed, this treatment would be delivered in the context of social inequality and bias that exists in society, including medical services. Those who are poor, elderly, lack access to good medical care or are members of minority groups will be at greatest risk.

CONCLUSION: EXPLAINING THE SUCCESSFUL LEGAL REFORM: WINNING THE FIGHT OVER THE IMPORTANCE OF VOLUNTARINESS

The slow progression from the moral and jurisprudential controversies over withholding versus withdrawing treatment, to "invasive" treatment versus artificial food and hydration, to the rights of competent versus incompetents, and now to patients who are on life support versus those who are not, depicts a dialectical pattern (Chambliss and Zatz 1993; DiChiara and Galliher 1994; McCann 1996).

This analysis of the interactive processes of judgment and reasoned intentionality, the dialectical nature of tactical efforts, and the contingent, indeterminate forces of political conduciveness, motivations, deliberations, and choice making attests to the significance of social agency in legal and moral change. From a broad viewpoint, the success of reform seekers in Oregon was contingent upon voter attitudes, neutralizing opposition strategies, and avoiding dissension within their own ranks. This paper has already described how proponents used appeals to voluntariness, as well as to voter opposition to religious and "outside" pressures, to maintain voter support and neutralize opposition forces.

The central issue in the Oregon debate was the assurance of voluntariness. That alone is not remarkable because voluntariness is a cultural norm manifested throughout 20 years of the development of a collective definition of death with dignity, as well as in many other American laws. But in these data, we observe the reconstitution of voluntariness to meet the conditions of care for the dying in Oregon.

Dr. Peter Goodwin and Barbra Coombs Lee deplored the tragic circumstances of instiutionalized death. They used their outstanding profesional integrity and community standing to mobilize others to form a coalition and back a ballot measure. They cultivated a pluralistic view of what is needed to address the problem of care for the dying. Goodwin conducted a survey of his colleagues and relied on the results to convicne the coalition to omit objections from the law. He also used the survey to help persuade the Oregon Medical Association to take an official position of neutrality on the measure. In order to hold the coalition together, Coombs Lee and Stutsman embraced Derek Humphry, yet dismissed his arguments that injections were a necessary component in aiding the dying. Claims and counterclaims manifested many political and legal concerns, but the central debate was between involvuntary suffering and involuntary death. The proponents barely won. Stustamn said they previaled because they assembled and held together a distinguished coalition of citizen professionals, not just a loose band of grass-roots organizers; because they sought only what patients wanted and physicians were willing to provide; and because they raised enough money to campaign hard right up until the end. Additionally, Coombs Lee said that "self-administering a pill" was the clinching image of voluntariness.

Proponents say their success was based on building a local coalition of professionals, crafting a law without injections, and raising extra money for a counterattack during the crucial final days of the campaign. They acuse their opponents, whom they believe are primarily Catholics, of politicking from the pulpit and unethically taking up collections for campaign funds. Catholic leaders counter that it was not their tactics as much as their equally secular message "not this law" that convinced many voters to reject the propsoed law.

Forming a coalition of professionals from within the polity helped create the perception that the measure was a sensible, compassion-driven effort to address a local need. By contrast, in Washington and California it seemed as if some backers of the initiatives were undisclosed national activists in search of a sympathetic polity. A substantial component of these campaigns included playing to the abstract fears of the general electorate (dying alone hooked up to machines versus involuntary euthanasia for the weak). In Oregon, however, many arguments and counterarguments were based on realistic concerns about recurring conditions in clinical settings and dilemmas and about making difficult choices in those settings. The ommission of injections is the best example.

Some opponents, and even Derek Humphry, claimed that omitting injections was political—that it was geared toward warding off a conflict with physicians. Our informants strongly denied that and countered that the decision to omit injections was reached without regard to the opposition. Dr. Goodwin, for example, stresses that while omitting injections from the legislation had a very favorable political impact, that is not why they were omitted. "They were omitted because doctors overwhelmingly felt like they could not and would not provide them, and patients expressed very little interest in having them available" (Goodwin 1996). Nevertheless, the opponents, particularly the Catholic chruches, were as sincere in their efforts to convince voters to defeat Measure 16.

Religious organizations, particularly the Catholic Church, played prominent roles in defeating earlier aid-in-dying initiative campaigns in Washington and California, and they were the primary opponent in Oregon. The Church provided funds for the opponents' campaign. By the time the campaign reached the crucial final days, the margin of support for the initiative had dwindled, largely because of the opponents' claims that Measure 16 lacked adequate assurance of voluntariness (Park 1997).

This dramatic narrowing of support indicates that early polls measured support for the idea more than for the proposed law. Many voters were already committed to one side or the other: Catholics had a lot of political and financial support from their membership; the proponents had a lot of the same from members of the Hemlock Society. The final days came down to the final media blitz aimed at uncommitted voters.

NOTES

1. We use the term "acquiescence" because Dolin publicly derides the need for physician participation in assisted suicide. "Anyone can obtain cyanide from a chemical supply store and be dead within a minute of swallowing just one teaspoon of it," he told me. Moreover, Dolin repeatedly stated that he was not associated with planning campaign strategy (Dolin 1996).

2. Some of the proponents' arguments and safeguards can be seen as related to the type of waiting period issues that became salient with abortion during the 1980s and 1990s. Polls have shown (Craig and O'Brien 1993) that the American public favored several types of limitations on access to abortion—parent notification or consent in the case of minors, waiting periods, even husband notification. The case of *Rust v. Sullivan* was centered on the requirement that federally financed clinics provide information on the alternatives to abortion to those seeking aboriton counseling. The 1992 U.S. Supreme Court ruling in *Casey* solidified the *Roe v. Wade* ruling of 1973 when a five-member majority of the court upheld the basic holdings of *Roe*, while allowing for the propriety of several limitations on access to abortion.

However, the ruling also gave support to the idea of some limitations on access, measures which have been enshrined in the Oregon Measure 16.

REFERENCES

Annas, G.J. 1994. "Death by Prescription: The Oregon Initiative." *The New England Journal of Medicine* (November 3): 1240-1243.

Anspach, R.R. 1993. *Deciding Who Lives: Fateful Choices in the Intensive-Care Nursery.* Berkeley, CA: University of California Press.

Bates, T., and M. O'Keefe. 1994. "On Suicide Measure, Oregon is a Maverick Again." *The Oregonian* (November 13): A1, A16.

Battin, M.P. 1994. *The Least Worst Death: Essays in Bioethics on the End of Life*. New York: Oxford University Press.

Bayer, R., and G.M. Oppenheimer, eds. 1993. *Drug Policy: Illicit Drugs in a Free Society*. Cambridge, UK: Cambridge University Press.

Becker, H.S. 1963. *Outsiders: Studies in the Sociology of Deviance*. Glencoe, IL: Free Press.

Belkin, L. 1993. *First, Do No Harm*. New York: Simon and Schuster.

Bonnie, R.J., and C. Whitebread, II. 1974. *The Marihuana Conviction*. Charlottesville, VA: The University of Virginia Press.

Calavita, K. 1992. *Inside the State: The Bracero Program, Immigration, and the I.N.S.* New York: Routledge.

Callahan, D. 1987. *Setting Limits: Medical Goals in an Aging Society*. New York: Touchstone/Simon and Schuster.

Callahan, D. 1990. *What Kind of Life?: The Limits of Medical Progress*. New York: Simon and Schuster.

Callahan, D. 1992. "'Aid-in-Dying': The Social Dimensions." *Commonweal* (Special Supplement, September): 12-16.

Callahan, D. 1993. *The Troubled Dream of Life: Living With Mortality*. New York: Simon and Schuster.

Campbell, C.S. 1994. "The Oregon Trail to Death: Measure 16." *Commonweal* (August): 9-11.

Campbell, C.S. 1995. "When Medicine Lost its Moral Conscience: Oregon Measure 16." Pp. 140-167 in *Arguing Euthanasia: The Controversy Over Mercy Killing, Assisted Suicide, and the "Right to Die,"* edited by J.D. Moreno. Bloomington, IN: Indiana University Press.

Cantor, N. 1993. *Advance Directives*. Bloomington, IN: Indiana University Press.

Capron, A.M. 1994. "Medical Futility—Strike 2." *Hastings Center Report* 24(5): 42-43.

Chambliss, W.J., and R. Seidman. 1982. *Law, Order, and Power*. Reading, MA: Addison-Wesley.

Chambliss, W.J., and M. Zatz. 1993. *Making Law*. Bloomington, IN: Indiana University Press.

Cohen, J.S., S.D. Filn, E.J. Boyko, A.R. Jonsen, and R.W. Wood. 1994. "Attitudes Toward Assisted Suicide and Euthanasia Among Physicians in Washington State." *The New England Journal of Medicine* 331(2, July 14): 89-94.

Condit, C.M. 1990. *Decoding Abortion Rhetoric: Communicating Social Change*. Champaign, IL: University of Illinois Press.

Coombs Lee, B. 1997. Interview, Seattle, WA, May 21.

Craig, B.H., and D.M. O'Brien. 1993. *Abortion and American Politics*. Chatham, NJ: Chatham House.

Currie, E. 1993. *Reckoning: Drugs, the Cities, and the American Future*. New York: Hill and Wang.

DiChiara, A., and J.F. Galliher. 1994. "Dissonance and Contradictions in the Origins of Marihuana Decriminalization." *Law & Society Review* 28: 41-77.

Dolin, L.C. 1995. "When Patients Have a Right to Die." *The Internist* (March): 16-18.

Dolin, L.C. 1996. Interview, Portland, OR, July 11.

Dombrink, J. Forthcoming. "Euthanasia and Legal Reform." *Law and Social Inquiry*.

Dombrink, J., and W.N. Thompson. 1990. *The Last Resort: Success and Failure in Campaigns for Casinos*. Reno, NV: University of Nevada Press.

Duncan, J. 1996. Interview, Portland, OR, July 10.

Duster, T. 1970. *The Legislation of Morality: Law, Drugs and Moral Judgment*. New York: Free Press.

Dworkin, R.M. 1993. *Life's Dominion*. New York: Alfred A. Knopf.

Dworkin, R.M. 1996. "Sex, Death and the Courts." *New York Review of Books* (August 8): 44-50.

"The Oregonian's Recommendations." 1994. *The Oregonian* (November 7): B10.

Foley, K. 1996. "Assisted Suicide in the United States." Hearing before the Subcommittee on the Constitution of the Committee on the Judiciary. House of Representatives, 104th Congress, April 19. Serial No. 78, pp. 12-34.

Galliher, J.F., and L. Basilick. 1979. "Utah's Liberal Drug Laws: Structural Foundations and Triggering Events." *Social Problems* 26: 284-297.
Galliher, J.F., and J.R. Cross. 1982. "Symbolic Severity in the Land of Easy Virtue: Nevada's High Marijuana Penalty." *Social Problems* 29: 380-386.
Galliher, J.F., J.F. McCartney, and B.E. Baum. 1974. "Nebraska's Marijuana Law: A Case of Unexpected Legislative Innovation." *Law & Society Review* 8: 441-455.
Garrow, D.J. 1994. *Liberty and Sexuality: The Right to Privacy and the Making of Roe. v. Wade*. New York: Macmillan.
Glick, H.R. 1992. *The Right to Die: Policy Innovation and Its Consequences*. New York: Columbia University Press.
Goodwin, P. 1996. Interview, Portland, OR, July 10.
Griffiths, J., H. Weyers, and A. Bood. 1998. *Euthanasia and Law in The Netherlands*. Amsterdam and Ann Arbor: Amsterdam University Press and University of Michigan Press.
Gusfield, J.R. 1996. *Contested Meanings: The Construction of Alcohol Problems*. Madison, WI: University of Wisconsin Press.
Herman, D. 1994. *Rights of Passage: Struggles for Lesbian and Gay Legal Equality*. Toronto, Canada: University of Toronto Press.
Hillyard, D.P., and J. Dombrink. Forthcoming. "Using the Law to Redefine Killing in Medical Settings." In *Research in Law and Policy Studies*, Vol. 6, edited by S.S. Nagel. Greenwich, CT: JAI Press.
Himmelstein, J.L. 1983. *The Strange Career of Marihuana*. Westport, CT: Greenwood Press.
Hoefler, J.M. 1994. *Deathright: Culture, Medicine, Politics and the Right to Die*. Boulder, CO: Westview Press.
"How Many Voted for Measure 16." 1994. *The Oregonian* (November 11): A16.
Humphry, D. 1991. *Final Exit*. Eugene, OR: The Hemlock Society.
Humphry, D. 1996. Interview, Portland, OR, July 9.
Jenness, V. 1993. *Making It Work: The Prostitutes' Rights Movement in Perspective*. New York: Aldine de Gruyter.
Jonsen, A.R. 1990. *The New Medicine and the Old Ethics*. Cambridge, MA: Harvard University Press.
Jonsen, A.R. 1997. Interview, Seattle, WA, May 20.
Kaplan, J. 1971. *Marijuana: The New Prohibition*. New York: Meridian Books.
Kingdon, J.W. 1984. *Agendas, Alternatives and Public Policies*. Boston, MA: Little, Brown.
Kleiman, M.R. 1992. *Against Excess: Drug Policy for Results*. New York: Basic Books.
Lempert, R. 1974. "Toward a Theory of Decriminalization." *Et Al.* 3: 1-14.
Logue, B.J. 1993. *Last Rights: Death Control and the Elderly in America*. New York: Lexington Books.
Luker, K. 1984. *Abortion and the Politics of Motherhood*. Berkeley, CA: University of California Press.
Macklin, R. 1993. *Enemies and Advocates of Patients*. New York: Oxford University Press.
Magleby, D.B. 1994. "Direct Legislation in the American States." Pp. 218-257 in *Referendums Around the World*, edited by D. Butler and A. Ranney. Washington, DC: The AEI Press,
Mapes, J. 1994. "Doctor-Aided Suicide Measure Shows Support." *The Oregonian* (September 8): C10.
McCann, M. 1994. *Rights at Work: Pay Equity Reform and the Politics of Legal Mobilization*. Chicago, IL: University of Chicago Press.
McCann, M. 1996. "Causal Versus Constitutive Explanations (or, the Difficulty of Being So Positive)." *Law and Social Inquiry* 21(2, Spring): 457-482.
McLaughlin, K. 1994. "History Points to Failure for Illegal Immigrant Initiative." *The Sunday Oregonian* (September 18): A19.
Meisel, A. 1992. "The Legal Consensus about Forgoing Life-Sustaining Treatment: Its Status and Its Prospects." *Kennedy Institute of Ethics Journal* 2(4): 309-345.

Musto, D. 1973. *The American Disease: Origins of Narcotic Control*. New Haven, CT: Yale University Press.

The New York State Task Force on Life and the Law. 1994. *When Death is Sought: Assisted Suicide and Euthanasia in the Medical Context*. New York: The New York State Task Force on Life and the Law.

Nuland, S. 1994. *How We Die: Reflections on Life's Final Chapter*. New York: Alfred A. Knopf.

"Offer Dignity Without Death" (Editorial). 1994 *The Oregonian* (November 2): C6.

O'Keefe, M. 1994a. "Catholic Leaders to Use Pulpit to Fight Initiative." *The Oregonian* (September 10): A1, A14.

O'Keefe, M. 1994b. "AMA's National Board Opposes Measure 16." *The Oregonian* (October 23): A1, A19.

O'Keefe, M. 1994c. "Founding Father: Derek Humphry Began the Assisted-Suicide Movement, But His Views May Be Too Extreme for Measure 16 Strategists." *The Oregonian* (November 2): C1, C8.

O'Keefe, M. 1994d. "TV Ad on Assisted Suicide Leaves Out Part of Story." *The Oregonian* (November 5): C1, C3.

O'Keefe, M. 1994e. "Churches Urge Voter Turnout: Their Way." *The Oregonian* (November 8): A1, A9.

O'Keefe, M. 1994f. "Opponents of Measure 16 Concede Defeat." *The Oregonian* (November 11): A1.

O'Keefe, M., and T. Bates. 1994. "Oregon Morality, Issues Divided." *The Oregonian* (November 10): A1, A20.

Oregon Secretary of State. 1994. *Election Guide*. Salem, OR: Oregon Secretary of State.

Park, S. 1997. Interview, Seattle, WA, May 22.

Preston, T.A. 1994. "Killing Pain, Ending Life." *The New York Times* (November 1): A15.

Quill, T.E. 1991. "Death and Dignity: A Case of Individualized Decision Making." *New England Journal of Medicine* 324(10, March 7): 693-694.

Quill, T.E. 1996. *A Midwife Through the Dying Process*. Baltimore, MD: The Johns Hopkins University Press.

Reagan, L.J. 1997. *When Abortion Was a Crime: Women, Medicine, and Law in the United States, 1867-1973*. Berkeley, CA: University of California Press.

Reinarman, C., and H.G. Levine. 1989. "Crack in Context: Politics and Media in the Making of a Drug Scare." *Contemporary Drug Problems* 16: 535-577.

Reinarman, C., and H.G. Levine. 1997. "The Crack Attack: Politics and Media in the Crack Scare." Pp. 18-51 in *Crack in America: Demon Drugs and Social Justice*, edited by C. Reinarman and H.G. Levine. Berkeley, CA: University of California Press.

Roby, P.A. 1969. "Politics and Criminal Law: Revision of the New York State Penal Law on Prostitution." *Social Problems* 17(1, Summer): 83-109.

Rothman, D. 1991. *Strangers at the Bedside: A History of How Law and Bioethics Transformed Medical Decision Making*. New York: Basic Books.

Rubenstein, S. 1994. "Voters Split over Initiative." *The Oregonian* (November 7): A1.

Schneiderman, L.J., and N.S. Jecker. 1995. *Wrong Medicine: Doctors, Patients, and Futile Treatment*. Baltimore, MD: The Johns Hopkins University Press.

Schur, E.H. 1980. *The Politics of Deviance: Stigma Contests and the Uses of Power*. Englewood Cliffs, NJ: Prentice-Hall.

Skolnick, J.H. 1978. *House of Cards: Legalization and Control of Casino Gambling*. Boston, MA: Little, Brown.

Skolnick, J.H., and J. Dombrink. 1978. "The Legalization of Deviance." *Criminology* 16(2): 193-208.

Staggenborg, S. 1991. *The Pro-Choice Movement: Organization and Activism in the Abortion Conflict*. New York: Oxford University Press.

"State Demos Urge Party to Support 3 Initiatives." 1994. *The Oregonian* (August 30): B6.

Steinhoff, P.G., and M. Diamond. 1977. *Abortion Politics: The Hawaii Experience*. Honolulu, HI: University of Hawaii Press.

Stutsman, E. 1996. Interview, Portland, OR, July 12.

Timberlake, J. 1963. *Prohibition and the Progressive Movement, 1900-1920*. Cambridge, MA: Harvard University Press.

Traynor, M.P., and S.A. Glantz. 1996. "California's Tobacco Tax Initiative: The Development and Passage of Proposition 99." *Journal of Health Politics, Policy and Law* 21(3, Fall): 543-585.

Tribe, L. 1992. *Abortion: The Clash of Absolutes*, 2nd edition. New York: W.W. Norton.

Vaid, U. 1995. *Virtual Equality: The Mainstreaming of Gay and Lesbian Liberation*. New York: Doubleday and Co.

Weiner, J.M. 1992. "Oregon's Plan for Health Care Rationing." *The Brookings Review* (Winter): 26-31.

Weitzer, R. 1991. "Prostitutes' Rights in the United States: The Failure of a Movement." *The Sociological Quarterly* 32(1, Spring): 23-41.

Zussman, R. 1992. *Intensive Care: Medical Ethics and the Medical Profession*. Chicago, IL: The University of Chicago Press.

TOWARD A GENERAL THEORETICAL-METHODOLOGICAL FRAMEWORK FOR THE SOCIOLOGY OF LAW:

ANOTHER LOOK AT THE EASTERN-EUROPEAN PIONEERS

A. Javier Treviño

ABSTRACT

In this paper, I aim to accomplish four objectives. First, I briefly discuss some of the key ideas proposed by the four Eastern-European pioneers of legal sociology: Eugen Ehrlich, Leon Petrazycki, Georges Gurvitch, and Nicholas S. Timasheff. Second, I identify and examine the five most salient theoretical themes (and their concomitant subthemes) that run through and inform the pioneers' major works in the sociology of law. Third, I comment on the methodological procedures which the pioneers advocate using in conducting sociolegal research. Fourth, based on the foregoing

Sociology of Crime, Law, and Deviance, Volume 1, pages 155-202.

ISBN: 0-7623-0282-8

remarks, I then draft a preliminary conceptual blueprint, in the form of a schematic diagram—the dual-polygonal paradigm—to be used in constructing a formal theoretical-methodological framework for the sociological study of law.

INTRODUCTION

In this essay, I argue that there are two intellectual endeavors that can contribute immeasurably to clarifying legal sociology's identity and to advancing its scientific knowledge. First, the sociology of law has yet to formally recognize its founding fathers or pioneers.[1] Only after a field of knowledge has properly acknowledged and saluted the classical authors responsible for laying its conceptual bedrock can it effectively and efficiently—that is to say, with disciplined rigor—begin the task of constructing its theoretical ideas and methodological strategies upon that foundation.[2] While it is doubtless true that the concepts and theories articulated by the three most influential social theorists of the nineteenth century—Karl Marx, Max Weber, and Émile Durkheim—have greatly enriched and enhanced our knowledge of legal sociology (Treviño 1996a, 1996b; Turkel 1996; Vago 1997), there has been no consensus among scholars that these three, individually or collectively, are the titular founders of legal sociology. This is largely explained by the fact that neither Marx nor Durkheim ever identified law as a major theoretical problem, and despite Weber's brilliant and numerous contributions to legal sociology, he has not commonly been regarded as its founder.

Second, and related, the sociology of law continues to await the formulation of an overarching paradigm, a conceptual scheme, that will guide and inform its theory and research. Some attempts have been made at developing a unified, general theory for the sociological examination of law (Renner [1904] 1949; Pashukanis [1924] 1989; Luhmann 1985); none, however, has been considered by the discipline as the leading, much less the authoritative, general theory. The most notable and systematic of these efforts has been undertaken by Black (1976). About such a general theory of law, Black states:

> The proper concern of legal sociology should be the development of a general theory of law. . . . To say that a theory of law is general means that it seeks to order law wherever it is found. It seeks to discover the principles and mechanisms that predict empirical patterns of law, whether these patterns occur in this day or the past, regardless of the substantive area of law involved and regardless of the society . . . unless we seek generality in our study of law, we abandon hope for a serious sociology of law (1972, p. 1096).[3]

In sum, then, the sociology of law has not identified its founders—its intellectual pioneers—and thus has neglected to build upon, extend, and elaborate their insights concerning theory and research. In addition, the sociology of law has not proffered a "grand theory" (Simon and Lynch 1989, p. 841), a wide-encompassing macro description or explanation of various sociolegal phenomena that can be accepted and utilized by most of its scholars and practitioners. In this paper, I identify four pioneers of legal sociology and offer their conceptualizations as an initial attempt at devising a general sociological theory of law.

EHRLICH, PETRAZYCKI, GURVITCH, AND TIMASHEFF

Several scholars have recognized the Eastern Europeans Eugen Ehrlich, Leon Petrazycki, Georges Gurvitch, and Nicholas S. Timasheff as pioneers of sociolegal theory.[4] Few legal sociologists, however, can claim true conversance with the Eastern-European pioneers' groundbreaking ideas. This paper represents the first effort to jointly and systematically analyze the sociolegal statements of Ehrlich, Petrazycki, Gurvitch, and Timasheff.

I here aim to accomplish four objectives: (1) to briefly discuss some of the Eastern-European pioneers' key ideas; (2) to identify and examine the five salient theoretical themes (and their concomitant subthemes) that run through and inform their major works in the sociology of law; (3) to comment on the methodological procedures which the pioneers advocate using in conducting sociolegal research; and (4) based on the foregoing remarks, to draft a preliminary conceptual blueprint, in the form of a schematic diagram—the dual-polygonal paradigm—to be used in constructing a formal theoretical-methodological framework for the sociological study of law. I begin by placing the four pioneers' and their foundational notions in their appropriate sociohistorical context. In so doing, a greater understanding is acquired of their contributions to the sociology of law.

The Sociohistorical Context

Perhaps of most significance in understanding the theoretical ideas of Ehrlich, Petrazycki, Gurvitch, and Timasheff is the fact that they had their formative biographical and intellectual experiences in the events and milieu of *fin de siècle* Eastern Europe. Near-contemporaries, they were all born within 32 years and about 1,600 kilometers of each other. Eugen Ehrlich (1862-1922) was born in Czernowitz in the province of Bukowina (Austro-Hungary), a region in the northeastern corner of the Carpathian mountains. Petrazycki, Gurvitch, and Timasheff were natives of Czarist Russia. The son of a Polish noble, Leon Petrazycki (1867-1931) was born near the city of Vitebsk in the province which formed the northeastern corner of the territory annexed by Russia from Poland in 1772. The fact that he was of Polish ancestry and that he belonged to the nobility seemed to have some bearing on the formation of his personality (Timasheff 1955, p. xxi). Georges Gurvitch (1894-1965) was born in the Russian port city of Norvorossisk, on the Black Sea; and Nicholas S. Timasheff (1886-1970), the son of the Minister of Trade and Industry, was born in St. Petersburg.

The Eastern-European pioneers also share several influences and locales concerning their education, careers, and political orientations. All of them acquired legal training in the university and spent most of their lives in academe. After receiving his doctorate in law from the University of Vienna Ehrlich became a *Privatdozent* and began teaching law at that institution in 1894. Three years later, he was appointed Extraordinary Professor of Roman Law at the University of Czernowitz. Ehrlich served as Rector of the University in 1906 and remained there the rest of his life. His interest in legal-sociological investigations in all likelihood "stemmed from his experiences with the legal situation in Bukowina, where every Volk-group possessed its own order below the surface of Austrian law" (Rottleuthner 1987, p. 19). During Ehrlich's time, Austria consisted of nine distinct Volk-groups or nationalities: Armenians, Germans, Jews, Rumanians, Russians (Lipowanians), Ruthenians, Slovaks, Hungarians, and Gypsies (Ziegert 1979, p. 229). The Austrian Civil Code, however, was in many important respects ignored by these various ethnic groups, and each of them obeyed totally different legal rules in all the legal relations of their daily lives (Kidd 1938, pp. 384-385; Ziegert 1979, p. 229). While Ehrlich did not belong to any political party, he nevertheless worked to preserve the Austro-Hungarian State with its multiplicity of ethnic minority groups (Rottleuthner 1987, p. 19).

Petrazycki received his master's degree in Roman Law from the University of Kiev. In 1883, while still a law student, he translated into Russian and published Baron's *Roman Pandects*. He later obtained a two-year grant to study at the University of Berlin under the great German scholar of Roman law, Heinrich Dernberg (Babb 1937, p. 794; Langrod and Vaughan 1970, pp. 306f). This was during the time that the new German Civil Code, the *Bürgerliches Gesetzbuch*, was in its final stages of completion, and Petrazycki had a hand in its preparation. Laserson explains that in "the atmosphere of the creation of new civil law which surrounded young Petrazhitskii it was only natural that a decisive criticism of dogmatic jurisprudence should develop. Here the reshaping and remaking of law, the *de lege ferenda*, became more important than the perception and interpretations of what written law commands or means, than the *de lege lata*" (1951, p. 61).

In 1897, Petrazycki was awarded the doctorate in law from the University of St. Petersburg, and the following year he was given the chair of jurisprudence at that institution. He was subsequently promoted to the rank of full professor and appointed Dean of the Faculty of Law. A constitutional democrat and active liberal Petrazycki joined the Constitutional Democratic (KD) party in 1906 and was elected to the Duma as a deputy. When the Duma was dissolved, Petrazycki—together with the other former deputies of the KD party—signed the Viborg Manifesto in protest against the dissolution. As a consequence of signing the Manifesto, which called for the population not to pay taxes to the Czarist government, to refuse conscription into the army, and to refuse to comply with other public obligations until the election of a new parliament, Petrazycki was imprisoned for three months and barred from all political activity (Laserson 1951; Langrod and Vaughan 1970; Górecki 1975; Timasheff 1981).

Disillusioned with the Bolshevik Revolution, Petrazycki, Gurvitch, and Timasheff fled Russia during the early 1920s. Clearly, none of the four pioneers was a political revolutionary. While they all exhibited strong reformist tendencies, they can perhaps best be described as "reform oriented right wing liberals" (Ziegert 1979, p. 227). This helps explain why Petrazycki, who was designated to take office in the provisional Kerensky government in Russia after the 1917 revolution, emigrated to Poland and in 1921 accepted the chair of sociology at the University of Warsaw.

Gurvitch and Timasheff produced their best-known works in legal sociology during their period of exile in the West. Both men taught at the University of Prague, spent time in the United States (Timasheff eventually settled there permanently), and obtained positions at Harvard University.

Gurvitch acquired university training at Dorpat, Estonia (then part of Russia). After receiving his *baccalauréat*, he studied law at the University of Petrograd, receiving his L.L.D. degree in 1917. Having become convinced that his hopes for a decentralized, pluralist form of democracy were not about to be realized, Gurvitch became disenchanted with the Russian Revolution. It is no doubt true, however, that the Revolution impressed upon Gurvitch the "elements of creativity, spontaneity and conflict which gave rise to a plurality of social forms" (McDonald 1979, p. 29).

In 1920, Gurvitch left Russia, never to return, and accepted a position at the University of Prague, where he taught for five years. In 1925, he became a Lecturer at the Slavonic Institute in Paris. Three years later, at the Sorbonne, he succeeded to the chair previously held by Émile Durkheim and in the 1930s was appointed a professor of sociology at the Universities of Bordeaux and Strasbourg. Between 1931 and 1940, he served as Secretary General of the International Institute of the Sociology of Law in Paris and as editor of the *Archives de Philosophie du Droit et de Sociologie Juridique*. During World War II, Gurvitch emigrated to the United States, where he taught sociology at the New School for Social Research, Columbia University, and Harvard. Unimpressed by the preoccupations of empirical research in America, he returned to France in 1945 and the following year organized the *Centre d'Études Sociologiques* with the intention of joining general sociological theory and empirical research (Bosserman 1968; McDonald 1979; Hunt 1979; Swedberg 1982).

Timasheff received his master's (magister) degree from St. Petersburg University in 1910. Four years later, he was awarded the doctorate and began teaching sociological jurisprudence at the university. Before long, he was appointed professor and dean of the Polytechnical Institute of St. Petersburg. He fled Russia in 1921 and went to Germany, where he wrote for French, Swiss, and Russian newspapers. In 1923, he became a professor of law at the University of Prague. Timasheff emigrated to the United States in 1936 and lectured on the sociology of law at Harvard until 1940. Shortly thereafter, he joined the faculty of arts and sciences at Fordham University and remained there until his retirement in 1958 (Bierstedt 1970).

Because the four pioneers had their formative biographical and intellectual experiences in spatial and temporal proximity, it is understandable that they would be closely acquainted with each others' key ideas. While it is not clear if Ehrlich and Petrazycki ever came into personal contact, they were doubtless familiar with each others' works. Indeed, one scholar claims that Ehrlich took over the notion of intuitive law from Petrazycki (see Podgórecki 1980-1981, p. 191, n. 10). We do know that Gurvitch wrote about Ehrlich (Gurvitch 1942a, pp. 148-156), Petrazycki (Gurvitch 1931, 1937a), and Timasheff (Gurvitch 1942a, p. 191) and made suggestions on the latter's completed manuscript on the sociology of law (Timasheff 1939a, p. vii). Timasheff (1937a, 1939a, 1955, 1981, 1942, 1957, 1967) also wrote extensively on the legal sociology of Ehrlich, Petrazycki, and Gurvitch. Furthermore, Timasheff and Gurvitch were students of Petrazycki at the University of St. Petersburg (Bierstedt 1970, p. 290; Coser 1977, p. 500; Hunt 1979, p. 190; Swedberg 1982, p. 45; Kojder and Kwasniewski 1985, p. 263; Sorokin 1963, p. 88).

While in some cases the four pioneers clearly agreed with each other's ideas, in many other cases they vehemently disagreed. Nonetheless, as a result of their professional connections and shared experiences—as well as the five theoretical themes common to them (to be discussed below)—the four Eastern-European pioneers' major works in legal sociology may legitimately be considered within a common conceptual framework.[5]

THE MAJOR WORKS

While many early sociologists exhibited an interest in law, none produced a self-contained volume on the study of the sociology of law proper.[6] By contrast, each of the Eastern-European pioneers' major works is, strictly speaking, devoted to a formal discussion of the sociology of law. The pioneers' major works in legal sociology, which have been translated into English, consist of the following books: Ehrlich's *Fundamental Principles of the Sociology of Law* ([1936] 1962), Petrazycki's *Law and Morality* (1955), Gurvitch's *Sociology of Law* (1942a), and Timasheff's *An Introduction to the Sociology of Law* (1939a).[7]

All through their major works in legal sociology, the Eastern-European pioneers had one basic objective: *the investigation of the dialectical interplay between positive law and living law.* Since these two antagonistic kinds of law are best understood vis-à-vis each other—the differences between the two types are relative rather than absolute—I will first briefly discuss positive law and then, in somewhat greater detail, the pioneers' notion of living law.[8]

Positive Law

Generally and simply, positive law (*jus positivum*), or formal law, consists of statutes enacted or recognized by an external authority, a political superior, or a sovereign (monarch, parliament, congress). As John Austin states, "Every positive law . . . is set, directly or circuitously, by a sovereign person or body, to a member or members of the independent political society wherein that person or body is sovereign or supreme" (1961, p. 405). Furthermore, positive law is also created by legislative, judicial, and administrative acts or by legal transactions (Kelsen 1945, p. 115). Positive law, or "lawyers' law" as Ehrlich sometimes calls it, is enforced in the courts and other tribunals (Ehrlich [1939] 1962, p. 493). According to Kelsen, the positivity of law "lies in the fact that it is created and annulled by acts of human beings" (1945, p. 114). Thus, we may say that the greater the amount of formal and authoritative interference in law, the greater its degree of legal positivity.[9]

Living Law

The term "living law" (*lebendes Recht*) is widely used by Ehrlich, who defines it as:

> the law which dominates life itself even though it has not been posited in legal propositions. The source of our knowledge of this law is, first, the modern legal document; secondly, direct observation of life, of commerce, of customs and usages, and of all associations, not only of those that the law has recognized but also of those that it has overlooked and passed by, indeed even of those that it has disapproved (1962, p. 493).

Petrazycki's "intuitive law" and Gurvitch's "intuitive spontaneous social law" refer to the same phenomenon. Timasheff, on the other hand, relies on the somewhat awkward phrase, "ethico-imperative coordination," in referring to the law's living *and* positive aspects.

Petrazycki's notion of intuitive law concerns "those legal experiences which contain no references to outside authorities and are independent thereof" (1955 p. 57). As is typically the case with intuitive law, "there are neither commands emanating from authorities nor normative facts of any kind" (1955, p. 155). Additionally, Petrazycki identifies four characteristics of intuitive law. First, it varies with each individual, its content being defined by each person's individual conditions and life circumstances. Second, the directions of intuitive law freely conform with the specific, individual circumstances of the given case and are not constrained by a preestablished pattern of corresponding precepts. Third, intuitive law is characterized by free variability and adaptability as it develops gradually and symmetrically, neither subject to fixation and fossilization nor dependent on arbitrary caprice. Finally, intuitive law has great scope and broad applicability—it is universal—being present always and everywhere.

Gurvitch only minutely defines social law (*droit social*) in his work. In general, he regards social law as the law of communion which emerges spontaneously in every active group and which can partially realize transpersonal values (Swedberg 1982, pp. 38-39). Social law is the nonpolitical law that is frequently neglected by jurists. It is created and embodied in collectivities of all types and found alongside and underneath individual law (Bosserman 1968, pp. 16-17). According to Gurvitch, as a law of objective integration in the "We," in the immanent whole, social law permits the subjects which it addresses to participate directly in the whole; that is why social law is based on confidence; being so based, it can never be imposed from without. Social law can only regulate from within, in an immanent way (Gurvitch 1942a, pp. 211-212). The one type of social law that most closely approximates Ehrlich's living law and Petrazycki's intuitive law is what Gurvitch calls "intuitive spontaneous" social law. Intuitive spontaneous social law is located in the most profound and dynamic—that is, the deepest level—of juridical reality and is based on the direct apprehension of unorganized normative facts (Gurvitch 1941a, p. 208).

Finally, Timasheff's characterization of law as ethico-imperative coordination brings together the concepts of power and ethics, thus revealing the law's positive and living qualities. On the one hand, the power phenomenon has a formalistic and positivistic stamp to it as it entails an "external excitation," such as the act of the dominator—imperative speech or gesture stimulus—or bodily domination (Timasheff 1938a, p. 503). The power phenomenon, moreover, requires organized active power centers, such as the state, as a necessary condition for the existence of law. On the other hand, the concept of ethics involves, for Timasheff, the idea of custom and morals, two forces having their origins in human notions, in the group-conviction, concerning duty of behavior.

In short, positive or formal law consists of legal propositions that are decreed by an external, organized authority. The law's positivity has to do with the extent to which it has been formally and logically manipulated—enacted, decided, ratified, and/or repealed. The living law (Ehrlich's concept will be used throughout this paper to also refer to Petrazycki's intuitive law, Gurvitch's social law, and the ethical aspect of Timasheff's ethico-imperative coordination), that is, the law as it actually lives in society, may generally be characterized as spontaneous, experiential, intuitive, customary, elastic, unwritten, latent, and de facto.[10] While the Eastern-European pioneers regard positive and living law as ideal types, it would also be profitable to consider them as dichotomies that are frequently, but not always, in tension. Chambliss and Seidman rightly contend that the "study of formal law and living law . . . embodies the study of the interaction—the dialectic, if you please—between law and society" (1982, p. 69). The pioneers' ideas about living law and how it sometimes supplements but usually contradicts positive law will be discussed in reference to the five theoretical themes running through their major works.

THE FIVE THEORETICAL THEMES

In examining the connection between positive law and living law, the pioneers base the bulk of their commentary on five theoretical themes that permeate their sociolegal writings. I will refer to these as: (1) antiformalism, (2) reciprocal social relationships, (3) functional control, (4) psychogenics, and (5) morality. It should be noted that while these themes remain constant throughout their works, the individual pioneers do not give the themes equal time or emphasis. For example, while Petrazycki discourses at length on the importance of morality in understanding legal relations and Timasheff talks about the involvement of custom and morals in law, Gurvitch addresses the notion of morality not so much in regard to law per se, but in regard to justice. As for Ehrlich, he only hints at the subject and does not mention it expressly.

Although the five theoretical themes are interrelated, we may, for analytical purposes, approach them as being distinct. I will discuss them in the order of the amount of attention and the degree of importance collectively given them by the four Eastern-European pioneers. Given space limitations, it is quite impossible to render any kind of detailed analysis of Ehrlich, Petrazycki, Gurvitch, and Timasheff's ideas; at best, only a most cursory and thus, grossly oversimplified discussion concerning the five most salient theoretical themes (and their concomitant subthemes) that repeatedly show up in their major works can be attempted here.

Antiformalism

Whatever their intellectual preferences and conceptual differences, one thing is certain: the pioneers' legal sociology emerged in direct opposition to the formalist jurisprudence prevalent during the nineteenth and early twentieth centuries.[11] The formalist legal view was perhaps best represented by Austin, who defined law, very simply and without regard to social factors, as the command of a sovereign. At the time that the pioneers were writing, legal formalism had created a system of law that was highly rational, autonomous, and conceptualist. Indeed, it was believed that through the process of formalism, judges could derive legal rules from abstract principles and then mechanically apply those rules, through logical and deductive reasoning, in deciding the outcome of a case. By contrast, the pioneers' legal sociology is antiformalist in that it focuses on the free, spontaneous, intuitive, and informal aspects of the law, the living law.[12]

Ehrlich's legal sociology is most evidently antiformalist when situated in the *Freie Rechtsfindung*, or "free finding of law" movement (Patterson 1931; Ziegert 1979; Rottleuthner 1987). This movement, of which Ehrlich was a founder and which first gained popularity in German-speaking Europe, was the intellectual forerunner of the early twentieth-century movement in law, sociological jurisprudence, as propagated by Oliver Wendell Holmes and Roscoe Pound (Stone 1972, p. 44; Friedmann 1967, p. 298).[13]

Ehrlich contends that it is the norms of conduct—those rules that regulate human behavior in a social association—and not the statutes found in the law books or enacted by the legislatures, that actually govern social life. The point that he continually advances is that the norms of conduct form the true law, the living law, that emerges naturally and spontaneously as people interact with each other in social associations. Consequently, the living law is of primary importance; it is "the center of gravity of legal development." The official command of a sovereign (i.e., positive law or lawyers' law), on the other hand, plays a secondary role and may be relatively insignificant because it is not of much use to people in the course of their daily lives. Accordingly, it makes the most sense to view the law as "something that is woven by the members of an association as they co-operate in their common business" (Partridge 1961, p. 9). The upshot is that a distinction must be made between "legal rules applied by the courts (*Rechtssätze*) and legal arrangements existing in society (*Rechtsverhältnisse, Rechtseinrichtungen*)" (Allen 1964, p. 123).

"The great mass of law," writes Ehrlich, "arises immediately in society itself in the form of a spontaneous ordering of social relations, of marriage, the family associations, possession, contracts, succession, and most of this Social Order has never been embraced in [legal propositions]" (1922, p. 136). Quite simply, Ehrlich posits that while law may be determined by the cultural pattern or "inner order" of associations (i.e., *gesellschaftlichen Verbände*, interest and pressure groups, etc.), the inner order of associations is never determined by law. Indeed, positive law, as defined in terms of statutes or judicial decisions, is simply unnecessary in many cases since most affairs work themselves out without any dispute. And when a dispute does arise, "it is often settled in a friendly manner either because the parties have reached a compromise or because they have renounced their claims because they dreaded the costs in time and money" (Ehrlich 1922, p. 141).[14]

Ehrlich's antiformalism emerges in yet another context. According to him, the ideal legal system was not that of the Continent with its civil codes; rather, it was the English one based on the common law. Contrary to the Continental legal systems which relied on a very rigid and "technical judicial method of decision" (Ehrlich 1969), the system of common law gave judges the freedom to consider the living law as a source for deciding their cases. Furthermore, only the common law allows: (1) the development of legal propositions (*Rechtssatz*) without the interference of a dogmatic and inflexible jurisprudence, such as is found in the codes; (2) the adaptation of legal practice to social needs; and (3) the correspondence of the court's "norms of decision" (*Entscheidungsnormen*)—those rules directing a judge how to decide a case—with the social associations' norms of conduct. Compared to the codified law of the Continent, the common law of England does not deduce a judicial decision from a restrictive set of general and fixed principles. Instead, the English judge engages in a free finding of law by considering the fluid living law. In this way, the judge (or the lawyer) is in a better position to respond to the legal needs of an ever-changing society.

As previously indicated, at the time that Ehrlich was writing, most jurists conceived of law as "a command given by the Government to the judge" (Ehrlich 1969, p. 49). Thus, the conventional wisdom held that the statute, as formulated by the legislature, was the predominant and perhaps the sole form of law. The legislature then gave the statute to the judges, who subsequently lost "all psychological capacity to find in a legal rule anything but a command" (Ehrlich 1969, p. 59). The statute, therefore, acquired a formal rigidity that prevented it from adapting to the practical and immediate needs of a dynamic society. Ehrlich, to the contrary, expressly endorses the *method of free decision* whereby the judge renders a verdict only on the basis of *stare decisis* and the traditional customs of the people. In this way, the judge is unencumbered by immutable legal dogma. Ehrlich distinguishes the method of free decision from the technical method used on the Continent:

> The difference between free decision and technical decision is . . . not so much that the former may go beyond the statute, but lies rather in the manner of doing so. For the technical method requires that its work of art be achieved only by means of certain devices of legal thinking from which no variation must be permitted; while free decision *counts also upon the element of creative thought by great individual minds* (1969, p. 73).

According to Ehrlich, the method of free decision had previously been practiced only in the praetorian law of ancient Rome and in the equity law of nineteenth-century England. In both cases, the law was adapted to the specific life situation under consideration and not the other way around. This type of free law, Ehrlich maintains, serves to safeguard against the formalistic statutes created by the political state, state law (*staatliches Recht*).

Like Ehrlich, Petrazycki also flatly rejects the notion of formalist jurisprudence that the law is a concrete, externally existing entity to be found in the legal codes, court opinions, law books, and other objective sources. Indeed, Petrazycki refers to these external manifestations of the law as nothing more than "phantasmata," naive projections of states of consciousness. He writes, "The content of traditional legal science is tantamount to an optical illusion: it does not see legal phenomena where they actually occur, but discerns them where there is absolutely naught of them—where they cannot be found, observed, or known—that is to say, in a world external to the subject who is experiencing the legal phenomena" (1955, p. 8).

According to Petrazycki, legal concepts like "obligation," "right," "property," and "contract" exist only in the human mind—or, to rely on Babb's (1937, p. 806) translation, the human psyche (*psikhika*). Langrod and Vaughn explain this idea by way of an illustration: "When a loan is contracted and its term comes, all that occurs is a series of mental pictures formed by the contracting parties and based on an anticipated assessment of their respective acts" (1970, p. 323). Thus, for Petrazycki all legal phenomena have their origins in people's subjective experiences and not, as Austin and similar others had suggested, in the external world "out there" (viz., in the organs of state authority).

Petrazycki's antiformalism resurfaces when he distinguishes between positive and intuitive law. Positive law refers to those written rules of a society that are enacted by the state and embodied in its constitutions, statutes, or codes. Intuitive law, on the other hand, emerges spontaneously from peoples' actions in a bilaterally imperative relationship and has no connection with external authority or coercion. For example, "if a husband experiences his duty and his wife's right to fidelity without even thinking about family code, religious command, or any other source establishing the obligation, his impulsion is intuitive" (Góreki 1975, pp. 7-8). The notion of *intuition*—of deep spontaneous conviction—is extremely important not only to Petrazycki but to all of the pioneers.[15] Both positive and intuitive law may be either "official" or "unofficial."

Positive official law consists of authoritative rules enacted by the legislature, recognized by the courts, and sanctioned by the state. Positive unofficial law is composed of the informal but written rules that are acknowledged by the people in a group, organization, or agency. An example of this latter type is found in the case of an arbitrator selected by a corporation so that he/she can settle a dispute between management and labor in accordance with the agreed-upon rules of arbitration. Intuitive official law is employed in an informal manner. The English Court of Chancery used it when it relied on the principle of equity. Intuitive unofficial law arises from people's spontaneous behavior guided by their legal intuitions. Timasheff provides as an example of intuitive unofficial law a situation of frontier justice where "men take the law in their hands and hang a 'bad man' because 'he deserves it'" (1955, p. xxix). In reality, the relationship between intuitive and positive law, along with their variations, "oscillates between minimal and maximal accord. The greater the accord, the better the law functions" (Babb 1938, p. 569).

In Gurvitch's view, the essential task of legal sociology is to study law in all its manifestations, from the realm of "symbols" where law is embodied in predetermined rules, formal procedures, and organized sanctions, to the realm of the "human spirit" (or noetic mind) where law is expressed in the spontaneous beliefs and intuitions of a particular grouping. Gurvitch's sociological orientation, therefore, is quite comprehensive as he considers the formalist as well as antiformalist features of law. Gurvitch addresses both of these aspects in his analysis of the forms of sociality and the types of law emerging from them.

In the forms of sociality that Gurvitch terms "mass" and "communion," the participants' behavior is primarily influenced by feelings of distrust and separation. In these situations, individual law coordinates interpersonal relations between opposing individuals. Alternatively, in the form of sociality that Gurvitch identifies as "community," the law of integration, or social law, emerges spontaneously from the reciprocal relations of the group members. With the doctrine of social law, Gurvitch advances what are perhaps the two most significant points of his legal sociology: (1) all law is social, and (2) social law exists before all other kinds of law. All law is social because it has as its primary source the *normative facts*, or the common values and behaviors, of the community members. Social law is ontologically prior to other forms of law because it resides at the deepest level of social reality: the level of normative facts, that is, those "facts penetrated by extratemporal values" (Swedberg 1982, p. 39). Gurvitch therefore rejects the ancient and popular notion that only the state could create law. Because social law arises directly from the normative facts of a community, it is informal, pluralistic, and democratic. Thus, while Gurvitch's approach to law is not exclusively antiformalist, it is primarily—that is, fundamentally and sequentially—so.

Another manner by which Gurvitch makes formalist and antiformalist distinctions between the different types of law is on the basis of the depth levels of jural reality. In this case, law may be classified according to the degree of organization. At the uppermost stratum, there is formal or organized law. This type of law is highly structured and revealed through symbolic communication (e.g., in the form of written documents). Gurvitch refers to organized law as "the most rigid and superficial level of jural reality" (1942a, p. 226). Organized fixed law, constituting a fixed body of rules backed by sanction, is similar to Ehrlich's lawyers' law (*Juristenrecht*), or statutes enacted by the state. At the other extreme, at the very lowest level of jural reality, we find intuitive spontaneous law. Intuitive spontaneous law emerges directly from the shared collective values—the normative facts—intuited by a living community. In other words, it is produced informally, unceremoniously, without the benefit of any technical procedure.

Like Gurvitch, Timasheff also appears to locate the law's antiformalism in the metaphysical realm of human spirit or, more precisely, in the realm of the collective ethical *ought*.[16] This metaphysical-like quality to his legal sociology is particularly evident in his concept of the self-limitation of power. According to Timasheff, a true legal order is possible to the extent that the political state engages in a self-limitation of power. Only in such a situation is there found the real union of ethics and power that characterizes the law.

In Timasheff's view, law exits only as long as it is recognized by an active power center, which in modern society is typically the state. International law, however, appears to lack the support of such a centralized power. In other words, because international legal rules constitute the highest forms of law, there are no higher legal rules to justify or enforce them. And, since Timasheff believes that a legal order must be engendered by power, by coercive sanctions, "the question arises as to how it can be maintained that [international laws] are of a truly legal nature" (Olivecrona 1948, p. 190). Timasheff's answer to this question is that there are sanctions (aside from those executed by an organized political power structure and socio-ethical pressure), stemming from the self-limitation of power, and numerous informal, extra-legal motives restrict the tendency of active power centers to violate the rules of international law (1939a, p. 265). Among these motives, which have their basis not in informal procedures but in ethical conviction, is the resistance of the people. Timasheff is convinced that the people (in the case of constitutional law) or the international community (in the case of international law) will not tolerate a situation of gross social injustice perpetrated by dominators who brazenly violate the self-limitation of power.[17] The point is that the law's free, intuitive, and customary aspects are evoked when "the people" or "the international community" are compelled, by moral belief, to suppress a perceived injustice.

Reciprocal Social Relationships

One major factor that gives the pioneers' legal theory a distinctively sociological bent is that they focus their study of law on reciprocal social interactions—that is to say, on bilateral exchanges consisting of a set of four corresponding rights (claims) and duties (obligations) between individuals.[18] Moreover, owing to their interest in the interactions occurring between two or more communicating parties, the pioneers' legal sociology is frequently pitched at the micro, or interactive, level of social investigation.

Ehrlich's sociology of law begins with an analysis of social association, which he describes as "a plurality of human beings who, in their relations with one another, recognize certain rules of conduct as binding, and, generally at least, actually regulate their conduct according to them" (1962, p. 39). An association may, broadly speaking, refer to any organized, formal or informal, human grouping where there exist reciprocal relations between people: the state, the economic institution, religious groups, corporations, trade unions, political parties, ethnic groups, the household, the family, and so on. Association also refers to simple, face-to-face relationships like those between parents and children, master and slave, and contractual partners. Ehrlich identifies four major *facts of the law* (*Rechtstatsachen*) or institutionalized standards, that give associations their inner ordering: (1) usage, (2) relations of domination and subjection, (3) relations of possession, and (4) declarations of will (in particular, contracts and testamentary dispositions).

By usage, and in reference to associations, Ehrlich means that "the custom of the past shall be the norm of the future" (1962, p. 85). Usage gives organization to an association like the family, by determining, for example, who will be the head and who will be its members. For reasons of expediency, traditional usage regulates the course of conduct among the members of an association by assigning them certain rights and duties within the context of that association. Usage tells people exactly what tasks and responsibilities they are required to perform in order to maintain the association which is beneficial to them all.

The relations of domination and subjection in an organized association refer to the interactions between superiors and subordinates. Ehrlich distinguishes between two kinds of such relations: those "that flow from the family relationship—the subjection of children to the power of the father, of the wife to that of the husband—and relations of subjection of a purely social origin, slavery and serfdom" (1962, p. 88).

Relations of possession have to do with utilizing a thing—property—for the purpose of deriving practical (economic) benefits from it. The farmer possesses a field to grow cabbage, the manufacturer possesses a loom to weave thread into cloth, the person possesses a slice of bread to appease hunger.

As concerns disposition of will (statements of desire), Ehrlich posits that, in the legal history of the world, there have only been two kinds that are of significance: contract and disposition of last will and testament.

Ehrlich maintains that the facts of the law always and everywhere precede legal propositions, or "the precise, universally binding formulations of the legal precept in a book of statutes or in a law book" (1962, p. 38):

> The [legal propositions] of marriage and family law pre-suppose the existence of marriage and the family. The [legal propositions] that constitute the law of possession could not possibly have been evolved before a system of possession was in existence. [Propositions] of law with reference to contract could not possibly have come about before the corresponding agreements had been made. And people had already inherited property for centuries when the first [legal propositions] with reference to the inheritance of property were being formulated (Ehrlich 1922, p. 139).

When written legal propositions turn into "a monstrous heap of hundreds and thousands of volumes full of contradictions and disputed points" (Ehrlich 1922, p. 136), it then becomes necessary to put them into codes like the *Corpus Iuris Civilis* and the French Civil Code of 1804. During the Middle Ages, Roman law, in the form of the *Corpus Iuris*, was adopted on the European Continent by Italy, Spain, France, Germany, and the Netherlands. Later, in the nineteenth century, there arose several state codes, many of which had their basis in the French Code of 1804: the Prussian *Landrecht*, the *Code Napoléon*, the Austrian Code, the German *Bürgerliches Gesetzbuch*, and the Swiss *Zivilgesetzbuch*. Ehrlich's point is that legal codes like the Roman and the French may, with some modifications, apply to and agree with a variety of social settings, the reason being that the same fundamental structured interactions (reciprocal social relationships) are found everywhere. "We find wherever we go marriage, associations, possession, contracts, succession. To this extent the society which created the [legal propositions] resembled that which adopted them, and the [legal propositions] of the one were thus to a certain extent applicable to the other" (Ehrlich 1922, p. 143).

Of the four Eastern-European pioneers, it is Petrazycki who places reciprocal relations at the center of his legal theory. Indeed, he contends that law introduces a bilateral relationship of rights and duties that is always present explicitly or implicitly. Petrazycki refers to this dual set of mutual claims and obligations as the *imperative-attributive* nature of law. In other words, in a legal relationship it is imperative that the interacting parties fulfill their duties; in the process they are attributed certain rights corresponding to those duties. Rudzinski explains this reciprocal, bilateral relationship:

> Legal "emotions" are complex psychological imperative-attributive experiences having a double passive (stimulus) and active (reaction) nature, where the image of an observed or imagined action releases an emotional repulsion or attraction and a conviction that actor A is obliged to behave in a certain manner (duty impulse) and that such behavior of A is due to person B as his right (1976, p. 113).

For Petrazycki, all legal phenomena—whether of a civil, criminal, administrative, or constitutional nature—are reducible to this imperative-attributive (claim- and obligation-oriented) relationship.[19]

Northrop (1956) charges that Petrazycki never identifies the means by which the imperative-attributive impulsions of the legal relationship are communicated between people. To be sure, Petrazycki fails to specify how individuals convey what their respective duties and rights are in relation to each other. Petrazycki's theory does, however, imply that a communicative process must occur, otherwise legal, and hence social, relations would be impossible. Without communication by means of symbols (body movements, facial expressions, language), neither law nor society can exist. At bottom, then, reciprocal legal relationships are possible through the process of communication.

Gurvitch refers to his brand of sociology as dialectical because he regards social phenomena as being characterized by tensions and conflicts. For Gurvitch, the object is to synthesize or balance the opposing forces creating these tensions and conflicts. In the context of social relations, Gurvitch sees people as experiencing a simultaneous consciousness that takes three forms and which he terms the "I," the "Other," and the "We." These three forms make up two types of social relations: the "*I-Other*" and "*We*" relations. In the experience of I-Other, or "interpersonal relations," people possess a strong individual consciousness that leads them to compare themselves with others and to see the differences and similarities existing between them and others. In such a social relationship, there exists a dialectical tension of "fusion" and opposition to the other. By contrast, in the We relation, individual consciousness is diminished and instead a strong collective mentality of togetherness is present. In real life, we find that there always exists a combination of I-Other and We relations in all social groupings, from the family to society as a whole.

In Gurvitch's view, social relations can be conceptualized as existing on different planes of social reality (the total social phenomena). He thus maintains that it is the sociologist's task to study the depth-levels (of which there are at least ten) as well as the types of social relations. In order to do this, Gurvitch analytically places social reality on two intersecting axes. The vertical axis corresponds to the levels of depth, while the horizontal axis corresponds to the types of social relations that "reside" in those levels of depth.

The vertical axis shows that social relationships are organized along a series of superimposed depth-levels running from the most surface manifestations, where social relations are highly structured and predictable, to the deepest stratum, where social relations are guided by a collective mentality and are highly spontaneous (see Sorokin 1966, pp. 471-472; Bosserman 1968, pp. 110-140; McDonald 1979, pp. 34-35). The horizontal axis shows the three types of social relations which potentially exhibit the degree of organization found in the depth levels. These three types of organized social relations constitute "forms of sociality," "groups," and "global societies." In the interest of space, I will here be primarily concerned with the forms of sociality.

The forms of sociality make up the most basic essence of all social groupings. They manifest themselves as the least structured and, hence, most unstable, spontaneous, and indeterminate of social relations. The forms of sociality are not social structures per se (i.e., associations, groups, or societies); rather, they are social bonds characterized by We-relations, or as Gurvitch puts it, they are "ways of being bound by the whole and in the whole [*par le tout* and *dans le tout*]" (1941a, p. 201, 1941b, p. 21). Gurvitch further distinguishes three primary forms of sociality which he classifies according to the intensity of We-relations or collective states of consciousness: mass, communion, and community (Gurvitch 1941c). Mass sociality occurs when there is a very low degree of We-relations, as evidenced, for example, by the activity of a lynch mob. In this case, the participants' feelings of unity are superficial and of short duration. At the other extreme, communion results when there is a very high degree of We-relations such as those found in a religious cult. Here, the intensity of the fusion results from the "states of collective ecstasy" and communion happens when the dialectical We and I-Other relations are balanced. Thus, even though the behavior of the members of a community is regulated, they are also given a certain amount of freedom to be spontaneous and creative. Gurvitch posits that the greater the intensity of regulation, the less intense the We-relations and vice-versa. Community is the most stable, common, and prevalent form of sociality.

Because law controls the various social relationships appearing at the various levels of depth, Gurvitch states that each level of social reality generates its own kind of law. Furthermore, the several different kinds of law generated correspond to the different forms of sociality and operate simultaneously at the different levels of social reality. He states, "Every form of active sociality which realizes a positive value is a producer of law. . . . Hence, microsociology of law must distinguish as many kinds of law as there are forms of active sociality" (1942a, p. 211). All told, Gurvitch maintains that, schematically speaking, 162 kinds of law can be found in all active social groups (*cadres sociaux*).

In mass sociality where I-Other relations are predominant, individual law coordinates interpersonal relations between contracting parties by informing them about the claims and duties they have relative to one another. We-relations are predominant in the form of sociality called community. In this case, the overemphasis on individualism is diminished as the mutual claims and duties of the community members interpenetrate and form a collective whole. Through their mutual participation, the members achieve "a partial fusion of minds" that produces for them a sense of togetherness or integration. The fusion is not total because there exists a balance that brings together equal measures of integration and regulation. Thus, social law arises, first and foremost, from the reciprocal relations of the members of the community.

Functional Control

Even the most casual reader of the Eastern-European pioneers' works is certain to notice that their legal theory repeatedly relies on the concept of social control as well as on a functionalist analysis of law and society. We may, in accordance with the pioneers' views, define social control as a power that imposes its authority on persons or groups for the express purpose of coordinating, regulating, and constraining their behavior. Moreover, this power may be—but is not necessarily—coercive (in the form of physical force or psychological pressure) in that it enforces social rules and punishes those who violate them.[20] Additionally, the pioneers' functionalist orientation allows them to view social control as having positive consequences, or benefits, for the whole of society. Thus, for them, social control leads to conformity and uniformity of behavior and helps, therefore, to develop and maintain order, integration, organization, and equilibrium in society.

Ehrlich's explanation of functional control begins with his analysis of social association. According to him, every association requires organization. Ehrlich considers organization to be the norm that orders and regulates social relationships by assigning every person a position and function in the association. Organizational norms, therefore, develop the inner order of an association; this inner order, in turn, provides the group with a certain degree of peace and harmony. The four major facts of the law are linked to the organizational norms. According to Ehrlich, "[t]he whole economic and social order of the human race is based upon [these four major facts of the law] . . . usage, domination, possession, disposition. . . . These facts by their very existence determine the rules of conduct for the human associations that are comprised in human society" (1962, p. 118).

The facts of the law determine the *norms of conduct* and the norms of conduct subsequently order social life and deter conflicts by giving structure and predictability to people's relations. Additionally, the norms of conduct may give rise to *norms for decision*, which are created either by the courts or the state in cases of dispute and carry with them specific sanctions. The norms for decision have two purposes in the judicial process. First, they provide guidelines for courts to follow in arriving at judicial decisions, and second, they regulate legal conflicts. As a consequence of these two functions, legal practice and jurisprudence develop and eventually predominate over other, less formal modes of dispute resolution which have their basis in the living law.

While Petrazycki clearly rejects the sanctions (coercion) theory of law (Rudzinski 1976, pp. 114-115), the concept of functional control is readily apparent in his jurisprudence as he examines law's constraining influence on individual behavior and its functions for the social structure. Indeed, Johnson plainly states that "Petrazycki was a kind of structural-functionalist theorist" (1975, p. 43).

According to Petrazycki, the law's imperative-attributive character allows it to regulate social relations and impact society in two significant ways (1955, pp. 93-100). First, it acts as a motivating force, stimulating the accomplishment of some actions. In this capacity, law "urges us to do our duty; it gives us the power to demand what we are entitled to by law; it makes us fight for our rights when they are transgressed and it urges a subject to a sense of obligation to do his duty" (Sorokin 1928, p. 702). Put another way, without law individuals would do little to maintain or improve their social condition.

Second, the law's motivating influence also encourages, inculcates, people to behave in a socially acceptable manner. This means that law plays an educational role in promoting conventional conduct through the process of socialization. Conduct violating conventional expectations is met by the law's negative internal sanctions of guilt or shame (Johnson 1975, p. 41). Through the various social institutions such as the family, church, and courts, individuals learn to comport themselves in a manner that is socially necessary. In this way, the law's educational influence also promotes a uniform system of behavior and contributes to social order.[21]

In Petrazycki's view, the law's two main social functions—the two ways in which law coordinates and regulates social conduct—are its *distributive function* and its *organizing function*. The law's distributive function, which pertains particularly to the nature of property, distinguishes clearly between what is mine and what is yours. Thus, the law distributes material goods (property) and ascribes the claims and obligations corresponding to those goods to all throughout society. The law's distributive function "results in the emergence of a coordinated system of behavior of group members with respect to goods on the market" (Lande 1975, p. 27). In this way, law produces the economic institution. What is more, the law's distributive function draws a boundary line between "mine" and "thine" not only in regard to material goods but also in regard to specific duties and roles among interacting individuals. As such, the law distinguishes between what each person is entitled or obliged to do. Were this not the case, no obedience of the subordinate to the superior, no orderly discharge of duties would be possible (Sorokin 1981, p. 677).

In order to prevent disputes about rights and duties, law fulfills its organizational function. This means that it must have an authoritative agency—such as the governmental legal system of courts, judges, police, prisons, and so forth—with the power to create law and enforce sanctions in cases where rights and duties are violated. Consequently, "there occurs a differentiation of powers" (Lande 1975, p. 28), between those in authority and those who must obey the commands of those in authority. The outcome is the formation of the political institution. Moreover, by performing the organizational function, law brings into existence a government-power capable of enforcing its distributive function and through that of maintaining an order in the group with a minimum of conflicts among its members

(Sorokin 1981, p. 679). In short, the law's distributive and organizational functions produce and maintain a stable social order. Both functions correspond to "tendencies of legal mentality and of the development of that mentality . . . to produce a stable and coordinated system of social conduct evoked by law—a firm and precisely defined order—with which individuals and masses can and should conform, and upon which there can be reliance and calculation as regards . . . the organization of life in general" (Petrazycki 1955, p. 121).[22]

Functional control is implied in Gurvitch's effort to define law as:

> an attempt to realize in a given social environment the idea of justice . . . through multilateral imperative-attributive regulation based on a determined link between claims and duties; this regulation derives its validity from the normative facts which give a social guaranty of its effectiveness and can in certain cases execute its requirements by precise and external constraint, but does not necessarily presuppose it (1942a, p. 59).

As is evident from the above definition, Gurvitch borrows Petrazycki's view of law as an imperative-attributive relationship. This means that Gurvitch, like Ehrlich and Petrazycki before him, does not see law only in terms of political coercion, that is, as simply emanating from the state's authority. Gurvitch does, however, acknowledge the law's very real ability to regulate people's behavior. Therefore, the various types of law—individual, social, and subordinative—control, to one degree or another, the diverse social relationships appearing at the different levels of depth.

Individual law is found in mass sociality where I-Other relations are pervasive. According to Gurvitch, the strong emphasis that the modern Western world placed on individualism came from Roman law, and since the reception of Roman law by most of Europe had occurred during the Middle Ages, European jurisprudence focused primarily on the isolated individual and their conflicts with other individuals. Thus, "[t]he law's function was purely negative—to prevent harm to the individual. Law per se had become so identified with individualism, Gurvitch argued, that anti-individualism was nearly always combined with hostility to the very notion of law" (Swedberg 1982, p. 38). As previously mentioned, individual law regulates relations between transacting parties by delimiting their claims and duties.

Social law, which "comes from the element of unity within the totality" (Bosserman 1968, p. 22), does not rely wholly or even principally on unconditional coercion. Although it has as one of its objectives the regulation of the life of the community, social law does not need an external political authority such as the state to exert pressure. And even though the complex community consists of a diverse population of many members, there must, from such a plurality, emerge a convergence of values. The union of these moral values is then embodied in the law. Hence, we may say that:

> [t]he starting point of [Gurvitch's] analysis is the proposition that, behind the daily experience of jurists, judges, claimants, legislators, voters, people who settle contracts or create associations, and the like, there is an "immediate legal experience" which gives a common meaning

to the separate experiences. The element common to every legal experience is the collective recognition of values (Timasheff 1942, pp. 710-722).

Subordinative law, or the law of domination, is a "perversion" of social law. It emerges as a result of combining social and individual law, but in a way that subjugates the former to the latter. Subordinative law expresses claims and duties in terms of the master-servant, superior-subordinate, or ruler-ruled relationship. It relies exclusively upon coercive force to ensure compliance. Subordinative law is therefore characteristic of totalitarian regimes (Nazi, fascist, communist). Indeed, at the height of World War II and in reference to Nazi Germany and Fascist Italy, Gurvitch wrote: "What is at stake in the decisive struggle for the fate of humanity, which in the present war is reaching its most accurate and tragic phase, can be formulated . . . as the struggle between the principle of social law—the foundation of pluralistic democracy—and the principle of the totalitarian state" (1941b, p. 25). Gurvitch characterizes the totalitarian state as "a closed organization without any contact with spontaneous sociality" (1941b, p. 30).

At the core of Gurvitch's definition of law is the notion of justice. To be sure, it is the very idea of justice that distinguishes law from other forms of social control such as morality, religion, aesthetics, and education. Justice, moreover, endows social control with a functional quality because it helps to maintain an equal balance between the normative facts—the reciprocal claims and duties—of the many community members; this is its imperative-attributive quality. In the process of doing this, justice stabilizes social relations and provides order, peace, and security for the community. In other words, justice, through law, resolves conflicts and tensions between people by assuring the realization of everyone's claims and duties. The role that justice plays then "is that of a go-between, an arbiter, a builder of equilibria" (Bosserman 1968, p. 42).

Two dialectical types of justice are said to exist: commutative and distributive. According to Gurvitch, commutative justice rests on the principle of individualism and operates at the personal level. Commutative justice is the business of the judge as he or she decides which punishments should be imposed and damages paid. Distributive justice, on the other hand, is premised on the principle of universalism and stresses the values of the whole. Distributive justice is the business of the legislator whose job it is to determine how political rights and goods should be apportioned. Social justice—that is, justice that has its basis in social law—balances the two types and thus addresses values at the transpersonal level, that is, at the level where social law is able to synthesize the individual *and* the universal. In this way, the parts and the whole interpenetrate. The judicial function is *social integration*:

> Justice is at once objective and subjective, real and formal, or rather it transcends these opposites because it integrates individuals in a transpersonal, antihierarchal order in which every individual maintains his/her own dignity precisely to the extent that s/he is an indispensable member of a community that cannot be reduced to the sum of its parts. Justice demands the realization of an order which is "neither communism, nor despotism, nor atomism, nor anar-

> chy, but liberty in order and independence in unity." It is through "mutualism," the interplay of collaborative associations and their federations, through the humanization of property by its transformation into a social function in the hands of cooperative associations, and finally, through the counterbalancing of the state by organized economic society, that justice can be best approximated (Gurvitch 1937b, p. 512).

Finally, Gurvitch's emphasis on the human spirit also reveals his functionalist orientation. Martindale posits that Gurvitch's "study of the human spirit or noetic mind is the study of cultural patterns, social symbols, and collective spiritual values and ideas in their functional relations with social structures and concrete historical situations in society" (1981, p. 577). Likewise, Hunt explains that Gurvitch's functional perspective "is one that is consistent with his pluralistic political philosophy, namely that of providing social regulation or maintaining the social equilibrium in such a way that the fundamental spiritual values of the collectivity are thereby protected" (1979, pp. 180-181).

The notion of functional control with its emphasis on equilibrium and social order finds its clearest and strongest exposition in Timasheff's legal sociology. As Hunt remarks, "[Timasheff] advances an 'equilibrium' or 'social order' model of society as a concrete system with an inherent tendency towards social equilibrium. He conceived society as responding with a Pavlovian reflex to anything that disturbs that equilibrium" (1979, p. 191). In addition to a Pavlovian influence, Timasheff's notion of social equilibrium is decidedly Paretian:

> The role of law securing equilibrium is obvious. Criminal law inhibits drives to violate it and, if the inhibition is sufficient, reinforces the totality of basic sentiments [behavior tendencies]. Civil law secures and, eventually, restores that distribution of goods and of services in which the social equilibrium is expressed. Constitutional law secures the distribution of dominance and submission within the social system. By many parts of modern "social law" the degree of co-operation attained in a given society is secured, etc. (Timasheff 1940, p. 149).

To begin with, Timasheff sees law as a "social force" that, with the support of an organized power structure, imposes on people certain norms of conduct. The purpose of these norms is to produce uniformity and conformity in the behavior of individuals. Only in this way can social order be realized. Timasheff describes order as "a set of rules of conduct which members [of a society] are supposed to follow and the violations of which are disapproved and reacted upon by the other members" (1946, p. 822).

Contrary to Petrazycki, Timasheff maintains that legal relations between people are possible in large measure because these relations entail a "situation of having to act under actual or potential coercion" (1939a, p. 331). Simply put, people sometimes fulfill their duties toward each other because they fear being punished. The fact remains, however, that uniformity of behavior is crucial to maintaining the equilibrium of society (see Timasheff 1939a, p. 21, 1940).

As concerns functional control, Timasheff distinguishes between three main types of social uniformities. Natural uniformities have to do with those sets of similar acts (e.g., crimes, suicides, divorces) caused by factors outside of the individual (e.g., poverty, rapid social change, unemployment); these are not acts to which individuals must conform in order to prevent disruption of society's equilibrium. Imitation uniformities are certain patterns of behavior that any number of individuals may freely choose to copy as, for example, with the introduction of a new fashion of clothing that is eventually adopted by some people. Finally, imposed uniformities occur when "a certain behavior is 'imposed' on group-members as an obligatory pattern for their behavior" (Timasheff 1939a, p. 8). An obligatory pattern of behavior may appear in a couple of ways: (1) as a concrete act or a series of similar acts, or (2) as an ideal structure, that is, as an "abstract description of behavior to which individuals should adjust their conduct" (Timasheff 1939a, p. 117). An example of the first variety is seen when the courts of a given country follow the decisions of their supreme court concerning a particular legal matter. An example of the second variety occurs when a new ritual is established by a church council and the priest and believers perform it. For Timasheff, the uniformity of behavior created by law is always of the "imposed" types.

The imposing of behavior patterns is accomplished by the activities of functionaries whom Timasheff calls "supporters of patterns" and which include magistrates, judges, administrative officials, and legislators. Behavior conforming to the obligatory pattern in force is regarded as normal and said to be "coordinated." On the other hand, behavior deviating from the obligatory pattern is considered "abnormal." The process of imposing preestablished behavior patterns is termed *social coordination*, and the purpose of coordination is to preserve social equilibrium. Put another way, the goal of coordination is the creation and preservation of social order.

Social coordination occurs in several forms. First, it may be classified as ethical or nonethical. Ethical coordination takes place when the imposition of patterns of conduct on individual wills is accepted by the ethical conviction of the group. A conviction is said to be an ethical one "insofar as its content is the evaluation of human behavior from a specific viewpoint, permitting the application of the term 'duty' to the behavior which is in conformity with a certain pattern, and of the term 'violation of duty' to the behavior noncomformable with it" (Timasheff 1939a, p. 13). On the other hand, nonethical coordination is not based on people's evaluation of behavior as being good or bad, right or wrong, just or unjust; rather, it relies on coercive sanctions alone to ensure desirable conduct. In this case, people obey the rules because they fear reprisal. Second, the forms of social coordination may also be classified as centralized or decentralized. In centralized coordination, we find within a larger social group, a smaller group which Timasheff calls the "active center of power-structures" (1938b, p. 868). This active power center—which in modern societies takes the form of the political state—exercises authority over the members of the passive periphery (e.g., the citizenry) as it imposes patterns of behavior on them in order to determine their conduct. Thus, owing to this power imbalance, the social interaction between the active power center and periphery is an unequal one. Timasheff refers to this process as "imperative coordination."

In a situation of decentralized coordination, there is no active power center and, thus, the imposition of behavior patterns takes place as individuals of equal standing influence each other's conduct. Because there is no display of organized power in this situation, Timasheff describes it as one of "non-imperative coordination." In this case, "every group-member influences all the others and every group-member is influenced by all the others" (Timasheff 1939a, p. 106). Hence, it is not coercion or the display of power in the form of official commands and sanctions that accounts for the imposition, but socio-ethical pressure. Socio-ethical pressure (which is the sole sanction in premodern societies and which is not yet legal regulation) arises from the group conviction that a person "ought" to act in a certain way in given circumstances. Those individuals who transgress the ethical rules will provoke a hostile attitude or punitive reaction from the group (Timasheff 1937c).

Timasheff derives four types of social coordination from its two pairs of forms discussed above. These are: (1) nonethical and nonimperative, (2) ethical but nonimperative, (3) imperative but nonethical, and (4) ethical and imperative. The nonethical and nonimperative type does not exist in reality because without group conviction and centralized power, there is no effort at securing uniform patterns of conduct, and without some patterns of conduct, society is not possible. Ethical but nonimperative (purely ethical) coordination relies on group conviction but not on centralized power. In this case, custom and morals alone determine individual behavior. Imperative but nonethical (purely imperative) coordination depends on an organized central power but not on group conviction. The despotic rule of a totalitarian government unconcerned with the moral sentiments of its people serves as an apt illustration. Finally, the ethical and imperative type of social coordination requires both group conviction and an organized social power to authoritatively impose patterns of behavior on group members. The ethical and imperative type of coordination, Timasheff contends, is created by law.

Based on the foregoing remarks, Timasheff concludes that ethics and power are the two major elements of social coordination. He distinguishes between the two elements: "The interaction resulting in giving force to ethical rules is an equal one: in this process everyone plays the same part, imposing the common will on others and feeling this will imposed upon him. Within power-structures, the social interaction is an unequal one—the waves of influence run only in one direction" (1939a, p. 171). Despite their differences, ethics and power combine to form a higher unity—law:

> Rules of behavior are created which are simultaneously ethical rules and general commands of an established power structure. They form a system of human behavior in society presenting simultaneously the features of efficient ethics and efficient power, of *law*. . . . Ethics and power are not two coordinated or subordinated phenomena. They may be thought of as two circles which cross one another. Their overlapping section is law (Timasheff 1939a, p. 248).

In other words, law is ethical because "every legal pattern of conduct can be expressed in a proposition with the predicate 'ought to be'" (Timasheff 1939a, p. 15). At the same time, law is also imperative because its "ought to be" is enforced by a centralized power-structure. The law, therefore, is an ethico-imperative coordination. As Timasheff puts it, "legal order is constituted by patterns of conduct enforced by agents of centralized power (tribunals and administration) and simultaneously supported by a group-conviction that the corresponding conduct 'ought to be'" (1939a, p. 17). The law's functional control brings about "the realization of a perfect coordination of human behavior" (1939a, p. 321).

Psychogenics

Although the Eastern-European pioneers have much to say about social institutions, social structures, and society in general, many of their more central concepts are psychogenically oriented. Accordingly, the pioneers frequently consider such "psychological" factors as personality, psyche, consciousness, impulsions, emotions, feelings, noetic mind, instincts, intuition, sentiments, and spiritual values. Greatly influenced by the behavioral psychology of their time, Petrazycki and Timascheff, in particular, premise their legal theory on the notions of conditioning, reinforcement, stimulus, and response.

Ehrlich's psychogenic technique is most evident when he discusses the method of free decision and underscores the "personal element" of justice. Ehrlich believes that, to a far greater extent than any legal doctrine, it is the judge's *personality* that, in the final analysis, influences how he decides a case. Ehrlich, to be sure, greatly admired the pronounced personalities of the great judges whom he regarded as "epoch-making in the history of English [and American] law and whose names are spoken of with reverence" (1962, p. 290). Among these he lists Sir Edward Coke, Sir George Jessel, John Marshall, James Kent, Joseph Story, and Oliver Wendell Holmes. In considering the judge's personality, Ehrlich anticipates, by a few decades, the psychological approach of adjudication employed by such American legal realists as Hessel Yntema, Joseph Hutcheson, Jerome Frank, and Karl N. Llewellyn (Nussbaum 1940, p. 194). For example, Frank (1930), in taking a psychoanalytical approach, argued that law is highly inconsistent because it is dependent on the judge's idiosyncratic biases (prejudices, sympathies, and antipathies). These biases reveal themselves in the way the judge interprets the "facts" of the case. Similarly, Hutcheson candidly admitted that as a judge, he decided cases "by feeling and not by judgment; by 'hunching' and not by ratiocination" (1929, p. 285). Thus, for legal realists like Frank and Hutcheson, as for Ehrlich, the judge's personality and intuitive mental processes of free interpretation have a highly significant determination on judicial outcome.

Petrazycki's orientation toward the law was, at least initially, heavily psychological.[23] As previously indicated, for him law is a psychological phenomenon because its origins lie in people's subjective experiences. Therefore, it is in psychology that Petrazycki finds "the basic facts and concepts in terms of which law is to be understood and analyzed" (Northrop 1956, p. 652), and it is through psychology that the nature of law is revealed.

At about the time that Petrazycki was formulating his psychological theory of law in St. Petersburg, Ivan Pavlov, also in that city, was constructing his stimulus-response theory (Timasheff 1981, pp. 743-744; Denzin 1975, p. 70). But whereas Pavlov's orientation toward psychology was strictly behaviorist, Petrazycki's orientation was behavioristic *and* introspective. Thus, he was interested not only in people's responses to the external stimuli in their environment but also in the subjective meanings of their *psychical experiences*.

Petrazycki believes that people's psychical experiences are constituted of psychic dispositions or "impulsions." Impulsions are bilateral, passive-active (stimulus-response) behavior-tendencies that motivate a person to respond (*Aktsiya*), or to refrain from responding (abstain), in a given situation. They are of two kinds, specific and abstract. Specific (or "special") impulsions refer to those automatic and unconscious biological responses that are determined by a stimulus. These include such motoric drives as hunger, thirst, the sexual drive, fear, and curiosity (Rudzinski 1976, p. 112). For example, a person experiences the stimulus of hunger pangs (passively) and reacts by going to the refrigerator to get food (actively). Abstract (or "blanket") impulsions, on the other hand, are products of culture. These include love, ambition, vanity, malice, and hatred. They have to do with the person having an "action idea"—a conscious awareness or mental image—that defines the character and direction of her behavior. Legal experiences belong in the category of abstract impulsions and, thus, we may speak of legal impulsions.

In analyzing people's psychical experiences, Petrazycki looks at the role that emotions play in the legal, imperative-attributive relationship. According to him, emotions motivate people to realize their rights as well as to fulfill their duties. Emotions as inner drives are what lead to the law's development. Further, emotional impulsions make the imperative-attributive legal relations "binding." That is to say, people obey the law because they feel committed to each other; they are bound by duty. As Babb puts it, "[a] legal phenomenon, a legal psychic act, may be an attributive norm or consciousness of 'ought' or of a legal claim, as belonging to another existing only in the mind of one man, with no acknowledgment or consent from social authority, court or anyone else at all, except the person experiencing these psychic conditions" (1938, p. 517). This notion is contrary to the explanation given by formalist jurisprudence that individuals obey the law because of some external constraint or because it is the command of a sovereign. For Petrazycki, the Austinian notion of the law as sovereign commands, or the power of the state, is only a metaphor, a projected symbol representing people's internal mental processes. In sum, "[t]he reality of law is in the mind of men *ascribing* rights and duties to others, not in the 'phantasmata' projected on persons and things with which the impulsions are concerned" (Olivecrona 1948, p. 173).

Relative to the other pioneers, Gurvitch's legal theory is the least psychogenic. Nevertheless, having been influenced significantly by Petrazycki, Gurvitch often speaks of law as having its origins in the intuitions of the community. As we have already seen, for Gurvitch the sociology of law has as one of its objectives the study of the *collective noetic mind* where law is expressed in the spontaneous beliefs and intuitions of the members of a community. Further, according to him, the power of social law is derived from the normative facts, the shared spiritual values of the community which can be apprehended directly through intuition. For Gurvitch, any "psychological attitude" like intuition or spiritual values can be examined in either "the individual or the collective subject" (1942b, p. 106). Since, in his legal sociology, Gurvitch's main concern is with the collective and transpersonal "We" relations of social law and distributive justice, he frequently opts to examine the psychological attitudes of the collective over the individual.

Timasheff bases his ideas about power and punishment on people's *biopsychic instincts* (basic sentiments). For example, in his view, ethics serve to sustain society's equilibrium by reacting against anti-social or unlawful behavior. This reaction, he claims, is a consequence of the instinctive emotional response to punish behavior violating the ethical convictions of the group. In premodern societies, punishment takes the form of private revenge and, thus, "retaliatory sanctions" like personal vengeance and blood feuds are the order of the day. In modern societies, by contrast, punishment is expressed as organized social retribution, and "restorative sanctions" like civil damages are introduced. Additionally, in modern societies, "[a]pplying punishment to transgressions of ethical rules becomes one of the functions of political power" (Timasheff 1937c, p. 402). Only through punishment can the ethical convictions of the group be reinforced in the minds of its members.[24]

Timasheff's reliance on many of the major concepts made popular by behavioral psychology is particularly evident in his explanation of the "process of polarization." According to him, the process of polarization is based on a natural division between people. This division is manifested in social groups as some individuals, possessing an active nature, exhibit the tendency to command, while the majority of individuals, possessing a passive nature, are inclined to obey. In this way, a relation of dominance-submission is created between dominators and subjects. The result is the emergence of a power structure, or "a complex of behavior tendencies and corresponding psychic dispositions in many interrelated individuals" (Timasheff 1939a, pp. 184-185). The commands of the dominators emanate from the power structure's active center and are received by the members of the passive periphery. In time, the subject's submission to the dominator's commands becomes habitual and automatic. The act of submission can thus be seen as a conditioned response to an external stimulus. Timasheff explains how the dominance-submission relationship molds the desired behavior:

> Why does the soldier behave "correctly?" Because during a certain length of time certain sounds accompanied the display of an already existing tendency of submission (inborn or acquired). In the beginning, our soldier was impressed by the meaning of the words he heard and by the sounds as such; these meanings, through the complex mechanisms of voluntary action, resulted in the corresponding bodily movements, which were, of course, carried out quite inaccurately; later on, the nervous current engendered in the sense organ by sound was directed immediately toward the centers ruling the commanded movements, and these movements were performed automatically and, therefore, with more accuracy (1939a, p. 181).

Timasheff's account of people's inborn instincts toward dominance or submission leads Alan Hunt to declare that "a distinctive feature of [Timasheff's] sociology of law is that he approaches the role of psychological factors in the study of legal phenomena" (1979, p. 192).

Morality

Morality, ethics, and kindred issues dealing with right and wrong inform much of the pioneers' sociology of law.

While Petrazycki comments extensively on morality, he treats the issue chiefly as a comparative index by which to delineate the sphere of legal phenomena. In his view, legal impulsions consist of the action ideas of right and duty that guide social relationships between people, and it is on this basis that he distinguishes law from morality. Petrazycki defines morality as those norms that "establish obligations free in respect to others: these authoritatively prescribe certain conduct for us but give others no claim or rights of any kind to fulfillment by us" (1955, p. 46). Thus, morality is one-sided; it is not attributive but only imperative—urging or recommending a given form of conduct. Morality stipulates the conduct that we should show toward others but does not recognize our entitlement to demand the same conduct from others. One example of a unilateral relationship is found in the imperative that one should come to the aid of a fellow human being who has been physically injured. Since there is no expectation that the victim should reciprocate, the individual's duty to help is here motivated only by *altruism* or good will. Another example of this kind of one-sided obligation is Jesus's injunction: "Whosoever shall smite thee on thy right cheek, turn to him the other also." In this case, the individual who is slapped has a moral duty to refrain from retaliating. The injunction, however, does not give the assaulter the right to strike. Law, on the other hand, is imperative *and* attributive (*pritiâzatel'nii)* and, thus, fundamentally based on the idea of quid pro quo. Babb explains that "imperativeness" and "attributiveness" are properties specifically of the emotional composition of ethical experiences (1938, p. 536). Moral and ethical experiences, therefore, are emotions of obligation, of duty. Gurvitch is quite right in stating that Petrazycki's goal was to "reconcile sociology and morality" (as quoted in Swedberg 1982, p. 157, n. 50).

Gurvitch's sociology, having been deeply influenced by Fichte's moral philosophy, makes repeated reference to moral experience and its relation to the total social reality. It is therefore no exaggeration to say that his general sociological works deal specifically with the sociology of the moral life. Likewise, in his sociology of law, Gurvitch is always concerned with the question of morality (juridical reality being one aspect of the total social reality) but in this case he addresses the question through his discussion of *social justice*.

While social justice is inextricably bound to the ideal realm of morality, social justice and morality may be distinguished from each other on the basis of their different structures. Simply put, Gurvitch, following Petrazycki, states that the structure of social justice is essentially bilateral; it consists of an imperative-attributive arrangement. On the other hand, the structure of morality is unilateral, or strictly imperative. What is more, morality is experienced as an action, a "volitive intuition," that is translated into law through logic. Logic, states Gurvitch, "arrests" the intuition-action of morality and "amalgamates" it into a judgment. Justice is thus situated midway between morality and logic. The direct relationship between morality and social justice consists of the former being experienced through the latter, as, for example, when justice is relativized to fit a community's normative facts—the common values intuited by a community and that characterize the reciprocal relationships between its members. The indirect liaison between morality and law is that law remains law only to the extent that it seeks social justice, and justice, as we know, is the active (action) experience of moral values.

Timasheff's legal sociology is also influenced by morality. For example, he divides ethics into three types: custom, morals, and law. In the case of custom, the individual complies with the system of rules only because of the *socio-ethical pressure* that she or he receives from others. Here, there is no power center exerting sanctions on the individual's behavior nor is the individual possessed of an inner conviction of duty. Custom, Timasheff contends, has to do with those rules of decency and politeness that inform our everyday behavior and interactions. An example of a customary rule is the expectation that we will greet acquaintances when meeting them. Alternatively, morals are connected to the great religious or philosophical movements such as Buddhism, Judaism, Christianity, Islam, ancient Greek philosophy, and Communism. Unlike custom, morals demand an "internal conviction" on the part of the individual. Consequently, in addition to socio-ethical pressure, another, more internal sanction is found in morals: *remorse*. Because remorse afflicts the conscience of the wayward individual, the first step which that individual must take toward reconciliation with the group is confession. Finally, law relies on the involvement of both custom and morals. This reliance, says Timasheff, gives law its ethical character.

CONCEPTUAL SUBTHEMES

In sum, the legal sociology of Ehrlich, Petrazycki, Gurvitch, and Timasheff revolves around five major theoretical themes. Each of these themes contains important conceptual subthemes that not only provide the language by which to more precisely discuss the theoretical themes but also give greater direction in guiding that discussion. The five major theoretical themes and their corresponding conceptual subthemes may be organized as follows:

I. *Antiformalism* refers to the sociological and judicial approach that considers the free, spontaneous, intuitive, and informal aspects of the living law. This theoretical theme is engendered by four conceptual subthemes.

   1. *The method of free decision* (fd) is the judicial technique that is adapted to the specific life situation under consideration as the judge, influenced by personality, precedent, and the customs of the people, renders a verdict. .
   2. *Intuition* (in) involves the irrational, perceptive-receptive, free-play given to inner psychical experiences in their relation to external social factors.
   3. *Normative facts* (nf), or the shared values and behaviors that are intuited by a living community.
   4. *The Ought* (ou) refers to the ethical conviction of what is considered by the collective to be just, good, and right.

II. *Reciprocal social relationships* are understood in the context of three conceptual subthemes.

   1. *The facts of the law* (fl) are the institutionalized standards that give associations their inner ordering. There are four facts of the law: usage, relations of domination and subjection, relations of possession, and declarations of will.
   2. *Imperativeness-attributiveness* (ia) characterizes the bilateral reciprocity of rights and duties between two parallel parties.
   3. *I-Other/We relations* (iw) refer to the dialectic occurring between individual consciousness and the collective mentality of togetherness.

III. *Functional control*, or the law's coercive and/or authoritative influence that coordinates behavior for the purpose of social integration, involves four subthemes.

   1. *Norms of conduct and for decision* (cd) refer, respectively, to: (i) those informal rules (customs and morals) that, independent of the legal institutions of the state, regulate human behavior in a social association, and (ii) those technical rules that direct a judge or other official how to decide a case.

2. *Distribution and organization* (do) concern the legal functions that bring about a coordinated system of behavior of group members with respect to property and each other, and that provide an authoritative agency with the power to create law and enforce sanctions in cases where rights and duties are violated.
3. *Social integration* (si) refers to the judicial function that promotes collaborative and cooperative associations. Social integration refers to the integration that occurs between associations (system integration arising from state control) and within associations (spontaneous social solidarity arising from normative facts).
4. *Social coordination* (sc) has to do with the sociolegal equilibrium—the balancing of interests—that is needed to bring about social change while preserving social order.

IV. *Psychogenics*, or those epistemologies that see the origins of sociolegal reality as residing in the individual or collective "mind" (psyche, Geist) and emotions. Psychogenics in the pioneers' legal sociology deals with four conceptual subthemes.

1. *Personality* (ps) refers the individual's (i.e., the subject/self and the object/other) character, personal sympathies, prejudices, and penchants.
2. *Psychical experiences* (pe) pertain to the subjective meanings given to the impulsions and emotions that are felt by individuals in reference to their rights and duties.
3. *Noetic mind* (nm) refers to the collective mentality expressed in the form of spontaneous beliefs and intuitions.
4. *Biopsychic instincts* (bi) are those inborn (biological) or acquired (learned) emotional reflexes that influence sociolegal behavior.

V. *Morality* considers three conceptual subthemes.

1. *Altruism* (al), or feelings of general good will, for the other (i.e., legal persons or social collectivities).
2. *Social justice* (sj) refers to the form of address that balances the individual (personal) and the social (universal) morals that have their basis in the parts (group-members) as well as the whole (group). It is the type of justice that combines the commutative and distributive functions.
3. *Socio-ethical pressure and remorse* (pr) refer, respectively, to: (i) the latent retributive disposition or actual retributive emotional response by a social group against a group-member who transgresses or threatens to transgress the common ethical (legal) rules, and (ii) the specific psychological punishment, in addition to social retribution,

experienced as a result of transgressing the social moral (obligatory) rules.

METHODOLOGIES

In this section, I briefly examine the various methodological directives advocated by the four Eastern-European pioneers.

Contrary to other legal sociologists, Ehrlich directs his commentary primarily to lawyers, for he believes that lawyers, not sociologists, can best implement his program, as a form of social engineering, in helping jurisprudence adapt to social change. As Roscoe Pound rightly points out, Ehrlich's sociology is "most useful from the lawyer's standpoint" (1971, p. 311). Similarly, Ziegert states that Ehrlich's "work dominated the lawyers' view of the intrusion of sociology into jurisprudence" (1979, p. 226).

Ehrlich spent a considerable portion of his career urging law students to go beyond the legal codes and the law books and search for the underlying living law in the reality of society, that is in the immediate facts dominating daily life. Consequently, he proposes the method of the *direct observation* of actual life, a technique that enables the researcher to find the living law in an inductive, empirical, and descriptive manner. Only in this way can the investigator determine how people organize their social relations (e.g., marriage, divorce, working relations, inheritance, etc.) based on legal norms. Ehrlich's methodology of direct observation also permits the researcher to contrast the actual social arrangements prevailing in everyday life with those arrangements set forth in the legal statutes. In light of the discrepancy that frequently exists between positive law and living law, it becomes necessary, says Ehrlich, "to open one's eyes, to inform oneself by observing life attentively, to ask people, and note down their replies" (1962, p. 498). Accordingly, Ehrlich proposes two major types of sociological method by which to investigate the living law: the *historiographical method* and the *questionnaire method.* Both methods involve researching the history of an association as well as interviewing its members. As a way of conducting investigations and avoiding the pitfalls of casual observation, Ehrlich recommends that the researcher speak with those older members of a community who have greater experience regarding the actual customs and moral views of their group. To be sure, Ehrlich sent his students to investigate the practices and attitudes of nearby communities, using a personal interview questionnaire, and thereby showing how widely familial customs of diverse racial groups of Bukowina differed from each other and from the supposedly sovereign Austrian legal code (Patterson 1931, p. 446).

Ehrlich further recommends that the investigator undertake archival research examining the facts of judicial reports and collections of business documents as well as obtain historical documents on which are recorded the community's statements of custom. "In this way," writes Ehrlich, "we could at last get a picture of what is taking place among us in the sphere of the document" (1962, p. 496). Moreover, in the case of an industrial neighborhood, the researcher may make an exhaustive study of the organization of the different forms of manufacturing and business which are carried on there (Page 1938, p. 831). All these techniques are used by the investigator to ascertain what is the living law. The bottom line is that the researcher:

> know what kinds of marriages and families exist in a country, what kinds of contracts are being entered into, what their content is as a general rule, what kinds of declarations by last will and testament are being drawn up, how all these things ought to be adjudged according to the law that is in force in the courts and other tribunals, how they are actually being adjudged and to what extent these judgments and other decisions are essentially effective (Ehrlich 1962, pp. 504-505).

Since Petrazycki's orientation toward psychology is behavioristic as well as introspective, he contends that the most suitable methods for obtaining knowledge about the true nature of law are internal and external observation. Whereas external observation enables the direct study of the concrete social behavior of people who are engaged in legal relationships, internal observation, or *introspection*, helps us to arrive at an understanding of these people's inner or psychic world and of their specific experiences in the context of legal relationships.[25] Introspection, states Górecki, involves "observation of one's own mental processes, and body movements resulting from them; and inferring contents of the mental processes of others, by analogy, from their body movements" (1975, p. 4). Laserson acknowledges Petrazycki's reliance on both internal and external observation in developing his theory of law: "Petrazhitskii widely used introspection and individual analysis of moral and jural emotions, but this went together with a deep inquiry into the societal and sociological research of legal behavior" (1951, p. 73, n. 25).

In addition, Petrazycki's methodology consists of "deductive inference on the basis of psychological premises, verified wherever possible by induction" (Babb 1937, p. 817). Thus, for Petrazycki, deduction and its empirical verification through factual data including statistics, is necessary for verifying and supplementing deductive inferences. Indeed, Petrazycki maintains that hypotheses as to the psychical experiences of others may also be based "on inference by deduction in concrete cases from general propositions (obtained inductively) as to outward manifestations of a certain category of psychic experiences, by bringing the actual movements of others within general propositions" (Babb 1938, p. 522). In sum, Petrazycki favors using both inductive and deductive methods.

Finally, as indicated above, Petrazycki also favors employing *statistical techniques*. According to Meyendorff, Petrazycki is "prepared to find a great variety of material, reducible, however, to averages correlated to age, sex, race, occupation, climate, degree of civilization, and so on" (1933, p. 24). In the final analysis, Petrazycki is first and last a "realist," stressing that all his findings were based on observation and inference, and not on a priori considerations (Timasheff 1981, p. 741).

McDonald describes Gurvitch's *Sociology of Law* as "rather metaphysical in tone" (1979, p. 24). She maintains that since Gurvitch insisted on simultaneously studying all the elements and all the levels of social reality as a whole, his legal sociology is sometimes regarded by his critics as being more philosophical than sociological. Despite Gurvitch's contentions that his sociological method is highly empirical ("dialectical hyperempiricism," as he terms it), his sociology is primarily concerned with the abstract and the ideal. As a result, there are no cause-and-effect relationships to be found or explained in his works. His is chiefly a sociology of description and analysis whereby he employs a multitude of concepts to formulate a highly abstract conceptual scheme. This gives his sociology added complexity and "[i]t is undoubtedly true that his works do not make easy reading" (Hunt 1979, p. 174). Nevertheless, McDonald is quiet correct in saying that before we dismiss Gurvitch's ideas as "too esoteric or complex, we might at least ask how legal sociology could ever have allowed itself to expect that its task would be simple" (1979, p. 52).

Gurvitch's abstract idealism notwithstanding, he does briefly state that in studying the full social reality of law in all its dimensional levels, the sociology of law must start with "the tangible and externally observable expressions of actual group conduct" (1941a, p. 200). Thus, similar to Ehrlich and Petrazycki, Gurvitch asserts that *external and direct observation* is necessary for analyzing established organizations, customary practices, traditions or behavioral innovations of law. Second, and without going into much detail, Gurvitch contends that the sociology of law must interpret the "material manifestations of law," which he states include "the spatial structure and the demographic density of juridical institutions" (1941a, p. 200). In other words, the legal sociologist as researcher must recognize the internal meanings (presumably requiring a kind of internal observation or subjective interpretation) of the "varying degrees of the intensity and actuality of the inter-individual relations of drawing nearer and separation, and of fusion in the mass, community, communion, etc." (1941a, p. 201). Gurvitch advocates for a nonsymbolic microsociology, a sociometry, that focuses on the intuitive union, the interpenetration, among minds and behaviors as they occur in the various forms of sociality and constitute "the collective mind" (Durkheim's *conscience collective*), the deepest level of juridical reality (1941c, pp. 486-487). Exactly how Gurvitch proposes to observe the collective mind of juridical institutions is not known. He does, however, maintain that an understanding of juridical experience requires the use of "spiritual data as well as tangible data of the life of law" (1941a, p. 215). It must be noted that Gurvitch's interest is largely with the spiritual, or noetic, and not with the tangible, or empiric, side of legal sociology. As Sorokin puts it, "All in all his system of sociology is largely abstract, formal, and fairly remote from concrete empirical realities" (1966, p. 487). To be sure, while in the United States during the 1940s, Gurvitch "was appalled by the over-use of technical skills, such as surveys, questionnaires and statistics, which could only lead to superficial descriptions." This is not to say that Gurvitch was inimical to empirical research, only that he felt "that empirical research in [American] sociology had declined in quality during the previous twenty-five years" (Bosserman 1968, p. 51). In the end, it is best to let Gurvitch himself explain the object and method of the sociology of law as he sees it: "The Sociology of Law is that part of the sociology of the human spirit which studies the full social reality of law, beginning with its tangible and externally observable expressions, in effective collective behaviors and in the material basis. . . . Sociology of law interprets these behaviors and material manifestations of law according to the internal meanings" (1942a, p. 61).

Timasheff (1937c) focuses principally on the law's causal reality and posits that the methods of individual observation, introspection, and mass observation be employed to show that law is, simply and concretely, "a fact of social life" that imposes uniform patterns of behavior on group members (1939a, p. 6; 1939c).

Through individual observation, the researcher directly studies how overt human behavior is related to law. Thus, for instance, human behavior may be seen as a set of conditioned reflexes (e.g., the reflexes of freedom and submission mentioned by Pavlov) determining which kind of social control the law will exert.[26]

Contrary to the behaviorism emphasized by individual observation, introspection involves an effort at reflexivity and employs the techniques of depth psychology. Timasheff describes introspection as the "accurate subsequent analysis of one's state of consciousness in so far as it is related to law (acting according to law, acting against the law, acting with the intent of transforming the law, reactions produced by another's acting in accordance with or against the law)" (1939a, p. 38). For example, introspection requires that the researcher—qua participating member of society—look within herself in order to recognize those patterns of behavior (ethical rules) that she supports and wishes to impose on others because, according to her sentiment, they ought to act in accordance with them. While Petrazycki's method of introspection is similar to Weber's *Verstehen* (see note 25), Timasheff states that his type of introspection is analogous to Freud's psychoanalytic method of investigating the unconscious.

Finally, *mass observation* is expressed in statistical data. In referring to this methodological procedure, Timasheff is obviously advocating the use of quantitative information as found, for example, in the Uniform Crime Reports and National Crime Survey.[27] At bottom, the object is to investigate: (1) the "immediate juridical experience" given in the acts of legislators, authorities, electors, contracting parties, and of persons taking part in the juridical life of corporate bodies, and (2) the "juridical mentality," which includes the primitive revenge mentality, the retributive emotion, and the relative force of norms of conduct.

THE DUAL-POLYGONAL PARADIGM

Relying on the Eastern-European pioneers' theoretical assumptions and research procedures, we are now in a position to cautiously but confidently begin sketching the contours of a theoretical-methodological framework for legal sociology. The objectives of this endeavor, which I will depict and refer to as *the dual-polygonal paradigm*, are twofold: (1) to serve as a temporary guide for legal sociology's further exploration of the dialectical interplay between positive law and living law, and (2) to serve as a blueprint by which to construct a general sociological theory of law.

The dual-polygonal paradigm is schematically represented as a polygon placed within a polygon (see Figure 1). The five vertices of the inside polygon represent the five theoretical themes (and their corresponding conceptual subthemes) on which the pioneers based their work: morality (**M**); psychogenics (**P**); reciprocal

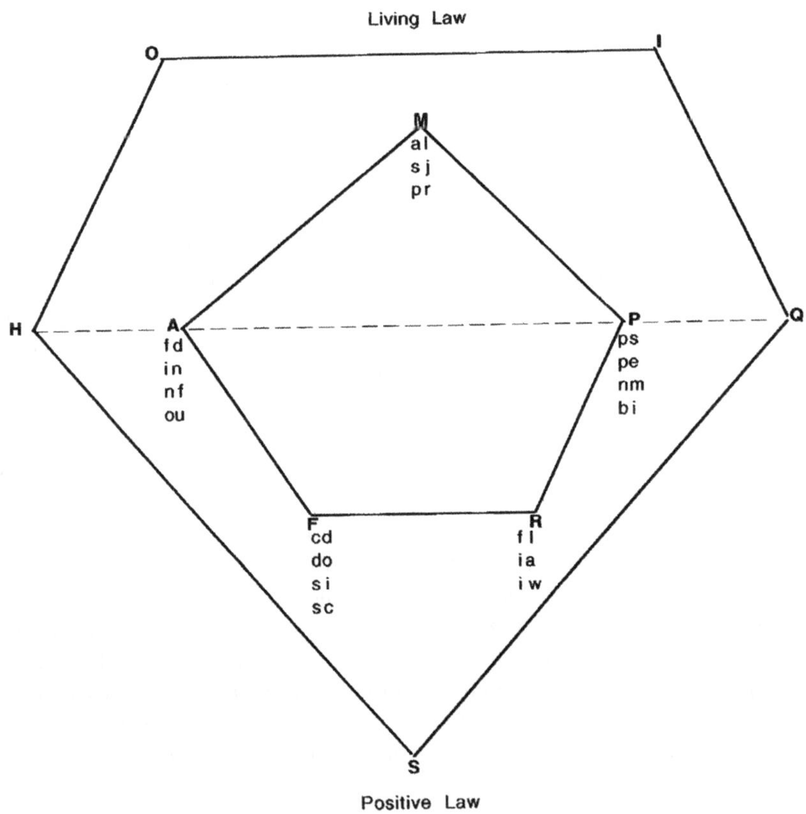

Figure 1. The Dual-Polygonal Paradigm

relations (**R**); functional control (**F**); and antiformalism (**A**). Similarly, the five vertices of the outside polygon represent the five main methodological directives proposed by the Eastern-European pioneers: external or direct observation (fieldwork) (**O**); introspection (Weber's *Verstehen* or Freud's depth psychology) (**I**); the questionnaire method or interviewing (**Q**); mass observation or statistical analysis (**S**); and the historiographical method (**H**).

The (sub)themes and methodologies occupying the upper halves of the two polygons—**O**; **M** (al, sj, pr); **I**—are ideally suited for analyzing the intuitive, spontaneous, and informal nature of living law. Those occupying the polygons' lower halves—**R** (fl, ia, iw); **S**; **F** (cd, do, si, sc)—are intended to help in empirical investigations of positive law. Finally, the (sub)themes and techniques located in the polygons' middle regions—**Q**; **P** (ps, pe, nm, bi); **A** (fd, in, nf, ou); **H**—are most useful in studying the relationship between the living law and positive law.

CONCLUSION

In this essay, I have reidentified Eugen Ehrlich, Leon Petrazycki, Georges Gurvitch, and Nicholas S. Timasheff as the Eastern-European pioneers of legal sociology and have offered a reappraisal of their major works. It may legitimately be asked why the pioneers' major works have not enjoyed greater appeal and utilization in the English-speaking world. Aside from the two most common arguments made against reading them—that their works are too metaphysical and too complex—two more substantial reasons account for their relative obscurity. First, as already indicated, the bulk of the pioneers' principal writings on the sociology of law remain to be translated into English from their original German, Russian, Polish, and French. Just as many of Weber's works had to await Parsons's translation, so do the pioneers continue to wait for their translators. Second, singly, each of the pioneers made an important but *limited* contribution to legal sociology. It is only when the most salient themes, and concomitant subthemes, and the main methodologies in the pioneers' works are considered *in tandem* that they yield a scheme that can inform contemporary sociolegal theory and research.

This conceptual scheme, this dual-polygonal paradigm, expressly contains those ideas, those essential elements, that must be considered by any general sociological theory of law. The dual-polygonal paradigm considers the law's consensual (functional) and coercive (conflictual) aspects; its positivistic (empirical) and normative (moral), rational and irrational features. It looks at legal as well as extralegal norms (customs, ethics, morality, norms of conduct, normative facts). The dual-polygonal paradigm address the processes of lawmaking (legislation) and lawfinding (adjudication, norms for decision, method of free decision). It is oriented toward psychological factors (intuition, personality, psychical experiences, biopsychic instincts) as well as sociological factors (social relationships, collective mentality, distribution and organization, social integration, social coordination). It allows treatment of the law as an autonomous, or semi-autonomous, agency in society as well as treatment of the law as a sociocultural product. It takes into account different forms of adjudication (formal rational, formal irrational, substantive rational, and substantive irrational). It considers different types of law (criminal, civil, constitutional, international). It considers social action (agency) and social structure (system). It explains the behavior of law and the behavior of individuals within various social units (bilateral social relationships, associations, social groups, nations, the international community). Finally, the dual-polygonal paradigm allows for the use of quantitative (questionnaires, statistical analysis, demographic data) and qualitative research methods (fieldwork, introspection, interviewing, historical analysis).

Timasheff (1952) has stated that a science is mature only if it has a solid foundation—a set of commonly accepted and well-defined concepts—in terms of which theories can be constructed. The purpose of this paper is to provide such a foundation for the sociology of law. As such, five theoretical themes, 18 conceptual subthemes, and five methodological techniques were distilled from the pioneers' works for the purpose of developing a blueprint, an analytical apparatus, to be used in formulating a theoretical-methodological framework for the further development of legal sociology. This is not to say that the concepts discussed herein are not ambiguous and contradictory; doubtless, they still require further elaboration and precision. Nevertheless, it is my belief that the dual-polygonal paradigm and its conceptual armament, as I have presented it here, will aid in developing a single, comprehensive framework which will pose new questions and answer them, or answer old questions in a new and better way. Until such time as this framework is fully realized, the dual-polygonal paradigm will serve to guide the legal sociologist's conceptual and empirical investigations of positive law and living law.

NOTES

1. In order to avoid perpetuating patriarchal imagery and terminology, I will, for the most part, use the terms "pioneers" or "founders" rather than "fathers" or "masters."

2. According to Merton, "the writings of classical authors in every field of learning can be read with profit from time to time, additional ideas and intimations coming freshly into view with each re-reading" (1965, p. 45). However, Merton also warns against excessive devotion to the ideas of intellectual predecessors, a dogmatic devotion that hinders scientific advancement:

> And because the words of the forefathers became final words, little was built upon their insightful suggestions. They were honored, not in the manner in which men of science do honor to their predecessors, by extending and elaborating their formulations on the basis of cumulatively developed problems and systematic researches bearing on these problems, but in the manner in which littérateurs honor their predecessors, by repeatedly quoting "definitive" passages from the masters' works (1968, p. 332).

In steering between the Scylla of Dogmatism and the Charybdis of Arrogant Innovation, in this essay I follow Merton's advice to follow my bent:

> Draw upon the wisdom of the past, to be sure, or else the implicitly arrogant claim to knowledge beginning with yourself will stand self-condemned. But do not confuse this dependence upon the corporate giants of the past with the merely learned repetition of what they have taught you. Instead, follow your bent where it leads (1965, p. 163).

3. For Black (1995), "generality" in a sociological theory of law means that it must consider "all conflicts, civil and criminal, at all stages of the legal process, in all societies, in all historical periods, wherever law is found." Generality also means that a theory of law must consider "legal variation in entire communities and societies, including the evolutionary emergence of law itself" (1995, p. 834). What is more, in Black's view, theory must be testable, that is to say, it must be subject to falsification. His critique of sociolegal theories, like that proposed by Luhmann (1985), is that they are not testable.

4. Ziegert (1979, 1980, pp. 75-77), Pódgorecki (1980-1981), and Scheuer (1965) have referred to Ehrlich, Petrazycki, and Timasheff, respectively, as the "founding fathers" of the sociology of law. (Ziegert claims that Ehrlich coined the term "sociology of law"—indeed, that he "invented" the field.) Bosserman (1968) implicitly attributes the same status to Gurvitch. Gurvitch (1942a, pp. 106-156) regards Ehrlich (along with Durkheim, Duguit, Levy, Hauriou, and Weber) as one of the European "founders" of the sociology of law. Sheskin (1978, p. 116) describes Timasheff as being "among the first to attempt the delimitation of the sociology of law." Hunt (1993, p. 63) describes Timasheff as "one of the earlier pioneers of theoretical sociology of law." Kelsen (1945, p. 25) calls Ehrlich "one of the founders of the sociology of law." Bierstedt (1970) identifies Pound, Ehrlich, Petrazycki, and Timasheff as the "founders" of the sociology of law. Rehbinder (1967) characterizes Ehrlich as the "founder of legal sociology." Later, Rehbinder (1977) names Ehrlich, Durkheim, Petrazycki, Hägerström, and Pound as virtually contemporary founders of legal sociology (as cited in Rottleuthner 1987, pp. 1, 31 f.1). As for Ehrlich, he considers Montesquieu's *L' Esprit des Lois* as "the first attempt to fashion a sociology of law" (1916, p. 583). Skapska (1987) describes Petrazycki as "the undisputed indirect 'father and founder'" of the sociology of law.

5. Alan Hunt makes the "common framework" argument for Gurvitch and Timasheff, stating that, among other things, they both "had in common the insistence upon the primary need to articulate a theoretical framework as a precondition for any successful sociological treatment of legal phenomena" (1979, p. 170).

Another argument that Hunt makes for placing Gurvitch and Timasheff's work on similar theoretical ground is that they both share an interest in the dualism affecting law. (This dualism, which I refer to as the dialectical interplay between positive law and living law, is discussed below):

> The common strand in [Gurvitch and Timasheff's] respective sociologies of law is at root a continuation of the efforts, very apparent in the work of Max Weber, to find a resolution or integration of the dualism which is conceived as so markedly affecting law. It is the apparent dualism between law as a positive institution resting upon the framework of social power, while at the same time being a system of values or norms having some compelling internal strength and validity. . . . In their efforts to deal with law as a manifestation of these two dimensions, both were greatly influenced by the Russian jurist Petrazhitzky (Hunt 1979, p. 170).

I concur with Hunt but extend his arguments to include not only Gurvitch and Timasheff's legal sociology, but Ehrlich and Petrazycki's as well. Doubtless, there are myriad theoretical and methodological points of divergence between the four pioneers; however, their similarities are more numerous and important than their differences, and for this reason I focus on the former.

6. The outstanding exception is, of course, Max Weber, whose formal sociology of law is found in Chapters 1, 3, and especially 8, of the second volume of his monumental work, *Economy and Soci-*

ety. Durkheim's splendid sociological insights on contract law and the evolution of the contract were not complied into a comprehensive volume until after his death, with the publication of a book titled *Professional Ethics and Civic Morals* (1957).

7. Many of the pioneers' major works are as yet unavailable in English. Ehrlich's *Fundamental Principles of the Sociology of Law* is a translation of *Grundlegung der Soziologie des Rechts* (1913). The volume *Law and Morality* is a translation (from the Russian) and abridgment of Petrazycki's *Introduction to the Study of Law and Morality* (*Vvedeniie v izucheniie prava i nravstvennosti*) published in 1905, and his two-volume work, *Theory of Law and State in Connection with a Theory of Morality* (*Teoriia prava i gosudarstva v sviazi s teoriei nravstvennosti*), published in 1907. The pioneers' minor works on the sociology of law which will also be considered here are: Ehrlich (1922, 1969), Gurvitch (1937b, 1941a 1941b, 1941c), Timasheff (1937b, 1937c, 1938a, 1938b, 1939b, 1939c, 1942, 1946, 1955, 1957, 1981).

8. The positive law/living law distinction is not unique to the Eastern-European pioneers. The distinction has a long tradition and is articulated in various forms; see, for example, Weber's (1978) formal rational law/substantive irrational law; Pound's (1910) law in books/law in action; Llewellyn's (1930) paper rules/real rules; Sumner's (1940) positive law/customary law; Kennedy's (1976) rules/standards.

9. It is noteworthy that Petrazycki and Luhmann both assess the maturity of law based on its degree of positivity, but from different points of view and with different conclusions. Taking a social-psychological point of view, Petrazycki (1955, p. 70) contends that in the child's legal mind, the law in operation is, for the most part, positive law. The legal experience of young children is positive—similar to statute law—in that it is restricted to external authority, namely, the directions of their elders. As children get older and mature intellectually, they develop an intuitive-law mentality; only then are they able to consider a system of stable, independent, intuitive, legal convictions. Luhmann (1985, p. 159f), by contrast, takes a strict sociological point of view and posits that in societies where complexity is low, the law is archaic in that the legal rules are not sophisticated and abstract. However, as societies evolve (i.e., develop toward greater complexity), their legal systems are characterized by greater positivity, which means that there is a more conscious and deliberate decision to make, select, validate, and change the law. In sum, for Petrazycki, legal evolution yields living law; for Luhmann, legal evolution produces positive law.

10. Unger writes that the "search for this latent and living law—not the law of prescriptive rules or of bureaucratic policies, but the elementary code of human interaction—has been the staple of the lawyer's art wherever this art was practiced with most depth and skill" (1976, p. 242). For a discussion of empirical studies illustrating the interaction between positive law and living law, see Cotterrell (1984, pp. 34-37). Cotterrell is one of the few legal sociologists who has paid serious attention to Ehrlich's sociology of law and his concept of living law. Elsewhere, Cotterrell argues that Black's (1989) recommendations about developing legal cooperative associations that would strongly encourage non-litigious forms of dispute resolution "evoke aspects of Eugen Ehrlich's classic theory of the living law of social associations" (Cotterrell 1995, p. 187). For further commentary on Ehrlich's ideas, see Vinogradoff (1928, pp. 41-422), Kelsen (1945, pp. 24-28), Allen (1964, pp. 28-32, 122-123), Friedmann (1967, pp. 247-252), Schur (1968, pp. 37-39), Stone (1968, 1972), Sheskin (1978), Johnson (1979), Ziegert (1980, pp. 75-77), and Luhmann (1985, pp. 19-20). Many of these treatments of Ehrlich's works are highly critical.

11. For detailed discussions of formalist jurisprudence in the American context see Horwitz (1975, 1977, 1992), Gilmore (1977), Kennedy (1980), Mensch (1982), Friedman (1985), and Treviño (1994, 1996a).

12. This antiformalism is similar to Weber's (1978) substantive irrational type of lawfinding, Twining's (1973) "Grand Style" of adjudication, and Llewellyn's (1960) "situation sense."

13. To be sure, Pound was responsible for introducing Ehrlich's ideas in the United States (see Pound 1922, 1971).

14. It is indeed the case that during the late nineteenth and early twentieth centuries, when Ehrlich was writing, relatively few disputes actually came before the courts. His legal theory as it applies to the various ethnic communities in rural Austro-Hungary therefore reflects the culture of a particular time and place, a culture that stands in sharp contrast to the most legalistic and litigious society the world has ever known—late twentieth-century America, a nation of competitive individuals and strangers. Auerbach (1983) has stated that the success of nonlegal forms of dispute settlement—namely, arbitration, mediation, and conciliation—has always depended on a strong coherent community vision, a community vision like that found among some immigrant ethnic groups in nineteenth-century America.

15. The notion of intuition is not uncommon, and is indeed taken quite seriously, in the psychological literature. Carl Gustav Jung, for example, saw intuition as one of the four functions of the personality (the other three being thinking, feeling, and sensation). For Jung and his followers, knowledge derived from intuition precedes thinking and suggests where thinking may go. It is the hunch which leads to the hypothesis. Intuition is the tendency to gain a total impression of a situation and also a sense of where it is leading. According to Jung, "Insofar as intuition is a 'hunch,' it is not the product of a voluntary act; it is rather an involuntary event, which depends upon different external or internal circumstances instead of an act of judgment" (1964, p. 49). While intuition has been ignored by sociologists because of its nonrational character, it was, for the legal realists, an important factor in adjudication (see, e.g., Hutcheson 1929).

16. Timasheff insists that his is a purely sociological explanation of the nature of law and that his treatment of law takes place within actual social reality. Olivecrona (1948), however, critiques him severely for abandoning the sociological conception of law and harboring the idea of law as an objective "ought." There are two reasons why Timasheff's (and the other pioneers') legal sociology should not be automatically dismissed as metaphysical balderdash in its attraction to the ideal and the "ought." First, there has never been a clear distinction between metaphysics and sociology. Simmel (1950, pp. 23-25), for one, was well aware of the almost inextricable connection between metaphysics and sociology. Furthermore, who is to say that the notion of human spirit (noetic mind) is more or less metaphysical than, say, Durkheim's highly useful conception of *sui generis* "collective representations," or his assumptions about human nature, the "constitutional duality" (*homo duplex*)? Second, the ideal and the "ought" have long been a part of the general study of law. Consider, for example, that even the legal realists, in their attack on formalist jurisprudence and in their pragmatic approach to understanding the law, maintained that jurists must put aside the philosophical question of the "ought" *but only temporarily* (Llewellyn 1931).

17. Although Timasheff made his theoretical statements prior to the Holocaust and other Nazi atrocities, much of what he says about international law found its practical expression in the Nuremburg Trials of 1945-1946. More recently, Timasheff's principle of the self-limitation of power as instigated by the international community was made evident in Bosnia. In this country, the killing of innocent civilians by warring factions, the Serbs, Croats, and Muslims, finally ended in 1995 after a 43-month war. This happened after the international community could no longer tolerate the genocide being committed in the name of ethnic cleansing, that is to say, after the international community felt an ethical conviction—a moral duty—to act. Accordingly, the "international community" imposed economic sanctions on Serbia, instigated a series of ceasefires, convened a peace conference in the Hague launched by the European Community, assigned United Nations peacekeepers including the deployment of an international force (IFOR), declared "safe areas" for Bosnian Muslims with the backing of the U.N. Security Council, conducted NATO air strikes, and, finally, brokered the Dayton peace agreement which eventually (for the time being, at least) brought an end to the war.

18. The idea that social interactions or "face engagements" have their basis in an exchange of rights and duties is common in the sociological literature. It has perhaps been most clearly articulated by Erving Goffman, who posits that, in coming together, persons make an implicit communication contract with one another:

> I have suggested some reasons why individuals, at least in our society, are obliged to keep themselves available for face engagements, and I have also suggested some of the dangers per-

> sons open themselves up to in so doing. These two opposing tendencies are reconciled in society, apparently, by a kind of *implicit contract* or *gentleman's agreement* that persons sustain: given the fact that the other will be under some obligation, often unpleasant, to respond to overtures, potential initiators are under obligation to stay their own desires. A person can thus make himself available to others in the expectation that they will restrain their calls on his availability and not make him pay too high a price for his being accessible. Their *right* to initiate contact is checked by their *duty* to take his point of view and initiate contact with him only under circumstances that he will easily see to be justified; in short, they must not "abuse" their privileges (Goffman 1963, p. 106, emphasis added).

Compare this statement by Goffman to the following explanation of Petrazycki's notion of what constitutes social order: "According to Petrazycki the social order is based on an elaborated network of interrelations between official and intuitive law . . . he maintained that . . . different networks of official laws—especially intuitive 'contracts,' 'gentlemanly agreements,' and accepted 'rules of the game' . . . constitute the very core of existing social order" (Podgórecki 1980-1981, p. 192).

A slightly different description of this bilateral exchange of rights and duties in social interaction is given by Parsons, who describes it as "the complementarity of role-expectations" and the "double contingency" (Parsons 1951, p. 38ff; Parsons and Shils 1951, p. 190ff). See also generally the literature on social exchange theory and rational choice theory; Coleman (1990, pp. 435f), for example, explains how a corporate actor, with a structure composed of positions rather than persons, must specify two sets of rights and obligations in relation to its agents. Finally, for an elaboration of the tetrad conception of law—the notion that law "is based on four reciprocal elements belonging to the parallel parties and containing two corresponding pairs of rights and duties"—see Pódgorecki (1974, p. 272ff).

19. Petrazycki identifies three types of imperative-attributive legal relationships. Rudzinski explains these three types:

> (1) The duty of the obligor may consist in doing something (paying a sum of money, delivering a merchandise, performing a service, or working) for the obligee; i.e., for the rightful claimant (*facere*). The corresponding right of the claimant consists in getting those goods or services (*accipere*). Or, on the contrary, (2) the duty of the obligor may consist in refraining from doing certain things; e.g., not to attack the life, health, liberty, property, or civil rights of another person or persons (*non facere*), and the other person or persons have the right not to tolerate such attacks (*non pati*). Finally, (3) the duty of the obligor may consist in tolerating certain rightful activities of a person or persons entitled to them (*pati*). The latter person or persons have a right to do certain things, they have certain areas of freedom—freedom of speech, press, assembly, and so forth (*facere*) (Rudzinski 1976, p. 117).

The most complete formulation of the imperative-attributive legal relationship is given by Petrazycki's student at St. Petersburg, Pitirim Sorokin (1981). Briefly, Sorokin identifies three classes of activities that exhaust all of the main forms of the objects of right and duty insofar as they are expressed in activities. On the one hand, the subject of right is entitled to: (1) *accept* (objects or services), (2) *do* (issue a command, give his property, marry), (3) *not tolerate* (violence, attack, insults, any violation of his rights). On the other hand, the subject of duty is obliged to: (1) *do* (work, deliver goods), (2) *tolerate* (reprimand, imprisonment, taking from him his property), (3) *not do* (not to kill, not to steal, not to violate law-norms). This threefold classification describes the actions-reactions of the subjects of right and duty and gives a clearcut map of conduct to the parties in each case (Sorokin 1981, p. 672). Elsewhere, Sorokin (1962, pp. 596-597) remarks that to the extent that imperative-attributive (ethicojuridical) convictions are homogeneous among the members of a society, a strong network of social relationships and a strong system of cultural values are established in such a society.

20. Because the pioneers sometimes downplayed the intensity of the law's coercive force, I prefer to use the term "control" in describing the law's internal (psychic) and external (social) regulating or

coordinating influences. While Kelsen (1945, pp. 28-29) critiques Ehrlich, Petrazycki, and Timasheff for arguing against coercion as an essential element in law, it must be made clear that all of the four Eastern-European pioneers were well aware of the law's consensual and coercive elements. It would therefore be a grave mistake to place any of the pioneers in either the power-coercion or the pluralist-consensus camp. Johnson (1979), in contradistinction to Sheskin (1978), argues persuasively that both the coercion and consensus images of law are quite evident in Ehrlich and Timasheff's legal sociology.

21. For an elaboration and extension of the motivational and educational functions of law, see Podgórecki (1974). To these, Podgórecki adds three other functions: integration, petrification, and reduction.

22. Petrazycki's notion of the law's functional control is most clearly articulated by Sorokin:

> Due to their precise and detailed definition of the actions of the subjects of right and of duty in each specific case and to the enormous emotional and volitional power with which a law-conviction is charged, the law-norms of every one of us constitute the main guide and the main motor-power of our conduct. . . . More than that. They are the essence—the skeleton, the heart, and the soul—of any organized group or institution. . . . Without such norms none of these organized groups would be possible. . . . Without them no order, no structure, no smooth functioning of these groups, indeed no continuity of their existence would be possible (1981, pp. 676-677).

23. A debate of sorts has arisen concerning whether Petrazycki was primarily a psychologist or a sociologist. Northrop sees Petrazycki as shifting his disciplinary orientation and maintains that "after constructing his legal science primarily in terms of psychological factors, [Petrazycki] turns implicitly and secondarily to sociological jurisprudence" (1956, p. 660). Pódgorecki takes pains to underscore Petrazycki's sociological orientation, arguing that "it is misleading to label Petrazycki as a psychological theorist, since his interest was predominantly in sociological questions." Pódgorecki further contends that referring to Petrazycki "as a psychologist neglects his shift to a more sociological expression of his thoughts and obscures his potential importance for the sociology of law" (1980-1981, pp. 185, 195-196). Skapska posits that "in spite of its assumed psychological one-sidedness, [Petrazycki's] theory is the starting point for the contemporary study of law in many aspects and on various planes: linguistic and logical, axiological, psychological, and sociological" (1987, p. 355). Denzin (1975, p. 63) credits Petrazycki's theoretical perspective with anticipating and overlapping with the underlying notions of symbolic interactionism. In any event, to a greater extent than the other Eastern-European pioneers (and, perhaps, than any other early sociologist, for that matter) Petrazycki created disciples, successive generations of legal sociologists, who devoted a significant part of their studies to the *sociology* of law, as his work greatly influenced further development in that field (Kojder and Kwasniewski 1985, p. 263; Skapska 1987, p. 353). What is more, Petrazycki's disciple M.A. Reisner took a strict sociological approach as he refashioned the concept of intuitive law and, by putting it on a Marxist foundation, developed "the most genuine class law which was worked out in the form of intuitive law (in the ranks of the oppressed and exploited mass)" (Reisner 1951, p. 85).

24. Similar ideas about penal evolution were held by Émile Durkheim (1984), who argued that the function of punishment is to strengthen a community's moral solidarity. Even more relevant are the ideas of G.H. Mead (1918) who, like Timasheff, paid special attention to the emotional reactions of the law-abiding members of society against the lawbreaker. And, like Petrazycki, Mead also wrote about the law-abiding members' "concrete impluses," their emotional attitudes, of attack and restraint toward the lawbreaker.

25. Petrazycki's technique of introspection is similar to Max Weber's concept of *Verstehen*. Weber argued that the logically formal type of legal thought, which he identified with the civilian codes of modern continental Europe, was especially rational because "the legally relevant characteristics of the facts are disclosed through the logical analysis of meaning" (Weber 1978, p. 657). In emphasizing *meaning*, Weber was alluding to the use of *Verstehen* as an "attitude-evaluation" or a "kind of interpre-

tation [that] seeks to construct the relations of the parties to one another from the point of view of the 'inner' kernel of their behavior, from the point of view of their mental 'attitudes'" (1978, p. 884). Weber regarded *Verstehen* as a type of *interpretive understanding* of cultural phenomena (actions and activity). Much like Petrazycki, Weber distinguished between two kinds of interpretive understanding. Direct *observational understanding* (Petrazycki's external observation), he wrote, involves "deriving the meaning of an act or symbolic expression from immediate observation without reference to any broader context," while *explanatory understanding* (Petrazycki's internal observation) involves placing "the particular act in a broader context of meaning involving facts that cannot be derived from immediate observation of a particular act or expression" (Weber 1978, p. 58, n.7). Denzin (1975, p. 69) contends that Petrazycki's introspection is a central methodology of G.H. Mead and symbolic interactionism.

26. Legal realist Karl Llewellyn (1930) also advocated a similar methodology, which he called the "behavior-content" approach. This approach involves the empirical study of the observable behavior of the courts and those affected by the courts.

27. Timasheff also suggests triangulating other methodologies. For example, he recommends that data obtained from ethnology, historical jurisprudence, comparative jurisprudence, and child psychology be used to test the validity of the results obtained through introspection and mass observation.

REFERENCES

Allen, C.K. 1964. *Law in the Making*. Oxford, UK: Oxford University Press.

Auerbach, J.S. 1983. *Justice Without Law? Resolving Disputes Without Lawyers*. New York: Oxford University Press.

Austin, J. 1961. "Lectures on Jurisprudence." Pp. 400-419 in *Society, Law, and Morality*, edited by F.A. Olafson. Englewood Cliffs, NJ: Prentice-Hall.

Babb, H.W. 1937. "Petrazhitskii: Science of Legal Policy and Theory of Law." *Boston University Law Review* 17: 793-829.

Babb, H.W. 1938. "Petrazhitskii: Theory of Law." *Boston University Law Review* 18: 511-578.

Bierstedt, R. 1970. "Nicholas S. Timasheff, 1886-1970." *The American Sociologist* 5(3): 290-291.

Black, D. 1972. "The Boundaries of Legal Sociology." *The Yale Law Journal* 81(6): 1086-1100.

Black, D. 1976. *The Behavior of Law*. New York: Academic Press.

Black, D. 1989. *Sociological Justice*. New York: Oxford University Press.

Black, D. 1995. "The Epistemology of Pure Sociology." *Law & Social Inquiry* 20(3): 829-870.

Bosserman, P. 1968. *Dialectical Sociology: An Analysis of the Sociology of Georges Gurvitch*. Boston, MA: Porter Sargent Publisher.

Chambliss, W., and R. Seidman. 1982. *Law, Order, and Power*, 2nd edition. Reading, MA: Addison-Wesley.

Coleman, J.S. 1990. *Foundations of Social Theory*. Cambridge, MA: Harvard University Press.

Coser, L.A. 1977. *Masters of Sociological Thought: Ideas in Historical and Social Context*. New York: Harcourt Brace Jovanovich.

Cotterrell, R. 1984. *The Sociology of Law: An Introduction*. London: Butterworths.

Cotterrell, R. 1995. *Law's Community: Legal Theory in Sociological Perspective*. Oxford, UK: Clarendon Press.

Denzin, N.K. 1975. "Interaction, Law, and Morality: The Contributions of Leon Petrazycki" Pp. 63-82 in *Sociology and Jurisprudence of Leon Petrazycki*, edited by J. Górecki. Urbana, IL: University of Illinois Press.

Durkheim, É. 1957. *Professional Ethics and Civic Morals*, trans. by C. Brookfield. London: Routledge & Kegan Paul.

Durkheim, É. 1984. *The Division of Labor in Society*. New York: Free Press.

Ehrlich, E. 1916. "Montesqieu and Sociological Jurisprudence." *Harvard Law Review* 29(6): 582-600.

Ehrlich, E. 1922. "The Sociology of Law." *Harvard Law Review* 36: 130-145.

Ehrlich, E. 1962 [1936]. *Fundamental Principles of the Sociology of Law.* New York: Russell & Russell, Inc.

Ehrlich, E. 1969. "Judicial Freedom of Decision: Its Principles and Objects." Pp. 47-84 in *Science of Legal Method: Select Essays by Various Authors*, edited by the Committee of the Association of American Law Schools. South Hackensack, NJ: Rothman Reprints.

Frank, J. 1930. *Law and the Modern Mind.* New York: Coward-McCann.

Friedman, L.M. 1985. *A History of American Law.* New York: Simon and Schuster.

Friedmann, W. 1967. *Legal Theory,* 5th edition. New York: Columbia University Press.

Gilmore, G. 1977. *The Ages of American Law.* New Haven, CT: Yale University Press.

Goffman, E. 1963. *Behavior in Public Places: Notes on the Social Organization of Gatherings.* New York: Free Press.

Górecki, J. 1975. "Leon Petrazycki." Pp. 1-15 in *Sociology and Jurisprudence of Leon Petrazycki,* edited by J. Górecki. Urbana, IL: University of Illinois Press.

Gurvitch, G. 1931. "Une Philosophie Intuitioniste du Droit: Léon Petrasizky" [An Intuitionistic Philosophy of Law: Leon Petrazycki]. *Archives de Philosophie du Droit et de Sociologie Juridique* 1: 403-420.

Gurvitch, G. 1937a. "Petrazhitsky, Lev Iosifovich (1867-1931)" [Petrazycki, Leon]. Pp. 103-104 in *Encyclopaedia of the Social Sciences*, Vol. 7, edited by E.R.A. Seligman and A. Johnson. New York: Macmillan.

Gurvitch, G. 1937b. "Justice." Pp. 509-515 in *Encyclopaedia of the Social Sciences*, Vol. 11, edited by E.R.A. Seligman and A. Johnson. New York: Macmillan.

Gurvitch, G. 1941a. "Major Problems of the Sociology of Law." *Journal of Social Philosophy* 6(3): 197-215.

Gurvitch, G. 1941b. "The Problem of Social Law." *Ethics* 52: 17-40.

Gurvitch, G. 1941c. "Mass, Community, Communion." *The Journal of Philosophy* 38: 485-495.

Gurvitch, G. 1942a. *Sociology of Law.* New York: Philosophical Library and Alliance Book Corporation.

Gurvitch, G. 1942b. "Magic and Law." *Social Research* 9(1): 104-122.

Horwitz, M.J. 1975. "The Rise of Legal Formalism." *The American Journal of Legal History* 19: 251-264.

Horwitz, M.J. 1977. *The Transformation in American Law: 1780-1860.* Cambridge, MA: Harvard University Press.

Horwitz, M.J. 1992. *The Transformation of American Law, 1870-1960: The Crisis of Legal Orthodoxy.* New York: Oxford University Press.

Hunt, A. 1979. "The Sociology of Law of Gurvitch and Timasheff: A Critique of Theories of Normative Integration." Pp. 169-204 in *Research in Law and Sociology,* Vol. 2, edited by S. Spitzer. Greenwich, CT: JAI Press.

Hunt, A. 1993. *Explorations in Law and Society: Toward a Constitutive Theory of Law.* New York: Routledge.

Hutcheson, J.H. 1929. "The Judgment Intuitive: The Function of the 'Hunch' in Judicial Decision." *Cornell Law Quarterly* 14(3): 274-288.

Johnson, H.M. 1975. "Petrazycki's Sociology in the Perspective of Structural-Functional Theory." Pp. 39-61 in *Sociology and Jurisprudence of Leon Petrazycki,* edited by J. Górecki. Urbana, IL: University of Illinois Press.

Johnson, A. 1979. "The Recognition of Differential Power in the Sociology of Law." *Mid-American Review of Sociology* 4: 57-70.

Jung, C.G. 1964. *Man and His Symbols.* New York: Dell Publishing.

Kelsen, H. 1945. *General Theory of Law and State.* New York: Russell & Russell.

Kennedy, D. 1976. "Form and Substance in Private Law Adjudication." *Harvard Law Review* 89(8): 1685-1778.

Kennedy, D. 1980. "Toward an Historical Understanding of Legal Consciousness: The Case of Classical Legal Thought in America, 1850-1940." Pp. 3-24 in *Research in Law and Sociology,* Vol. 3, edited by R.J. Simon. Greenwich, CT: JAI Press.

Kidd, A.M. 1938. "Book Review: Fundamental Principles of the Sociology of Law by Eugen Ehrlich." *Columbia Law Review* 38(2): 383-386.

Kojder, A., and J. Kwasniewski. 1985. "The Development of the Sociology of Law in Poland." *International Journal of the Sociology of Law* 13: 261-272.

Lande, J. 1975. "The Sociology of Petrazycki." Pp. 23-37 in *Sociology and Jurisprudence of Leon Petrazycki*, edited by J. Górecki. Urbana, IL: University of Illinois Press.

Langrod, G.S., and M. Vaughan. 1970. "The Polish Psychological Theory of Law." Pp. 299-362 in *Polish Law through the Ages*, edited by W.J. Wagner. Stanford, CA: Hoover Institution Press.

Laserson, M.M. 1951. "The Work of Leon Petrazhitskii: Inquiry into the Psychological Aspects of the Nature of Law." *Columbia Law Review* 51: 59-82.

Llewellyn, K.N. 1930. "A Realistic Jurisprudence—The Next Step." *Columbia Law Review* 30:431-465.

Llewellyn, K.N. 1931. "Some Realism about Realism—Responding to Dean Pound." *Harvard Law Review* 44(8): 1222-1264.

Llewellyn, K.N. 1960. *The Common Law Tradition: Deciding Appeals*. Boston, MA: Little, Brown.

Luhmann, N. 1985. *A Sociological Theory of Law,* trans. by E. King and M. Albrow, edited by M. Albrow. London: Routledge & Kegan Paul.

Martindale, D. 1981. *The Nature and Types of Sociological Theory,* 2nd edition. Prospect Heights, IL: Waveland Press.

McDonald, P. 1979. "The Legal Sociology of Georges Gurvitch." *British Journal of Law and Society* 6: 24-52.

Mead, G.H. 1918. "The Psychology of Punitive Justice." *American Journal of Sociology* 23: 577-602.

Mensch, E. 1982. "The History of Mainstream Legal Thought." Pp. 18-39 in *The Politics of Law: A Progressive Critique*, edited by D. Kairys. New York: Pantheon Books.

Merton, R.K. 1965. *On the Shoulders of Giants: A Shandean Postscript*. New York: Free Press.

Merton, R.K. 1968. *Social Theory and Social Structure*. New York: Free Press.

Meyendorff, A. 1933. "Leo Petrazycki (1864-1931)." Pp. 21-37 in *Modern Theories of Law*. Oxford, UK: Oxford University Press.

Northrop, F.S.C. 1956. "Petrazycki's Psychological Jurisprudence: Its Originality and Importance." *University of Pennsylvania Law Review* 104: 65-662.

Nussbaum, A. 1940. "Fact Research in Law." *Columbia Law Review* 40(2): 189-219.

Olivecrona, K. 1948. "Is a Sociological Explanation of Law Possible?" *Theoria* 14: 167-207.

Page, W.H. 1938. "Professor Ehrlich's Czernowitz Seminar of Living Law." Pp. 825-839 in *Readings in Jurisprudence*, edited by J. Hall. Indianapolis, IN: The Bobbs-Merrill Company.

Parsons, T. 1951. *The Social System*. New York: Free Press.

Parsons, T., and E.A. Shils. 1951. *Toward a General Theory of Action*. New York: Harper & Row.

Partridge, P.H. 1961. "Ehrlich's Sociology of Law." Pp. 1-29 in *Studies in the Sociology of Law,* edited by G. Sawer. Canberra, Australia: The Australian National University.

Pashukanis, E.B. 1989 [1924]. *Law and Marxism: A General Theory,* trans. by B. Einhorn, edited and introduced by C. Arthur. Worcester, UK: Pluto Press.

Patterson, E.D. 1931. "Ehrlich, Eugen (1862-1922)." Pp. 445-446 in *Encyclopaedia of the Social Sciences,* Vol. 5, edited by E.R.A. Seligman and A. Johnson. New York: Macmillan.

Petrazycki, L. 1955. *Law and Morality.* Cambridge, MA: Harvard University Press.

Pódgorecki, A. 1974. *Law and Society.* London: Routledge & Kegan Paul.

Pódgorecki, A. 1980-1981. "Unrecognized Father of Sociology of Law: Leon Petrazycki." *Law and Society Review* 15: 183-202.

Pound, R. 1910. "Law in Books and Law in Action." *American Law Review* 44: 12-36.

Pound, R. 1922. "An Appreciation of Eugen Ehrlich." *Harvard Law Review* 36(2): 129-130.

Pound, R. 1971. "Sociology of Law." Pp. 297-341 in *Twentieth-Century Sociology*, edited by G. Gurvitch and W. Moore. New York: Books for Libraries.

Rehbinder, M. 1967. *Die Begründung der Rechtssoziologie durch Eugen Ehrlich* [The Founding of Legal Sociology by Eugen Ehrlich]. Berlin: Duncker und Humblof.

Rehbinder, M. 1977. *Rechtssoziologie* [Sociology of Law]: Berlin: de Gruyter.

Reisner, M.A. 1951. "Law, Our Law, Foreign Law, General Law." Pp. 83-109 in *Soviet Legal Philosophy*, trans. by H.W. Babb. Cambridge, MA: Harvard University Press.

Renner, K. 1949 [1904]. *The Institutions of Private Law and their Social Functions*, edited by O. Kahn-Freund. London: Routledge & Kegan Paul.

Rottleuthner, H. 1987. "Three Legal Sociologies: Eugen Ehrlich, Hugo Sinzheimer, Max Weber." Institute for Legal Studies, Working Papers Series 2, Institute for Legal Studies, University of Wisconsin—Madison Law School.

Rudzinski, A.W. 1976. "Petrazycki's Significance for Contemporary Legal and Moral Theory." *American Journal of Jurisprudence* 21: 107-130.

Scheuer, J.F. 1965. "Nicholas S. Timasheff and the Sociology of Recurrence." *Thought* (Autumn): 432-448.

Schur, E.M. 1968. *Law and Society: A Sociological View*. New York: Random House.

Sheskin, A. 1978. "A Critical Review and Assessment of the Sociology of Law." *Mid-American Review of Sociology* 3: 109-124.

Simmel, G. 1950. *The Sociology of Georg Simmel*, trans. and edited by K.H. Wolff. New York: The Free Press.

Simon, R.J., and J.P. Lynch. 1989. "The Sociology of Law: Where We Have Been and Where We Might Be Going." *Law & Society Review* 23(5): 825-847.

Skapska, G. 1987. "The Sociology of Law in Poland: Problems, Polemics, Social Commitment." *Journal of Law and Society* 14(3): 353-365.

Sorokin, P.A. 1928. *Contemporary Sociological Theories*. New York: Harper & Brothers.

Sorokin, P.A. 1962. *Social and Cultural Dynamics: Fluctuations of Systems of Truth, Ethics, and Law*, Vol. 2. New York: The Bedminster Press.

Sorokin, P.A. 1963. *A Long Journey: The Autobiography of Pitirim A. Sorokin*. New Haven, CT: College and University Press.

Sorokin, P.A. 1966. *Sociological Theories of Today*. New York: Harper & Row.

Sorokin, P.A. 1981. "The Organized Group (Institution) and Law-Norms." Pp. 668-695 in *Interpretations of Modern Legal Philosophies: Essays in Honor of Roscoe Pound*, edited by P. Sayre. Littleton, CO: Fred B. Rothman & Co.

Stone, J. 1968. *The Promise and Function of Law: A Study in Jurisprudence*. Buffalo, NY: William S. Hein & Co.

Stone, J. 1972. *Social Dimensions of Law and Justice*. Holmes Beach, FL: Wm. W. Gaunt & Sons.

Sumner, W.G. 1940 [1906]. *Folkways: A Study of the Sociological Importance of Usages, Manners, Customs, Mores, and Morals*. Boston, MA: Ginn and Company.

Swedberg, R. 1982. *Sociology as Disenchantment: The Evolution of the Work of Georges Gurvitch*. Atlantic Highlands, NJ: Humanities Press.

Timasheff, N.S. 1937a. Book Review: "Fundamental Principles of the Sociology of Law by Eugen Ehrlich." *American Sociological Review* 2(1): 120-124.

Timasheff, N.S. 1937b. "The Retributive Structure of Punishment." *The Journal of Criminal Law and Criminology* 28: 396-405.

Timasheff, N.S. 1937c. "What is 'Sociology of Law'?" *American Journal of Sociology* 43(2): 225-235.

Timasheff, N.S. 1938a. "The Power Phenomenon." *American Sociological Review* 3(4): 499-509.

Timasheff, N.S. 1938b. "Law as a Social Phenomenon." Pp. 868-873 in *Readings in Jurisprudence*, edited by J. Hall. Indianapolis, IN: Bobbs-Merrill.

Timasheff, N.S. 1939a. *An Introduction to the Sociology of Law*. Cambridge, MA: Harvard University Committee on Research in the Social Sciences.

Timasheff, N.S. 1939b. "The Crisis in the Marxian Theory of Law." *New York University Law Quarterly Review* 16(4): 519-531.

Timasheff, N.S. 1939c. "The Sociological Place of Law." *American Journal of Sociology* 44(2): 206-221.

Timasheff, N.S. 1940. "Law in Pareto's Sociology." *American Journal of Sociology* 46(2): 139-149.

Timasheff, N.S. 1942. "Gurvtich's Philosophy of Social Law." *Thought* 17: 709-722.

Timasheff, N.S. 1946. "The Sociologist's Contribution to the Law." *Virginia Law Review* 32: 818-834.

Timasheff, N.S. 1952. "The Basic Concepts of Sociology." *American Journal of Sociology* 58(2): 176-186.

Timasheff, N.S. 1955. "Introduction." Pp. xvii-xl in *Law and Morality*, by L. Petrazycki. Cambridge, MA: Harvard University Press.

Timasheff, N.S. 1957. "Growth and Scope of Sociology of Law." Pp. 424-449 in *Modern Sociological Theory: In Continuity and Change*, edited by H. Becker and A. Boskoff. New York: The Dryden Press.

Timasheff, N.S. 1967. *Sociological Theory: Its Nature and Growth*. New York: Random House.

Timasheff, N.S. 1981. "Petrazycki's Philosophy of Law." Pp. 736-750 in *Interpretations of Modern Legal Philosophies: Essays in Honor of Roscoe Pound*, edited by P. Sayre. Littleton, CO: Fred B. Rothman & Co.

Treviño, A.J. 1994. "The Influence of Sociology on American Jurisprudence: From Oliver Wendell Holmes to Critical Legal Studies." *Mid-American Review of Sociology* 18(1-2): 23-46.

Treviño, A.J. 1996a. *The Sociology of Law: Classical and Contemporary Perspectives*. New York: St. Martin's Press.

Treviño, A.J. 1996b. "The Place of a General Theory of Law in Social Problems Inquiry: A Marxist-Oriented Approach." Pp. 199-248 in *Perspectives on Social Problems,* Vol. 8, edited by J.A. Holstein and G. Miller. Greenwich, CT: JAI Press.

Turkel, G. 1996. *Law and Society: Critical Approaches*. Boston, MA: Allyn and Bacon.

Twining, W. 1973. *Karl Llewellyn and the Realist Movement*. Birkenhead, UK: Willmer Brothers.

Unger, R.M. 1976. *Law in Modern Society: Toward a Criticism of Social Theory*. New York: Free Press.

Vago, S. 1997. *Law and Society*, 5th edition. Upper Saddle River, NJ: Prentice Hall.

Vinogradoff, P. 1928. *The Collected Papers of Paul Vinogradoff*, Vol. II. Oxford, UK: Oxford University Press.

Weber, M. 1978. *Economy and Society*, Vols. I-II, edited by G. Roth and C. Wittich. Berkeley, CA: University of California Press.

Ziegert, K.A. 1979. "The Sociology behind Eugen Ehrlich's Sociology of Law." *International Journal of the Sociology of Law* 7: 225-273.

Ziegert, K.A. 1980. "A Sociologist's View." Pp. 60-85 in *Law and Social Control,* edited by E. Kamenka and A.E-S. Tay. New York: St. Martin's Press.

DOCUMENTING DISPUTES

LAW AND BUREAUCRACY IN ORGANIZATIONAL DISPUTING

Gale Miller

ABSTRACT

This paper analyzes how legal and bureaucratic concerns are interrelated in organizational dispute processing. Using data on dispute emergence in a Work Incentive Program and administrative hearings intended to adjudicate the disputes, the analysis focuses on the ways in which staff-client disagreements evolved as they were considered in different intra- and inter-organizational dispute resolution settings. Of special concern is the ways in which staff members' routine, organizationally mandated record-keeping practices anticipated the possible escalation of staff-client disagreements into formal disputes by providing staff members with documentary resources for justifying their actions to legal adjudicators. The staff's prospective orientation is contrasted with the shorter-term and relational orientation of most clients, which left them poorly prepared for the argumentative demands of legal adjudication, even when they were represented by legal counsel. Finally, the implications of the findings for reforming dispute processing in public bureaucracies are discussed.

Sociology of Crime, Law, and Deviance, Volume 1, pages 203-229.

ISBN: 0-7623-0282-8

INTRODUCTION

Analysis of organizational disputing must be sensitive to the subtle ways that organizational structure and culture are implicated in disputing processes. Not only do the explicit ground rules associated with diverse organizational settings shape and constrain the disputing process, but the mere knowledge of disputing possibilities within an organization may affect the disputing process. Anticipating the interpretive and discursive requirements of a dispute resolution setting shapes the way complaints are initially formulated and advanced. Miller and Holstein (1995, 1996) analyze these requirements as aspects of dispute domains which consist:

> of the practical circumstances to which organization members orient in formulating and pressing their complaints about others, responding to others' complaints about themselves, and intervening in others' disputes. . . . They are not so much geographical locations as interpretive and discursive orientations. Dispute domains are constituted from disputants' and dispute interveners' typical orientations to the purposes of social interactions, their social roles within the interactions, the issues that may be properly considered within them, and available resolutions to the disputes at hand (Miller and Holstein 1996, p. 12).

These concerns are especially germane to conflicts between organization members and outsiders. As more or less permanent fixtures, members are more likely to be aware of organizational disputing possibilities, resources, and demands, while outsiders lack such knowledge. This, of course, works to the insiders' advantage, even if the same rules apply to both sides. For example, anticipating the need for documentation in a formal dispute domain may lead organization members to routinely keep records of all pertinent interactions, even though no specific dispute is foreshadowed. Conversely, outsiders—including clients—may be less familiar with such downstream possibilities (Emerson 1991) and not consider what might be needed if a future dispute should develop.

These issues are significant for the sociological study of law because formal legal redress is often the response of last resort (Emerson 1981) to conflicts emergent in organizations. So viewed, legal proceedings are distinctive dispute domains, and downstream possibilities to which organization members may orient in their interactions with outsiders. A major practical consequence of this organization member orientation is the blending of the rule of law with routine organizational processing and governance. Law and organization become one, even when the intervening legal body is formally separate from the organization in which it intervenes. One possible result of this circumstance is that some disputants may enter legal proceedings better prepared to satisfy the distinctive requirements of these dispute domains than other disputants.

FOCUS AND ORGANIZATION OF THE STUDY

The analysis is informed by two perspectives in sociolegal studies. The first is Felstiner, Abel, and Sarat's (1980-1981) "naming, blaming, and claiming" approach to dispute transformation. They analyze how potential disputes emerge and evolve as potentially aggrieved parties first develop vocabularies for describing themselves as injured (naming), then blame concrete others for their injuries (they now have a grievance), and finally voice their grievances (claiming). According to Felstiner et al. (1980-1981), these developments are stages in the development of predisputes which become full-fledged disputes when the parties accused of wrongdoing reject the claims made against them.

While drawing from Felstiner et al.'s (1980-1981) approach, this analysis focuses on organizations as distinctive environments for the emergence and transformation of disputes. This focus makes it possible to consider how predisputes emerge within particular organizational settings and how they evolve as they are considered within different—but related—dispute domains. Organization members often regard dispute domains as components of a potential dispute's organizational horizons (Emerson and Paley 1992; Emerson 1992). They project the downstream consequences (Emerson 1991) of their own and others' actions, and may modify their actions in anticipation of the consequences.

In attending to these concerns, organization members may blend legal and bureaucratic orientations. They may, for example, adopt a prospective orientation that justifies greater attention to record-keeping that is likely to be emphasized in the dispute domains to which current disagreements may eventually be taken. A predispute, then, may be analyzed as having an anticipated trajectory of evolution from an organization member's point of view. Commonsense knowledge of this trajectory may influence members' actions, both directly within disputing interactions and in terms of actions that are ancillary to ongoing interactions but which might eventually become significant.

The second sociolegal perspective that is relevant to this analysis is recent discursive studies of dispute resolution in legal settings. Conley and O'Barr (1990), for example, analyze how disputes considered in small claims courts may be organized, contested, and resolved within a legalistic discourse that emphasizes rules of evidence and assigning culpability to one disputing party, or within a relational discourse which stresses the interpersonal issues at stake in the disputes. The latter discourse focuses disputants' and judges' attention on developing dispute resolutions that address all disputants' concerns and are mutually agreeable to them. Merry (1990) stresses similar themes in her discursive analysis of how conflicts between family members and neighbors (problems) are transformed into cases when they are considered in legal settings. She states:

> Cases have beginnings, middles, and ends, while problems often do not. Closure or "resolution" of problems does not make much sense, since problems are simply aspects of social rela-

> tionships. Problems do not have the definiteness of substance, the smooth development, or the certainty which a retrospective view of a completed or ended case suggests (p. 88).

A major theme in these analyses of legal settings is a concern for the ways in which disputing discourses may place some disputants at an advantage over others by stressing some concerns, rhetorical styles, and forms of knowledge, and devaluing others. The legal discourse of rules and cases, for example, favors disputants who are knowledgeable about legal procedures and evidence and skilled at legal argumentation, and who have access to the types of documents that are usually honored in legal proceedings. These factors are less likely to be similarly honored in dispute domains involving other disputing discourses, such as mediation settings. Discursive studies of legal settings, then, sensitize us to the ways in which related intra- and inter-organizational dispute domains may reconfigure the issues at stake in emergent disputes, and the conditions under which they are argued (Miller and Holstein 1995, 1996).

I explore these issues in this paper by analyzing how staff members and clients in a Work Incentive Program (WIN) oriented to, and managed, conflicts emergent in their relationships. The next three sections deal with the setting of the study, how dispute processing was organized in the Work Incentive Program, and how staff-client conflicts were transformed as they moved through the WIN disputing process. We then turn from WIN staff-client orientations to the potential downstream consequences of the conflicts. We also consider how WIN hearings were organized and conducted and the implications of the hearings for staff-client conflicts and relationships. Finally, I discuss the implications of the study for analyzing and changing dispute processing in public bureaucracies.

The analysis emphasizes how disputes emerged from predisputes in WIN, forming a trajectory of escalating conflict that staff members anticipated in their dealings with clients. The process of naming, blaming, and claiming analyzed by Felstiner et al. (1980-1981), then, was an institutionalized feature of WIN dispute processing. I also stress how WIN staff members' organizational interest in producing records attesting to their professionalism melded with the legal requirement that disputants provide documentary evidence supporting their claims against others. This blending of organizational and legal interests in WIN produced social conditions which privileged a rule-oriented discourse of organizational records over alternative—including relational—discourses in legal confrontations between WIN staff and clients. While perhaps unintended, these social conditions usually placed staff members at a considerable advantage over their clients in formal dispute resolution settings.

The data analyzed below have been slightly altered to protect the confidentiality of the parties involved. The changes focus on information that might be used to identify WIN clients, staff members, and hearings officers. Specifically, all names, addresses, telephone numbers, and related identifying information have been altered.

SETTING OF THE STUDY

The Work Incentive Program (WIN) was a publicly funded program designed to help recipients of Aid to Families With Dependent Children (AFDC) find jobs and become economically self-supporting. AFDC supports dependent children by providing modest financial benefits when their parents are unemployed and (in some cases) when their parents' earnings do not meet designated levels. All AFDC recipients were obligated to enroll in WIN unless they qualified for one of the following exceptions:

> children under [the] age of 16 or attending school; those ill, incapacitated, or of advanced age; those so remote from a project as to preclude participating; those caring for a member of the household who is ill or incapacitated; a mother in a family where the father registers; and a mother of a child under age six (Rein 1974, p. 115).

Most WIN clients were required to look for jobs, keep records detailing their job-seeking activities, and regularly meet with their WIN workers (the staff member who supervised the client and to whom the client was directly accountable) about their employment situations. Other clients were assigned to programs designed to increase their employability (such as educational and training programs), and a few were temporarily excused from employment-related activities while they sought help with physical, emotional, and/or family problems. The WIN program provided clients with funds to meet some of their job-seeking expenses (mostly to pay for gasoline and one meal per day) and for hiring baby sitters to watch their children while they competed their WIN assignments. These funds were provided in addition to those provided by the AFDC program.

The data analyzed here are based on 13 months of observation in a WIN office and informal interviews with staff and clients. The WIN office studied was located in a city of approximately 90,000 people with a highly industrial local economy that was experiencing a major recession during the research period. The city was located between two major urban centers in which clients were also encouraged to look for jobs. During most of the research period, the WIN staff consisted of seven WIN workers, a WIN supervisor, and three social workers who represented the County Welfare Department. The data also include transcripts of 73 WIN hearings in which clients appealed staff members' decisions to expel them from the program for noncompliance with WIN rules. The hearings were conducted in a wide variety of WIN offices across the state.

A major WIN staff member responsibility involved monitoring clients' compliance with WIN rules and procedures, particularly rules requiring that clients fulfill the assignments made by staff members. The assignments included requiring clients to keep accurate records of their job-seeking activities, see doctors about their physical problems, find babysitters so that the clients could look for jobs, and keep their appointments with their WIN workers. When, in the judgment of staff members, clients were not meeting their WIN obligations, staff members investigated and assessed the circumstances associated with the clients' noncompliance. For example, staff members sometimes assessed clients as not adequately grasping the rules and expectations of the program, and at other times as unable to meet program requirements because of health, family, or related problems beyond the clients' control. Staff members responded to clients assessed in these ways by instructing them on WIN rules and expectations and by temporarily exempting the clients from normal WIN activities.

Occasionally, however, WIN staff members assessed clients' noncompliance as a long-standing pattern of uncooperative behavior reflecting the client's intention to avoid meeting their WIN responsibilities. Staff members were required to seek reconciliation with clients so assessed. If reconciliation was unsuccessful, the clients were expelled from the program, although they could apply for readmission to WIN once the expulsion period passed (usually 30 days). Depending on their WIN statuses, expelled clients lost all or significant portions of their AFDC grants during the expulsion period. The following statement by a staff member is typical of how staff members explained their decisions to expel clients from WIN:

> A lot of these people [uncooperative clients] are like alcoholics. They have to hit bottom to see [that] they have a problem, to feel pain. Then they look at their lives and decide that they hafta make some changes. They'll put it off as long as they can, though. It's only when they don't have any choice that they look at themselves in the mirror. That's what we're doin' here, forcing them to look at their lives and make some changes.

The vast majority of grievances expressed in the WIN office that I studied were initiated by staff members against clients whom they portrayed as uncooperative—that is, clients who did not fulfill the assignments made by their WIN workers. When clients disagreed with staff members' decisions regarding their WIN activities and statuses, the clients could request WIN hearings to adjudicate the matters. Staff member decisions to expel clients from the program were the actions most likely to trigger such a request by clients.

It is important to emphasize that only a small minority of WIN staff-client predisputes escalated into formal legal disputes. First, most staff-client disagreements were managed without expelling the clients from the program. Also, most expelled clients did not appeal the staff members' actions. Using Galanter's (1974) typology of disputing parties, the WIN clients were "one shotters," meaning that they only occasionally chose to take legal action against staff members. Staff members might be classified as "repeat players" (Galanter 1974) because they were more likely than their clients to have previously participated in WIN hearings. This difference between WIN staff members and clients should not be overstated, however, since WIN hearings were unusual events for both parties.

The hearings were conducted by attorneys (hearings officers) associated with the State Hearings Office. They traveled to local WIN offices to conduct the hearings, in which they took sworn testimony from witnesses for both sides and considered documents presented to them as legally admissible evidence. Clients could be represented by legal counsel in the hearings. This happened in less than 10% of the hearings. Hearings officers rendered legally binding decisions that either upheld staff members' actions or overturned them. The transcripts analyzed here were made from tape recordings routinely made by hearings officers. The tapes were kept at the State Hearings Office in case of further appeal, a rare occurrence. I also attended several hearings as a part of my fieldwork and informally interviewed the hearings officers who conducted hearings in the fieldwork site.

While the WIN program no longer exists, it is typical of the welfare-to-work programs that preceded and have followed it. These programs also require clients to look for jobs or complete other employment-related tasks. Staff members are also required to identify clients who are not meeting minimal organizational expectations and to take actions holding the clients accountable for their noncompliance. Finally, most if not all welfare-to-work programs allow for client appeals of staff members' decisions to outside legal adjudicators.

WIN DISPUTE DOMAINS

The Work Incentive Program was organized as five major dispute domains involving differing degrees of formalization of staff-client predisputes and disputes. The most formal dispute domain was WIN hearings. Each WIN dispute domain also had somewhat different implications for staff members' and clients' roles, the opportunities provided to them for advocating for their positions, and organizing the issues at stake. These differences are summarized in Table 1 and discussed below.

Routine staff-client meetings in WIN included clients' first encounters with staff members when they registered with the program, as well as orientation sessions conducted a few days after a client registered in WIN. Registration meetings were largely organized as information gathering interactions in which staff members asked questions designed to assess the applicants' suitability for WIN and to determine the most appropriate assignments for the applicants judged by staff members to be appropriate for WIN. Orientation sessions involved groups of new clients who were instructed on WIN rules, procedures, and expectations by one staff member. Most routine staff-client meetings, however, consisted of the regular interactions between clients and their WIN workers. These meetings focused on whether clients were fulfilling their WIN assignments and on developing new strategies for solving clients' employment problems.

Clients sometimes raised questions about their WIN assignments in these meetings, including whether they should be involved in WIN at all. Staff members usually responded to clients' questions by assessing whether the clients were able to fulfill their WIN assignments and/or whether the assignments were appropriate for clients' circumstances. Staff members displayed most interest in client claims that they could not fulfill their WIN assignments because of family or personal (usually health) problems. Staff members sometimes made adjustments in clients'

Table 1. WIN Conflict and Dispute Settings

Interactional Setting	*Setting Organizer*	*Institutional Question at Issue*	*Preferred Responses*
Routine staff-client meetings	Client's WIN worker	Can and is the client fulfilling his or her WIN assignments?	Claims of personal and/or family troubles
Pattern of behavior meetings	Client's WIN worker	Does the client understand WIN expectations?	Promises of future cooperation
Conciliation meetings	Conciliation team	Does the client deserve another chance?	Promises of future cooperation
WIN hearings	Hearings officer	Were proper procedures followed in expelling the client or refusing readmission, and what conditions must the former client meet in order to be readmitted?	Legally admissible support for staff and client claims, and specification of conditions clients must meet in order to be readmitted to WIN
Readmission meetings	Worker or the WIN supervisor	Does the client understand and will he or she fulfil WIN expectations?	Documentation of promises of future cooperation

WIN assignments (including occasionally exempting clients from WIN) based on their assessments of these claims. Once these issues had been dealt with to staff members' satisfaction, however, they treated ongoing client complaints as possible signs of uncooperative client attitudes. Staff members responded to these clients by calling pattern of behavior meetings.

Pattern of behavior meetings usually involved clients and their WIN workers but differed from routine staff-client meetings in their primary focus on staff members' complaints against clients. For staff members, the central issue at stake in these predisputes was making certain that clients understood the WIN rules and expectations to which they were being held accountable. A related issue involved staff members' solicitation from clients of promises of future cooperation. Staff members also used pattern of behavior meetings to anticipate possible movement of the predisputes into a more formal setting because they could not refer clients to conciliation meetings unless they could show that clients had been offered pattern of behavior meetings. According to staff members, predisputes with clients became serious matters when conciliation meetings with the clients were requested.

The requests were directed to another WIN staff member who served as an adjudication specialist and made the final determination about whether conciliation meetings should be held. In addition to the adjudication specialist who directed the meetings, conciliation teams included a social worker associated with both WIN and the County Welfare Department. Further, complaining staff members and conciliation teams held preconciliation meetings which did not include clients. The major focus of these meetings was the negotiation of agreements about how to respond to clients' noncompliance in conciliation meetings. These negotiations turned on whether the clients deserved another chance to fulfill their WIN responsibilities. While staff members and conciliation teams sometimes decided that the clients' actions warranted immediate expulsion from the program, they usually agreed that the clients should be given one more chance. A major part of giving clients "one last chance" was soliciting promises from clients that they would fulfill all WIN assignments in the future. Should clients fail to keep the promises made in conciliation meetings, they were routinely expelled from WIN without another meeting being called.

WIN hearings were distinctive because they reversed prior disputing roles. Previously, staff members voiced complaints against clients, who were asked to account for their behavior. In WIN hearings, however, clients were the complainants and the onus was on staff members to show that they had acted properly. The central issues of WIN hearings focused on whether staff members had followed proper procedures in dealing with clients and on the conditions that clients would need to meet in order to be readmitted into WIN. In considering these issues, hearings officers only considered sworn testimony and legally admissible evidence submitted by both sides to the disputes.

While organized as formal legal proceedings, many normal legal restrictions on evidence and hearsay testimony were relaxed in WIN hearings. For example, the hearings officers often accepted unsubstantiated claims by WIN staff members when clients did not contest the claims. When clients objected, the hearings officers asked staff members to document their claims. Hearings officers also treated "normal business records"—documents created and maintained by WIN staff members as part of their everyday jobs—as admissible evidence, rarely seeking any further verification of their authenticity. The records included forms completed by clients and staff members about clients' life circumstances and efforts to find employment, and case narratives written by staff members. The case records dealt with clients' employment troubles and participation in WIN, as well as staff members' reasons for treating clients as they did. Hearings officers disallowed documents that might have been specifically created "based on a concern for collecting evidence to be used at a hearing."

Clients expelled from WIN could seek readmission to the program once the expulsion period had passed. These meetings constituted the fifth WIN dispute domain. Expelled clients were required to meet the same eligibility requirements as other WIN applicants, and their registration meeting with staff members involved the same questions and concerns as other registration meetings. Expelled clients were also sometimes required to meet with the WIN supervisor prior to being readmitted to the program. The supervisor could extend the expulsion period by insisting that expelled clients display their commitment to future cooperation prior to being reregistered in the program. A readmission condition sometimes specified by the supervisor in the WIN office that I studied was that former clients participate in paid and unpaid community service programs operated by several local human service agencies. Of course, clients who objected to staff members' readmission conditions could also request WIN hearings on these matters.

DISPUTE TRANSFORMATION

Routine staff-client meetings, pattern of behavior meetings, conciliation meetings, WIN hearings, and readmission meetings were interconnected parts of an organizational process through which the predisputes might escalate and be transformed into disputes Routine staff-client meetings and pattern of behavior meetings, for example, were predispute settings in which staff members' blamed clients (routine meetings) and made claims against them (pattern of behavior meetings). If clients rejected staff members' portrayals of them as uncooperative and offers to "resolve" the conflicts, then these disputes-in-the-making were forwarded to the next dispute domain. Full-fledged disputes sometimes emerged in conciliation meetings when clients rejected staff members' portrayals of them as uncooperative and staff members responded by expelling the clients from WIN. More typically, however, these were predispute interactions in which staff members sought to eliminate any possible future client claims to extenuating circumstances that would justify further noncompliance with staff members' directives.

WIN hearings, on the other hand, were clearly dispute resolution proceedings. They were defined and justified by disputed claims and counter-claims, and hearings officers' roles as adjudicators of the disputes. The disputes were transformed once again when expelled clients reenrolled in WIN. While previously expelled clients were closely watched by staff members, newly emergent conflicts between the reenrolled clients and their WIN workers involved the same process and trajectory as other staff-client predisputes. That is, WIN staff members responded to predisputes with previously expelled clients by first calling pattern of behavior meetings and then requesting conciliation meetings.

Officially, then, WIN dispute processing was organized as a cycle that offered most clients multiple "second chances" to participate in the program. The cycle began with predisputes in routine staff-client interactions, escalated into full-fledged disputes in WIN hearings, and then cycled back to predisputes in readmission meetings. It should be emphasized, however, that each of these steps in WIN dispute processing involved potentially significant consequences for clients and staff members. For example, clients who were warned and threatened in early stages of the process and in readmission meetings were less likely than other clients to be "forgiven" by staff members for subsequent rule violations and disagreements.

Staff members also treated the disputing process as consequential, emphasizing that one of their major professional responsibilities involved holding uncooperative clients accountable to WIN rules and procedures. Thus, WIN hearings were significant events for staff members who treated them as contests about their professionalism and right to sanction noncompliant clients. Staff members in the WIN office that I studied also objected when hearings officers found against them, stating that they did not expel clients from the program unless the clients' really "deserved" such action. Indeed, on one occasion, a hearings officer chastised the WIN supervisor for complaining about a decision that supported the client. He told the supervisor that she should not treat the hearings process or outcomes as personal matters. She replied, "Of course, it's personal." The issues in contention in the hearings for the supervisor involved more than whether the staff had met the technical requirements of the law. Her professional identity and that of her staff were also at stake in WIN hearings.

Because WIN hearings were mainly concerned with the procedural correctness of actions taken by WIN personnel, the disputants were required to formulate their positions within a discourse of organizational policy, procedure, and rules. This new orientation was evident, for example, when a hearings officer advised a staff member about how he and his colleagues might better prepare for future hearings. The interaction took place in the WIN office, just prior to the start of a hearing. It began as a discussion about a recent hearing in which another hearings officer had found in favor of the client. The hearings officer began by describing the hearings as very simple and straightforward matters, stating that staff members tend to "ramble on and on because they don't understand what the legal issues are." The hearings officer continued:

> Here's what you have to do to prove your case. You must demonstrate that the client has knowledge of the rules, and that he's broken them. You also must demonstrate that the client's been informed of the implications of further rule violation. That's it. It's not necessary to review the whole case for me. Just focus on those parts that are directly pertinent.

Each of these WIN hearings requirements might be met by eliciting sworn testimony from witnesses, but such testimony is always potentially subject to rebuttal by clients and witnesses called by clients. Clients might testify, for example, that WIN staff members never properly explained clients' rights and responsibilities during registration and orientation meetings. They might also testify that clients were not given the WIN assignments in question, or that staff members improperly conducted pattern of behavior and conciliation meetings. Under these circumstances, hearings officers would have to decide between the disputing parties, because legal adjudication involves upholding one disputing position against the other.

It is perhaps not surprising, then, that WIN hearings officers sought and accepted organizationally produced documents into evidence and relied on them in making their decisions. The hearings officers treated such documents as objective evidence verifying the claims made by staff members and clients. Hearings officers also assumed that the documents accurately represented clients' and staff members' understandings about their relationships and their responsibilities in WIN. The content of the documents only became matters of negotiation in WIN hearings if staff members and clients offered conflicting documents as evidence or if clients challenged staff members' claims that their documents were "normal business records." These were rare occurrences in WIN hearings.

I have no data on clients' preparations for the hearings, although their actions in the hearings suggested that they had devoted little time to preparing for the hearings. Staff members, on the other hand, clearly prepared for WIN hearings. I attended several pre-hearing meetings, much of which involved assembling documents on clients' WIN participation. Clients' seeming lack of preparation and staff members extensive preparation for WIN hearings are indicative of other important differences in their orientations to conflict and disputing. We turn to these differences next.

STAFF-CLIENT ORIENTATIONS

Staff members and clients took different orientations to, and had different practical interests in, their predisputes. Staff members' practical interests shifted from a primary concern for forestalling serious future conflicts in routine staff-client and pattern of behavior meetings to justifying their recommendations to conciliation teams. Staff members were also much more likely than clients to take a prospective orientation to their predisputes with clients, even when the disagreements were "resolved" in routine and uneventful meetings with clients. Staff members occasionally directly voiced this orientation to one another, as when a staff member announced in a loud voice after a client with whom she had had a disagreement left the office, "You all heard that. You heard what he said and what I said. If there's a hearing, I expect you to testify about what happened here."

More often, however, staff members expressed a prospective orientation by informing clients of the practical, downstream implications of noncompliance. Clients were informed by staff members in pattern of behavior meetings, for example, that failure to cooperate in the future could result in conciliation meetings and possible expulsion from WIN. Staff members also informed clients of their right to WIN hearings during conciliation meetings, and the written notices sent to clients formally informing them of their expulsion from the program noted clients' right to legal redress. New clients were told during the orientation sessions that they had the right to make grievances against their WIN workers, and the procedures for doing so were described for them. Finally, the orientation sessions included discussion of staff members' expectations of client cooperation and the usual ways in which staff members responded to "uncooperative" clients.

Staff members anticipated these potential future disputes by maintaining case files on their clients. Staff members were required to maintain the files as a normal part of their everyday work activities. The files summarized aspects of staff members' dealings with clients, including notations about the times when clients failed to fully comply with staff members' demands. Equally significant, however, was the routine and unremarkable information solicited from clients by staff members about clients' past and present lives. The information focused on clients' employment histories, family circumstances, possible health problems, and employment plans.

Staff members used this information in developing strategies for responding to clients' employment problems. Staff members also routinely requested that clients sign documents summarizing their assessments of, and plans for, clients. This request might become significant in the future because, in signing the documents, clients agreed to the conditions specified in the documents. Perhaps the most politically important of these documents was the WIN Rights and Responsibilities form that all WIN applicants were required to sign in order to be enrolled in the program. In signing the form, clients stated that they understood their responsibilities in WIN and agreed to fulfill them.

The files constructed and maintained by staff members were periodically reviewed by the WIN supervisor, who noted when pertinent information was missing. One aspect of the WIN supervisor's evaluation of staff members' performances was her assessments of the completeness of their case files. Staff members' interest in constructing and maintaining files, then, was both prospective and practical. The files provided evidence that staff members were properly discharging their responsibilities to clients and anticipated possible charges of staff incompetence or unfairness that might emerge in the future. Here, we see the confluence of bureaucratic and legal concerns in WIN staff members' everyday professional practices. Being a competent organization member involved constructing and maintaining documents that might be used—and honored—in other dispute domains.

Specifically, when called on to do so, staff members could assemble aspects of clients' case files into patterns of uncooperative behavior that had discernible beginnings and involved escalating trajectories of serious client noncompliance. The histories also detailed staff members' attempts to bring closure to the predisputes and documented clients' refusals to resolve them or failures to comply with agreements made in prior conflict resolution meetings. Consider, for example, the following staff member portrayal of a client's file during a preconciliation meeting:

> OK, back in [date] she quit a good job at [a local business] that paid $8 an hour, and got herself on welfare. I'm not sure about the circumstances of her leaving, but I heard that she didn't get along with her new supervisor. She either quit or was fired, I'm not sure about that either. [The client's] record is funny because she has a lot of secretarial experience, but her tests don't show that she's a very good typist or would be a good secretary. She also doesn't present

herself very well either. That's why I arranged a work experience [volunteer work] for her at [a local social service organization]. But she made it clear at the interview that she didn't really want to be there, and so they didn't ask her to stay. That really upset me 'cause I'm sure that they would have offered her a job [at the end of the work experience]. Then I asked her to go to the [Alternative Education Center] to take a typing test and she didn't. She just hasn't been showing any serious effort at job search.

Clients, on the other hand, were more likely to treat each predispute as a discrete event involving few or no downstream consequences. They were less likely than staff to describe their actions as aspects of patterns of behavior, preferring instead to emphasize that their seeming noncompliance was related to such practical contingencies as family problems, inoperable automobiles, no money, or forgetfulness. Nor did clients ask for written summaries of their negotiations with staff members or make certain that their WIN workers recorded the times when they kept their promises of future cooperation. In some cases, clients might not have understood that staff members maintained such records, although they were routinely given copies of many of the documents kept in their WIN files. When staff members told clients about their record-keeping activities (indeed, they sometimes read selected entries to clients), most clients expressed little interest in the contents of the records.

Clients' typical orientation to their predisputes with staff members may be characterized as relational (Conley and O'Barr 1990) because they emphasized the interpersonal issues at stake in the disagreements. This orientation served clients well in routine staff-client meetings and pattern of behavior meetings in which staff members usually accepted clients' explanations for their actions and promises to "do better in the future." It was less useful in conciliation meetings, where staff members treated prior client explanations as excuses and demanded that clients make unconditional promises to cooperate in the future. Clients also encountered a new emphasis on documentary evidence in conciliation meetings where conciliation teams responded to clients who could not produce any documentation for their claims as making excuses.

The differences in WIN client and staff member orientations to their predisputes and disputes are clearly evident in the following exchange which occurred during a conciliation meeting. The exchange began when a conciliation team member asked the client why she had refused to complete an assignment made by her WIN worker. Notice how the client (CL) responds by emphasizing the bad attitude of the WIN worker (SM) toward clients (a relational claim), and how her WIN worker responds by constructing a dispute history emphasizing the times when the client has broken WIN rules.

CL: He [indicating her WIN worker] has a bad attitude toward us [pause] lower-class people. He doesn't care about us, he thinks he's better than we are.

SM: Well, let's see what sort of attitude you've had toward WIN. [He reads portions of her WIN record dating back several years. The emphasis is on the times when the client has missed appointments with her WIN worker and failed to

> complete her assignments.] Now, if I have a bad attitude toward you, it may be because of your record.

On the other hand, when clients did respond to staff members' complaints by offering documentation of their claims, staff and conciliation team members honored the claims. They did so even when the veracity of the documents offered by clients could not be substantiated by anyone else. For example, one client stated in a conciliation meeting that while he had not kept his WIN appointments, he was still looking for work. He then pulled a small spiral notebook from his pocket and showed staff members the entries that noted when and where he had looked for jobs. The staff members accepted the entries as truthful and accurate, praised the client for his commitment to finding a job, but stated that he was still responsible for keeping his WIN appointments.

Clients' relational orientation was especially ill suited to the demands of WIN hearings in which the documentation of disputant claims was stressed. Staff members, on the other hand, were usually well equipped to manage the demands of this dispute domain, despite the charges against them.

WIN HEARINGS

WIN hearings involved four major phases of argumentation. The hearings began with hearings officers' introductory remarks, which included formal specification of clients' charges against staff members. WIN representatives (usually a member of the local conciliation team) were then asked to respond to the charges by calling witnesses (usually other WIN staff members) and presenting documentary evidence supporting their position. Following this questioning, hearings officers asked questions of the WIN representatives and their witnesses and provided clients and their counsel with opportunities to cross-examine WIN representatives and witnesses.

The third phase of the hearings dealt with clients' sides to the disputes. They, too, were required to present their arguments as question-answer sequences and to submit documents supporting their claims, although virtually no clients offered such documentation. Because few clients called witnesses or were represented by counsel, the hearings officers conducted the direct examination of the vast majority of clients. WIN representatives were invited to cross-examine clients and their witnesses at the completion of the direct testimony. The hearings were concluded by the hearings officers, who asked the disputants if they would consider informally settling their differences (both parties agreed to this option in only one hearing) and then described the procedures to be followed in adjudicating the disputes.

WIN hearings turned on staff members' abilities to construct legally persuasive cases. Thus, staff members played a more central role in WIN hearings than clients. They either satisfied the demands of hearings officers and "won" the disputes, or they failed to satisfy the hearings officers and "lost." This circumstance is reflected in the disposition of the 73 hearings considered in this study. Hearings officers affirmed WIN staff members' actions in 57 of these hearings and reversed them in 15, and one resulted in a mutual conciliation. Nine of the reversals were based exclusively on procedural grounds relating to the filing of letters sent to clients informing them of their expulsion from WIN. In these instances, the hearings officers ruled that the clients were not properly informed about the reasons for their expulsion from the program. Hearings officers also justified the other reversals on procedural grounds, but they cited hearing testimony and evidence as the central factors in determining these outcomes.

An emphasis on constructing staff-client disputes as cases (Merry 1990) was also evident in the typical argumentation practices of WIN representatives and witnesses. They argued from the outset of the hearings that the disputes at hand involved clear beginning stages in which clients were fully informed of their responsibilities in the program and were given several opportunities to correct their noncompliant behavior. They further stated that despite staff members' efforts to resolve their predisputes with clients, the conflicts escalated due to clients' continuing noncompliance with WIN rules. Staff members built these histories by offering aspects of clients' WIN files as documentary evidence of their professionalism and clients' culpability. The histories defined the major issues at stake in the hearings, issues to which complaining clients might be held accountable in subsequent phases of the hearings.

MAKING CASES IN WIN HEARINGS

The opening questions asked by WIN representatives of witnesses focused on the witnesses' professional backgrounds and qualifications to speak on the matters at hand. The representatives followed these questions with others which introduced clients' files into evidence, justified the actions in question, and chronicled clients' noncompliance with WIN rules. WIN representatives introduced clients' files into evidence by asking witnesses to identify and explain the documents that they brought to the hearings. It is difficult to overstate the micropolitical significance of these questions and answers because they provided legal grounds for treating virtually all aspects of clients' WIN files as matters of fact. Once this assertion was accepted by hearings officers and clients, WIN representatives were no longer required to substantiate the claims recorded by staff members in clients' files. The following exchange is typical of how WIN representatives (WR) and staff members (SM) cast clients' WIN files as normal business records:

WR: And what is the document you have before you?

SM: It is our standard work, WIN registrant history folder.

WR: And how is it generated?

SM: Um, it comes about when people or when a person as Mr. Ciati [the complaining client] is registered and appraised for the WIN program and, um, [pause] it contains, um, all records, status changes, notes, um, case notes.

WIN representatives then displayed selective entries in the files by asking staff members to provide information about clients' life circumstances and involvement in WIN. They included questions about clients' home addresses, family composition, and WIN statuses. WIN representatives also sometimes asked staff members to describe clients' activities prior to the troublesome incidents at issue in the hearings. The following exchange is typical of this phase of the hearings process:

WR: OK, what is the document you have before you?

SM: It is the folder of the WIN registrant-participant folder on Ricardo Ibarra. It is a normal document we keep on all of the WIN clients.

WR: OK, what is the registrant's name?

SM: Ricardo Ibarra, [spells Ibarra].

WR: And what is the registrant's address?

SM: The last address we have on him is 1875 York Street, Ralston.

WR: Is there a phone at the residence?

SM: No, but we have a message for him at 288-5310.

WR: What is the registrant's family situation?

SM: The registrant is currently married [pause] with 2 children.

WR: What type of assistance is the registrant receiving and what county is administering the grant?

SM: The registrant is receiving AFDC unemployed parent, um, his last grant approval we have amount $529 per month is administered through the Ralston County welfare department. [pause]

WR: Is this a voluntary or mandatory registrant?

SM: Um, Mr. Ibarra is a mandatory registrant in the WIN program.

WIN representatives turned to the legal grounds justifying staff members' actions by asking witnesses to provide documentary evidence of their claim that complaining clients were aware of relevant WIN rules. Central to making this claim was offering the WIN Rights and Responsibilities form as evidence. The following exchange illustrates how this was accomplished. Notice, also, how the staff member casts the Rights and Responsibilities form as a normal business record by describing how it was a normal part of the registration of new clients in WIN.

WR: Were his rights and responsibilities, and the consequences of failure or refusal to participate in the program, explained to [the client] at the time he entered [the program]?

SM: Yes, they were.

WR: . . . I hand you a document marked Exhibit #1, could you identify this for the record, please?

SM: This is a WIN program's Rights and Responsibilities form which [the client] signed on the day he was registered into the program. And this consists of all of the obligations, rights, responsibilities, and so forth that people who are registered into the program are made aware of at the time that they are appraised and registered with us.

WR: Is there anything in there specifically regarding the registrant's responsibilities about keeping appointments or calling and canceling?

SM: Yes, right in the very first paragraph, um, it deals with the idea of keeping all appointments with the WIN program and, um, it makes mention that all appointments are necessary and if a person isn't able to keep an appointment that they do need to call ahead of time so that the appointment can be rescheduled for them.

WR: Is there any requirement in there regarding registrants' obli-, responsibility to notify the WIN office of any change in their address, mailing address?

SM: Yes, the last paragraph does state that they are required to notify their local WIN office of any change in their mailing address.

In entering these documents into evidence, staff members confirmed that they had fulfilled their responsibility to fully inform clients of WIN regulations before clients committed themselves to participation. But the full significance of the notification of this information only became apparent later, when accusations of irresponsibility, failure to cooperate, and/or refusal to participate were made.

Typically, WIN representatives asked the first witness several other questions about the client's background with WIN, job readiness evaluations, interests and goals, and WIN assignments. With this information on record, WIN representatives inquired into the circumstances which prompted the action under appeal. In an almost formulaic fashion, WIN representatives led witnesses through a sequence of questions and answers to elicit documented histories of client noncompliance. For example, in the following case, the client had been scheduled for a routine meeting with her WIN worker to pick up job referrals and confer about her ongoing job search. The staff member testified (based on entries in the client's file) that the client missed one appointment but had called ahead of time, saying she was sick. Thus, he scheduled another appointment for April 6.

WR: Did she report to that appointment with you or call to indicate that she otherwise could not keep the appointment?

SM: She did not call [and] she did not show for the appointment on April 6.

WR: Did you send her or notify her in any way of any further appointments?

SM: Yes, I sent her out an appointment notice for (pause) April 9. (pause)

WR: Did she come in or call for April 9? (pause)

SM: She did not.

WR: Did not report to the appointment. Did she call to indicate that she would not be able to keep the appointment?

SM: It was no show, she did not show and she did not call.

WR: OK. So after that missed appointment then on April 9, what did you do?

SM: I rescheduled another appointment for POB [pattern of behavior meeting].

[Staff member explains the purposes of pattern of behavior meetings, emphasizing that it was the organizationally prescribed and routine way of responding to such client noncompliance.]

WR: And did she report to that interview or call in?

SM: She did not show, she did not call.

WR: What did you do next?

SM: Then I referred her to . . . for further adjudication [conciliation meeting].

In this interaction, the WIN representative and staff member provide the hearings officer with the beginnings of a dispute history by noting the client's failure to keep her appointment on April 6. The prior missed appointment is discounted because the client "called ahead of time" to cancel it. The staff member elaborates by noting other times when the client failed to meet her WIN obligations and by noting his responses to her noncompliance (first calling a pattern of behavior meeting and then referring her for conciliation). This dispute history was further extended by the subsequent witness who also made frequent reference to entries in the client's WIN file.

Through these interactional procedures, WIN representatives and witnesses constructed cases that explained and justified the expulsion of clients from WIN, and provided hearings officers with reasons for upholding staff members' decisions to expel clients from the program. This pattern of questioning was repeated in virtually all hearings. The sequence of events, and information about times, places, persons, and circumstances were elicited, but peripheral details were ignored, both in the questions and the answers. Specific questions were used to invite specific answers.

Hearings officers usually questioned each WIN witness upon the completion of his or her direct testimony. The hearings officers' questions were not designed to cross-examine the witnesses but to elaborate on, and clarify, information already in evidence. For example, hearings officers asked for more detailed information about the events and dates in question, and sometimes inquired about staff members' and client's interactions. When hearings officers finished questioning WIN witnesses, clients were given the opportunity to cross-examine the witnesses. Most clients declined the invitation, to which hearings officers sometimes responded with mild encouragement, such as "Are you sure?" When clients continued to decline, hearings officers moved to the next witness.

PRESENTING CLIENTS' SIDE

When clients chose to cross-examine WIN witnesses, the ensuing exchanges were often problematic for hearings officers (HO). As in the following interaction involving Jim Epps (JE), this was because clients used their designated turn at talk to "tell their side of the story."

> JE: . . . What I want to know is uh, (pause) on this form uh, (pause) exhibit 3 it says here that um, (pause) if I refuse to take the full-time work I could be in a 30-day conciliation period. And if he still refuses by Friday, April 3, they will sanction me. OK, now (pause) that gives, that just about tells everybody here that I had til, actually I had til that Friday (pause) to make up my mind whether I wanted to work full time or not. But, uh, (pause) what happened is they harassed me into, uh, well they, they didn't harass me, they threatened me, they said either you sign this, (pause) uh, paper and go to work immediately or (pause) you'll be cut off your grant and everything. . . .
>
> HO: What's your question Mr. Epps?

Here, Mr. Epps started to formulate a question, but then veered into a paraphrase of a WIN document that had been placed into evidence. He then initiated a reformulation of the circumstances that the WIN witness had described, at which point the hearings officer asked the client to ask a question. Later, when Mr. Epps directed the question to the hearings officer, the officer instructed the client to address the question to the witness. Mr. Epps finally developed the question, which lead to a competent, somewhat contentious, exchange of questions and answers with the witness. Occasionally, the hearings officer had to remind the client, "Just questions, Mr. Epps."

This exchange also illustrates how the procedural guidelines of WIN hearings constrained clients' efforts to provide alternative understandings of the matters previously alleged (Merry 1990; Conley and O'Barr 1990). The constraints persisted even when hearings officers aided clients by rephrasing their unacceptable responses to WIN witnesses as questions. These constraints were often exacerbated by clients' prior inattention to the routine record-keeping practices of staff members. Clients almost never brought documents provided to them by staff members to their hearings, and some clients seemed surprised at the significance of the documents in the hearings. Like Mr. Epps, most clients were inclined to tell their stories within a relational discourse focused on their interactions with staff members.

These difficulties were also evident in clients' direct testimony, which usually involved answering questions posed by hearings officers. After clients were sworn in, hearings officers asked them to identify themselves, and then asked a series of questions dealing with clients' addresses, family statuses, and some details about their histories with AFDC and WIN. Hearing officers usually followed with questions regarding evidentiary exhibits, asking clients to identify documents and verify that they had been correctly entered into evidence. Hearings officers also verified that clients had read and signed the Rights and Responsibilities form and were familiar with other forms that had been submitted as evidence.

Hearings officers' questions usually followed chronologically from the first events that WIN witnesses described as troublesome, through the entire sequence of events reported by WIN. Typically, hearings officers asked if an event took place as WIN witnesses contended, if clients had anything to add to, or change, from the WIN description, and if clients could explain their actions. Through such questioning, the hearings officers cast the cases previously constructed by staff members as the central issues at stake in the hearings. Clients were required to legally refute the cases made against them or have their appeals denied. As in the following interaction, hearings officers' questioning sometimes involved a critical tone. I designate simultaneous talk by the hearings officer and client (Cl) with //.

HO: Did you show up for this job search group on November ninth?

Cl: No, I, I honestly thought it was the Monday prior to it so I was going to do some other things and stuff.

HO: You thought it was the Monday prior to November ninth?

Cl: This was on

HO: The week before?

Cl: This was on it, yes.

HO: This [a document in the client's file] says (pause) "started intensive job search group 7:45, Monday November ninth." And this is signed on November 5.

Cl: Well, (pause) //I have no excuse for

HO: //Look at the calendar

Cl: I see you're right.

HO: Its date is November 5 and then the following Monday was when you'd start.

Cl: Right, you're right.

HO: Now why didn't you go in that week?

Cl: Well, at the time I didn't know, I honestly thought that when I heard him talk, I didn't read the paper which was my fault so I had no excuse for it I know I don't. But that's what I thought when I'd taken it back. It's my fault, I should've read it, I had the paper in front of me.

HO: I'm concerned with what you thought it read or what you understood.

Cl: I understood it to be.

HO: What?

Cl: The previous Monday. (pause)

HO: Well, that's impossible though, isn't it?

Cl: No, it isn't//

HO: //If he just talked to you about it on the fifth how could he already tell you to start something the Monday before when that day is already //past?

Cl: //I haven't understood this program from the word go. (pause)

In this sequence, the officer sought confirmation of events recounted in prior testimony, then asked the client for an explanation of the event in question. In almost all instances, such sequences provided multiple opportunities for clients to explain their actions, but hearings officers also implicitly passed judgment on the explanations through further comments and questions. While the displays of apparent disapproval did not insure that the clients' appeals would be rejected, they signaled that the explanations were not heard to be very compelling. Notice also that when the client in the above interaction did offer an explanation, he described his noncompliance as a misunderstanding for which he had "no excuse." This response was sufficient to resolve disagreements in other WIN dispute domains, but hearings officers took it as an admission of client culpability.

Further, the hearings officer's questioning discouraged elaborate narrative answers. Only occasionally did hearings officers explicitly ask for extended responses, or even invite them implicitly. For example, it was quite uncommon for a hearings officer to ask about an event with a question like "Can you relate what you did at that time?" The more common questioning technique was to paraphrase WIN witnesses's descriptions of events, and then ask "Is that correct?" or "Was that what you did?" The usual opportunity for clients to expand on their testimony came at the end of the hearings officers' interrogation. They asked an open-ended question like "Do you want to say anything more?" or "Do you have something else you'd like to say?" Most clients declined these opportunities.

When clients called witnesses, a single witness was usually called, almost always a family member or friend. Hearings officers asked clients why the witnesses had been called, then began questioning them by focusing on the issues indicated by clients. Like their interrogation of WIN witnesses and clients, hearings officers' questions for clients' witnesses focused on the details of the dispute histories at hand, matters about which the witnesses usually had limited knowledge. For example, in one case, the client indicated that he wanted to call a witness—his brother-in-law—to substantiate the client's claim that he had given a WIN staff member a good reason for refusing to apply for a job. "I got a witness to verify [my story]," the client explained. The hearings officer asked the witness (Wi) to come forward, swore him in, and asked his connection with the client, then proceeded with the interrogation.

HO: Were you present at, uh, Mr. Hackman's house on the day that he talked to Mr. Smith?

Wi: Yes, I was.

HO: Where were you at the time?

Wi: I was sitting on his car with my mom. (pause)

HO: What information do you recall Mr., um, Smith giving about why he was there or what his job involved?

Wi: Well, he, uh, came to the door and rang the doorbell. He said that, uh, he wanted Wilbur to pick tobacco so I went to the bedroom and got him up and told him somebody had a job for him and went outside. I seen my mom outside coming up the sidewalk and so I went out to talk to her. He says, uh, that he had a job picking tobacco for $4.50 an hour (pause) and, uh, Wilbur said, "Well, I don't really want it, besides I can't, I can't take the heat and my ankles give out anyway." (pause)

HO: What was Mr. Smith's response to that?

Wi: Well, he says, "Well, OK." And got in his car with somebody else and left. (pause)

HO: Mr. Hackman, since this is your witness, you have the right to question him. Do you have any further questions for him?

WI: No ma'am.

Client witnesses usually testified to a very narrow range of issues. For example, several clients had witnesses testify about the unreliability of their mail delivery service, which prevented their timely response to mailed requests for meetings. Others called witnesses to substantiate other explanations for missed appointments—often confirming that the client had been out of town, or at the doctor. As in the above exchange, clients were given the opportunity to question their own witnesses, but most declined.

By the time the hearings officers finished questioning clients and their witnesses, most of the issues raised in the WIN testimony had been reexamined. Hearings officers always offered WIN representatives opportunities to cross-examine clients and their witnesses, although they frequently declined. When they did cross-examine, they usually asked only a question or two, seeking clarification on prior answers.

DISCUSSION

It is in WIN hearings, then, that we see the full downstream implications of staff members' record-keeping practices and how they blended legal and bureaucratic interests. The records displayed the professionalism of staff members to the WIN supervisor and were resources for constructing dispute histories in WIN hearings. Further, staff members' record-keeping involved a prospective orientation to dispute emergence, even when they were not explicitly mindful of the potential downstream implications of their actions. Indeed, this orientation to dispute emergence might be analyzed as provided by routine organizational practices. These practices also included clients who were required to submit various WIN forms to their WIN workers, who added them to clients' WIN files.

The blending of bureaucratic and legal interests in WIN also helps to explain some of the ironies associated with WIN dispute resolution. For example, the ostensible reason for having formal adjudication proceedings was to protect clients' rights, yet the mechanism for this protection was most effectively manipulated by staff members, not by clients. The hearings' focus on procedural correctness put a premium on rhetorical resources, with which staff members were well-stocked. Placing the burden of accountability on WIN also tended to exacerbate a more general transformation promoted by WIN hearings, one that greatly diminished the possibility of compromise. The requirements of a discourse of documented accusations all but obliterated alternative discourses of accommodation and reconciliation.

Outcomes in previous settings were more open-ended and included a variety of plausible resolutions. WIN hearings, on the other hand, required a binding, immutable resolution involving "winners" and "losers." This had the effect of changing disputants into full-blown adversaries. In other dispute domains, their arguments were geared toward persuading the other disputing party to accept a different point of view. In WIN hearings, however, they were interested in convincing the hearings officer of their correctness. The almost universal rejection of hearings officers' offers to conciliate clearly underscored the now formalized antagonism.

A final irony associated with this disputing process involves clients' right to legal counsel. While considered a procedural safeguard against letting the appeals system overwhelm clients, the presence of an advocate for clients had little effect on the proceedings. Counsels' cross-examinations of WIN witnesses, for example, were usually brief, focusing on the types of clarifications and elaborations sought by hearings officers. When clients' counsel took a more aggressive approach, their questions focused on staff members' training and expertise in areas related to the issues at hand and on whether staff members had properly informed clients of their rights and responsibilities. Counsel also asked for clarification of events, times, places, and other facts presented in direct testimony.

Clients' counsel usually allowed hearings officers to conduct the initial direct examination of their clients. They followed with their own questions which, again, asked for clarification and elaboration of prior testimony. On the rare occasions when clients' counsel conducted the initial examination, they usually proceeded chronologically through the events noted in WIN testimony, asking for clarifications, elaborations, and reinterpretations. Hearings officers then followed with their own questions.

Certainly, the tone of counsels' questioning was more sympathetic to clients than was the interrogation by hearings officers. Counsel invited clients to elaborate on prior explanations and refrained from negatively judging the explanations. The questions often focused on clients' evaluations of staff members' conduct in the matters under appeal, thus treating staff—rather than clients—as the source of trouble. Counsels' questions also allowed clients to demonstrate alignment with the ideals of WIN and to rebut aspects of prior testimony given by WIN witnesses. Still, the presence of legal counsel for clients did not have any direct affect on the likelihood of a successful appeal. Clients represented by counsel were no more likely than other clients to have their appeals upheld in WIN hearings.

CONCLUSION

WIN exemplifies how dispute processing is often organized in public bureaucracies. Predisputes between organization members and clients—or other outsiders—may escalate and evolve as they are considered in different dispute domains, which are often controlled by organization members. Like WIN clients, other organizational outsiders' ultimate appeal against their treatment by organization members often involves formal legal proceedings which privilege documentary evidence over other rhetorical forms with which the insiders are more likely to be familiar. Thus, some readers might conclude that legal adjudication of disputes between members of public bureaucracies and outsiders should be eliminated, perhaps replaced by independent mediation.

But this recommendation also involves problems. It would, for example, deny organizational outsiders the right to legal redress of their grievances against staff members, even if their understandings of disputes are given short shrift in administrative hearings. Staff members also have an interest in maintaining the adjudication option. So long as public bureaucracies require that staff members punish clients whom they believe to be severely opposed to organizational interests, staff members should have the right to defend their actions. I believe this analysis points to two other possible responses to inequities in dispute processing in WIN and other public bureaucracies. The responses also serve the public's interest in keeping clients involved in programs designed to help them improve their lives.

The first change involves eliminating staff member control over conciliation. It was at this point that an independent mediator might have helped staff members and clients to redefine the issues in contention, and identify mutually agreeable solutions. Mediation would have given clients a chance to help define the conditions of their WIN participation, while not requiring that staff members agree to solutions that were contrary to WIN's interests. Mediators might have informed clients of the dire downstream consequences of failing to keep their agreements without threatening them in the manner of conciliation teams. Finally, clients could have complained about their WIN workers without always being required to document their complaints, as in WIN hearings.

Should clients or staff members fail to keep their mediation agreements, they should have the opportunity to grieve. Staff members might complain to their supervisors or a body similar to WIN's conciliation team. The mediation agreement might also serve clients' interests, because they would have a basis for making legally acceptable complaints against staff members. Clients might argue that they made good faith commitments to resolving their differences with staff members which staff members failed to honor. Further, the argument would change WIN hearings by making prior patterns of client misconduct less relevant, as the purpose of mediation agreements is to get beyond past troubles.

Finally, the analysis shows that opportunities for alternative dispute resolution were routinely overlooked by WIN hearings officers. In acting as legal adjudicators, hearings officers were required to discount most client appeals to extenuating circumstances and promises to do better in the future. The appeals were, at best, irrelevant to the matters at hand. But the adjudicators' role might be modified to allow for the encouragement of alternative dispute resolution. They could simultaneously gather information that might be useful in determining which parties' actions were legally warranted, and serve the public interest by trying to find grounds for keeping clients in social service programs as long as possible. At the very least, they could provide more than perfunctory queries about alternative dispute resolution, and might go so far as to suggest where clients and staff members might look to find common ground for conciliation.

ACKNOWLEDGMENT

Part of this research was supported by the Fund for Research for Dispute Resolution, grant no. G4-90-32 and by the National Institute for Dispute Resolution. The research was also partially supported by grants from the American Sociological Association and Marquette

University. This is a revised version of a paper presented at the annual meetings of the Law and Society Association, Chicago, 1993.

REFERENCES

Conley, J.M., and W.M. O'Barr. 1990. *Rules vs. Relationships*. Chicago, IL: University of Chicago Press.

Emerson, R.M. 1981. "On Last Resorts." *American Journal of Sociology* 87: 1-22.

Emerson, R.M. 1991. "Case Processing and Interorganizational Knowledge." *Social Problems* 38: 198-212.

Emerson, R.M. 1992. "Disputes in Public Bureaucracies." Pp. 279-307 in *Studies in Law, Politics, and Society,* Vol. 12, edited by S.S. Silbey and A. Sarat. Greenwich, CT: JAI Press.

Emerson, R.M., and B. Paley. 1992. "Organizational Horizons in Complaint-Filing." Chapter 7 in *The Uses of Discretion*, edited by K. Hawkins. Oxford, UK: Oxford University Press.

Felstiner, W., R.L. Abel, and A. Sarat. 1980-1981. "The Emergence and Transformation of Disputes." *Law and Society Review* 15: 631-654.

Galanter, M. 1974. "Why the 'Haves' Come Out Ahead: Speculations on the Limits of Legal Change." *Law and Society Review* 9: 95-160.

Merry, S.E. 1990. *Getting Justice and Getting Even*. Chicago, IL: University of Chicago Press.

Miller, G., and J.A. Holstein. 1995. "Dispute Domains." *The Sociological Quarterly* 36: 37-60.

Miller, G., and J.A. Holstein. 1996. *Dispute Domains and Welfare Claims*. Greenwich, CT: JAI Press.

Rein, M. 1974. *Work and Welfare?* New York: Praeger.

PART III

DEVIANCE: CONSTRUCTIONS, ACTS, AND CONSEQUENCES

A CULTURAL-IDENTITY THEORY OF DRUG ABUSE

Tammy L. Anderson

ABSTRACT

The purpose of this paper is to outline a new theory of *drug abuse*, that is, the cultural-identity theory. It seeks to inform substance abuse etiology by understanding how individual (i.e., micro) and environmental (i.e., meso and macro) phenomena influence the construction of drug-related identities and drug abuse. The theory proposes that drug abuse is an outcome of a drug-related identity change process featuring three micro-level (*personal marginalization, ego identity discomfort*, and *lost control in defining an identity*), two meso-level (*social marginalization* and *identification with a drug subcultural group*), and three macro-level (*economic opportunity, educational opportunity*, and *popular culture*) concepts. Together, they describe a motivation for drug-related identity change and an opportunity structure for that change. The theoretical model contains 12 hypothetical relationships that describe the links between the micro, meso, and macro-level concepts. The paper begins with a review of leading theories of drug use and abuse that identifies a niche the cultural-identity theory proposes to fill. Suggestions for empirical investigation of the theory conclude the paper.

Sociology of Crime, Law, and Deviance, Volume 1, pages 233-262.

ISBN: 0-7623-0282-8

INTRODUCTION

Current data on drug abuse paints an increasingly dismal picture as we approach the twenty-first century. Both the adult (middle-aged people mostly in their 30s and 40s) and the school-aged drug abuser population has grown in size following years of relative stability. Currently, at least 4.6% of high school seniors are daily marijuana users, as are about 1% of eighth graders, suggesting that the average abuser is getting younger (Johnston, O'Malley, and Bachman 1995). Still other prevalence data estimate that 12.4 million people used illicit drugs in the past month during 1994 (SAMHSA 1995) and that in 1993, 2.1 million were heavy cocaine users and between 444,000 and 600,000 were heavy heroin users (Rhodes et al. 1995).

Constrained by the rhetoric and ideology of the latest "War on Drugs," discourse about the social problems associated with drug abuse in the last quarter of this century has suffered from political campaigns targeting less-problematic drug use, especially that of "softer" drugs (e.g., marijuana). Such thinking and policymaking overlooks the considerable scholarly evidence that distinguishes *drug use* and *drug abuse* as separate phenomena, suggesting different explanations for each. Males (1997, p. 5) recently explained:

> Current drug policy ignores the lessons of the 1960s: Moderate drug, particularly marijuana, experimentation is normal and widespread among the young—and will abate without frantic suppression measures. However, the smaller number of habitual users of harder drugs and multiple drugs require urgent and focused attention regardless of their ages.

The current leading etiological theories concerning drug use do not effectively resolve this matter. They have tended to focus more on drug users rather than abusers or not to distinguish between the two. Also, they have depended on micro-level factors (individuals and small groups) which can result in pathologizing the problem or in further stigmatizing the population in question. The purpose of this paper is to offer a new theory—that is, the cultural-identity theory of drug abuse—that attempts to broaden this literature.

Unlike the leading etiological theories (see below), the cultural-identity theory is specifically concerned with drug abuse. It also attempts to link three levels of analysis (i.e., micro, meso, and macro) for a more comprehensive explanation of drug abuse. This kind of approach departs from most existing work, which usually has elaborated explanatory factors at one level of analysis, especially the micro level, instead of exploring and/or specifying links between phenomena measured at the micro, meso (mid-range social group), and macro (broad sociocultural) levels that affect lived experience on a daily basis. As such, it promises to increase our understanding of how the relationship between individual and environmental factors explains drug abuse and drug-related identity change so that improved prevention and treatment strategies can be forthcoming.

A REVIEW OF LEADING ETIOLOGICAL THEORIES

Etiological reviews (Lettieri, Sayers, and Pearson 1980; Hawkins, Catalano, and Miller 1992; Petraitis, Flay, and Miller 1995) or special journals devoted to this topic (e.g., *Journal of Drug Issues*, Spring 1996) have identified the following eight theories as dominant in the field: (1) problem behavior theory (Jessor and Jessor 1977; Jessor, Donovan, and Costa 1991; Donovan 1996); (2) the theory of reasoned action (Ajzen 1985; Ajzen and Fishbein 1980; Fishbein and Ajzen 1975); (3) social learning theory (Akers 1977; Akers and Lee 1996; Bandura 1977); (4) social control theory (Hirschi 1969; Kandel 1980, 1985, 1996); (5) self-derogation theory (Kaplan 1975, 1996; Kaplan, Martin, and Robbins 1984, 1986; Kaplan and Johnson 1992); (6) the integrated delinquency model (Elliott, Huizinga, and Ageton 1985); (7) social development theory (Catalano and Hawkins forthcoming; Hawkins and Weis 1985; Catalano et al. 1996); and (8) the theory of triadic influence (Flay and Petraitis 1994). The following paragraphs briefly review four of these theories (i.e., self-derogation theory, the integrated delinquency model, social development theory, and the theory of triadic influence) in an attempt to forge links between various individual and more environmental factors, integrate ideas from the first four listed theories, and offer a useful comparison to the cultural-identity theory.[1]

Four matters frame this review. They are limitations of extant etiological theory that the cultural-identity theory attempts to address, including confusion surrounding drug use and drug abuse, failure to link the micro, meso, and macro levels of analysis, and an overreliance on narrowly defined peer group concepts and behavioral outcomes.

Drug Use versus Drug Abuse

The persistent focus in etiological theory on drug use instead of drug abuse may be due, in part, to complications that arise from attempts to identify a large enough pool of drug abusers through survey research methods that employ a prospective design with national population samples. Scholars investigating the four theories mentioned above have typically employed this kind of methodology. Such population studies tend to focus on drug use while clinical studies focus more on drug abuse (Institute of Medicine 1996). The result is that most studies of psychosocial etiological factors do not distinguish between the two.

Moreover, there seems to be a tendency in etiological theory to use the words "use" and "abuse" together or interchangeably. Many also attribute credibility to the "gateway" theory of drug use (i.e., that the use of "softer" drugs eventually leads to the abuse of "harder" ones) without discussing the processes involved in that transition. This assumption or oversight is repeatedly called into question by other research. For instance, the Institute of Medicine (1996, p. 117) has noted that it may be incorrect to assume that the factors involved in the initiation of drug use are important in the escalation of it. Also, Johnston and colleagues show large discrepancies between monthly or annual use and daily use rates (which can serve as a proxy for abuse) and suggest that only a small portion of eighth graders, for instance, who use drugs (about 21% in 1995) would likely become daily abusers of them by twelfth grade (4.6%), all else being equal (Johnston, O'Malley, and Bachman 1995). Furthermore, Waldorf, Reinarman, and Murphy (1991) reported that the NIDA surveys, for example, show that the majority of cocaine users in the U.S. are "ceremonial" users (i.e., they use it occasionally) and do not become abusers. Drug prevention strategies would be greatly improved if "risk" or "protective" factors that distinguished between drug *users* and drug *abusers* in the larger population could be identified.

The cultural-identity treats drug use and abuse as separate phenomena. The theoretical tenets described below are meant to explain how certain environmental and individual factors interact to influence drug-related identity change for people who *abuse or reach crisis points with drugs*. The theory does not propose to do the same for those who use drugs in a non-abusive or unproblematic fashion, which several studies (Waldorf et al. 1991; Granfield and Cloud 1996) have shown is possible over an extended period of time. It would, therefore, be inaccurate to call the cultural-identity theory an explanation of drug use. On the contrary, the theory seeks to address the scholarly inattention to diverse etiologies for drug use and abuse by simply focusing on drug abuse.

Linking the Micro, Meso, and Macro Levels

Etiological theory's overreliance on micro-level influences has hindered its ability to understand and, therefore, to predict how macro-level or sociocultural factors cause drug abuse. The scarcity of work that offers a theoretical or empirical account on the link between micro and macro phenomena further speaks to this matter. Elsewhere, U.S. ethnographers (e.g., Bourgois 1989, 1996; Hamid 1991a, 1991b, 1991c; Waterston 1993; Dunlap and Johnson 1992) and scholars from the Birmingham School of Cultural Studies (Brake 1985; Clarke et al. 1976; Hebdige 1979; Willis 1976, 1977; McRobbie 1991) have described how various macro-level phenomena, like economic and social inequality, and social marginalization result in many social ills, including drug abuse. However, this more macro-focused work has not yet explained how it is that most people who experience such conditions do not become drug abusers. Recent theories like Flay's theory of triadic influence stand out as an exception and are discussed in more detail below.

The cultural-identity theory attempts to bridge these two literatures. It elaborates on micro-, meso-, and macro-level phenomena and the links between them. It seeks to avoid overly reductionist and deterministic claims by insisting on an integrative environmental and individual explanation that guards against a micro- or macro-level bias. Furthermore, an approach like this could result in more a more integrated and comprehensive prevention strategy consisting of several programs at different levels (i.e., schools, families, and communities) instead of single programs located at one level of analysis.

Peer Groups versus Drug Subcultures in Abuse Etiology

Third, these four theories, especially the work of Kandel, Elliott, and Dishion, pinpoint peer groups as a major explanatory factor in drug use. However, the question of how peer culture operates to influence drug use versus drug abuse is left unanswered. Kaplan et al. (1986) have noted that the peer-based research has not effectively addressed the role of peer groups in the transition from drug use to abuse. This kind of inquiry is important for drug prevention policies, especially recently, since Gorman (1996) has noted the influence of the peer group variable in prevention policies.

The cultural-identity theory focuses on drug subcultural groups (e.g., potheads, dopers, gangs, etc.) instead of peer groups, which highlights identification with specific social groups and the patterns of activity among them (see also Fishkin et al. 1993; Mosbach and Leventhal 1988). It also addresses the subcultural meaning attached to specific drugs (see McRobbie 1991; Hebdige 1979; Willis 1976), which transcends any particular set of individuals and persists over time. These drug-related meaning systems and the identities that youth create in group settings may be the more important factors for drug abuse etiology and prevention.

Identity versus Behavioral-Oriented Variables

Fourth, most etiological theories focus solely on predicting behavioral outcomes—for example, frequency or amount of drug use. The cultural-identity theory studies, in addition, the acquisition of drug-related identities and other identity changes during involvement with drugs—for example, drug-related identity change (see Anderson 1993; Anderson and Mott 1998). Behaviors like actual drug abuse are conceptualized as part of the identity change process from non-drug user to drug abuser.

Interactionists exploring deviant behaviors and careers have noted the importance of identity change in the initiation, persistence, and termination of drug addiction (Ray 1968; Biernacki 1986; Becker 1963; Pearson 1987; Waldorf 1983; Hawkins and Wacker 1983; Jorquez 1983; Waldorf et al. 1991), alcoholism (Denzin 1987; Brown 1991), crime (Shover 1983; Miesenhelder 1982; Schmid and Jones 1991), mental illness (Goffman 1961), and obesity (Dehger and Hughes 1992). This work consistently underscores the notion that "undesirable" behaviors escalate with increased "deviant" identification and lesson with identity change toward non-deviance.

The cultural-identity theory acknowledges this relationship between identity (e.g., drug-related identities) and behavior (drug abuse). It speculates that drug-related identification may ultimately distinguish drug use from drug abuse. Future empirical work seeks to determine if drug-related identity change mediates the relationship between such behaviors. This approach allows for a deeper understanding of the drives toward drug abuse and my offer new approaches to drug abuse prevention strategies.

Kaplan's Self-Derogation Theory

Of the eight etiological theories mentioned above, the cultural-identity theory has most in common with Kaplan's theory of self-derogation. Kaplan (1975, 1996) and colleagues (Kaplan and Johnson 1992; Kaplan, Robbins, and Martin 1984, 1986) maintain that self-derogation plays a central role in determining drug use and abuse. For them, negative feelings and statements about oneself and the socially devaluing experiences that set it up *motivate* individuals to behave in ways that minimize self-derogation and maximize positive self attitudes. They propose that this explains why individuals reject the normative structure and embrace that which is "deviant" (e.g., drug use, drug peers, and drug subcultures). Cultural-identity theory both compliments and enhances these premises. It proposes that negative self-evaluations are part of the etiological process, but articulates a specific mechanism through which such negative self-evaluations lead to drug abuse. It is two social and largely external factors (i.e., *personal* and *social marginalization*) that help produce this identity discomfort and can lead to drug-related identity change. Kaplan and colleagues have not delineated the same. These theoretical differences about identity or self-definition and the sources of it could account for an important risk factor that distinguishes drug users from abusers.

The most significant difference between self-derogation theory (and the other four theories discussed below) and the cultural-identity theory, however, pertains to the presence of meso- and macro-level concepts in the explanatory model. Kaplan (Kaplan and Johnson 1992; Kaplan 1996) has recently discussed more macro-level influences (e.g., social controls) on drug abuse, but his theoretical model does not yet contain specific concepts and, therefore, does not directly discuss a link between them. Finally, another major difference between the two is Kaplan's focus on "deviant" acts (see Kaplan 1996) rather than identities and identity change.

Elliott's Integrated Delinquency Model

Elliott et al. (1985) have proposed an integrated sociological theory of drug use that draws from social control theory (Hirschi 1969), strain theory (Merton 1938, 1957), and social learning theory (Akers 1977). They posit that strong bonding with "deviant" peers is the primary cause of drug use. "Deviant" peer bonding, they maintain, is a result of weak conventional bonds with parents and school, prior delinquent behavior, and social disorganization.

Given the recent significance of the peer group concept in drug prevention efforts (Gorman 1996) and in etiological research (see Ennett and Bauman 1991; Kandel 1996), it makes sense to explore more about the ways in which youth peer groups influence or cause undesirable behavior in individuals. Elliott's focus on bonding with "deviant" peers differs substantially from the cultural-identity theory's emphasis on drug subcultural groups. It is important to understand whom individuals interact with (e.g., who become their friends), because research and theory has repeatedly shown that such associations and attachments are predictors of behavior. This was part of what Bandura called "modeling"; individuals often model or do what people around them do—for example, use drugs. However, both drug users and abusers usually report bonding with "deviant" peers (see Kandel 1996 for a discussion of the overstatement of the impact of "deviant" peers in drug research). Therefore, the overall meaning-system that the peers embody and the new definition of the self that individuals get from interacting in "alternative" youth subcultures might comprise the more important explanatory factor and may ultimately distinguish between drug use and drug abuse. For instance, Ennett and Bauman (1991) and Harton and Latane (1997) have recently noted the importance of the "social approval" function that peers play in the etiological process instead of an individual's association with them.

Hawkins and Catalano's Social Development Theory

Social development theory is also an integrated approach that combines social learning, control, and differential association theories. It has much in common with Elliott's approach, with the exception that it elaborates on the developmental processes in both pro-social and anti-social (e.g., drug use) behavior. Bonds develop between the individual and socializing agents (family, schools, religious and community institutions, and their peers) during development. An individual's behavior will, therefore, be antisocial or pro-social depending on the behavior, norms, and values of those socializing agents to which he or she is bonded.

Like Kaplan's and Elliott's theories, the general model of social development theory does not specify micro-, meso-, and macro-level variables. Instead, Hawkins, Catalano, and colleagues focus on the individual and his or her perceptions about opportunities and interactions in the environment around them. Jessor and Jessor (1973) made an earlier observation on the possible ways in which factors outside the individual (environmental or "contextual") may impact behavior. They concluded that the perceived environment was a more important predictor of individual behavior than the "actual" or "objective" one. Social development theory is in agreement on this matter.

Flay's Theory of Triadic Influence

Flay and Petraitis' (1994) theory of triadic influence (TTI) is a complex web of factors that prior research has tied to drug use. To date, TTI is the only drug use theory that acknowledges the various streams (i.e., cultural, social-situational, and interpersonal/biological) that affect all human behavior. Furthermore, within each causal stream, Flay and colleagues identify three levels of influence—proximal, distal, and ultimate. Doing so has provided them with a theoretical model that can investigate sophisticated kinds of causal relationships—for example, mediating and moderating ones—on drug use. This is a second quality of TTI that distinguishes it from the theories described above.

The cultural-identity theory differs from TTI in two major ways. First, TTI does not specify which variables or relationships predict drug use versus drug abuse. Second, TTI is a theory about behavioral outcomes. It is not a statement about the drug-related identity change process that begins with no drug use for many and ends in drug abuse for some.

A CULTURAL-IDENTITY THEORY OF DRUG ABUSE

The cultural-identity theory proposes that drug abuse is an outcome of a drug-related identity change process that is set in motion by three micro-level (*personal marginalization, ego identity discomfort*, and *lost control in defining an identity*), two meso-level (*social marginalization* and *identification with a drug subcultural group*), and three macro-level (*economic opportunity, educational opportunity*, and *popular culture*) concepts[2]. These concepts describe a motivation for drug-related identity change and an opportunity structure for that change. The theoretical model contains 12 hypothetical relationships, which are diagramed in Figure 1.

Hypothesis 1. *Personal marginalization* has a direct and positive effect on *ego identity discomfort* (before drug use or during early childhood and adolescence).

Hypothesis 2. *Personal marginalization* has a direct and positive effect on *lost control in defining an identity.*

Hypothesis 3. *Ego identity discomfort* (before drug use or during early childhood and adolescence) has a direct and positive effect on *lost control in defining an identity.*

Hypothesis 4. *Lost control in defining an identity* has a direct and positive effect on *identification with a drug subculture.*

Hypothesis 5. *Ego identity discomfort* (before drug use or during early childhood and adolescence) has a direct and positive effect on *identification with a drug subculture.*

Hypothesis 6. *Identification with a drug subculture* has a direct and negative effect on later *ego identity discomfort* (i.e., during drug abuse).

Hypothesis 7. *Economic opportunity* has a direct and negative effect on *social marginalization.*

Hypothesis 8. *Educational opportunity* has a direct and negative effect on *social marginalization.*

Hypothesis 9. *Popular culture* has a direct and positive effect on *identification with a drug subculture.*

Hypothesis 10. *Social marginalization* has a direct and positive effect on *identification with a drug subculture.*

Hypothesis 11. *Social marginalization* has a positive correlational relationship with *ego identity discomfort* (before drug use or during early childhood and adolescence).

Hypothesis 12. *Earlier Ego identity discomfort* (before drug use or during early childhood and adolescence) has a positive and direct relationship with *later ego identity discomfort* (i.e., during drug abuse).

To date, research on this theory has taken place in clinical-type settings, that is, with people involved in treatment programs and who had reached crisis points with drug abuse (Anderson 1991, 1994, 1998a, 1998b, 1998c; Anderson and Mott 1998). Therefore, the theory started with observations from more clinical samples, and current work on it attempts to develop it in order to explain the larger population of drug abusers. Still other components of the theory come from literature reviews on drug abuse and addiction (Anderson 1995).

Cultural-identity theory uses a multi-dimensional definition of drug abuse that distinguishes it from drug use. This definition features the following: (1) a pattern of regular and heavy use over a significant period of time, (2) a set of drug-related problems (at work or with interpersonal relationships, one's own health, and formal social control agencies), (3) previous and failed attempts to terminate drug consumption, and (4) self-identification as having a drug and/or alcohol problem.

The theory maintains that the concepts and hypothesized relationships are significant for drug abusers. It may be that drug users experience some part of this process but may exit it at different points. They may also experience high "risk" on some concepts after other "risk" factors have disappeared. This is a conclusion that Waldorf et al. (1991) reached with heavy cocaine users. The cultural-identity theory does not propose to explain progressions in drug use behaviors per se, such

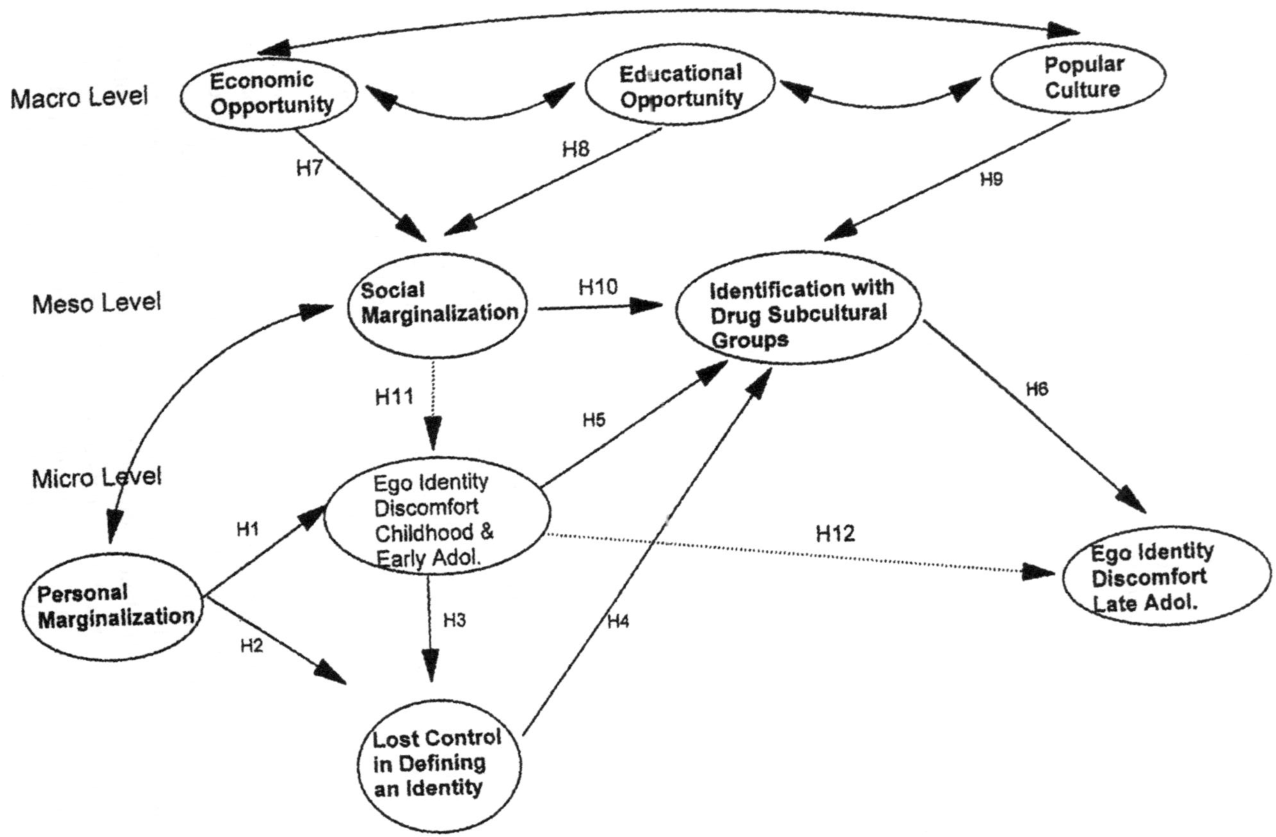

Figure 1. Cultural-Identity Theory of Drug Abuse

as simple frequency or pattern changes in the consumption of drugs, or movement from no drug use to drug abuse. However, the change in behavioral indices of *no drug use* and *drug abuse* are implied by the theory.

IDENTITY CHANGE MOTIVATIONAL CONCEPTS

Motivation refers to the state of an individual at a particular time and in relation to his/her environment. Consequently, many different factors can influence particular motivations. Identities are a major influence on behavioral motivation (cf. Hewitt 1991). Cultural-identity theory is primarily concerned with identity change motivations that characterize late childhood and early adolescence, while individuals are dependant on caretakers and attending primary and secondary school, since previous work (see Kandel 1980 for a review) has documented the onset of drug use between 11 and 15 years of age. An underlying premise of the theory is that individuals are motivated toward drug-related identity change because of socially defined problems with existing ego identities (*ego identity discomfort* and *lost control in defining an identity*) in childhood and early adolescence, and that certain meso-level, (e.g., *identification with drug subcultural groups*) and macro-level phenomena (e.g., *economic opportunity, educational opportunity, popular culture*), that they encounter provide an opportunity structure for that change (Anderson 1994, 1995; Anderson and Mott 1998). Cultural-identity theory pinpoints four identity change motivational concepts: *personal marginalization, social marginalization, ego identity discomfort*, and a *felt loss of control over one's identity*.

Two Types of Marginalization

Two types of marginalization (personal and social) help to initiate the drug-related identity change process. *Personal marginalization* emerged in the original qualitative study (Anderson 1991, 1994). *Social marginalization* is borrowed from the cultural reproduction theory (e.g., Bourgois 1989, 1996; Waterston 1993; Bordieu 1980; Bordieu and Passeron 1977). Before distinguishing between the two and the role they occupy in the present theory, a few words are necessary to clarify marginalization.

Marginalization has two main components. The so-called "actual" side of the concept refers to the stigmatized or devalued social status of certain experiences or traits that may have been assigned to the individual at birth or during the socialization process. They act to place him or her outside the boundaries of what is considered acceptable and desirable in a given social context, within the larger society, or both. Goffman (1963) called them "blemishes of character." For Erickson (1970), they were instances of "violating the boundaries of normal behavior."

Most people have experienced or possessed some of these at one time or another in their lives. And the definition of any one of them as a stigma may also have changed over time. Cultural-identity theory maintains that the greater the number of marginalizing experiences, traits, or statuses one has, the greater the risk for drug abuse. The theory also specifies that the salience or degree of stigma attached to each one also matters. Some experiences, statuses, and traits are more stigmatized than are others; therefore, the greater the stigma, the greater the risk for drug abuse, ultimately. This also varies geographically and by social group (peers versus adults).

The other necessary aspect of marginalization is the "feeling/affective/subjective" component, which may ultimately be the more salient one for predicting drug abuse. This refers to the negative feelings that "actual/objective" marginalization can generate for the individual. Usually, these feelings emerge when the individual compares him or herself to others or when he or she is compared to others (these are social comparisons) because of "actual" marginalization. When "actual" marginalization is coupled with "felt" or "affective" marginalization—for example, feelings of not belonging with or mistreatment by others—the drug-related identity change process is set in motion and the risk for drug abuse escalates.

Both concepts of personal and social marginalization contain the two components of "actual/objective" and "feeling/affective/subjective" marginalization. The key to understanding them lies in connecting the individual to the sociocultural environment, because definitions of experiences, statuses, and traits as negative/undesirable or positive/desirable are part of the structure and culture in which all individuals live and learn to define themselves.

Personal Marginalization

Personal marginalization is a micro-level concept that helps initiate the drug-related identity change process.[3] It refers to various early (childhood and adolescence) experiences that can sever individuals from norms or what is socially acceptable in their worlds. Children have no awareness of relationships or social structures until they become conscious of variations in social linkages between themselves and others (Couch 1989). *Personal marginalization* features these kinds of ties. The events and experiences described below often act to differentiate children from others in a negative fashion, fracturing the positive linkages to others they once had. These experiences and events can change the individuals' social status from a more socially acceptable one to a more stigmatized one (Glaser and Strauss 1971).

There are likely many such experiences, traits, and statuses that could potentially operate in a similar fashion. To date, work on the cultural-identity theory (Anderson 1994, 1998a, 1998b, 1998c; Anderson and Mott 1998) has tied 14 such events to the drug-related identity change of non-drug user to drug abuser. Existing research substantiates their ties to drug abuse. These events include the separation or divorce of parents, the death of someone significant (Hoffman 1993), frequent geographic moves of the family, inappropriate sexual activity with an adult (Barrett, Trepper, and Stone-Fish 1991; Russell 1986; Herman, Russell, and Tracki 1986; Singer, Petchers, and Hussey 1989; Briere and Zaidi 1989), caretaker responsibilities for siblings and other relatives, rigid and regular domestic responsibilities (cleaning the house, cooking for members, earning money to support family—see Baumrind 1971, 1983, 1985), individual's early parenthood (i.e., biological reproduction), physically punished or beaten by caretakers, strict caretaker guidelines and expectations (Baumrind 1971, 1983, 1985), frequent physical and/or verbal punishment at school, school suspension, placement into different school or program, frequent participation in fights, and police contact or arrest.

Parental divorce is one phenomena whose marginalizing or stigmatizing potential may be less salient than other factors and may have changed over time. For instance, Anderson's (1994) respondents, who were on average 35 years old, recalled it as an important marginalizing factor before they began to use drugs (in the early to mid-1970s). However, social norms regarding divorce have changed since then. Future analyses may not uncover the same relationship. Cultural-identity theory hypothesizes direct and positive relationships between *personal marginalization* and *ego identity discomfort* (Hypothesis 1) and *lost control in defining an identity* (Hypothesis 2).

Social Marginalization

Social marginalization is an important concept in cultural reproduction theory (see, e.g., Bourdieu 1980; Bourgois 1989, 1996; Waterston 1993). It refers to an individual's disadvantaged or oppressed economic, social, and cultural situation in comparison to important groups and/or entities around him or her. It is similar to relative deprivation, where the substance of the deprivation pertains to various socioeconomic and cultural phenomena. Its degree is measured by the individual's socioeconomic and cultural position with respect to various social groups around that individual. This concept, therefore, meets the criteria for a meso-level factor (Feree and Hall 1996; Maines 1994). Cultural-identity theory maintains that *social marginalization* is an outcome of *economic opportunity* (Hypothesis 7) and *educational opportunity* (Hypothesis 8) and contains a negative and direct relationship with each. In turn, it directly predicts *identification with a drug subculture* (Hypothesis 10). Therefore, it serves as a mediating variable between the theory's micro and macro-level concepts. Although not previously specified theoretically or empirically tested, cultural-identity theory posits a positive correlational relationship between it and *ego identity discomfort* (Hypothesis 11). It is feasible to speculate that individuals' social alienation may cause them discomfort with their existing ego identities.

Ego Identity Discomfort (Before Drug Use)

Ego identities are individuals' feelings about their most personal self-definitions (Goffman 1963; Anderson 1994). Ego identity discomfort represents a significant level of dissatisfaction with how one feels about who one is. Cultural-identity theory maintains that *personal marginalization* directly and positively impacts ego identity discomfort and that social marginalization is positively correlated with it. Marginalization and the negative affect it engenders (e.g., feeling out of place and different from others—see also Peluso and Peluso 1988), becomes central to the description of the self and can lead to identity dissatisfaction in childhood or early adolescence and before drug use. *Ego identity discomfort* is, therefore, a socially-based consequence for the individual. It is, therefore, a second source of motivation of drug-related identity change. The theory posits a direct relationship between it and *lost control in defining an identity* (Hypothesis 3) and *identification with drug subcultural groups* (Hypothesis 5).

Lost Control in Defining an Identity

Lost control in defining an identity is the third identity change motivational concept in the cultural-identity theory. It concerns a loss of individual control over positive and gratifying identity construction. Such a loss of control can be problematic for some and escalate the risk for drug abuse. Therefore, the perceived inability to define a satisfactory identity for oneself because of external pressure to define oneself in some socially proscribed fashion is also part of this concept and the process of drug-related identity change.

One commonly reported source of *lost control over defining an identity* found in previous work (Anderson 1994, 1998b) was unrealistic parental expectations and/or extreme parent authoritativeness. Baumrind (1983) noted previously the relationship between these two factors and drug use. Couch (1989) explains that adults bring their conceptions of how children and adults should relate to each other, to their encounters with children. These conceptions structure but do not determine their behavior toward the child. Large discrepancies between children's actions and identities and adult and significant others' expectations of them is problematic. Anderson and Mott (1998) recently found that *lost control in defining an identity* directly and positively predicted *identification with a drug subcultural group* (Hypothesis 4).

OPPORTUNITY CONCEPTS

Opportunity is a second underlying theme in the cultural-identity theory. It refers to the various openings and possibilities to individuals for such things as identity construction, behavior, and experience. Individuals exist within environments defined by previous interaction, and which will change with present and future interaction. Opportunity, then, varies temporally. It also varies geographically, socially, and economically. Opportunities are located in the many social situations that individuals pass through on a daily basis. Cultural-identity theory is interested, then, in those opportunities that typically characterize early childhood through late adolescence in the latter twentieth century in the United States.

Cultural-identity theory contains four concepts that help to provide an opportunity for drug-related identity change and which play a necessary role etiological role: *identification with a drug subcultural group* (meso-level), *economic opportunity, educational opportunity*, and *popular culture* (macro-level). Other macro-level factors might also play a similar role, however, the theory pinpoints these because research has consistently documented their salience in creating drug subcultural groups (see, e.g., Clarke et al. 1976). In other words, *economic opportunity, educational opportunity*, and *popular culture* explain the number and nature of drug subcultural groups that are available to a given youth population at certain historical moments. *Identification with a drug subcultural group*, in turn, provides the individual with an important opportunity to resolve his or her socially defined ego identity problems. Cultural-identity theory maintains that the higher an individual scores on the four identity change motivational concepts, the more likely it is that he or she will identify with drug subcultural groups and experience drug-related identity change. Furthermore, the theory also maintains that individuals exposed to environments with high risk levels on the three macro concepts will have more opportunity to identify with drug subcultural groups and will be at increased risk for drug abuse. The theory does not contend that all individuals involved with drug subcultural groups will become drug abusers or experience drug-related identity change. It maintains that those who experience high levels of the four motivational concepts and high exposure to drug-conducive opportunity structures will be at greater risk for it.

The cultural-identity theory attempts to show how limits in economic and educational opportunity and increased pro-drug messages from popular culture can foster increased identification with drug subcultural groups. The theory proposes an indirect and negative relationship between *economic opportunity, educational opportunity*, and *identification with drug subcultural groups* through the *social marginalization* concept and a direct and positive relationship between *popular culture* and *identification with drug subcultural groups*. Cultural-identity theory also speculates that these three macro-level factors may be mediated through identification with drug subcultural groups to indirectly affect more micro-level concepts such as ego identity discomfort during drug abuse.

Identification with a Drug Subculture

The subculture concept has enjoyed widespread popularity in sociological studies of deviance and drugs, ranging from early Chicago School research (see Bennett

1981 for a review) to Cohen's (1955) classic study of delinquent boys to Birmingham School scholars. This kind of focus helps expand on the peer group concept that researchers have consistently tied to individual drug use (Dishion et al. 1995).

Drug subcultural groups are part of youth culture; they involve a common set of values and interests, and a tactic ideology among young people without a dependency on regular face-to-face interaction. Individuals learn about opportunities from the groups (primary and secondary) they encounter in everyday situations. Here, they are socialized toward certain groups (e.g., normative and socially acceptable ones) and away from others (alternative or "deviant" groups). The *identification with a drug subculture* concept embraces this opportunity theme. It maintains that drug subcultures provide, for those who eventually reach crisis points with drugs, important opportunities for drug-related identity change and an improved level of satisfaction with an ego identity. Thus, a direct and negative relationship to later *ego identity discomfort* (e.g., during drug abuse) is hypothesized (Hypothesis 6). It is important to note, however, that not all drug use takes place within identifiable drug subcultures, nor do all interactants in such contexts become drug abusers or seek resolution of identity problems within them (Waldorf et al. 1991; Granfield and Cloud 1996; Beck and Rosenbaum 1995). To further underscore this point, Anderson and Mott (1998) found that the three concepts of *personal marginalization, ego identity discomfort,* and *lost control over identity* explained 23% of the variance in *identification with a drug subculture*. Clearly, drug subcultures are varied entities.

The cultural-identity theory also utilizes observations from other researchers that subcultures also provide a readily accessible solution to employment and school dilemmas by uniting youth in resistance of the conventional and in alternative identity creation (Schwartz, Turner, and Peluso 1973). Salient components of the alternative meaning systems in drug subcultural groups hinge on such things as drug use, drug-specific languages, drug-related merchandise (e.g., magazines, music), activities of the drug lifestyle (rituals, patterns of use, ways to purchase drugs), and the construction of ingroups (those who use drugs) and outgroups (those who do not use drugs).

Economic Opportunity

Cultural-identity theory maintains that *economic opportunity* has a direct and negative relationship with *social marginalization* (Hypothesis 7) and an indirect and negative effect on *identification with a drug subcultural group* (Hypothesis 10). It may also affect ego identity matters (see dotted arrows on Figure 1). The theory maintains that limits on *economic opportunity* help foster *identification with drug subcultural groups* (see Anderson 1995; Anderson and Mott 1998). *Economic opportunity* can, for instance, be altered by market transformations—for example, the latter twentieth-century industrial change from manufacturing-based to service-sector jobs. Increases in working- and lower-class unemployment, and a declining standard of living for working and lower-class families, are still other examples of limits on *economic opportunity* that may affect *identification with drug subcultural groups.*

The drug abuse literature reveals support for the premise that macro-level economic factors influence the growth of drug subcultures, rates of abuse, and etiological matters (Dunlap and Johnson 1992; Hawkins et al. 1992; Merton 1938, 1957; Cloward and Ohlin 1960; Menicucci and Wermuth 1989; Edwards and Arif 1980; Preble and Casey 1969). According to Bourgois (1989) and Hamid (1991a, 1991b, 1991c), inner city residents experience a significant level of unemployment and personal anxiety over their ability to provide for a minimum standard of living for their families. They lack a viable economy and legitimate opportunity structure. This, they claim, can often result in drug abuse.

It is important to note, at this point, that middle- and upper-class people also become drug abusers. Cultural-identity theory does not contend otherwise. It simply maintains that the greater the limits on *economic opportunity,* the greater the risk for drug-related identity change and drug abuse. It may be that economically induced expectations and stress are more salient for middle- and upper-class drug abusers. This is also a matter for empirical investigation and may alter the theoretical premises outlined here.

Educational Opportunity

Educational opportunity plays a similar role in identification with drug subcultural groups and drug abuse. Cultural-identity theory's claims about *educational opportunity* and its impact on *identification with drug subcultural groups* and ego identity matters come from the Birmingham School of Cultural Studies (Brake 1985; Clarke et al. 1976; Willis 1977; Hebdige 1979, McRobbie 1991) and cultural reproduction theory (Bourdieu 1980; Bourdieu and Passeron 1977; Brice-Heath and McLaughlin 1993; MacLeod 1987). Schools reproduce social class position while teaching a meritocratic ideology. For instance, lower-class youth are encouraged toward vocational programs where they will learn skills for blue-collar or service-sector employment. Middle- and upper-class kids are encouraged toward and selected for academic-oriented programs. Youth encounter different kinds of opportunities based on their social class, with lower-class white and ethnic minority girls and boys receiving the most limited ones—that is, a diploma and training for blue-collar and service sector jobs. This is especially salient now as the economy of the twenty-first century will likely offer lower-class youth far more lower-paying service-sector jobs than skilled employment or industrial ones. This would may put lower-class youth at greater risk for drug-related identity change and drug abuse.

Research has also documented a link between race- and gender-based limits in educational opportunities and increases in drug abuse (Guyette 1982; Wurzman, Rounsaville, and Klever 1982; Harvey 1985). For instance, research shows increased levels of drug and alcohol use and abuse among ethnic and racial minorities with increased pressure to adopt white-centered cultural norms (Mendes de Leon and Markides 1986; Caetano 1987; Sue 1987; Galan 1988; Kitano et al. 1988; Castro et al. 1991). Some have shown that such so-called cultural conflict is an underlying causative factor of drug abuse (Yee and Thu 1987; Beauvis and LeBoueff 1985; Harvey 1985; Wurzman et al. 1982). Identification with drug subcultural groups would, according to cultural-identity theory, mediate the effects of these educational opportunities and the individual drug abuser because they would provide an opportunity structure for the validation of culturally specific norms, language, and values that schools would not provide. The male-centered structure and sexist socialization practices of educational systems in the United States may also explain the appeal of drug subcultural groups to today's women and girls in a similar fashion (Wilsnack and Wilsnack 1979; Alicea and Friedman 1994; Henderson and Boyd 1992; Ettore 1992; Pohl and Boyd 1992; McRobbie 1991; Mitic, McGuire, and Neumann 1987; Rosenbaum 1981). *Educational opportunity*, thus, emerges as a second important macro-level influence on *identification with drug subcultural groups* and drug abuse. The theory hypothesizes that it will have a direct and negative impact on *social marginalization* (Hypothesis 8) and an indirect and negative effect on *identification with a drug subcultural group* (Hypothesis 10).

Popular Culture

According to Gans (1974), popular culture consists of a set of materials and activities that are commercially exchanged and which are consumed or enjoyed by a large number of people. Literature, film/video, music, and fashion comprise the essential cultural forms that disseminate these messages and others. Gans (1974) claims that social groups (by social class, race or ethnicity, or neighborhood) select particular cultural forms which serve their focal concerns and define their group identity. He calls these "taste publics" and maintains that they characterize the local environments in which people are socialized. At an early age, then, children are brought up in neighborhoods that have specific "taste publics" which will influence their identities and behaviors. Young people's choice of music, literature, and cinema are, therefore, indicative of the "taste publics" to which they have been exposed. Cultural-identity theory currently maintains that these popular culture forms can foster pro-drug attitudes (e.g., directly through drug-specific lyrics or indirectly through the association of drugs with certain musicians) and play an active part in promoting identification with drug subcultural groups.

Birmingham School scholars (Hebdige 1979, Brake 1985; Clarke et al. 1976) note that drug subcultural groups are where these cultural forms or "taste publics" become transformed into identities that individual members will learn to embrace. For instance, consider the relationship between music and drugs. Sussman et al. (1994) recently noted that adolescent identification with discrete youth peer groups or youth subcultural groups (which are geographically situated) delineates preferences for music, style, language, and social experience. For Willis (1976), there is a homology between the values and lifestyle of a group, its subjective experience, and the musical forms it adopts. Music expresses the meanings that correspond to all aspects of group life. It influences the group's relationships with drugs. Therefore, cultural-identity proposes that pro-drug *popular culture* messages will likely have a direct and positive relationship with *identification with a drug subculture* (Hypothesis 9) and an indirect and negative relationship with *ego identity discomfort* (e.g., during drug abuse)—that is, it will help reduce it (Hypothesis 6).

Popular culture has not previously appeared in empirical work on the cultural-identity theory, although it has been discussed theoretically (Anderson 1995). Moreover, the field of drug abuse, in general, contains little evidence to date of an empirical relationship between *popular culture's* pro-drug messages and drug use or abuse. This kind of argument has recently, however, become politically popular and has ignited considerable empirical data in other social problems' debates—for example, crime and violence (see Barak 1994; Barlow, Barlow, and Chiricos 1995; Ledingham, Ledingham, and Richardson 1993; Reeves and Campbell 1994).

THE MEANING OF DRUGS

Goode (1993) has observed that drug-taking is nearly a cultural universal—that is, almost every society has substances that are consumed for many reasons, and there are no consistent "objective" criteria that make one a drug and another not. Instead, "drugs" are cultural and social constructs. Their meaning is largely symbolic and their contexts (culturally, geographically, and historically) are specific. The cultural-identity theory's tenets about the meaning of drugs begins with this premise. Scholars from the Birmingham School of Cultural Studies agree with Goode's position. Willis (1976, p. 107) states:

> The importance of drugs did not lie in their direct physical effects, but in the way they facilitated passing through a great symbolic barrier erected over against 'straight' society.

The theory proposes that drugs serve three functions for abusers and that these functions are part of the identity change process—that is, the concepts and pathways of the theoretical model explain why drugs may be used in these fashions. This point underscores the notion that drugs are attempts to resolve identity-related problems. It is important to mention, however, that research (e.g., Waldorf et al. 1991) has identified still other functions that drugs play for the individual consumer (e.g., to be "cool" or "fashionable"). The cultural-identity theory does not exclude consideration of them.

Material Symbolism

Given the theory's tenets about the meso and macro-level concepts, drugs can function as a mechanism to pursue economic and leisure activities, especially the marketing of illicit ones. According to Bourgois (1989), inner city residents seek their income and subsequently their identity and the meaning of their life through what they perceive to be high-powered careers on the street enmeshed in illicit drug markets as dealers and consumers. Interaction in such arenas and with drugs often leads to abuse. Also, what drugs represent in terms of status and prestige with respect to economic well-being (money and possessions, property), fashion and other popular culture artifacts (e.g., music), and leisure activity is also very important to the potential abuser.

Affect Control

This is perhaps the best documented function of drugs for the abuser and is most closely tied to the theory's micro-level concepts. It refers to consuming drugs to deal with feelings, usually negative, about the self and/or others in one's immediate environment or in the larger society. Drugs often quell ill feelings or provide an escape from them. Feelings of helplessness and powerlessness can foster the search for completeness through drugs and alcohol (see also Henderson and Boyd 1992; van den Bergh 1991). Furthermore, they can also provide an increased sense of personal freedom from constraining social structures.

Identity Creation

This function of drugs features a new definition of the self that is likely related to both material symbolism and affect control. Anderson's (1993) work on "temporary" identity changes found that drug euphoria helped facilitate negations of existing identities and reconstructions of new identities for her addict respondents. These new self-definitions were typically viewed as more positive by the respondent and those in his/her immediate environment. Drug euphoria, then, delivers much more than personal pleasure from an altered state. Earlier, Becker (1963) observed a similar function with drug euphoria. Furthermore, this identity is defined by group reference (i.e., drug subcultural groups, drug using others/peers, knowledge about the drug lifestyle, and media institutions).

SUMMARY OF THEORY

To sum up, events and experiences that sever young people from normative ideals and positively sanctioned statuses create feelings of alienation or social isolation within them and earn them undesired statuses and treatment from important others (*personal marginalization*). *Social marginalization*—that is, people's relative economic, employment, educational, and cultural deprivation compared to those around them—works in a similar fashion to provide a second source of alienation from mainstream society. These two types of marginalization lead to an extreme discomfort in how individuals feel about who they are (*ego identity discomfort*). This discomfort, coupled with a strong sense of not being able to construct a definition of themselves (because external sources are exerting too much control) that will be positively sanctioned (*lost control in defining an identity*) motivate them to identify with alternative social groups (*identification with a drug subcultural group*). These groups provide opportunities to resolve identity problems.

Economic opportunity, *educational opportunity*, and *popular culture* set the stage for the appearance and growth of drug subcultural groups and help define the substance of the identity-based solutions which such groups will offer to those who are motivated to participate in them. Their effects on identification with a drug subcultural group are mediated by social marginalization. Consequently, *identification with a drug subcultural* group reduces young people's *ego identity discomfort* or helps them, in the short term, to solve their identity problems. Drugs are sought as the solution because they provide, for the abuser, material symbolism, affect control, and identity creation. It is through this process that young people change from non-drug users to drug abusers.

Differences by Race, Gender, and Class

Scholars today increasingly note the importance of centering basic elements of social organization (race, ethnicity, gender, and social class) in theory and research. Discussed below are some preliminary observations about how these phenomena might alter the cultural-identity theory. Researchers studying the leading etiological theories have attempted to evaluate the explanatory power of their models across population subgroups (i.e., testing for differences between certain groups as an external validity question), but few have considered how the "substance" of the concepts or variables which comprise their models may differ by the same (an internal validity question). The cultural-identity theory attempts to address both matters.

Consider, for example, the 14 experiences which currently characterize the "actual" component of *personal marginalization*. It may be that blacks, whites, Hispanics, males, females, and lower- and middle-class individuals experience them differently. For instance, Anderson (1998b) recently found that *personal marginalization* for black females stemmed largely from the pre-adolescence assumption of adult-like responsibilities, sexual and physical abuse victimization, and birthing a child and/or becoming a substitute parent for younger siblings. White females' *personal marginalization* pertained more to parental loss (divorce or death), repeated geographic moves by the family, and the assumption of various adult responsibilities. Black males most frequently linked their drug use to the assumption of various adult-like responsibilities, which reportedly marginalized them from typical and more desirable childhood experiences. For white males, *personal marginalization* resulted from heavy adult responsibilities or rigid parental expectations. Anderson (1998b) also found that blacks were more likely to experience *personal marginalization* at school than their white counterparts, which may imply an increased likelihood of *ego identity discomfort* among blacks and greater risk for drug abuse.

Anderson (1998b) also found gender differences in the *ego identity discomfort* concept. *Ego identity discomfort* came from the perceived departure from gender scripts—that is, not acting masculine or feminine enough, or not doing the things a girl or boy was supposed to do. Since a fundamental aspect of the socialization process is the acquisition of sex-appropriate social identities—that is, gender identities—it makes sense that problems in or resistance to this process may be a source of *ego identity discomfort* that results in later drug use. The same might also be expected for race/ethnicity and social class.

Regarding the theory's macro-level concepts, Anderson (1998c) found that the composition of drug subcultural groups differed between blacks and whites. Blacks described neighborhood- and high-school-based groups. These groups secured members an improved social status and reputation. For many, such groups provided a necessary source of protection from a sometimes "tough" (i.e., aggressive/violent) environment and the people located therein. Marijuana, cocaine, crack, and alcohol were commonly used drugs by them during early drug use. Later on, crack cocaine dominated. The use and sale of such drugs often gave blacks an impression that they could improve their material well-being in addition to gaining an important source of peer acceptance and a new identity.

Anderson (1998c) found that the drug subcultural groups reported by whites differed. They were located at nightclubs and bars, college and high school, and around the neighborhood. Some of the drug subcultural groups were "other" activity-oriented (e.g., college groups or the entertainment industry) and had a very strong interest in drugs. Whites reported using many different drugs—that is, alcohol, cocaine (powder), marijuana, heroin, PCP, and LSD.

It is important to point out possible structural roots of these race-related differences. Formal social control policies, such as federal and state government anti-drug strategies, may shape the creation and activity of drug subcultural groups and identification with them. In addition, economic trends that worsen and perpetuate racial disparities in income can also help define such groups (Anderson 1995; Anderson and Laundra 1995).

Anderson (1998c) also found that both whites and blacks linked drug use and identification with drug-using groups to some sort of socioeconomic status-seeking. Such status-seeking was largely symbolic for whites. They reported experiencing increased prestige and social worth by having expensive drugs or associating with publicly-esteemed friends. For blacks, it was a different matter. They reported that participation in the drug world initially promised to alleviate financial stress and promote material well-being. Poverty at home and in the neighborhood and a lack of legitimate opportunities helped create a climate conducive to the flourishing of an illicit crack trade.

These differences by race and gender may, therefore, alter the meaning of each of the theory's eight concepts and the overall explanatory power of the theory across race and gender population subgroups. Future theorizing and empirical investigation of the ideas discussed here should explore this diversity. Furthermore, although no empirical evidence exists to date, differences by social class also likely alter the theory and should, therefore, be given similar attention.

CONCLUSIONS

Cultural-identity theory is about how the interaction between socially and culturally constructed meanings, symbols, and institutions interact with the individual to produce drug abuse. Its eight concepts are meant to help explain who will likely become an abuser of drugs. Thus far, the theory holds that abusers are likely to be individuals who experience a significant amount of personal and social marginalization and whose ego identity discomfort escalates because of it. They are people who likely feel that they have little control over defining a gratifying identity for themselves. They also more often live in areas that have significant limits on economic and educational opportunity and environments that are conducive to the growth of drug subcultural groups.

It is important to remember that this theory and the process it describes is about resolving socially induced identity problems that often exist between individuals and the larger social structure and culture in which they live. The theory does not propose that drug abuse is an individual pathology. Instead, it views drug abuse as an unfortunate outcome of an attempted solution to socially and largely externally induced problems with one's identity and being. Here, drugs and identification with drug subcultural groups are "temporary" (Anderson 1993) or "symbolic" (Clarke et al. 1976) solutions which ultimately fail to resolve real problems and which often create still others. Such problems will, therefore, exist and/or persist when the abuser terminates drug use. Efforts to rectify these problems must acknowledge this point.

The cultural-identity theory describes a process that individuals can get off and on at different times in their lives. Doing so might ultimately help it to distinguish between drug users and drug abusers. For instance, some of the users whom Waldorf et al. (1991) described may fit into the drug-related identity change process described here but may have exited it at different points before becoming full-fledged abusers according to the criteria discussed above. They found that some heavy users managed to control and moderate their use, some developed abusive patterns, some experienced serious health problems, and others became socially dysfunctional or stopped using drugs with simple commonsense strategies. Most of their respondents increased their use gradually over time, a fact they explain through increased exposure to drugs, which is similar to Anderson's (1994) previous concept of *social climate conducive to drug use* (popularity and availability of drugs in a given geographical location and historical moment). Empirical investigation of the ideas discussed here, therefore, should be mindful of these observations.

Empirical Investigation

Any methodology that attempts empirical investigation of the concepts and hypotheses discussed here will have to consider how to capture the multiple levels of influence on individuals and how they change over a significant period of time. This is a challenging undertaking, but there are many ways of achieving this goal. For instance, researchers desiring to conduct large-scale population-based surveys in pursuit of verifying the theory's overall explanatory power would likely have to collect data at a minimum of four points (see Figure 1) over about a 10-year span (i.e., from late childhood to early adulthood) or longer. When employed in a prospective fashion and with a national random sample, such a design would provide, perhaps, the best evidence for the causal ordering of the concepts and the theory's fit with drug abusers. The limitations of such an approach would include attrition (sample mortality), data management complications, and considerable financial support. A case-control survey research design that compared non-users, users, and abusers might resolve some of these limitations and achieve similar goals. Both strategies would have to reconcile issues related to self-report and retrospective data.

Qualitative approaches, on the other hand, would help enhance the internal validity of the theory. These studies (e.g., in-depth interviews and ethnographies) might uncover new factors and relationships of importance to the identity change process and show how the proposed concepts and relationships may differ by various dimensions of social organization.

NOTES

1. The cultural-identity theory attempts to articulate the social bases of drug abuse. Discussion of the considerable literature on genetic or physiological-based correlates of drug abuse (see Tarter 1988 for a review) is, therefore, beyond the scope of the theory and will not be discussed here.

2. This claim acknowledges that all socially constructed phenomena, such as those discussed here, have roots or ties to other levels of analysis.

3. Please note that the cultural-identity theory does not purport that *personal marginalization* is the only factor that can set this process in motion—that is, it is a sufficient condition for the initiation of drug-related identity change. Empirical work (Anderson and Mott 1998) on it to date implies that there are likely to be others.

REFERENCES

Ajzen, I. 1985. "From Decisions to Actions: A Theory of Planned Behavior." Pp. 11-39 in *Action-Control: From Cognition to Behavior*, edited by J. Kuhl and J. Beckmann. New York: Springer-Verlag.

Ajzen, I., and M. Fishbein. 1980. *Understanding Attitudes and Predicting Social Behavior.* Englewood Cliffs, NJ: Prentice-Hall.

Akers, R.L. 1977. *Deviant Behavior: A Social Learning Approach*, 2nd edition. Belmont, CA: Wadsworth.

Akers, R.L., and G. Lee. 1996. "Empirical Validation of the Applicability of an Integrative Theory of Deviant Behavior to the Study of Drug Use." *Journal of Drug Issues* 26(2): 317-344.

Alicea, M., and J. Friedman. 1994. "Women, Heroin and Resistance: Rethinking the Deviance Paradigm." Paper presented at the Annual Meetings of the American Sociological Association, Los Angeles, CA.

Anderson, T.L. 1991. "Identity Transformation in Drug Addiction." Unpublished Ph.D. dissertation, The American University, Washington, DC.

Anderson, T.L. 1993. "Types of Identity Change in Drug Using and Recovery Careers." *Sociological Focus* 26(2): 133-145.

Anderson, T.L. 1994. "Drug Abuse and Identity: Linking Micro and Macro Factors." *Sociological Quarterly* 35(1)" 159-174.

Anderson, T.L. 1995. "Toward a Preliminary Macro Theory of Drug Addiction." *Deviant Behavior* 16(4)" 353-372.

Anderson, T.L. Forthcoming a. "Drug-related Identity Change Processes: Uncovering Race and Gender Differences, Part 1: "Explanations of Drug Misuse and a New Identity-Based Model." *Substance Use & Misuse.*

Anderson, T.L. Forthcoming b. "Drug-related Identity Change Processes: Uncovering Race and Gender Differences, Part 2: "Micro-Level Motivational Concepts." *Substance Use & Misuse.*

Anderson, T.L. Forthcoming c. "Drug-related Identity Change Processes: Uncovering Race and Gender Differences," Part 3: "Macro-Level Opportunity Concepts." *Substance Use & Misuse.*

Anderson, T.L., and K. Laundra. 1995. "Theoretical Models of Drug Abuse and Addiction and Anti-Drug Policy: The Case of a Missing or Micro-Link." Paper presented at the Annual Meetings of the Midwest Sociological Society, Chicago, IL, April 6-9.

Anderson, T.L., and J.A. Mott. Forthcoming. "Drug-related Identity Change: Theoretical Development and Empirical Assessment." *Journal of Drug Issues.*

Bandura, A. 1977. "Self-efficacy: Toward a Unifying Theory of Behavior Change." *Psychological Review* 84: 191-215.

Barrett, M.J., T. Trepper, and L. Stone-Fish. 1990. "Feminist Informed Family Therapy for the Treatment of Intra Family Child Sexual Abuse." *Journal of Family Psychology* 4: 151-166.

Baumrind, D. 1971. "Current Patterns of Parental Authority." *Developmental Psychology Monograph* 4(1, Part 2).

Baumrind, D. 1983. "Rejoinder to Lewis's Reinterpretation of Parental Firm Control Effects: Are Authoritarian Families Really Harmonious?" *Psychological Bulletin* 94: 132-142.

Baumrind, D. 1985. "Familial Antecedents of Adolescent Drug Use: A Developmental Perspective." In *Etiology of Drug Abuse: Implications for Prevention*, edited by C.L. Jones and R. J. Battjes. NIDA Research Monograph 56. Rockville, MD: National Institute on Drug Abuse.

Beauvis, F., and S. LaBoueff. 1985. "Drug and Alcohol Abuse Intervention in American Indian Communities." *The International Journal of Addictions* 20: 139-171.

Beck, J., and M. Rosenbaum. 1995. *Pursuit of Ecstasy.* New York: SUNY Press.

Becker, H. 1963. *Outsiders.* New York: The Free Press.

Bennett, J. 1981. *Oral History and Delinquency: The Rhetoric of Criminology.* Chicago, IL: University of Chicago Press.

Biernacki, P. 1986. *Pathways from Heroin Addiction: Recovery Without Treatment*. Philadelphia, PA: Temple University Press.

Bourdieu, P. 1980. *The Logic of Practice*. Stanford, CA: Stanford University Press.

Bourdieu, P., and J.C. Passeron. 1977. *Reproduction in Education, Society, and Culture*. London: Sage.

Bourgois, P. 1989. "In Search of Horatio Alger: Culture and Ideology in the Crack Economy." *Contemporary Drug Problems* 16(4): 619-649.

Bourgois, P. 1996. *In Search of Respect*. New York: Cambridge University Press.

Brake, M. 1985. *Comparative Youth Culture*. London: Routledge and Kegan Paul.

Brice-Heath, S., and M.W. McLaughlin 1993. *Identity and Inner-City Youth*. New York: Teachers College Press.

Briere, J., and L.Y. Zaidi. 1989. "Sexual Abuse Histories and Sequelae in Female Psychiatric Emergency Room Patients. *American Journal of Psychiatry* 146: 1602-1606.

Brown, J.D. 1991. "Preprofessional Socialization and Identity Transformation." *Journal of Contemporary Ethnography* 20(2): 157-178.

Caetano, R. 1987. "Acculturation and Drinking Patterns among U.S. Hispanics." *British Journal of Addiction* 82: 789-799.

Castro, F.G., E.V. Sharp, E.H. Barrington, W. Walton, and R.A. Rawson. 1991. "Drug Abuse and Identity in Mexican Americans: Theoretical and Empirical Considerations." *Hispanic Journal of Behavioral Sciences* 13(2): 209-225.

Catalano, R.F., and J.D. Hawkins. In press. "The Social Development Model: A Theory of Antisocial Behavior." In *Delinquency and Crime: Current Theories*, edited by J.D. Hawkins. New York: Cambridge University Press.

Catalano, R.F., R. Kosterman, J.D. Hawkins, M.D. Newcomb, and R.D. Abbott. 1996. "Modeling the Etiology of Adolescent Substance Use: A Test of the Social Development Model." *Journal of Drug Issues* 26(2): 429-456.

Clarke, J., S. Hall, T. Jefferson, and B. Roberts. 1976. "Subcultures, Cultures, and Class: A Theoretical Overview." Pp. 9-74 in *Resistance Through Rituals: Youth Subcultures in Post-War Britain*, edited by S. Hall and T. Jefferson. London: Hutchison.

Cloward, R.A., and L. Ohlin. 1960. *Delinquency and Opportunity*. New York: Free Press.

Cohen, A.K. 1955. *Delinquent Boys: The Subculture of the Gang*. London: Collier MacMillian.

Couch, C. 1989. *Social Processes and Relationships*. Dix Hills, NY: General Hall Press.

Denzin, N.K. 1987. *The Recovering Alcoholic*. Beverly Hills, CA: Sage.

Dishion, T.J., D. Capaldi, K.M. Spracklen, and F. Li. 1995. "Peer Ecology of Male Adolescent Drug Use." *Development and Psychopathology* 7: 803-824.

Donovan, J.E. 1996. "Problem-Behavior Theory and the Explanation of Adolescent Marijuana Use." *Journal of Drug Issues* 26(2): 379-404.

Dunlap, E., and B. Johnson. 1992. "The Setting for the Crack Era: Macro Forces, Micro Consequences, 1960-1992." *Journal of Psychoactive Drugs* 24(4): 307-321.

Edwards, G., and A. Arif, eds. 1980. *Drug Problems in the Sociocultural Context*. Geneva: World Health Organization.

Elliott, D.S., D. Huizinga, and S.S. Ageton. 1985. *Explaining Delinquency and Drug Use*. Beverly Hills, CA: Sage.

Ennett, S.T., and K.E. Bauman. 1991. "Mediators in the Relationship Between Parental and Peer Characteristics and Beer Drinking by Early Adolescence." *Journal of Applied Social Psychology* 21: 1699-1711.

Ettore, E. 1992. *Women and Substance Abuse*. New Brunswick, NJ: Rutgers University Press.

Erickson, K. 1970. "The Sociology of Deviance." Pp. 709-725 in *Social Psychology Through Symbolic Interaction*, edited by G.P. Stone and E.A. Farberman. Walthow, MA: Xerox College Publishing.

Feree, M.M., and E. Hall. 1996. "Gender, Race and Class in Mainstream Textbooks." *American Sociological Review* 61(6): 929-950.

Fishbein, M., and I. Ajzen. 1975. *Belief, Attitude, Intention, and Behavior: An Introduction to Theory and Research.* Reading, MA: Addison-Wesley.

Fishkin, S.A., S. Sussman, A.W. Stacey, C.W. Dent, D. Burton, and B.R. Flay. 1993. "Ingroup Versus Outgroup Perceptions of the Characteristics of High-Risk Youth: Negative Stereotyping." *Journal of Applied Social Psychology* 23(13): 1051-1068.

Flay, B., and J. Petraitis. 1994. "The Theory of Triadic Influence: A New Theory of Health Behavior with Implications for Preventive Interventions." Pp. 19-44 in *Advances in Medical Sociology, Vol. 4: A Reconsideration of Health Behavior Change Models,* edited by G. Albrecht. Greenwich, CT: JAI Press.

Galan, F.J. 1988. "Alcoholism Prevention and Hispanic Youth." *The Journal of Drug Issues* 18: 49-58.

Gans, H. 1974. *Popular Culture and High Culture.* New York: Basic Books.

Glaser, B.G., and A.L. Strauss. 1971. *Status Passage.* Chicago, IL: Aldine.

Goffman, E. 1961. *Asylums.* New York: Doubleday and Company.

Goffman, E. 1963. *Stigma.* Englewood Cliffs, NJ: Prentice-Hall.

Goode, E. 1993. *Drugs in American Society,* 4th edition. New York: McGraw-Hill.

Gorman, D.M. 1996. "Etiological Theories and the Primary Prevention of Drug Use." *Journal of Drug Issues* 26(2): 505-520.

Granfield, R., and W. Cloud. 1996. "The Elephant that No One Sees: Natural Recovery Among Middle-class Addicts." *Journal of Drug Issues* 26: 45-61.

Guyette, S. 1982. "Selected Characteristics of American Indian Substance Abusers." *The International Journal of Addictions* 17: 1001-1014.

Hamid, A. 1991a. "From Ganja to Crack: Caribbean Participation in the Underground Economy in Brooklyn, 1976-1986," Part 1: "Establishment of the Marijuana Economy." *The International Journal of the Addictions* 26(6): 615-628.

Hamid, A. 1991b. "From Ganja to Crack: Caribbean Participation in the Underground Economy in Brooklyn, 1976-1986," Part 2: "Establishment of the Cocaine (and Crack) Economy." *The International Journal of the Addictions* 26(7): 729-738.

Hamid, A. 1991c. "Crack: New Directions in Drug Research," Part 3: "Differences Between the Marijuana Economy and the Cocaine/Crack Economy." *The International Journal of the Addictions* 26(8): 825-836.

Harton, H.C., and B. Latane. Forthcoming. "Social Influence and Adolescent Lifestyle Attitudes." *Journal of Research on Adolescence.*

Harvey, W.B. 1985. "Alcohol Abuse and the Black Community: A Contemporary Analysis." *Journal of Drug Issues* 15: 81-91.

Hawkins, J.D., and N. Wacker. 1983. "Verbal Performances And Addict Conversion: An Interactionist Perspective on Therapeutic Communities." *Journal of Drug Issues* (Spring): 281-297.

Hawkins, J.D., R.F. Catalano, and J.Y. Miller. 1992. "Risk and Protective Factors for Alcohol and Other Drug Problems in Adolescence and Early Adulthood: Implications for Substance Abuse Prevention." *Psychological Bulletin* 12(1): 64-105.

Hawkins, J.D., and J.G. Weis. 1985. "The Social Development Model: An Integrated Approach to Delinquency Prevention." *Journal of Primary Prevention* 6: 73-97.

Hebdige, D. 1979. *Subculture: The Meaning of Style.* London: Methuen & Co Ltd.

Henderson, D., and C. Boyd. 1992. "Masculinity, Femininity, and Addiction." Pp. 153-166 in *Drugs, Crime and Social Policy,* edited by T. Mieczkowski. Boston: Allyn and Bacon

Herman, J., D.E.H. Russell, and K. Tracki. 1986. "Long-term Effects of Incestuous Abuse in Childhood." *American Journal of Psychiatry* 143: 1293-1296.

Hewitt, J.P. 1991. *Self and Society,* 5th edition. Boston: Allyn and Bacon.

Hirschi, T. 1969. *Causes of Delinquency.* Berkeley, CA: University of California Press.

Hoffman, J.P. 1993. "Exploring the Direct and Indirect Family Effects on Adolescent Drug Use." *Journal of Drug Issues* 23: 535-557.

Jessor, R., J.E. Donovan, and F.M. Costa. 1991. *Beyond Adolescence: Problem Behavior and Young Adult Development.* New York: Cambridge University Press.

Jessor, R., and S.L. Jessor. 1973. "The Perceived Environment in Behavioral Science." *American Behavioral Scientist* 16(6): 801-828.

Jessor, R., and S.L. Jessor. 1977. *Problem Behavior and Psychosocial Development.* New York: Academic Press.

Johnston, L.D., P.M. O'Malley, and J.G. Bachman. 1995. "The Monitoring the Future Study 1975-1994." Monograph, Institute for Social Research, University of Michigan, Ann Arbor.

Jorquez, J.S. 1983. "The Retirement Phase of Heroin Using Careers." *Journal of Drug Issues* (Spring): 343-365.

Kandel, D.B. 1980. "Drug and Drinking Behavior among Youth." *Annual Review of Sociology* 6: 235-85.

Kandel, D.B. 1985. "On Processes of Peer Influences in Adolescent Drug Use: A Developmental Perspective." *Advances In Alcohol and Substance Abuse* 4(Spring/Summer): 139-163.

Kandel, D.B. 1996. "The Parental and Peer Contexts of Adolescent Deviance: An Algebra of Interpersonal Influences." *Journal of Drug Issues* 26(2): 289-316.

Kaplan, H.B. 1975. "Sequelae of Self-derogation: Predicting from a General Theory of Deviant Behavior." *Youth and Society* 7: 171-197.

Kaplan, H.B. 1996. "Empirical Validation of the Applicability of an Integrative Theory of Deviant Behavior to the Study of Drug Use." *Journal of Drug Issues* 26(2): 345-378.

Kaplan, H.B., and R.L. Johnson. 1992. "Relationships Between Circumstances Surrounding Initial Illicit Drug Use and Escalation of Drug Use: Moderating Effects of Gender and Early Adolescent Experiences." In *Vulnerability to Drug Abuse*, edited by M. Glantz and R. Pickens. Washington, DC: American Psychological Association.

Kaplan, H.B., S. Martin, and C. Robbins. 1984. "Pathways to Adolescent Drug Use: Self-derogation, Peer Influence, Weakening of Social Controls, and Early Substance Abuse. *Journal of Health and Social Behavior* 25: 270-289.

Kaplan, H.B., S. Martin, and C. Robbins. 1986. "Escalation of Marijuana Use: Application of a General Theory of Deviant Behavior." *Journal of Health and Social Behavior* 27: 44-61.

Kitano, H.H.L., J.E. Lubben, and I. Chi. 1988. "Predicting Japanese American Drinking Behavior." *The International Journal of the Addictions* 23: 417-428.

Lettieri, D.J., M. Sayers, and H.W. Pearson, eds. 1980. *Theories on Drug Abuse: Selected Contemporary Perspectives*. NIDA Research Monograph 30. Rockville, M.D: National Institute on Drug Abuse.

MacLeod, J. 1987. *Ain't No Makin It: Leveled Aspirations in a Low Income Neighborhood*. Boulder, CO: Westview Press.

Maines, D.R. 1994. "In Search of Mesostructure: Studies in the Negotiated Order." Pp. 277-286 in *Symbolic Interaction,* edited by N. Herman, and L.T. Reynolds. Dix Hills, NY: General Hall Press.

McRobbie, A. 1991. *Feminism and Youth Culture*. Boston, MA: Unwin Hyman.

Mendes de Leon, C.F., and K.S. Markides. 1986. "Alcohol Consumption and Physical Symptoms in a Mexican American Population." *Drug and Alcohol Dependence* 16: 369-379.

Menicucci, L.D., and L. Wermuth. 1989. "Expanding the Family Systems Approach: Cultural, Class, Developmental and Gender Influences in Drug Abuse." *The American Journal of Family Therapy* 17(2): 129-142.

Merton, R.K. 1938. "Social Structure and Anomie." *American Sociological Review* 3: 672-683.

Merton, R.K. 1957. *Social Theory and Social Structure*. Glencoe, IL: The Free Press.

Mitic, W.R., D.P. McGuire, and B. Neumann 1987. "Adolescent Inhalant Use and Perceived Stress." *Journal of Drug Education* 17(2): 113-121.

Morgan, P., ed. 1996. "Unknown, Unexplored, and Unseen Populations: An Introduction to the Truly Hidden Worlds of Drug and Alcohol Research." *Journal of Drug Issues* 26(1, Special Issue).

Mosbach, P., and H. Leventhal. 1988. "Peer Group Identification and Smoking: Implications for Intervention." *Journal of Abnormal Psychology* 97: 238-245.

Peluso, E., and L.S. Peluso. 1988. *Women and Drugs: Getting Hooked and Getting Clean*. Minneapolis, MN: Compcare Publishers.

Petraitis, J., B.R. Flay, and T.Q. Miller. 1995. "Reviewing Theories of Adolescent Substance Use: Organizing Pieces in the Puzzle." *Psychological Bulletin* 117(1): 67-86.

Pohl, J., and C. Bôyd. 1992. "Female Addiction: A Concept Analysis." Pp. 138-152 in *Drugs, Crime and Social Policy*, edited by T. Mieczkowski. Boston, MA: Allyn and Bacon.

Preble, E., and J.J. Casey. 1969. "Taking Care of Business: The Heroin Street User's Life on the Street." *International Journal of the Addictions* 4: 1-24.

Ray, M.B. 1968. "Abstinence Cycles and Heroin Addicts." In *Deviance/The Interactionist Perspective*, edited by E. Rubington and M.S. Weinberg. London: MacMillian Publishing.

Reeves, J.L., and R. Campbell. 1994. *Cracked Coverage: Television News, the Anti-Cocaine Crusade, and the Reagan Legacy*. Durham, NC: Duke University Press.

Rhodes, W., P. Scheiman, T. Pittayathikhun, L. Collins, and V. Tsarfaty. 1995. *What America's Users Spend on Illegal Drugs, 1988-1993*. Prėpared for the Office of National Drug Control Policy, Washington, DC.

Rosenbaum, M. 1981. *Women on Heroin*. New Brunswick, NJ: Rutgers University Press.

Russell, D.E.H. 1986. *The Secret Trauma: Incest in the Lives of Girls and Women*. New York: Basic Books.

Substance Abuse and Mental Health Services Administration (SAMHSA). 1995. *National Household Survey on Drug Abuse: Population Estimates 1994*. Washington, DC: U.S. Department of Health and Human Services.

Schwartz, G., P. Turner, and E. Peluso. 1973. "Neither Heads nor Freaks: Working Class Drug Subculture." *Urban Life and Culture* 2(3): 288-313.

Schmid, T.J., and R.S. Jones. 1991. "Suspended Identity: Identity Transformation in a Maximum Security Prison." *Symbolic Interaction* 14(4): 415-432.

Shover, N. 1983. "The Later Stages of Ordinary Property Offender Careers." *Social Problems* 31(2, December): 208-218.

Singer, M.I., M.K. Petchers, and D. Hussey. 1989. "The Relationship Between Sexual Abuse and Substance Abuse among Psychiatrically Hospitalized Adolescents." *Child Abuse and Neglect* 13: 319-325.

Sue, D. 1987. "Use and Abuse of Alcohol by Asian Americans." *Journal of Psychoactive Drugs* 19: 57-66.

Sussman, S., C. Dent, L. McAdams, A. Stacy, D. Burton, and B. Flay. 1994. "Group Self-Identification and Adolescent Cigarette Smoking: A 1-Year Prospective Study." *Journal of Abnormal Psychology* 103(3): 576-580.

Tarter, R.E. 1988. "Are There Inherited Behavioral Traits that Predispose Substance Use?" *Journal of Consulting and Clinical Psychology* 56: 189-196.

Van Den Bergh, N. 1991. *Feminist Perspectives on Addictions*. New York: Springer.

Waldorf, D. 1983. "The Social-Psychological Processes of Control And Recovery from Substance Abuse." *Journal of Drug Issues* (Spring): 237-280.

Waldorf, D., C. Reinarman, and S. Murphy. 1991. *Cocaine Changes*. Philadelphia, PA: Temple University Press.

Waterston, A. 1993. *The Street Addict in the Political Economy*. Philadelphia, PA: Temple University Press.

White, H.R. (Ed.) 1996. "Empirical Validity of Theories of Drug Abuse." *Journal of Drug Issues* 26(2, Special Issue): 345-378.

Willis, P. 1976. "The Cultural Meaning of Drug Use." Pp. 106-118 in *Resistance Through Rituals: Youth Subcultures in Post-War Britain*, edited by S. Hall and T. Jefferson. London: Hutchison.

Willis, P. 1977. *Learning to Labour*. London: Saxon House.

Wilsnack, S.C., and R.W. Wilsnack. 1979. "Sex Roles and Adolescent Drinking." Pp. 183-227 in *Youth, Alcohol, and Social Policy*, edited by H.T. Blane and M.E. Chafetz. New York: Plenum Press.

Wurzman, I., B.J. Rounsaville, and P. Kleber. 1982. "Cultural Values of Puerto Rican Opiate Drug Addicts: An Exploratory Study." *American Journal of Drug and Alcohol Abuse* 9: 141-153.

Yee, B.W.K., and N.D. Thu. 1987. "Correlates of Drug Use and Abuse Among Indochinese Refugees: Mental Health Implications." *Journal of Psychoactive Drugs* 19: 77-83.

GENDER DIFFERENCES IN CONSEQUENCES OF ALCOHOL USE AMONG ADOLESCENTS

Celia C. Lo and Gerald Globetti

ABSTRACT

Feminists have raised questions about gender bias embedded in many past and current social studies. Methodological difficulties related to gender bias have impeded the accurate study of males' and females' drinking experiences (Kline 1990; Wood, Nagoshi, and Dennis 1992) and have led to a search for new and more reliable measures of young people's drinking behavior. This study constituted a semi-structured interview approach to the study of female and male drinking, in which the respondents were encouraged to describe their drinking behavior and its consequences in their own words. The responses were then categorized and analyzed, reversing the usual methodological technique in which youth are asked to reply to questions on alcohol use with fixed and sometimes cant alternatives. Results show that males tend to report problems classifiable as either physical discomfort, strain in relationships, or encounter with law enforcement. Females, on the other hand, apparently experience more guilt feelings, believe they engage in irresponsible or inappropriate

Sociology of Crime, Law, and Deviance, Volume 1, pages 263-276.

ISBN: 0-7623-0282-8

behavior, and are more apt to feel emotional and psychological effects from drinking. Although both gender groups often experience similar problems and expectations, their accounts of their experiences differ qualitatively. The present data supports recent research demonstrating that gender plays a part in the kinds of alcohol-related problems adolescents experience (Lo 1996). The results also confirm a suspicion voiced by many feminists that established measures of alcohol-related problems should be revised to represent female as well as male experiences and perceptions.

INTRODUCTION

Feminists have alerted the research community to the possibility that, in subtle and not-so-subtle ways, science is a "gendered enterprise" (Harding 1986) rather than a thoroughly objective one. Women have not had an equal chance to participate in the production of scientific knowledge (Rose 1987; Tomm 1989), so science's "androcentric culture" has determined the problems to investigate (Keller 1987). Women's experiences at best are considered to be the same as men's, or at worst, virtually insignificant (Bart et al. 1989; Chesney-Lind 1989; Tomm 1989). Scientific research has largely been conducted as if the study of men is analogous to, and can be simply generalized to, women (Holmes and Jorgensen 1971; Dan and Beekman 1972; Bailly, Carman, and Forslund 1991).

Gender roles and sexual politics have changed markedly in the last three decades. More women are in the academy and involved in the production of scientific knowledge. Yet, the ratio of male to female researchers remains very unequal, with typical measures to remedy the imbalance tending to prove ineffective. Thus, it is important to scientific enterprise that conscious steps be taken to minimize the androcentric bias that still underlies the research process. The quality of empirical data and conclusions is weakened as long as androcentric assumptions go unscrutinized.

For example, studies of crime and deviance are essentially studies of male behavior in which females are treated in either a stereotypical or an incidental way (Barkan 1997). One such problem is the practice of extrapolating, from all-male (or nearly so) samples to the whole population (Chesney-Lind 1986, 1989). Commonly in delinquency research, findings consider only men, who are the primary respondents in most studies. Or, the few women included are assumed to respond along the same lines as men.

For the central focus of this study, alcohol use, the problem of bias involves not only this "single standard" methodology but a double contrivance that may be just as problematic to collecting reliable data. Traditionally, male behavior has been the primary focus of alcohol studies (Annis and Liban 1980; Hoar 1983; Vannicelli and Nash 1984; T. Hughes 1990). This focus obviously results from the fact that data, to this point, demonstrate that males are the heavier users of alcohol (Barnes and Welte 1986; Engs and Hanson 1985). Thus, female alcohol use is marginalized, while the consequences and issues of male drinking are central to the alcohol research effort. Similar to delinquency research, after the initial correlation regarding gender and alcohol abuse establishes that males are more problematic drinkers, the less-involved female problem users are either treated as incidental to the male population or are just ignored. Until recently, alcohol use and abuse among females have been characterized as either insignificant in comparison to male drinking, and consequently not warranting special study, or as narrow research objectives reflecting women's sexuality and its relation to pregnancy risks (Clemmons 1985; Gomberg 1986; T. Hughes 1990).

While male alcoholics' health and welfare has received primary research attention, it is not at all certain that men actually experience more problems from alcohol use than do women in this society. Attempts to measure problems alcoholics experience have been criticized as gender-biased (Ferrence 1980; Blume 1987). Measurements generated by assumptions about male experiences have been employed repeatedly to assess females' behavior as well. For instance, the apparently simple measurement "quantity of alcohol consumed," though ubiquitous in alcohol-use studies, is a gender-biased value in that it ignores physiological differences between the sexes in terms of body weight and water content (Vogel-Sprott 1983; T. Hughes 1990).

The present interview study, which was intended to examine gender differences in the perceptions young people have about the consequences of drinking, took into account the difficulties of past research. Several approaches were employed in an attempt to enhance the quality of the data collected and to make the investigation more sensitive to females' experiences and perceptions. In the study, an almost equal number of male and female subjects were interviewed (59 males and 65 females). Interview questions were open-ended, encouraging respondents to discuss their drinking experiences (Smith 1994) in their own words and way.

REVIEW OF LITERATURE

Alcohol is the drug most commonly used by teenagers in the United States. The results of a national survey (Johnston, O'Malley, and Bachman 1995) conducted in 1994 show that the annual prevalence of alcohol use by 12th-graders is 73% (74.1% of male and 72.1% of female respondents). In addition to the growing general prevalence of alcohol use, heavy drinking has become a specific concern of alcohol research during the last two decades. However, definitions of "heavy drinking" differ from study to study, making comparisons difficult. One example definition of a heavy drinker is a person who consumes five or more drinks more often than once a week (Engs 1977; Engs and Hanson 1985; Sherry and Stolberg 1987). Estimates and extrapolations from the data suggest that 20% to 30% of those surveyed can be considered heavy drinkers (Engs 1977; Wechsler and McFadden 1979; Engs and Hanson 1985; Gonzalez 1986; Sherry and Stolberg

1987). Among these heavy drinkers, males greatly outnumber females and subsequently experience more adverse consequences as a result of alcohol use (S. Hughes and Dodder 1983; Gadaleto and Anderson 1986; Haworth-Hoeppner et al. 1989). Yet, these findings may be deceptive. Although women drink less than men per sitting, the effects of these smaller amounts may actually be greater because of male/female physiological differences in metabolizing alcohol. If body weight is taken into account in defining individual drinking behavior, greater numbers of females may be identified as heavy drinkers, even though males may continue to be found to consume the larger quantities (Lo and Globetti 1995).

In order to address this issue, Lo in a recent study (1996) measured three dimensions of the drinking act—namely, the duration of the drinking episode, the quantity of alcohol consumed per typical sitting, and respondents' body weight—which she combined in a "blood-alcohol concentration" measure. Results showed that females were heavier drinkers than demonstrated by previous research, although they did not attain as high a blood-alcohol concentration as males did during typical drinking episodes. Quantity of alcohol consumed, therefore, is not an equally accurate measure of drinking levels for the two gender groups. This shortcoming was notably recognized in a 1993 survey of college students in which the authors expressed the need for distinct definitions of "binge drinking" for males and females (Wechsler et al. 1994; Wechsler et al. 1995). This recommendation was based on two observations: (1) that females would be more likely to experience a particular kind of alcohol-related problem if a single definition of "binge drinking" was used for both genders; and (2) females and males typically have different body masses and are differentially affected physically by alcohol.

In studies by Wechsler and his associates, as in other studies (Engs 1977; Engs and Hanson 1985), a fixed list of alcohol-related problems was used to measure individuals' experience of alcohol-related problems. However, the alcohol-problems indexes included in most studies have tended to be male-oriented (including problems such as getting into fights and damaging property), suggesting that the researchers expect males than females to experience problems related to drinking(Engs and Hanson 1985). But when blood-alcohol concentration (not simply quantity consumed) is used to measure drinking level, gender as well as drinking level is a significant predictor of the occurrence of certain kinds of alcohol-related problems (Lo and Globetti 1995; Lo 1996). These findings suggest that females behave differently than males under the influence of alcohol, leading them to experience alcohol-related problems of a different type.

METHODS

This paper grew out of a study designed to explore how perspectives on alcohol use vary between young male and female high school students. The study specifically focused on first-person accounts of the effects of alcohol reported by the students in face-to-face interviews (these interviews can be considered semistructured). All respondents who acknowledged using alcohol at least once were asked the following question: "What were the experiences you encountered as a result of drinking?" The interviewers were instructed to make sure that respondents mentioned both positive and negative experiences. If respondents were confused by the question, interviewers were instructed to restate the question as follows: "Have you experienced anything comfortable or uncomfortable as a result of drinking (both feelings and behaviors)? What kinds of things?" Further instructions to the interviewers were that they could encourage respondents to think about three kinds of experiences: physical, psychological, and social. Interviewers were also instructed to ask respondents "What else?" whenever there was a pause during the interview, in pursuit of complete answers.

The goal of the study was exploratory. We sought from members of both genders oral accounts of consequences resulting from drinking. A small, manageable sample was sufficient to achieve the goal. One hundred twenty-two 10th to 12th-grade students (two 9th-grade students who were interested in the study were also interviewed) from a public high school with an enrollment of 1,100 constituted the sample. The school is situated in a rural county in Michigan, with median household income around $35,000. (It is the only public high school in the city where the first author and her affiliated university are located.) Most of the respondents classified themselves as white, except for nine who reported they were Native American, Hispanic, or Caucasian and Native American. Since the purpose of this research was to secure different perspectives of the two genders, ethnic diversity was not consciously pursued in this study.

The interviews were begun in November and finished in December 1995. Interviews were conducted by trained graduate students. Males interviewed males, and females interviewed females, based on the observation that students are more relaxed and truthful with people of their own gender and approximate age. Five graduate students (three males and two females) studying with the first author were trained to frame and explain (when requested) the scheduled questions; they were also trained to use probing skills to help respondents express themselves fully. The training also focused on issues including the requisite confidentiality of the information obtained in the study. Finally, the interviewers were cautioned about the possibility of respondents' having feelings of sensitivity about the questions. They were instructed in ways to resolve any related discomfort expressed by respondents.

Early in November 1995, the first author visited about 10 classes suggested by the principal of the high school, in order to explain the study. Students were told that the study was about gender differences in adolescent drinking behavior. The purpose of the study was clearly stated in both the parent's informed consent and child's assent forms. Students who volunteered to participate in the interviews made appointments and received a parent's consent form. Students who received parent's permission to participate in the project were then interviewed. In addition, a student consent form was signed by each respondent before the interview began. The entire interview was tape-recorded and required about 20 minutes to complete.

RESULTS AND DISCUSSION

Since the study was exploratory in nature, we relied on the students' own responses to devise categories that suitably describe alcohol-related problems and perceived positive consequences of drinking. While reading through each respondent's transcribed interview, the researchers, following suggestions from Strauss and Corbin (1990), first used students' descriptive phrases to indicate perceived positive and negative consequences of drinking. Next, conceptual labels were developed describing some commonalities among the descriptive phrases. Eventually, categories such as "removal of inhibitions" and "strain in relationships" were developed, grouping together concepts applied for the same phenomena. The categorization was basically an inductive process, shaped by ideas generated from prior research (Berg 1995). The central idea was that the usual measure of blood-alcohol concentration can only partly explain the experience of alcohol-related problems. After blood-alcohol concentration is controlled, males are more likely to engage in male-oriented behavior, such as fighting, whereas females are more likely to experience female-oriented behavior, such as feeling less attractive (Lo 1996). But the researchers remain well aware of the intention of this study, remaining true to the oral accounts of the respondents as we developed inductive categories.

Once the lead author had developed the categories from the raw data, copies of the transcribed conversations and the analysis results were provided to the second author. The second author was responsible for assessing the categories generated by the lead author and devising any other categories deemed appropriate. These response categories agreed upon by both authors were retained for use in further analysis.

The data on the positive and negative consequences of drinking were compared by gender, in an effort to determine: (1) whether the two gender groups gave qualitatively identical oral accounts that could be classified in identical categories (such as strain in social relationships and scrapes with the law), and (2) whether, for the two genders, different rates of incidence are associated with a particular category. Of the 124 respondents, 59—that is, 48%—were male. Fifty of those (85%), as well as 53 of the 65 female respondents (82%), had consumed alcohol at some time. Among the males, 71% reported drinking in the year prior to the interview. Females were somewhat less likely to have taken a drink, with 65% of those interviewed reporting at least one drinking episode in the year before the interview. Females also attained lower blood-alcohol concentrations than males during typical drinking episodes within the year (.115% for males and .077% for females). In this study, respondents' typical blood-alcohol concentrations were calculated using reported information about body weight, height, age, duration of drinking episodes, and quantity of alcohol consumed at typical sittings (Alcohol Research Documentation 1983; Sutker et al. 1983; Watson, Watson, and Batt 1980).[1]

Positive Consequences of Drinking

Positive consequences of drinking cited by the respondents were classified in five categories: relaxation and physical enhancement, removal of inhibitions, increased confidence and forgetting problems, enlightenment, and other. Males (16%) were less likely than females (23%) to indicate relaxation and physical enhancement as a positive result of drinking. When a male respondent reported this type of positive effect, his response was likely to be expressed in the form "I like to drink—it calms me down." Females reported similar feelings in words to the effect that drinking prompted them to slow down and relax. This finding is not surprising, in that the literature shows that one of the principal reasons people in Western cultures use alcohol is to relieve stress and tension (Bales 1946; Ullman 1960).

Another belief widely cited by Americans who drink is alcohol's ability to facilitate communication and social interaction that does not come easily to them. Males and females in our study were almost equal in citing as a positive result of drinking the social-lubricating effect of alcohol and the freeing from inhibitions to social interaction (44% of males and 45% of females). When drinking, males and females found it easier to open up to peers and enjoy socializing with others. However, males appear to view disinhibition as a way to personal emancipation—simply having more fun—while females seem to see disinhibition as a means to develop social links. One female respondent reported that her drinking helped her in "meeting people that you don't know, [and] I think you get closer to your friends. Probably a lot of people say that, but it's true. You share things that you don't usually share."

Another category of positive consequences, generated from the respondents' own words, was increased confidence and forgetting problems. A minority of both men and women (18% of males and 13% of females) mention this type of effect. Males in the group seem most interested in being accepted by friends and having better experiences with the opposite sex. A male respondent stated, "I can't really think of anything positive besides meeting a lot more people and feeling a lot more at ease when you're drinking." Females, on the other hand, focused on themselves, for example, "when I do drink, like when I go out to a party or something, I know I feel a lot more self-confident."

Four out of 53 females suggested that drinking "enlightened" them somehow; no males made this claim. One respondent said that drinking made her a bit more self-aware. Another described feeling that drinking prompted her to think about issues she usually did not think about.

Negative Consequences of Drinking

The following categories were devised from the students' descriptions of negative experiences: physical discomfort, guilt, strain in relationships, irresponsible or inappropriate behavior, escape and dependency, psychological and emotional effects, and involvement with law enforcement. A higher proportion of males (54%) than females (43%) reported experiencing negative physical effects from drinking. These results correspond with other, large survey studies in the field (Engs and Hanson 1985). Since males were more likely than females in this study to attain a high blood-alcohol concentration (on average, males during a typical drinking sitting attained a .115% blood-alcohol concentration), physical discomfort such as hangover or vomiting/nausea more commonly were mentioned by male respondents. Males also named loss of coordination as a problem much more often than their female counterparts did. Other physical effects mentioned by both gender groups included feeling drunk and feeling tired or fatigued.

Almost three times more female (21%) than male (8%) respondents felt guilty after drinking. Statements indicating this effect included: "Sometimes I feel guilty about lying to my parents about where I am and what I'm doing" and "It doesn't make you feel good. It makes you feel guilty." Keep in mind that females, as compared to males, seem to be relatively light drinkers in this study. Individuals in the United States are socialized to believe that males are more able to tolerate alcoholic beverages, especially liquor and beer; indeed, this is considered a trait of masculinity. Consequently, males are given more societal permission to consume and abuse alcohol, supporting a double standard relative to the drinking act. Changes in gender roles in recent years may have led to increased female drinking while nevertheless leaving many females guilt-ridden even when drinking small amounts.

Disruption in relationships when drinking, such as getting into arguments with friends or family, has been cited frequently by past studies (Wechsler and McFadden 1979; Wechsler and Rohman 1981) as an alcohol-related problem that young people often experience. In the present study, 30% of males and 17% of females reported incidents indicating disruption of or strain in relationships resulting from drinking. Male respondents tended to see their drinking as a cause of their behavior, making them fight with friends and parents. Alcohol is thus an excuse for inappropriate or aggressive behavior. Females, though they reported fewer incidents of aggressive behavior (fighting), did indicate that drinking increased tension between themselves and their significant others. A remark from one female was that her parents stopped trusting her after she lost her virginity because of drinking. A male respondent described his fighting with friends and others in the following statement: "Well, I had somebody's boyfriend chase me once. I've gotten beat up because I picked a fight with somebody once. That's the worst of it."

Consistent with the finding that females are more apt than males to feel guilty after drinking, the data also revealed that females were more likely to say they engaged in irresponsible or inappropriate behavior (such as engaging in sexual acts and other risk-taking behavior) as a result of drinking. About one-third of the females (32%) reported they had engaged in such acts, whereas fewer than one-fifth of the males (16%) said so. This again suggests that, for some females, the drinking act in itself may be regarded as inappropriate behavior.

Females were more likely to mention inappropriate sexual behavior as a negative consequence of drinking. For example, one female stated, "Well, one time I almost got raped and stuff. I didn't like it. I had been drinking and stuff, and I guess I went too far and almost got raped. I went home crying." Males described themselves as becoming more aggressive or risk-taking than usual when drinking. One male stated, "Well, a couple of my friends, it was an apartment with an upper floor, there was these bushes outside, and we decided we'd go bush jumping, so we were jumping off the balcony into the bushes."

Only one female and one male indicated that they drank primarily to escape or because they had become dependent on alcohol. The female indicated that she "used to want to get drunk," while the male responded that "people got down on [him] . . . that [he] had used alcohol as an escape or something." The low numbers reporting this kind of consequence are not surprising, since most adolescents are really beginners at drinking and see alcohol use as a social phenomenon. Moreover, for youth as for adults, there is a strong tendency to deny that one may be dependent on alcohol, since our society views such dependency as a weakness.

More than one-third of the females (34%) brought up psychological or emotional effects when they described the negative consequences of their alcohol use. Males were much less likely to report these effects (10%), although a few males described their drinking episodes as bad experiences. Drinking seems to stimulate more psychological and emotional effects among females, and these effects are sometimes unpredictable. For example, several females said that they drank to improve their mood but had found that drinking made them feel worse instead of better. One female said, "Sometimes I get emotional, any little thing can set me off, like if I think someone has done something bad around me."

While 12% of the males had had at least one run-in with law enforcement as the result of drinking (or were scared of having such an encounter), no female in the sample reported experiencing this kind of consequence. A male described an experience as follows: "I guess sometimes I was scared. We were at a friend's house and the neighbors complained we were loud. We were at this party, me and a couple of guys. The police pulled up and just told us to keep the noise down. But I still snuck out the back door." Another male was involved in a more serious incident: "There was once when I was younger, when we were all drunk, we decided to go watch baseball, and we got in trouble by the cops and brought to the station, and they called our parents and we all got in trouble. We got a year probation, 400 hours of community service. We had to pay for all the mailboxes we broke, too."

SUMMARY

Feminist researchers have criticized the disregard of female experiences and extrapolation of males' experiences to females in many past and current studies. This study of gender differences in consequences of alcohol use among adolescents was based on the observation that alcohol research, as with a great deal of the research in the field of deviance, is generally biased toward male behavior and subsequently obscures the picture of female drinking (Beckman 1993). Usual research measures such as quantity of alcohol consumed per sitting, as well as problem-drinking indexes loaded toward "acting out" and risk-taking such as fighting, vandalism, and driving while intoxicated, create artifacts that underestimate females' problems with alcohol (Lo 1996). It is little surprise that males usually appear to be the more abusive and problematic drinkers. Moreover, since the research focus is generally drawn toward those who abuse alcohol, the initial correlation with gender which shows a predominate male pattern means that the female who abuses alcohol often disappears from the more intensive subsequent analyses. This study was designed to have female and male high school students respond to a series of questions about alcohol use in a narrative way, in order to develop more sensitive measures of gender differences in drinking. This procedure reversed the traditional survey method whereby youth are presented a checklist of drinking circumstances that assume male behavior as the norm (Beckman 1993).

The data revealed that the adolescent males and females interviewed were similar in some aspects. For example, respondents of both genders reported experiencing the removal of inhibitions and enhancement of confidence as a result of drinking. Male and female respondents also shared experiences with alcohol making them feel more talkative and open.

However, the results also showed some gender differences in the students' perceptions and experiences of alcohol use. The results showed that females tend to be overrepresented in certain categories, such as drinking to relax and to enhance physical sensations. Males, in turn, are overrepresented in such negative categories as physical discomfort, strain in relationships, and encounters with law enforcement.

Several subtle qualitative differences within the categories devised for this study should be mentioned. While males as well as females expressed some concerns about engagement in inappropriate behaviors while drinking, these behaviors were in the form of aggression and/or vandalism. Females were more concerned about engaging in inappropriate sexual acts. In addition, female students were more apt to carry a greater sense of guilt about drinking, even drinking in moderation. Females also expressed more affective problems with alcohol use, in the form of negative emotional and psychological effects. In contrast to females' accounts, none of the male respondents mentioned their suffering from depression after consuming alcohol.

These differences indicate that males and females behave and feel differently while and after they drink. Studies using traditional male-biased instruments suggest that females do not experience as many alcohol-related problems as males (Haworth-Hoeppner et al. 1989). But perhaps young women do have similar numbers of problems with alcohol, just different problems than young men have. The present study supports the feminist argument that researchers should consciously realize the danger of using established lists of alcohol-related problems developed long ago, by male researchers examining male samples for male-oriented behaviors.

CONCLUSION

Males and females are socialized about alcohol differently when growing up. Thus, alcohol-related behaviors may be partly physical reactions, but they are also driven by our social norms and gender expectations (MacAndrew and Edgerton 1969). Traditionally, acting out has been perceived to be more in the male character than in the female character. As a result, male behavior relative to alcohol use (as well as abuse) has been tolerated to an extent, as part of the "sowing wild oats" syndrome. Despite changes in gender roles, we still find residues of guilt and opinions that drinking is inappropriate for females. It is time to start taking such norms into account, so that females' as well as males' perspectives and experiences are considered as prevention and treatment strategies developed for adolescents.

Gender differences in alcohol use and concomitant behaviors exist among youth. One research need, then, is to develop measurements which accurately reflect females' drinking behavior. Instruments and samples biased toward males show them to be much more involved with alcohol and to experience more problematic drinking. However, as Lo (1996) has shown in her quantity drinking index, the difference in heavy drinking between the sexes is actually smaller than normally shown by the data. The difference in magnitude of problem drinking for males and females may also be shown to be smaller when instruments sensitive to females are employed.

This study suggests that an index including female-oriented items as measures of problem drinking is needed. Respondents might be asked to choose from the following positive and negative consequences of drinking:

1. Have you ever felt guilty about your drinking?
2. Has drinking caused you embarrassment?
3. Have you felt ashamed after drinking?
4. Does drinking make you more self-confident?
5. Does drinking enlighten some part of your life?
6. Has drinking hurt your reputation in any way?
7. Has drinking ever put you in a sexual situation you usually avoid?
8. Do you feel closer to your friends after drinking?

9. Do you usually wish you had not drunk, after doing so?
10. Do you usually say you plan to quit drinking, after doing so?
11. Does drinking increase tension between you and your friends?
12. Does drinking increase tension between you and your parents?
13. Have you ever experienced a bad mood after drinking?

The results of the present study suggest that the inclusion of such questions may correct part of the measurement errors leading to gender bias in assessing alcohol-related problems. But problems or negative consequences, it should be remembered, are only part of the picture. Adolescents report experiencing positive consequences from drinking, changes they look forward to. Perhaps these changes can be elicited in some other way than drinking. The present study's findings may help suggest "substitutions" for use in prevention programs.

ACKNOWLEDGMENT

The authors wish to thank Drs. Kathryn Feltey and James Ross for their valuable suggestions for the writing of this paper.

NOTE

1. The explicit calculations used are available from the lead author.

REFERENCES

Alcohol Research Documentation. 1983. *How to Use the Alco-Calculator.* New Brunswick, NJ: Center of Alcohol Studies.

Annis, H.M., and C.B. Liban. 1980. "Alcoholism in Women: Treatment Modalities and Outcomes." Pp. 385-422 in *Alcohol and Drug Problems in Women: Research Advances in Alcohol and Drug Problems.* Vol. 5, edited by Oriana Josseau Kalant. New York: Plenum.

Bailly, R.C., R.S. Carman, and M.A. Forslund. 1991. "Gender Differences in Drinking Motivations and Outcomes." *The Journal of Psychology* 125(6): 649-656.

Bales, R.F. 1946. "Cultural Differences in Rates of Alcoholism." *Quarterly Journal of Studies on Alcohol* 6: 480-499.

Barkan, S.E. 1997. *Criminology: A Sociological Understanding*. New York: Prentice Hall.

Barnes, G.M., and J.W. Welte. 1986. "Patterns and Predictors of Alcohol Use among 7-12th Grade Students in New York State." *Journal of Studies on Alcohol* 47(1): 53-62.

Bart, P.B., P.Y. Miller, E. Moran, E.A. Stanko. 1989. "Guest Editors' Introduction." *Gender & Society* 3(4): 431-436.

Beckman, L. 1993. "Alcoholics Anonymous and Gender Issues." Pp. 233-250 in *Research on Alcoholics Anonymous: Opportunities and Alternatives,* edited by B.S. McCrady and W.R. Miller. New Brunswick, NJ: Rutgers Center of Alcohol Study.

Berg, B.L. 1995. *Qualitative Research Methods for the Social Sciences,* 2nd edition. Boston, MA: Allyn and Bacon.

Blume, S.B. 1987. "Women's Health: Issues in Mental Health, Alcoholism, and Substance Abuse." *Public Health Reports Supplement* 102: 38-42.

Chesney-Lind, M. 1986. "Women and Crime: The Female Offender." *Signs: Journal of Women in Culture and Society* 12(1): 78-96.

Chesney-Lind, M. 1989. "Girls' Crime and Woman's Place: Toward a Feminist Model of Female Delinquency." *Crime & Delinquency* 35(1): 5-29.

Clemmons, P. 1985. "Reflections of Social Thought in Research on Women and Alcoholism." *Journal of Drug Issues* 15(1): 73-80.

Dan, A.J., and S. Beekman. 1972. "Male versus Female Representation in Psychological Research." *American Psychologist* 27(November): 1078.

Engs, R.C. 1977. "Drinking Patterns and Drinking Problems of College Students." *Journal of Studies on Alcohol* 38(11): 2144-2156.

Engs, R.C., and D.J. Hanson. 1985. "The Drinking Patterns and Problems of College Students: 1983." *Journal of Alcohol and Drug Education* 31(1): 65-83.

Ferrence, R.G. 1980. "Sex Differences in the Prevalence of Problem Drinking." Pp. 69-124 in *Alcohol and Drug Problems in Women: Research Advances in Alcohol and Drug Problems*, edited by O.J. Kalant. New York: Plenum.

Gadaleto, A.F., and D.S. Anderson. 1986. "Continued Progress: The 1979, 1982, and 1985 College Alcohol Surveys." *Journal of College Student Personnel* 27(6): 499-509.

Gomberg, E.S.L. 1986. "Women: Alcohol and Other Drugs." *Drugs and Society* 1(1): 75-109.

Gonzalez, G.M. 1986. "Trends in Alcohol Knowledge and Drinking Patterns among Students: 1981-1985." *Journal of College Student Personnel* 27: 496-499.

Harding, S. 1986. *The Science Question in Feminism*. Ithaca, NY: Cornell University Press.

Haworth-Hoeppner, S., G. Globetti, J. Stem, and F. Marasco. 1989. "The Quantity and Frequency of Drinking among Undergraduates at a Southern University." *The International Journal of the Addictions* 24(9): 829-957.

Hoar, C.H. 1983. "Women Alcoholics—Are They Different from Other Women?" *The International Journal of the Addictions* 18(2): 251-270.

Holmes, D.S., and B.W. Jorgensen. 1971. "Do Personality and Social Psychologists Study Men More than Women?" *Representative Research in Social Psychology* 2: 71-76.

Hughes, S.P., and R.A. Dodder. 1983. "Alcohol Consumption Patterns among College Populations." *Journal of College Student Personnel* 24: 256-264.

Hughes, T.L. 1990. "Evaluating Research on Chemical Dependency among Women: A Women's Health Perspective." *Family and Community Health* 13(3): 35-46.

Johnston, L.D., P.M. O'Malley, and J.G. Bachman. 1995. *National Survey Results on Drug Use from Monitoring the Future Study, 1975-1994*, Vol. I. Rockville, MD: National Institute on Drug Abuse.

Keller, E.F. 1987. "Feminism and Science." Pp. 233-246 in *Sex and Scientific Inquiry*, edited by S. Harding and J.F. O'Barr. Chicago, IL: The University of Chicago Press.

Kline, R.B. 1990. "The Relation of Alcohol Expectancies to Drinking Patterns among Alcoholics: Generalization across Gender and Race." *Journal of Studies on Alcohol* 51(2): 175-182.

Lo, C.C. 1996. "Are Women Heavier Drinkers Than We Thought They Were?" *Journal of Studies on Alcohol* 57(5): 531-535.

Lo, C.C., and G. Globetti. 1995. "Are Males Actually Heavier Drinkers than Females?" *Addiction* 90: 1547-1551.

MacAndrew, C., and R.B. Edgerton. 1969. *Drunken Comportment: A Social Explanation*. Chicago, IL: Aldine.

Rose, H. 1987. "Hand, Brain, and Heart: A Feminist Epistemology for the Natural Sciences." Pp. 265-282 in *Sex and Scientific Inquiry*, edited by S. Harding and J.F. O'Ban. Chicago, IL: The University of Chicago Press.

Sherry, P., and V. Stolberg. 1987. "Factors Affecting Alcohol Use by College Students." *Journal of College Student Personnel* 28(4): 350-355.

Smith, M.D. 1994. "Enhancing the Quality of Survey Data on Violence Against Women: A Feminist Approach." *Gender & Society* 8(1): 109-127.

Strauss, A., and J. Corbin. 1990. *Basics of Qualitative Research: Grounded Theory Procedures and Techniques*. Newbury Park, CA: SAGE.

Sutker, P.B., B. Tabakoff, K.C. Goist, and C.L. Randall. 1983. "Acute Alcohol Intoxication, Mood States and Alcohol Metabolism in Men and Women." *Pharmacology, Biochemistry, and Behavior* 18(S1): 349-354.

Tomm, W. 1989. "Introduction." Pp. 1-12 in *The Effects of Feminist Approaches on Research Methodologies*, edited by W. Tomm. Waterloo, Ontario, Canada: Wilfrid Laurier University Press.

Ullman, A.D. 1960. "Ethnic Differences in the First Drinking Experience." *Social Problems* 8(1): 45-56.

Vannicelli, M., and L. Nash. 1984. "Effect of Sex Bias on Women's Studies on Alcoholism." *Alcoholism: Clinical and Experimental Research* 8(3): 334-336.

Vogel-Sprott, M. 1983. "Response Measures of Social Drinking: Research Implications and Applications." *Journal of Studies on Alcohol* 44(5): 817-836.

Watson, P.E., I.D. Watson, and R.D. Batt. 1980. "Total Body Water Volumes for Adult Males and Females Estimated from Simple Anthropometric Measurements." *The American Journal of Clinical Nutrition* 33: 27-39.

Wechsler, H., A. Davenport, G. Dowdall, B. Moeykens, and S. Castillo. 1994. "Health and Behavioral Consequences of Binge Drinking in College: A National Survey of Students at 140 Campuses." *JAMA* 272(21): 1672-1677.

Wechsler, H., G.W. Dowdall, A. Davenport, and E.B. Rimm. 1995. "A Gender-Specific Measure of Binge Drinking among College Students." *American Journal of Public Health* 85(7): 982-985.

Wechsler, H., and M. McFadden. 1979. "Drinking among College Students in New England: Extent, Social Correlates and Consequences of Alcohol Use." *Journal of Studies on Alcohol* 40(11): 969-996.

Wechsler, H., and M. Rohman. 1981. "Extensive Users of Alcohol among College Students." *Journal of Studies on Alcohol* 42(1): 149-155.

Wood, M.D., C.T. Nagoshi, and D.A. Dennis. 1992. "Alcohol Norms and Expectations as Predictors of Alcohol Use and Problems in a College Student Sample." *The American Journal of Drug and Alcohol Abuse* 18(4): 461-476.

Printed and bound by CPI Group (UK) Ltd, Croydon, CR0 4YY

16/09/2026

14963399-0003